Key Debates in Anthropology

Every year, leading social anthropologists meet in Manchester to debate a motion at the heart of current theoretical developments in their subject. *Key Debates in Anthropology* collects together the first six of these debates, spanning the period from 1988 to 1993. For each debate there are four principal speakers: one to propose the motion, another to oppose it, and two seconders. These debates give unprecedented insight into the process of anthropological theory in the making, as the many contributors both engage with each other's positions and respond to wider intellectual currents of the time.

The first debate addresses the disciplinary character of social anthropology: can it be regarded as a science, and if so, is it able to establish general propositions about human culture and social life? The second examines the concept of society, in relation to such terms as individual, community, nation and state. In the third debate the spotlight is turned on the concept of culture, and on the role of culture in people's perception of their environments. The fourth debate focuses on the place of language in the formation of culture, highlighting the problematic distinction between verbal and non-verbal communication. The fifth takes up the question of how we view the past in relation to the present, touching on the difference between history and memory. Finally, in the sixth debate, the concern is with the cross-cultural applicability of the concept of aesthetics. Can there be an anthropology of aesthetics, or is the term so wedded to Western standards of evaluation as to make any such endeavour hopelessly ethnocentric?

With its unique format, *Key Debates in Anthropology* addresses issues that are currently at the top of the theoretical agenda, and registers the pulse of contemporary thinking in social anthropology. The presentations, by leading anthropologists of both older and younger generations, are clear, original and provocative.

Tim Ingold is Max Gluckman Professor of Social Anthropology at the University of Manchester.

Key Debates in Anthropology

Edited by Tim Ingold

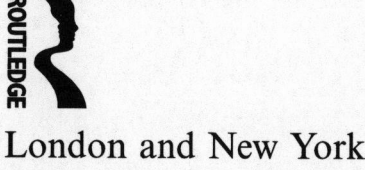

London and New York

First published 1996
by Routledge
11 New Fetter Lane, London EC4P 4EE

Simultaneously published in the USA and Canada
by Routledge
29 West 35th Street, New York, NY 10001

© 1996 Tim Ingold, selection and editorial matter; individual
chapters, the contributors.

Typeset in Times by Routledge
Printed and bound in Great Britain by
TJ Press (Padstow) Ltd, Padstow, Cornwall

British Library Cataloguing in Publication Data
A catalogue record for this book is available from the
British Library

Library of Congress Cataloguing in Publication Data
Key debates in anthropology/edited by Tim Ingold.
    Includes bibliographical references and index.
    1. Ethnology – Philosophy.   2. Ethnology – Methodology.
    I. Ingold, Tim, 1948–
    GN345.K49   1996
    306'.01–dc20   96–7493
                                                            CIP

ISBN   0–415–15019–1 (hbk)
ISBN   0–415–15020–5 (pbk)

Contents

Preface   ix

General introduction   1
Tim Ingold

1988 debate   **Social anthropology is a generalizing science
                  or it is nothing**   15

Introduction   17
Tim Ingold

Part I   The presentations   21

               For the motion (1)   21
               Keith Hart

               Against the motion (1)   26
               Anthony P. Cohen

               For the motion (2)   30
               Anthony Good

               Against the motion (2)   36
               Judith Okely

Part II   The debate   41

1989 debate   **The concept of society is theoretically obsolete**   55

Introduction   57
Tim Ingold

Part I   The presentations   60

              For the motion (1)   60
              Marilyn Strathern

              Against the motion (1)   67
              J. D. Y. Peel

              For the motion (2)   72
              Christina Toren

              Against the motion (2)   76
              Jonathan Spencer

Part II   The debate   83

1990 debate   **Human worlds are culturally constructed**   99

Introduction   101
Roy Ellen

Part I   The presentations   105

              For the motion (1)   105
              Wendy James

              Against the motion (1)   112
              Tim Ingold

              For the motion (2)   118
              Roland Littlewood

              Against the motion (2)   123
              Paul Richards

Part II   The debate   129

1991 debate   **Language is the essence of culture**   147

Introduction   149
Tim Ingold

Part I   The presentations   154

              For the motion (1)   154
              David Parkin

Against the motion (1)   159
Alfred Gell

For the motion (2)   166
Brian Moeran

Against the motion (2)   171
James F. Weiner

Part II   The debate   176

1992 debate **The past is a foreign country**   199

Introduction   201
Tim Ingold

Part I   The presentations   206

For the motion (1)   206
David Lowenthal

Against the motion (1)   212
Gillian Feeley-Harnik

For the motion (2)   218
Penelope Harvey

Against the motion (2)   224
Susanne Küchler

Part II   The debate   229

1993 debate **Aesthetics is a cross-cultural category**   249

Introduction   251
James F. Weiner

Part I   The presentations   255

For the motion (1)   255
Howard Morphy

Against the motion (1)   260
Joanna Overing

For the motion (2)   266
Jeremy Coote

	Against the motion (2) *Peter Gow*	271
Part II	The debate	276
Index		294

Preface

In any academic discipline, the intensity of debate concerning its theoretical and intellectual foundations is a good measure of its current vitality. Ten years ago, I had the feeling that if the pulse of my own discipline, of social anthropology, had been measured by this criterion, it would have been found to be virtually moribund. I had no idea, at the time, whether my feeling was widely shared, or whether it was a symptom of a purely personal frustration. But three things worried me in particular. The first was that the subject was becoming fragmented into narrow specialisms whose practitioners, while they might converse among themselves, seemed to have less and less to say to colleagues in other fields. Second, after a decade in which virtually no new appointments had been made to departments of anthropology in British universities, the discipline – at least on this side of the Atlantic – was being starved of new ideas. The so-called 'younger generation', myself included, seemed to be growing older all the while, without ever being replaced. Third, I was concerned about the widening gap between anthropology as it was practised and the way the discipline was being publicly presented and taught to students. Why should it be supposed that all the great debates of anthropology, the debates from which the discipline draws its substance and its identity, took place in the ever more distant past? Was nothing of equal significance going on in contemporary work? Why were anthropologists not at the forefront of public and academic debate on the great issues of the day?

It was with these concerns in mind that, in May 1987, I wrote to a number of colleagues, all of them established academic anthropologists in British university departments, to find out whether they shared my feeling of despondency and, if so, whether there might be something to be said for establishing a forum in the UK for the regular discussion of topical issues in anthropological theory. Their responses varied. Some took exception to my assessment of the state of the discipline. In reality,

x *Preface*

they argued, there was plenty of exciting and innovative work going on. Indeed, in view of the strains under which the entire university system was labouring, British social anthropology had not been doing so badly, though admittedly much could still be done to raise the public profile of the discipline, and in particular to counter the tendency – which still persists in North America and to some extent in continental Europe – to identify British anthropology with the era of Malinowski, Radcliffe-Brown and Evans-Pritchard, as though nothing had happened since. Others, however, concurred with my judgement and expressed strong support for the proposal to set up some kind of 'Group for Anthropological Theory'. Overall, the responses were sufficiently positive to encourage me to go ahead with it. A meeting was arranged in Manchester to launch the group, and was intended to take the form of a round-table discussion on the theme: 'What are theories in anthropology and why do we need them?'

The meeting, held in January 1988, was a flop. For one reason and another, hardly anyone came. Nevertheless, it produced one good idea. This was a suggestion that we should hold a major annual event, open to all, in which a motion bearing centrally on concerns in current anthropology would be formally debated. A leading anthropologist would be invited to propose the motion, and another to oppose it. The opening addresses would be followed by a free debate from the floor, a summing-up by each side, and finally a vote. We thought that such an event, apart from being a lot of fun, would generate much serious discussion, and would help to focus attention on issues at the heart of our work. It would make a refreshing change from the standard format for academic events of the 'distinguished lecture' type, which involve minimal audience participation and where debate, if any, follows only years later, after publication.

It was with this suggestion that the Group for Debates in Anthropological Theory (GDAT) was born. In highlighting the element of debate, the intention was to stress the importance not so much of constructing theories as of arguing theoretically. The significance of this distinction is a matter to which I turn in the general introduction; suffice it to say at this point that the Group was not to become associated with any particular tendency or 'school of thought'. Rather, its purpose was to promote a continuing dialogue between the many and divergent viewpoints that make up contemporary anthropology. For then, as now, it is in this dialogue and not in any contrived theoretical consensus that the unity of the subject resides. Moreover, there is good reason to believe that theory in anthropology consists not in some separate corpus of propositions about the social world, but rather in the practices of persuasion through which each of us seeks to draw the other's way of attending to, or engaging with, that world along the same paths as our own. Debate, in short, is the very *modus vivendi* of theory. And theory, since it is about how we engage with the world and not just about how we represent it, is inherently political.

The first debate to be staged by GDAT took place in Manchester on 29 October 1988, before an audience of more than seventy individuals drawn from eighteen institutions around the UK. It was, by all accounts, a successful and enjoyable occasion. The second debate, a year later, drew an even larger crowd. The annual GDAT debate has now become an established fixture in the calendar of anthropological events in the UK. The debates continue to be held in Manchester, and to be closely associated with Manchester University's Department of Social Anthropology. Attendance has varied from a low of around 60 to a high of over 120, but there has been a tendency, over the years, for the proportion of students to faculty in the audience to increase. One reason for this trend may lie in the policy, adopted by the Group, of publishing the proceedings of each debate in the form of a separate booklet. Established faculty preferred, perhaps, to stay at home and read about it afterwards!

Six consecutive debates were held in the years 1988 to 1993. The published versions of these debates, reproduced with minor editorial amendments in the order in which they took place, make up this book. In 1994 there was no debate, partly because the energies of everyone, in that year, had been taken up with the nationwide review, by the Higher Education Funding Council, of the quality of teaching in social anthropology. A new series of debates was inaugurated in 1995, under the direction of the present chairman of GDAT, Peter Wade. There is every indication that the debates continue to fulfil a need in British anthropology for a regular forum for the discussion of leading theoretical issues; moreover, there are signs that the model established by GDAT is being taken up elsewhere, both inside and outside of anthropology. As far as I know, however, a volume of this kind, consisting of a collection of such debates, is quite without parallel. It represents a new departure in anthropological publishing, one that – for the first time – gives due recognition to the contemporary understanding of anthropology (some would prefer to call it 'post-modern') as a polyphonic texture of multiple voices, each responding critically to the others and reacting to changes in the world around them. Anthropology, after all, is not some kind of Durkheimian superorganism with a life of its own, over and above those of its individual contributors. It is, rather, the name of a conversation in which all of us are engaged – professionals, students, not to mention the countless individuals who assist with our inquiries in the field – and which turns around the conditions of human life in the world.

As for my earlier despondency about the moribund state of British social anthropology, this has all but melted away. I would like to think that GDAT has played some small part in the reinvigoration of the discipline that has undoubtedly taken place over the last few years. But there are other significant factors. There are more jobs in university departments of anthropology, albeit less secure ones. A new generation of anthropologists, equipped with a degree of theoretical sophistication and field expertise that would put many of their seniors to shame, is making its mark. The great figures of the past are still there in our collective memory, but they no longer cast such a shadow over present work. And after a period of rather introverted self-reflection, which was perhaps necessary and inevitable with the collapse of the certainties of modernism, anthropologists seem to have regained some confidence in their ability to draw on the meagre resources at their disposal to tackle some of the great questions that presently confront human life.

It remains for me to thank the very many individuals and organizations that made the debates, and hence also this book, possible. The Group for Debates in Anthropological Theory has been supported throughout, both financially and in other practical ways, by the Association of Social Anthropologists of the Commonwealth, to which the Group is formally affiliated. In the first two years, the debates were additionally sponsored by the Royal Anthropological Institute, which provided a grant from the William Campbell Root Fund. The University of Manchester has generously made available the Muriel Stott Centre, in the John Rylands University Library, for each annual debate, and the support of the University Librarian, as well as of the Library's technical and portering staff, is gratefully acknowledged. Special thanks are due to the successive secretaries of GDAT – Nigel Rapport (1988–9), Matthew McKeown (1990) and Jackie Taylor (1991–3) – all of whom put a great deal of work into organizing the debates, as well as in otherwise managing the affairs of the Group. The 1993 debate was organized by James F. Weiner, who took over as chairman of GDAT for the year 1993–4, prior to his departure to Australia. He was responsible for much of the initial editorial work in bringing this debate to its published form. Over the years, Patti Peach has put in many hours of thankless labour in transcribing the tapes of the debates, and Jean Monastiriotis, Steven Sharples and Karen Egan have all had a hand in typing up various drafts. Gustaaf Houtman and Dominique Remars did a wonderful job in converting the typescripts into camera-ready copy.

Most of all, I should like to take this opportunity to thank all those who submitted to having their arms twisted to perform as principal speakers in the debates – no doubt in many cases against their better judgement. Their co-operation in providing texts of their contributions, and in the subsequent editing, has been much appreciated. Last but not least, I want to thank everyone who attended the debates, and especially those who contributed to the discussion. It is of course due to their participation that the debates were so successful. Many will find their comments in discussion recorded here, though perhaps in a form so heavily edited as to be barely recognizable. I can only hope that they will not be too dismayed, and perhaps even pleasantly surprised, by the result.

Tim Ingold
Manchester, April 1996

General introduction

Tim Ingold

THE NATURE OF ANTHROPOLOGICAL THEORY

Anthropology is at once the most resolutely academic and the most fiercely anti-academic of disciplines. Its commitment is to human understanding of a very fundamental kind, and it continues to exist and thrive only thanks to a university system which – at least in principle, if no longer in practice – is dedicated to the production of knowledge for its own sake. Yet at the same time, anthropologists have been foremost in challenging the claims of academia to deliver authoritative accounts of the manifold ways of the world, along with the implicit ranking of such accounts above those that might be offered by 'ordinary folk' whose powers of observation and reason have supposedly not been cultivated to the same degree. This challenge commonly appears in the form of a critique of the assumptions of so-called 'Western discourse', a discourse founded upon a claim to the supremacy of human reason and whose natural home and breeding ground is the academy. Through the practice and experience of fieldwork, anthropologists have been more inclined to privilege the kinds of knowledge and skill that are generated in the course of people's practical involvements with one another and with their environments, in their everyday lives. The paradox is that by doing so, they are undercutting the intellectual foundations of an organization of knowledge without which anthropology, as a discipline, could not exist.

This paradox manifests itself in countless ways. One would have thought, for example, that having so effectively demonstrated the limited and historically contingent purchase of Western thought and science, and having thoroughly cleansed its own conceptual equipment of so-called Western bias, anthropology could move on to other things. Yet it seems that we are perpetually at it, caught in a groove of disciplinary auto-critique from which it sometimes appears there is no escape. The reason, of course, is that the bias we are so anxious to avoid, and the conceptual dichotomies that seem to hamstring our thinking, are continually reproduced in our own academic practice. Another manifestation of the paradox lies in the well-known fact that students encountering anthropological writing for the first time find it very difficult to understand, even though the quantity of jargon or specialist terminology is no greater – and probably a great deal less – than in most other academic disciplines. Why should it be so phenomenally hard to write about the stuff of ordinary experience in terms that others can readily comprehend? Novelists and poets often seem to make a better job of it, since they are not bound by the convention that what they write should take the form of definitive, context-independent propositions. They can guide readers into a world of shared experience, rather than seeking to represent it on an abstract, conceptual level. In attempting to convey everyday, local knowledge of an essentially non-propositional form in a decontextualizing language of abstract propositions, anthropologists cannot help but tie themselves in knots. Students quickly grasp the difficulty if asked to write an account of such a routine task as tying shoelaces. The simple knot soon becomes a verbal labyrinth.

A third manifestation of the paradox, which is of prime concern here, has to do with the status of 'theory'. Celebrated as the most advanced products of human reason, theories hold pride of place in the academic pantheon. Theoreticians are ranked above observers, experimentalists and laboratory technicians, much as architecture is ranked above housebuilding, or intellectual over manual labour. All of these rankings are instances of a more profound dichotomy, heavily institutionalized in the Western academy, between *design* and *use*: the first a rational creation of the absolutely new; the second a mechanical execution of pre-existing plans. Thus it seems that theories are made by some for others to apply. Do anthropological theorists, then, design conceptual structures for lower ranking ethnographers (or research students) to carry with them into the field? Is the field merely an empirical testing ground for abstract theory? Most anthropologists would nowadays feel profoundly uncomfortable about such a division of labour. They would point out that their own ways of thinking, far from having been fully constituted in advance and then *applied* to field data, actually continue to grow and take shape within those ongoing dialogues with local people that go by the name of 'fieldwork', and that most so-called 'data' consist of their own experiences of, and reflections on, these dialogues. They might observe that the division between theory and data is just one of those artefacts of academic discourse that gets in the way of a proper understanding of human-lived worlds. Yet at the same time it is assumed that anthropology, like any self-respecting academic discipline, should have its theory, without which it would cease to have any intellectual coherence, becoming nothing more than an assortment of ethnographic narratives. In what, then, can this 'theory' possibly consist?

The present volume is offered in response to this question. I do not mean that answers can be found *in* the book, as though it were a showcase for the higher products of the anthropological imagination. I would rather suggest that the book be regarded as part of the answer, concrete testimony to the fact that anthropological theory consists, in the first place, not in an inventory of ready-made structures or representations, to be picked up and used as it suits our analytic purposes, but in an *ongoing process of argumentation*. In this sense, theory is an activity, something we do. The problem remains, however, of how to characterize more precisely the nature of this activity. We could begin by distinguishing between two arenas of activity in which most anthropologists are involved, whether serially or in parallel: the field and the academy. It would be fair to say that the settings for theoretical work are normally located in the academic arena; they include conferences, lectures and seminars, as well as the solitary spaces of the library or study. The field, by contrast, is not usually a locus for theoretical dialogue: thus the voices of local or native people do not figure in the exchanges recorded in this book and would certainly be out of place here. Admittedly the distinction is not hard and fast. The settings of academic debate are no more ring-fenced than the settings of fieldwork, and may even overlap to a degree. Both are situated in a social world in which we all participate. It can still be argued, nevertheless, that the kind of work we do in the academy differs fundamentally from the kind we do in the field, along the lines of a contrast between production and collection. According to this argument, the field is a site for the extraction of empirical information ('data') which is then processed by means of conceptual tools ('theory') perfected in the academy.

The point of departure for this volume is a different one. It is that the forms anthropological knowledge takes do not arise *de novo* as the creation of superior academic minds, whence they are handed down for application by the rank and file of researchers and students, but rather emerge and are sustained within the contexts of our mutual, dialogic engagement in social and intellectual life. True, engagements in the field do have a different character and dynamic from dialogues in the academy. But far from the one being extractive and the other productive, both are dialogues through which knowledge is *generated*. The difference is that the contexts of engagement in the field lie in the efforts of ethnographers to learn the skills of action and perception appropriate to particular forms of life, whereas the contexts of academic dialogue are removed from such practical endeavours and are framed by formal structures of teaching and learning. It is solely within these latter structures, themselves indifferent to what is learned or taught, that skills acquired in the field take on the appearance of *information* – that is, empirical content for the ideal forms of theory.

But in reality, anthropologists enter the arena of theoretical debate with far more than 'data'. They come to it with a set of intuitions, sensibilities and orientations that have been decisively shaped by the field experience. The dialogue in the field, in short, is not just a source of ethnographic facts: for the fieldworker it is also an *education*. By the same token, there is more to anthropological theory than the fashioning of conceptual tools for use in the analysis of data. We should rather understand the process of theory as one in which the education provided by the field experience, or more generally by life, is brought to bear in a systematic interrogation of the foundational terms of Western academic discourse – terms like individual and society, culture and nature, language, art and technology, individuality and personhood, history and memory, equality and inequality, even humanity itself. And the engine that drives the theoretical process is the tension, intrinsic to the anthropological endeavour, between abstract philosophical speculation about what human life *might* be like, and our experience of what life *is* like, for particular people at particular places and times.

To outsiders, particularly perhaps to people accustomed to the ways of natural science, anthropologists seem to spend an inordinate amount of time quibbling about the finer meanings of words, instead of getting on with the job of explaining the data. There is plenty of that in this book. But I want to insist that there is more to such arguments than mere quibbling. For every word carries, compressed within it, a history of past usage, and it is only by unravelling such histories that we can gauge the appropriateness of particular words for current or projected purposes. In general, the meanings of words are shaped within contexts of dialogue, and this is no less true of the contexts of anthropological debate. The debates that make up this volume testify to the attempts of the several participants, educated through their field experience as well as by their formal academic training, to seek out a common vocabulary in which to cast the particularities of this experience, by stretching to the limits (and sometimes beyond) the potentials of an academic discourse which often seems singularly ill-suited to the task. The process of theory, as we read it in these pages, is tantamount to the fashioning of an anthropological language dedicated to establishing the commensurability of radically contrasting forms of knowledge and experience. This is why theory is an activity that we cannot and must not do without. A theory-free anthropology would be one that had reneged on its mission to bring academic scholarship and practical know-how into a productive and mutually enhancing engagement.

TROUBLESOME DICHOTOMIES

Despite the diversity of specific content, the debates reproduced here are connected in very many ways. Participants often commented, off the record, that it felt as though the arguments of each debate always appeared to turn, ultimately, on the same underlying problem. No one, however, seemed able to put their finger precisely on what that problem was. In editing the texts I have had the same feeling, and the same difficulty. On reflection, it seems to me that the source of the problem lies in the contradiction I have already identified at the heart of the anthropological endeavour, between the claim – central to anthropology's constitution as an academic discipline – to be able to make representative statements about the conditions of human life in the world, and the essentially anti-academic critique of the supposedly 'Western' notion that it is by representing the social world that we come to know it. The way in which the problem generally manifests itself, regardless of the particular topic under discussion, is in the trouble we always seem to have with dichotomies. Academic discourse is notorious for its tendency to operate in terms of conceptual dichotomies, which are not so much accepted uncritically as indefinitely multiplied in the effort of their resolution. Even as (some) anthropologists set themselves up as champions of non-Western holism against the insistent dualism of Western thought, they cannot avoid reproducing the master dichotomy of anthropology itself, between Western and non-Western societies, characterized respectively as people who think in terms of dichotomies and people who don't! Short of becoming poets, painters or novelists, there seems to be no way out.

The first debate, on the proposition that social anthropology is a generalizing science, at once plunges us into the midst of the problem with its focus on two of the most frequently invoked dichotomies: between science and the humanities, and between the general and the particular. Let me begin with the latter. Though explicitly raised in the first debate, the question of the distinction between the general and the particular lay also, if implicitly, at the heart of the second, on the concept of society. The parallel is this: both the concept of the general and the concept of society, at least in one of its senses, rest on a certain view of part–whole relations. Both assume a world that primordially consists of naturally indivisible entities or events – that is, of 'individuals' – which may be added together to yield a totality of a higher order, a 'whole'. Conversely, the whole may be divided up into its individual parts. A generalization is a covering statement about the whole, as opposed to statements about its parts; likewise statements about society refer to the whole comprised of the sum of its individual members. But if we understand the world to be one continuous process of becoming, of which our own lives are a part, and if our knowledge of the world is built up against the background of our active involvement in this process, then this logic of part–whole relations – and with it the oppositions both between the general and the particular and between society and the individual – disintegrates. Each one of us may be different, but these differences are constituted in and through our mutual involvement in the generative process of social life, they do not exist in spite of it. By contrast, to point to similarities – that is, to generalize across multiple instances – is to presuppose a world already fragmented into its minimal constituents. In short, it is difference that connects, whereas similarity divides.

What, then, becomes of the distinction between science and humanism? Or more specifically, what is entailed in the claim that anthropology is a 'human science'? One answer might lie in a particular interpretation of the motion for the third debate, that 'human worlds are culturally constructed'. While natural scientists set themselves up as disinterested observers of the phenomena of nature, anthropologists might see their task as one of registering the multiple ways in which these phenomena are apprehended within the representational schemata, or 'world views', of diverse cultures. These two projects are perfectly compatible, since they both place the observer – whether natural scientist or social anthropologist – at a point doubly removed from the phenomenal world. Ordinary human beings are one step removed, since they alone are said to reconstruct the world in their social discourse, along lines laid down by the categories of culture, whereas all other animals merely get on with the business of living in it. But scientists and anthropologists can be no ordinary humans, since to perceive cultural constructions *as such*, and to recognize the 'real' reality of nature that lies behind them, they must have taken a second step – not just out of the one natural world, but also out of the several worlds of culture that all other mortals inhabit. Where the first step marks the transcendence of humanity over nature, the second marks the triumph of reason over the forces of tradition.

It is possible, however, to argue for anthropology as a human science, and to support the motion that human worlds are culturally constructed, without having to endorse this claim to the superiority of reason. To do so requires a broader conception of science as knowledge, one that refuses to draw an absolute distinction between the processes of mind and nature, or between the knower and the known. Such a science would begin from the premise of our initial engagement with the world of nature, instead of our detachment from it. And in place of the idea that human beings ordinarily inhabit worlds of culturally constructed meaning, one could argue – as did the proposers of the motion for the third debate – that people 'live culturally'. To take this view is to conceive of the life process not as accommodated within ready-made structures of knowledge, but rather as the very process wherein knowledge is *generated*. This conclusion would tally with my earlier remarks regarding the generation of anthropological knowledge within the dialogic contexts of both the field and the academy. And it would place the anthropological quest for meaning in human affairs on a par with that of people everywhere.

But if human beings do not just live, like other animals, but live *culturally*, what is it that enables them to do this? It was the search for an answer to this question that motivated the fourth debate. Human beings can live culturally, argued the proposers of the motion for this debate, thanks to language. For whether our concern be with the evolution of our species or with the ontogenetic development of every human individual, it is language that makes possible the transition from sign to symbol, that is from non-verbal gestures whose meanings lie in the material effects they bring about in the particular contexts of their production to verbal utterances which take their meanings from concepts and ideas in the minds of speakers. To have made the transition, according to this argument, is to be in a position to enter that traffic in representations technically known as the 'cultural construction of reality'. As the debate revealed, however, there are two major difficulties with this argument.

First, a great deal of what we would normally take to be integral to living culturally apparently does not depend upon linguistic articulation, and seems indeed to be fundamentally resistant to expression in words or symbols. One has only to think of my earlier example of tying shoelaces. Language use, in short, appears to mark only the tip of the iceberg of cultural life. If language is the essence of anything, it is not of culture, but of the specialized practices of academic writing by which we seek to represent it. This conclusion, however, only serves to highlight the second difficulty, which lies in the extent to which these academic practices have influenced our idea of what language *is*. Once we cease to regard language as a domain of affect-free, context-independent propositions, modelled on that of the printed word, and focus instead upon speech as a situated social activity, the conventional dichotomy between language and non-verbal communication seems much less secure.

Arguably, both speaking and tying shoelaces are instances of skilled practice whose meanings lie in the effects they secure in the world. But surely the same goes for the skilled activities of non-human creatures. If so, there can be no radical contrast between the cultural life of humans and the natural life of other animals. The contrast, if it can be made at all, must be a soft or 'fuzzy' one, rather than hard and fast.

The root of the problem seems to lie in understanding the relation between the development of practical skills of perception and action, on the one hand, and the reconstruction of experience through verbal narrative, on the other. This was the central theme of the fifth debate, on the proposition 'The past is a foreign country'. It figured in terms of an opposition between historical and memorial approaches to the past. As an object of historical narrative, the past seems cut off from the present: one can only talk *about* something that is already finished. Yet story-telling is itself a skill, which like any other skill depends upon the work of memory – that is, of capacities of feeling and response shaped through past experience. In this sense, then, the past is active in the present. Despite their differences, both sides in this debate were aware of the dangers of divorcing human capacities from the historical process of social life in which they come into being, that is of appealing to 'universals' of human nature that are somehow pre-specified as the properties of individuals, in advance of their entering into any kinds of relationships at all. The so-called 'capacity for language' is one such frequently posited universal. Another, which figured centrally in the final debate on the category of the aesthetic, is the capacity to make evaluative judgements of the impact of externally induced stimuli upon the senses.

Such capacities, it is widely supposed, must have become established through the evolution of our species, and must therefore be equally present in all human beings, ancient and modern. But if the past is indeed a foreign country, as the proposers of the motion for the fifth debate argued, then it cannot be populated by characters like ourselves, equipped with all the same capacities, propensities and dispositions. Recalling the argument against the opposition between the general and the particular, we are connected to the people of the past not by our similarities to them – by what we have in common – but by the fact that they, like us, were as much caught up as we are now in the overall historical process of social life. And if that is so, then human feelings and responses, just as much as skills and capacities of action, must be constituted within that process, rather than given independently and in advance of it through some kind of universal genetic specification.

This is to call into question yet another troublesome dichotomy, which turned out to be central to the argument in favour of the motion that aesthetics is a category that may be generalized across cultures: namely between the aesthetic and the semantic. Aesthetics, it was argued, is about the judgement of sensation, whereas semantics is about the attribution of meaning. The first, in other words, gives an answer to the question 'How does it feel?', the second answers the question 'What does it represent?' Yet as opponents of the motion pointed out, it is difficult to see how these two questions can be separated without presuming some kind of split between mind and body. If meaning is not added on by the mind to the world, but is rather gathered from the contexts of our engagement with its manifold constituents, then to feel things is indeed to discover what they mean. In place of the dichotomy between aesthetics and semantics we would then have a single anthropology or perception. But it is surely still the case that human beings can represent, in the imagination, what they perceive, and that these representations may, in turn, feed back to the activity of perception itself. Perhaps, if there is an overall conclusion to be drawn from these debates, it is that the most fundamental problem for anthropology lies in understanding this dialectic of perception and representation.

SETTING UP THE DEBATES

One of the challenges, in setting up these debates, has been to identify motions and to phrase them in such a way as to touch on a genuine division of opinion. It was easy enough to think of snappy propositions that would have commanded general assent or dissent within the profession, much more difficult to find ones around which compelling arguments could be made both for and against. Coupled with this was the logistical problem of finding four speakers, all available on the same day, two of whom were prepared to propose the motion and two to oppose it. The rather cumbersome and impossibly ambiguous wording of the motion for the first debate, 'Social anthropology is a generalizing science or it is nothing', was the result of protracted negotiation among the four speakers in an attempt to find a mutually acceptable formula. Science, of course, is one thing, generalization another, and the majority who opposed the motion were free to adopt their own, doubtless diverse and discrepant views of what anthropology might be, if *not* a generalizing science. Learning from experience, in subsequent debates we made it clear to potential speakers that the wording of the motion was not open to negotiation; at the same time, however, we encouraged speakers to take the otherwise rather unusual step of presenting only one point of view, even to the extent of acting as devil's advocate, and to go out of their way to be deliberately provocative. In many cases, speakers could have argued as convincingly on one side or the other: Marilyn Strathern, for example, gracefully left it to us to determine whether she was to argue for or against the proposition that 'the concept of society is theoretically obsolete'. And more than one speaker was set up to argue for a motion that, given the choice, they might have been more inclined to oppose: David Parkin's defence of the proposition that 'language is the essence of culture' is a brilliant example.

There is a risk that to set arguments up in this way is to manufacture purely artificial divisions and disagreements, and thereby to generate more heat than light. The best insurance against this risk lay in the participation of the audience in the open debate following the four presentations. If the motion resulted in a contrived opposition, they would be the first to object; and object they did. By and large, contributors from the floor wisely resisted attempts to polarize the issues, pointing to areas in which both sides appeared to be in perfect agreement. However, when these areas of apparent consensus were further probed in discussion, it almost always turned out that behind them were more profound disagreements which had not been anticipated in the framing of the debate, and which came as a genuine surprise. For example, in the debate on the motion 'Human worlds are culturally constructed', the anticipated opposition from the socio-biological quarter did not materialize, and for a while it seemed that with minor allowances for differences in idiom, both sides were saying the same thing – until it transpired that the actual source of the argument lay not in the opposition between culture and biology but in the meaning to be attributed to the notion of construction. And in the debate on 'Language is the essence of culture', the real problem turned out to hinge on the issue of whether language exists at all as a discrete capacity of human minds, or whether the idea of such a capacity is the result of attempts by linguists to create for themselves a distinctive object of study (in a manner strictly analogous to the anthropological invention of 'culture'). And on this issue, both the proposer and the opposer of the motion found an unlikely ally in the seconder on the opposite side!

In the course of these debates, then, the initial issues were often significantly reframed. Old arguments were found to hang on illusory differences, while new divisions opened up in unexpected places. It was in this respect that each debate was a genuinely productive exercise. Not much significance, however, should be attached to the ballot taken at the end of every debate. The point of the ballot was in part to get a sense of where opinion lay, and in part to enhance the entertainment value of the event. There is no suggestion that intellectual issues can or should be settled by these means. The assumption that a particular position must be right because the majority think so has a long and dishonourable history in Western academia. Anthropologists, who are used to swimming against the tide, should have no truck with it. Just for the record, however, the voting figures are appended to this introduction, along with a warning that they should not be taken seriously. If they indicate one thing, it is that our efforts to phrase the motions in a way that allowed convincing arguments to be marshalled both for and against, were largely successful.

If there really existed an 'average' British social anthropologist (BSA), who adhered in every respect to the majority opinion, he or she would be perversely inconsistent! On the one hand, taking a stance against generalization and anthropology-as-science, our standard BSA would deny that language is the essence of culture, would rule out the cross-cultural application of the notion of aesthetics, and reject as obsolete the concept of society. On the other hand, this BSA would point to the centrality of language and aesthetic judgement in the constitution of culture, and to the distinctiveness of human social relations, in arguing that human beings live in culturally constructed worlds, and that their constructions of the past in the present are radically cut off from the pasts experienced (as *their* presents) by predecessors of earlier times. But while the standard BSA is, of course, a fictional character, theoretical inconsistency is nothing new in anthropology, nor is it necessarily a bad thing. For inconsistency is also a sign of movement, of a willingness to try out new ideas. Complete theoretical consistency, on the other hand, spells intellectual stagnation.

CONVERTING THE DEBATES TO WRITTEN TEXT

After every debate took place, the four principal speakers were asked to supply written texts of their contributions. These texts, slightly edited, make up the first part of the published record of the proceedings. The second part consists of an edited text of the open debate following the presentations, rounding off with final comments from the speakers. Preceding both parts is a short introduction, written after the event by the chairperson, and serving to draw attention to the main themes and to the significance of the debate as a whole.

The second part of the proceedings for each debate is very far from being a word-for-word transcription of what was said on the day. Rather, it has been constructed by first producing such a transcription (from audio-tape), and then completely rewriting each contribution so as to make the same point in the clearest and most economical way – even to the extent of reconstructing what the speaker *would* have said if he or she had had the opportunity to think it out more carefully. Wherever appropriate or possible, the words and phrases that speakers actually used have been incorporated into the rewritten text, but I have felt under no obligation to keep to them. In some cases the material has been reordered, to make for a more logical and coherent sequence of challenge and response; some contributions have even been split up into two or more segments and reinserted in different places. My overriding aim in this editorial work has been to produce a text that reads well, and that captures the spirit of the argument and the specific points at issue, rather than one that reproduces exactly what was said. Cutting out redundant material has generally led to a reduction (by comparison with the original transcript) of around one-quarter to a third. Unfortunately, due to technical problems, one or two contributions were lost from the debate 'Human worlds are culturally constructed', as were the final minutes of the debate 'The past is a foreign country'.

The text of each debate is followed by endnotes including bibliographic references. The decision to include endnotes was taken while editing the first debate for publication: this, then, established a precedent which subsequent speakers have followed – with the result that the number of endnotes has tended to increase from one debate to the next! Where appropriate and helpful, I have also introduced endnoted references into the second part (the open debate).

READING THE DEBATES

Perhaps a few words are in order about how these debates should be read. The first point is that while readers will search in vain for ready-made theories, they are afforded unprecedented access to the normally invisible process of theory in the making. Each debate should be taken as an invitation to readers to join in, and to develop informed positions of their own. Second, rules of criticism that would normally apply to published work cannot be so strictly applied to the contributions reproduced here. Different rules, of course, apply to oral presentations such as in lectures and seminars. Indeed, the value of the seminar lies precisely in the opportunity it affords to launch ideas that are still so rough-cut or unrefined that one would never dare venture them in published form. But precisely because only the refined product ever makes it into print, the dialogic process of 'working up' remains hidden and mysterious to all but those fortunate enough to have been present and able to participate. This volume is intended to remove some of the mystery and to widen the scope of participation. In reading it, however, it would be wise to imagine oneself placed within the debating chamber, much as in reading the script of a play you might imagine yourself in the theatre. That is to say, read the words as if you were hearing them spoken.

There is one other reason why the debates reproduced here are closer to the improvised, oral discussion of the seminar than to the carefully controlled debates that typically appear in the pages of learned journals. This has to do with the dimension of time. In print, an author might criticize an argument published years previously by another; later on the latter may publish a further response to the former. The whole debate reads like a conversation among whales, echoing throughout the academic ocean in excessively slow motion. The debates reproduced here, by contrast, took hours, not years. However, the various positions taken by the opposed sides in each debate are still situated in the long-term flow. Thus each side develops its position in response to a view that is already established in the literature and is inclined to attribute that view to its opponents, while the latter vigorously deny any such attribution on the grounds that their position has been developed in response to something else! It is this feature of what could be roughly called 'synchronic' rather than 'diachronic' debate that leads to the impression, in many cases, that arguments are being conducted at cross-purposes. This can be frustrating, yet argument at cross-purposes is surely better than no argument at all, since only by first revealing misunderstandings can they be addressed and corrected.

The participants in these debates, however, are not responding only to currents of thought within anthropology. They are also sensitive to the events taking place around them. In reading the debates, therefore, it is important to bear in mind the year in which they took place, and what was going on in the world at the time. This is most obviously the case in the debate on the concept of society, held in 1989, when British academics were coming to terms with the wholesale destruction of the social fabric wrought by Thatcherite policies at home, and witnessing the collapse of communist Eastern Europe and the revival of nationalist fervour abroad. All of this lent a special urgency to our thinking about what was being done, or thrown out, in the name of 'society'. But although contemporary world events thread their way through the following pages, this does not mean that the debates have been overtaken by history, or that their salience has been in any way reduced by the passage of time. The themes they address remain at the top of the theoretical agenda, and the debates themselves effectively register the pulse of contemporary thinking in British social anthropology.

APPENDIX

Reproduced below are the results of the ballots following each debate. Note that these figures give nothing more than a glimpse of the balance of opinion, and should not be regarded as an index of the relative merits of alternative arguments.

Social anthropology is a generalizing science or it is nothing

For 26
Against 37
Abstentions 8

The concept of society is theoretically obsolete

For 45
Against 40
Abstentions 10

Human worlds are culturally constructed

For 41
Against 26
Abstentions 7

Language is the essence of culture

For 24
Against 47
Abstentions 8

The past is a foreign country

For 26
Against 14
Abstentions 7

Aesthetics is a cross-cultural category

For 22
Against 42
Abstentions 4

1988 debate

Social anthropology is a generalizing science or it is nothing

Introduction

Tim Ingold

Is social anthropology a scientific endeavour? Does it aim to establish general propositions about the conditions of human culture and social life? These questions are as old as anthropology itself; indeed, the tensions they imply – between science and humanism, between the general and the particular – are vital to the constitution of the discipline. Nevertheless their salience has changed, not only due to developments within the subject, but also on account of new pressures and expectations whose source lies in the societies to which we ourselves – as anthropologists – belong. At a time when we are increasingly conscious of the implications of our involvement with the peoples among whom we study, the gap between our own scholarly aspirations and what is practically required of us has grown wider than ever. In this situation, the questioning of the nature and objectives of anthropological inquiry has gained an added urgency. The motion for the first in this series of debates was phrased to reflect this sense of urgency.

Of course the question concerning science is, to some extent, separate from the issue of generalization, and the nature of the link between them depends both on what is meant by science and on the kind of generalization one has in mind. Apropos the latter, the debate reveals two rather different approaches. The principal target of Anthony Cohen's critique, in his opposition to the motion, is the kind of generalization that screens out individual differences and idiosyncrasies, leaving only those characteristics that the members of some collectivity or other appear to have in common. This is what enables anthropologists to attribute beliefs and practices not to particular persons, but to entire ethnic groups like Nuer, Inuit or Australian Aborigines, or even to categories of people which exist only in the anthropological imagination such as hunter-gatherers, peasant farmers, or 'Euro-Americans'. Behind this critique is a more deep-seated unease about the way we tend to speak of 'societies' or 'cultures' as collectivities whose members have more in common with one another than with members of other, equivalent groupings. For surely those differences that make every life-history unique do not appear in spite of people's engagement in social and cultural life, but *because* of it. Yet the question remains: if societies or cultures cannot be defined by the limits of consensus among their members, then how can they be defined at all? And if they cannot be defined, except in the most arbitrary or provisional way, what becomes of the traditional anthropological project of cross-cultural or cross-societal comparison?

The second kind of generalization is closer to what is normally meant by the notion of the hypothesis in science. It is a statement to the effect that where certain conditions obtain, a certain result may be expected. An example of such a generalization might be that in agricultural societies with land-intensive techniques of cultivation, and where land rather than labour is a scarce resource, property will devolve to both men and women and marriage will be monogamous. That this is a general statement is undeniable, but whether it has been derived through a process of generalization is another matter altogether. The issue here hinges on the contrast between induction and deduction. Arguably, the notion of generalization implies an inductive procedure whereby certain regularities or patterns are drawn from the systematic review of a large number of empirical cases. But in supporting the motion, Anthony Good favours the kind of deductive procedure most prominently advocated by Karl Popper. According to Popper, every hypothesis is derived from a theory, but theoretical innovation is a matter of inspired conjecture, not scientific method. Hypotheses cannot be proven, but they can be refuted through testing against the evidence. When it comes to critical testing, Good argues that anthropologists are far more conscientious than many natural scientists (his example is chemistry); furthermore, anthropologists are a good deal more aware that such testing necessarily involves dialogue and debate within the scientific community.

However, Judith Okely, opposing the motion, objects to the Popperian version of anthropology-as-science, with its image of the fieldworker as technician, testing hypotheses and recording facts in the 'natural laboratory' furnished by other cultures. Anthropologists are involved in multiple conversations, both in the field and among academic colleagues. But it is hard to say of any conversation that it is one thing or the other, either an episode of theory building or an episode of critical testing. It is, however, to the language of positivism in which so much of contemporary science is couched that Okely directs her principal critique. Her objections, in other words, are not so much to science as to *scientism*. She would have nothing against the idea of anthropology as science if science were taken in its original sense, meaning simply 'knowledge'. But scientism blocks knowledge by closing down or discrediting the work of the creative imagination. Okely makes it very clear that the source of this blockage is political. Mainstream science, with more power and resources at its disposal than anthropologists could ever dream of, can celebrate the genius and inspiration of its great thinkers. But in the public perception of anthropology, reliance on the imagination tends to be dismissed as evidence of 'soft' or sloppy thinking.

Though Keith Hart and Judith Okely contribute on opposite sides in the debate, Hart's support for science resonates to some extent with Okely's rejection of scientism. Like Okely, Hart objects to positive science's obsession with method, at the expense of an awareness of what knowledge is *for*. Moreover, he is sensitive to the way in which the meaning of science has changed over the centuries. His strategy for revealing such changes is to show how successive generations have responded to the question of what science is *not*. Where once the antitheses of science were myth and religion, now they are the humanities and creative arts. Even the creativity involved in theoretical conjecture, according to the Popperian model, is supposed to lie beyond the purview of scientific investigation. However, positivism, Hart argues, is already obsolescent within mainstream natural science, and the rather jaded view that many anthropologists have of science – with its vision of men in white coats – is increasingly out of date. Attending to matters of history, reflexivity, language and so on should amount not to a rejection but to a reform of science, a reform that must ultimately lead to the dissolution of the disciplinary barriers between the natural sciences, the arts and the humanities that currently carve up the academic arena. In this, Hart argues, anthropology has a unique role to play.

Overall, the contributors to this debate seem virtually united in their dislike – indeed detestation – of the methods and presumptions of positivism, yet the relation between positivism and generalizing science is contested. Many would agree that modern science has become so corrupted by its association with positivist methodology, and by its subservience to commercial and military interests, that it has forsaken its original, humane objectives of creating a better and more just society – objectives to which social anthropology might very well subscribe. But do we embrace these objectives in the name of science or by projecting our discipline as a counter-science? On the one hand, it may be argued that we should not dismiss science simply because some of the work that goes on in the name of science strikes us as thoroughly disreputable. After all, anthropology's record, too, is not exactly untarnished. On the other hand, even if a distinction is made between 'real' science and 'pseudo' science, a good deal of 'social science' in Britain is of the latter kind, as is the view of science enshrined in the dominant discourse of our society, and imposed upon us by our political and bureaucratic paymasters. How, then, should we respond to these imposed definitions? Do we collude by presenting a public image of anthropology as a social science, whatever our private practice, simply as a strategy of survival in a philistine and competitive environment? Or do we justify our claims to be practising 'real' science? Or do we abandon science altogether, adopting a critical stance unequivocally rooted in the humanities? These are just some of the issues raised by the following exchanges. They make compelling reading for all who are concerned with the future direction of social anthropology.

Part I The presentations

FOR THE MOTION (1)

KEITH HART

The reason I have for taking part in this debate is not to rehash inconclusive arguments over methodology, but rather to revive interest in the objectives of anthropology. It is appropriate to be concerned with the means of acquiring knowledge if we are confident that the established ends of our collective efforts are sound. But, when our social purpose is uncertain and our discipline reflects a general intellectual malaise, preoccupation with means rather than ends becomes self-defeating.

I take British social anthropology today to be marginal, fragmented, confused; to be obsessed with its own internal affairs more than with any larger conception of the purposes of knowledge. The demoralized descendants of Radcliffe-Brown and Malinowski are now increasingly given to insular reflection on the sources of their own anxiety, an anxiety induced by the loss of empire and with it the closure of that window on the world which once gave British anthropology its breadth and global vision.

We are not alone in this. The great project of modern social science with which our century began is manifestly in disarray. The West is now facing for the first time, in the shape of Asia's resurgence, a challenge to its intellectual and practical ascendency. If we wish to situate our dilemmas within these epochal events, it will not do to dwell on the methodological legacies of those who wrested a niche for social anthropology in the British academy half a century ago. Rather, we must take a broader view of our place in world history, the better to devise a strategy for making a constructive contribution to understanding modern society's next phase.

There are two great ideas driving modern history and they are inextricably linked – democracy and science. The first of these says that societies fit for human beings to live in must guarantee the freedom and equality of all citizens so that the people may be self-governing. The second says that such societies can only flourish if knowledge in them is based on the discovery of what is objectively real.

Science has two great objects – nature (everything out there that we did not consciously make up) and society itself (which is both a part of nature and the result of human intentions, however misguided). A democratic society has to break down intrinsic barriers to its own development – poverty, ignorance, injustice. To do so it needs science. Whatever we plan to do is more likely to succeed if we employ reason to find out how essential things work.

Moreover, the principles on which society is founded must be common to all of us; they must touch what is 'natural' in us, as opposed to what is merely conventional or arbitrary. This is the core of the modern quest for human, civil or natural rights. Equally, science thrives on democratic social organization. It is above all a communal enterprise, relying on the painstaking, cumulative efforts of generations towards shared ends. When science is merely an elite exercise, cut off from the general impulses of ordinary people, it is in danger of atrophying. The idea that links the two sides is education. Free and equal citizens must be knowledgeable. And science must be sustained by a general culture which values truth, learning and practical invention.

There is only one modern revolution and it is far from finished. It began in earnest in seventeenth-century England, which Veblen once described as 'an isolation hospital for science, technology and civil rights'. The discoveries of Locke and Newton were made general in the eighteenth century by the European Enlightenment and were realized as a living social experiment in the United States of America. Since then, the French and Russian revolutions have dominated the thinking of progressive intellectuals. And, as the Western industrial nations became more wealthy and, it must be said, more equal, the pursuit of knowledge has often become more esoteric and personal.

Of late it has been claimed that we are already in a post-modern, post-industrial or post-scientific phase. I doubt if this is true even of the richest countries; but it is manifestly untrue of world society as a whole, where poverty, ignorance and the starkest inequalities are normal for the vast majority. The task of building a world fit for human beings to live in has barely begun.

Two attitudes predominate among our intellectual and political elites: one turns its nose up at 'bourgeois' democracy and science, declaring them a sham, without enquiring too deeply into institutional realities;

while the other rejoices in the apparent achievements of 'free' Western states whose citizens remain at this time extremely unfree and unequal, being governed by remote rulers for whom science is largely an aspect of the military budget, rather than a means of general emancipation.

It may be objected that my idea of science is old-hat, that the world has moved on in the last three hundred years. And so it has. Keywords like nature, society and science move with history. This is a dialectical process and its principle is negation. What science is supposed not to be, its place in a set of terms referring to what it is not, offers a better guide to historical shifts in its meaning than positive definitions taken in isolation.

There can be little doubt that what science originally was *not* was mystical beliefs – religion, superstition, stories – uninspected traditions referring human existence to a supernatural cause; in a word, it was not 'myth'. After five thousand years of agrarian civilization, the main task of modern societies is to found knowledge on a truly secular footing. Even a century ago the political drive sustaining science was largely anti-clerical; and, in a world where fundamentalist Christianity and Islam flourish (not to mention the Catholic Church), this crusade is still necessary.

Yet, in this century, for most Western intellectuals that battle may appear to have been won. What science principally is not has shifted ground to embrace the oppositions which sustain an expanded academic division of labour. The negation of science is now most commonly the creative arts – literature, poetry, the critical imagination – reflecting the division between natural science and the humanities (the separation of matter and spirit) which has spawned, as a hybrid experiment, social science.

Today's debate could be taken as a referendum on the social sciences and on anthropology's place as one of them. Most of this audience probably came to it with the word 'science' already fixed in mind as a positive or negative notion defined by one of several linked oppositions, all of them retained in present-day usage. For the founders of British social anthropology, our science of ethnography had as its principal negation 'history' or Victorian evolutionism. Now ethnography may be appropriated by the advocates of anthropology as writing and reflection, the very antithesis of science. Meanwhile scientific anthropologists are likely to insist that their subject matter is largely historical.

It is for this reason that I have sought to rescue the original and, I would hope, unifying conception of science as one of the two great objects of modern development. I feel sure that, if we concern ourselves with the method of knowing rather than with the object of knowledge, we will repeat the mistake which has led twentieth-century social science into a blind alley; and our debate will be hopelessly confused. Science undoubtedly rests on the premiss that it is possible to know what is objectively real. But to be committed to that idea is not to be forced to sign up for an ossified seventeenth-century epistemology, as, for example, economics has (thereby revealing itself to be more secular religion than science).

The intellectual achievements of the last three hundred years, in both science and the humanities, have necessarily altered our conception of subject–object relations and of ways of knowing. A modern science must incorporate notions of history, reflexivity, relativity, linguistic and logical traps, Western ethnocentrism, the need for self-knowledge and much else. The best twentieth-century scientists have already done so. The ideal type 'science' – the positivist stereotype of the man in the white coat – cannot capture what scientists, the best and the worst of them, actually do.

The mistake is to emulate scientific method, while forgetting what science is supposed to be for – to be so wrapped up in the problem of one's own ability to know or communicate anything that the priorities determining what needs to be known are lost. If modern anthropologists can often be seen to fall into this error, they are no more guilty than most modern intellectuals. We have lost our way; and this may be because we can no longer see the connection between the social purposes of knowledge and the pursuit of knowledge for its own sake.

Our problem is that the natural scientists can no longer relate what they do to the complex character of human existence, including their own; while the humanists have given up trying to understand how the world works. The social scientists have proved incapable of spanning the gap, for a number of reasons, but mainly because they tried to behave like scientists without seeking to alter what natural scientists think or being able to learn fast enough from what they have discovered. As a result they (including ourselves, as British social anthropologists) have nothing to say about the reciprocal interdependence of nature and society.

My contention is that our civilization desperately needs to reconstitute the original Enlightenment goal of progress through the systematic application of reason, in a world where nature and human society are understood to be interdependent. The prevailing division of intellectual effort within the universities stands in the way of such a development. But the progress of humanity on a world scale will demand a new concept of scientific knowledge and of its constituent branches. The mechanization of brains is one aspect of our phase of the modern revolution which is already requiring such a reorganization.

Even as I contend that anthropology must be part of the great modern project to institute democratic societies on a firm basis of objective knowledge, I would still argue that the experiment known as social science has been a failure and that we would be well advised to distance ourselves from it as fast as we can. Otherwise we will soon go down with sociology, economics and other benighted 'pseudo-sciences' into that dustbin of history reserved for disciplines which failed to move with their times.

The task of our generation is to bring knowledge of nature and society once more into an active, mutually reinforcing relationship. This means mediating and ultimately transcending the opposition between science and the humanities. Anthropologists are uniquely placed to begin such a task. We retain vestiges of an evolutionary anthropology which combines the study of humanity's nature, societies and cultures. Even within social anthropology we combine both the scientific tradition of social theory and humanistic scholarship, as well as our own distinctive hybrid style of ethnographic writing, of abstract generalization pursued through concrete description. Above all our subject matter is the vital, inclusive middle ground – humankind as a whole.

Our virtue as an eclectic anti-discipline is that we are (or should be) open to all the currents which will make the next intellectual synthesis. It would be absurd to tie ourselves to the analytical relics of the last synthesis, to the social sciences that were formed in the early twentieth century. I do not know what this next synthesis will call itself, but I suspect that it may be 'science', perhaps 'human sciences'. The rhetorical power of the word is too strong for us to abandon it lightly. If Derrida and the deconstructionists are human scientists – and I take their synoptic review of the history of Western thought to be a scientific enterprise – then current academic divisions cannot be taken seriously as a guide to whatever science may become in the next century. It is only through the dialectical synthesis of what science is and what it is not that progress in the pursuit of knowledge can continue. What matters is that we should seek to play an active role in the ongoing redefinition of what knowledge is centrally thought to be in our society. If we do not, we deserve to go under in the global upheaval that is building to a climax under our noses.

The task of a science is to generate replicable knowledge; to help others to do difficult things more easily and reliably; to get something right again and again; and, when it is no longer right enough, to think again. Anthropology as an academic discipline must be a part of science. We are in the public domain and we must fight for our place there. The rhetoric of serious public discourse concerns science. We have plenty to say about what that ought to be. We are not artists, even less priests. We have nothing to gain by declaring ourselves to be against science.

AGAINST THE MOTION (1)

ANTHONY P. COHEN

The 'opposition' will divide its labour: Judith Okely will deal with the issues of 'science'; I will limit myself to the question of generalization.

It is undeniable that, throughout most of its history, social anthropology has been a generalizing discipline. Indeed, one might well go so far as to say that if our predecessors did not generalize, they did nothing. But our concern today is not to debate historical facts. Rather, we must address ourselves to contemporary truths.

Our subject is not what the discipline has been in the past, but what it should be *now*, this normative view informed both by developments which have transformed anthropology especially during the last twenty years or so, and by the intellectual and political circumstances within which we are presently working.

Whatever the ambivalence with which any of us approach this motion today, I am certain that none of us will be tempted into the kind of soggy compromise offered recently by Peacock in his *The anthropological lens*. There, he tells us that anthropology deals 'exquisitely' (his word) with individuals – but sees them as representative of their societies. 'Ethnography,' he says, 'reveals the general through the particular. . . . From the Kula ring, we learn about order and integration; from the shaky-handed circumciser, about the interplay of tradition and conflict; and from the cockfight, about hierarchy.'[1] The adjacency of these two latter examples would have intrigued Freud, but there is nothing very intriguing about Peacock's contention: it is nonsense. We have been *taught* to make sense of the Kula as if it was ordering process; and to see Ndembu circumcision as an exemplary case of ritual mediating conflict – in other words, to use the general as a matrix with which to de-particularize the particular; and thereby to validate itself. Generalization becomes a self-confirming hypothesis – a classic instance of what Ardener might have characterized as text becoming genre.

While we will not ape the ploys of formal debate, we are entitled to test a little the terms of the motion. While we do not feel that it is incumbent upon us to reject generalization out of hand, we *do* dispute that generalization is the defining activity or competence of anthropology. Indeed, although we accept that there may be circumstances in which, and audiences to which, generalization might be appropriate, we deny that it is among the more important qualities of the anthropological exercise. Furthermore, we do not regard it as necessary to show by repeated example that generalization can be vacuous. What strikes me as curious is the notion that we should aspire to generality, for generalization is such a dull, such an unambitious, mode of discourse – rather like regarding any performance of a Bruckner symphony as if it were an unvarying reproduction of Bruckner's notes; or, as in the critic's version, as if it were merely an expression of the conductor's reading, ignoring the hundred or so musicians who do the actual bowing and blowing, the plucking and banging.

No wonder orchestral musicians view the maestro through such jaundiced eyes. With what tinge of yellow should we regard our respected colleague who tells us, in a near-orgy of generalization, that Sinhalese abhor individualism as an affront to the cosmic integrity of the State and hierarchy; while Australians regard the State as an offence to the individualism which they venerate, and therefore, drink excessively in celebration of their personal autonomy?[2]

Well, if von Karajan can have *his* Bruckner, we must allow Kapferer *his* Australia, so long as we are clear that it is a figment of his vivid and ingenious imagination, whatever claims may be made for its 'ontologies'. We, on this side, prefer to think of Australians rather than of Australia, and see no reason to suppose that they are any more generalizable than we are. Are there groups whose members are *less* comfortable with generalization about themselves than departments of anthropology? Let me repeat to you an instructive observation, arising out of a consideration of literature on American and Indian kinship: 'Blanket considerations... involve so much selectivity and systemization by the analyst, that they cannot reflect indigenous thinking to the extent claimed.' This is a caution I applaud, and was made in an excellent article on the anthropology of kinship by my opponent today, Anthony Good.[3]

It may reasonably be objected that generalization does not have to take such crude, all-embracing forms. I agree. What kind or degree of generalization might we then regard as acceptable? To the extent that we think with categories – of gender, age, ethnicity, class, and so forth – we know we cannot eschew typification altogether; thinking and intellectual discourse could not proceed without it. But that is not to say that the proper objective of anthropology is to generalize. I would prefer to say that anthropologists use generalization pragmatically as an essential weapon in their struggle to beat a path through generalities towards some greater sensitivity and enlightenment. In this regard, we can measure ourselves against the politician, the journalist, the advertiser, the survey researcher, whose entire enterprise depends upon their capacity to make the grossest kinds of generalization, and to make them stick. But we may also distinguish ourselves from those scholars who are content to ignore, or to miss, the inconvenient qualification, the exceptions to the rule – those devastating pieces of information which, when once revealed, turn out not to be quite so exceptional after all, and, indeed, to show the general statement to be a travesty. Our own experience surely leaves us in no doubt that the ubiquitous failure of development projects, of urban plans, indeed, of strategic planning of all kinds, often results from the planners' neglect of, or disdain for, the vital differences among people which their generalizing models obscure. Social scientists, from econometricians to ethnomethodologists, are obsessed with the postulation of pattern, or rules which purportedly govern behaviour, or some contrived regularity, or with testing their unfalsifiable metaphysics of regularity. But what strikes us so forcibly through ethnographic observation are the *ir*regularities among people. If anthropology's concern is not with complication, with complexity, with differentiation, with non-generalizability, we might just as well retreat to the positivistic pleasures of number-crunching, of social surveys and statistical sampling; take refuge in comfortable, but mindless statements about 'human nature'; or indulge in the pernicious kinds of formulation that we castigate in less liberal minds than our own as racism, sexism, ageism, and so forth.

Let me make it clear that I am not pleading for a redefinition of the objects of study, from societies to individuals; and far be it for *me* to wish to bring into disrepute the notion of 'culture'. But I do insist that we can treat societies, cultures, as barely generalizable aggregates of difference rather than as fictive matrices of uniformity. Plainly, what is at issue here is not simply the highly specific topic of generalization but, rather, the more fundamental, perhaps irresolvable question of the nature of anthropology itself. I am anxious that we should not tumble over that precipice. However, I will put this to you: we can reject generalization as an essential activity without succumbing to the vagaries of 'post-modernist' ethnographic representation, if indeed that is a path you wish to avoid, or without leaving material life for the more elusive realms of symbology, if *that* is the route you dread. It is not a matter of choosing between 'theoretically hard' and 'methodologically soft' anthropology. It *is* a matter of recognizing Hobbes's postulate that societies and cultures are constructs of individuals (*not* the other way around). If we recognize that, then we have no choice but to slash and burn wherever we encounter the generalizing bush.

The alternative is an anthropology to which people – individuals – are almost purely incidental; indeed, are ignorable if they cannot be generalized into some category or other.

Holy's *Comparative anthropology*[4] has some helpful pointers for us. Holy himself notes the move away from the search for cross-cultural uniformities towards cultural specificities – a progress which, as he and other contributors separately observe, liberates us from the tedious search for variations on a theme; and, by focusing on the relationship within any culture between structure and agency, enables us instead to treat people as culturally creative. There is a major difference between Geertz's view of culture as 'webs of significance' collectively spun by its members; and Parkin's as the means by which they individually spin 'endless perspectives' out of the cultural fleece.[5] Generalization is thereby declared redundant – not merely because it is out of fashion or because of political malaise, but because it is intellectually barren, perhaps even bankrupt.

Replying to his invitation to attend this debate, a distinguished anthropologist commented that he was intrigued to learn what 'concealed solipsisms' would be employed to oppose this motion. There is no need for me to conceal them: since self-knowledge seems to me quite unattainable, I do not use them. The essential self is frustratingly elusive, the generalizable self insubstantial; considerations which, in themselves, must suggest the absurdity of general statements about societies or their collective constituents. Contemporary concerns with reflexivity do not suggest necessarily a 'self-indulgence', or what a respected reviewer recently referred to in *Man*, perhaps a little intemperately, as 'the soppy drivel of self-analysis'. The call for an awareness of the anthropological self is not an end in itself (a misrepresentation perpetrated by several writers, such as Friedman)[6] but, rather, an injunction to us as ethnographers to recognize that those whom we study are, like ourselves, composites of selves, as complex as we are, as uncomfortable as we are ourselves with generalization about ourselves. The fruitfulness of such sensitivity is superbly illustrated in Wendy James's account of Uduk personhood in her *The listening ebony*.[7]

What consciousness of the self and of the philosophical problems of personhood *should* have taught us is that, by failing to extend to the 'others' we study a recognition of the personal complexity which we perceive in ourselves, we are generalizing them into a synthetic fiction which is both discredited and discreditable. We fall back too easily on the assumption that in important matters the members of collectivities think alike. That is why we talk blithely about ethnic strategies, about cultural attitudes and values, about how the Azande or the peasants of the Bocage regard witchcraft, about how the Huichol and the Tallensi contemplate their destinies. With what arrogance and insensitivity do we presume to speak about the aspirations, sentiments and sensibilities of tribes, lineages, ethnic groups, sects, or other, even more general categories: pastoralists, hunters, indigenous peoples?

Let me sum up. I do not stand for an anthropology without generalization but, rather, for one which uses it to expose the falsity and superficiality of the general statement. Roger Keesing has recently shown how scratching the surface of Kwaio general statements about ghosts and the Land of the Dead reveals an infinity of contradiction and diversity, a diversity which, he concludes, 'seems to me to render deeply problematic premises about culture as systems of shared meaning'.[8]

Symbols mean different things to different people, different things to the same people at different times. What then can be the status of the generalized claims we make for the most arcane and elusive aspects of social behaviour, wrapped in the mysteries of ritual and myth, cloaked in the fog of kinship ideology? If our aspiration is to reveal and display the genius of those whom we study, rather than *our* cleverness in inventing *them*, then we must be bold, ambitious, and look beyond the blandness of the general to the sharpness of the particular – or, at least, know how to treat the general with the very greatest scepticism and caution.

FOR THE MOTION (2)

ANTHONY GOOD

Anthony Cohen chose in his presentation to focus almost exclusively on stereotyping in formulating his critique of generalization. I agree entirely with his comments on the limitations and undesirable features of cultural stereotyping, but stereotypes are of course not the only kinds of generalization possible in anthropology. I intend to deal with generalization from a rather different, broader point of view. I have been encouraged to be as polemical, unscholarly and controversial as I like, and intend to try and take full advantage of that offer. The motion is that 'social anthropology is a generalizing science or it is nothing'. I myself wish to claim something slightly different: namely, that if anthropology is not a generalizing science, it is *not worth doing*.

My main qualification for speaking today is that I have actually done something you will all agree *is* 'generalizing science', namely physical chemistry. Yet the differences between chemistry and anthropology, it seems to me, are not very great. The point is not that social anthropology is more like physical chemistry than you may think – you know as well as I do what anthropology is like – but that physical chemistry is more like social anthropology than you may think.

It is a truism that the crucial distinction between the physical and social sciences lies in their objects of study. Unlike atoms and molecules, people are reflexive: in Weberian terms, they don't merely behave, they behave meaningfully, they act. Social science is the study of meaningful human behaviour.

Most of us would agree that anthropology is concerned with meaningful behaviour, with action, with actors' understandings of 'facts' rather than 'facts' themselves, though this is more true methodologically than theoretically. That is, although we subject much of our information to criticism and re-interpretation by informants, we allow ourselves the option of rejecting these critiques, for sound reasons such as the more systematic nature of our own observations, which transcend the perspective of any one social role.

So far so good: but this argument goes off the rails if it leads to the conclusion that – because of its concern with meaning – anthropology cannot be scientific. For some, indeed, the allegedly 'non-scientific' character of anthropology is not merely accepted as a regrettable but inevitable deficiency, but glorified, and made a matter for rejoicing. I find this view unintelligible, and indeed dangerous both for what we teach our students, and for the utility of anthropology outside the academic context. I shall refute it by showing that anthropology *is* a thoroughly scientific enterprise, if the nature of 'science' is properly understood.

First, it stands in a clear relationship to other sciences with regard to its subject matter. Let me illustrate this by means of an admittedly over-simple just-so story, as follows.

There are a number of levels at which the world can be understood. Each is the concern of one of the basic sciences. The nature of the most elementary components of the physical universe is controversial, but for simplicity let us label them sub-atomic particles. Whatever they are, the discipline which studies them is nuclear physics. More broadly, physics generally studies the behaviour of single, monadic particles. When such particles combine to form more complex entities – molecules – these prove to have bulk properties which are more than the sum of their parts. These molecules are the subject matter of chemistry. They combine in turn to form cells, whose properties – most dramatically, the property of life – are again not the mere aggregation of the properties of their component molecules. Cells are the subject matter of biology. They combine into organisms, which have properties and possibilities infinitely greater than mere aggregations of cells. These include the phenomena of mind, studied by psychology. Finally, of course, human organisms combine into societies with attributes such as power, authority, hierarchy, and so on, not present in individual human beings. Such societies also share collective representations – emergent properties whose peculiarities lie at the heart of today's debate, and which form the most distinctive subject matter of anthropology.

The interrelationships of these basic sciences are clear: each studies those bulk properties which arise when the objects of study of the science preceding them in order of presentation are combined together in distinctive structures. A further methodological principle is that, as the properties studied by each science emerge only at that particular level of structural complexity, they cannot be fully accounted for in terms of properties at any earlier level. That is, they cannot be explained by any form of reductionism. Each of these sciences thus has its own autonomous level of competence, and it should not surprise us, therefore, if it also has its own distinctive methodology. Finally, all these approaches are equally valid ways of understanding events in the real world, though their respective relevance changes drastically according to the nature of the questions asked and the answers sought. Thus, although any human interaction is simultaneously a process of interaction for countless billions of sub-atomic particles, this fact is not particularly relevant if our concern lies with the social implications of what is going on.

So social anthropology stands in a clear relationship to the other basic sciences, because it is concerned with studying phenomena at one clearly discriminable level *vis-à-vis* those other sciences. This does not mean, of course, that anthropology as presently practised, still less the work of any particular anthropologist, is *ipso facto* scientific; but it does mean, I suggest, that anthropology has the potential to be scientific.

My next point takes this argument a stage further: social anthropology, I shall show, has already realized its scientific potential. Despite its distinctive subject matter and methodology, anthropology as presently practised fits comfortably under the rubric of 'science'.

So what do we mean by science? *Chambers Dictionary* gives the following definitions: 'knowledge' (presumably we all agree that anthropology is a form of knowledge); 'a skilled craft' (again, we all agree that skill is involved). But presumably the definition closest to what our motion has in mind is the following: 'knowledge ascertained by observation and experiment, critically tested, systematized and brought under general principles'. With the possible exception of 'experiment', if very narrowly defined, it seems undeniable that social anthropology is all these things. Consider them in turn:

(a) *observation*: participant observation is what we always say is our characteristic method.
(b) *critical testing* operates at all stages. During fieldwork, there is what Holy and Stuchlik[9] call 'test by praxis', namely our growing ability to take part in local events, and advance opinions on them which are taken seriously by local people. During writing, our analyses are tested in many ways: against our own data, for internal coherence, and against the ethnographies and analyses of others.
(c) *systematized*: all ethnography, however 'reflexive', 'autobiographical' or 'post-modern' – to mention only a few terms of abuse – is undeniably subject to systematization.
(d) *brought under general principles*: not all anthropologists set out to do this all the time, but I cannot imagine any justification for anthropology, any reason why it might be worth devoting one's life to, and trying to teach to others, if it did not hold out the possibility of generalization. If it is in the end merely a means of 'finding ourselves' then it is pure self-indulgence and not worth doing.

If we wish to characterize 'science' rather more precisely, one of the most satisfactory and influential ways of doing so is that offered by Popper. As you will know, Popper argues that scientific method is founded not upon induction, but upon deduction. Moreover, science is not concerned with 'proving' – or as he says 'verifying' – laws once and for all, but only with (temporarily) corroborating them, by showing that certain hypotheses deduced from them account for the observations made so far. There is an asymmetry here, though: one can never finally 'verify' a generalization, but one *can* falsify it.[10]

Science as a method applies only to the testing of hypotheses: theory-development itself is wholly non-scientific, and arises through intuition, or genius. Moreover, even the assessment of observations, to decide whether or not they corroborate or falsify the hypotheses in question, is almost never a simple, clear-cut matter, even for the most trivial hypothesis, and has to be resolved by debate within the scientific community. Popper himself, of course, was a methodological individualist, but most of *us* would wish to see this inter-subjective testing as a pre-eminently social process. The contributions of Polanyi, Kuhn, Ziman and others lend extra force to such a modification of Popper's account and add further to its general credibility.

All the features Popper describes are explicitly present in social anthropology, where we debate such issues all the time – much more so, in fact, than in chemistry, where the inductive delusion is still widely, if implicitly, held, and where the debate of inter-subjective testing is generally perfunctory. Physical chemistry, I was assured by my chemistry PhD supervisor, was merely colouring in 'little patches of blue sky' in the grand design of scientific knowledge. In the fields of debate and questioning, anthropologists behave far more like Popperian scientists than chemists do!

Arguments about the significance of evidence, and the inferences legitimately drawn from it, lie at the heart of virtually all anthropological debates. The central process of Popper's model, falsification, also features clearly in anthropology. If you doubt this, compare our present state of knowledge with that prevailing in the last century. Surely we can say with confidence that – whatever the validity of our present views – certain approaches then adopted, certain assumptions made about specific other cultures, and about 'others' in general, were wrong?

A familiar, but none the less excellent example is provided by Sahlins's[11] writings on primitive affluence. We do not necessarily have to accept in detail his notion of the 'Zen road to affluence', but it is surely undeniable that a necessary precondition for the study of hunter-gatherer behaviour or ideology is the realization that they are in fact *not* perpetually on the brink of starvation.

It is true that anthropologists rarely formulate universal, descriptive and predictive laws, but it would be wrong to regard this as evidence that anthropology is non-scientific, for several reasons:

(a) Most would-be laws in anthropology have ultimately proved to be tautologies: definitions or typologies masquerading as predictions. But precisely the same is true of science: thermodynamics, for example, is a closed logical system in which apparently predictive statements of interrelationship follow automatically from the definitions of such metaphysical notions as 'heat' and 'energy'. Many scientific 'laws' are themselves metaphysical statements.

(b) 'Laws' – even scientific ones – are not merely descriptive and predictive, but morally *pre*scriptive, too. Laws which are primarily of this latter type are found in every society, and occupy a great deal of any fieldworker's attention. We study such laws, and our conclusions are necessarily different in character from the laws themselves – just as the laws of physics differ from the phenomena which they describe. Social anthropology, you might say, is *above the laws*!

I have argued that, as a matter of fact, anthropology *is* a science with regard to both methodology and practice. I shall now argue further that strategically, in our own interests, in the interests of the discipline, but above all in the interests of those we study and with whom we claim such unusual closeness and mystical participation, it is incumbent upon us not only to accept that social anthropology is scientific, but to proclaim from the rooftops that it is.

I am concerned now with anthropology as expertise, with the role of the anthropologist as expert, for example in the field of development. This role is often not particularly glamorous or intellectually exciting, but it is useful. Involvement in such situations may confront anthropologists with uncomfortable moral dilemmas, and certainly it is right for us to question forcefully, where necessary, the underlying assumptions and practices of development. But such dilemmas are inescapable in any practical situation, and it is better for us to be involved than to allow such processes to go on without us. We may at least ameliorate their wilder excesses.

There is a dilettante notion, fashionable in some quarters, that anthropology can have no practical relevance. I disagree: indeed, in the polemical context of debate, I would suggest that such attitudes might justifiably be viewed as almost obscene. Anthropologists above all, precisely because of our claim to specially close, intense personal relationships with those about whom we write, operate under a moral imperative which requires us to involve ourselves in developmental processes initiated from outside but affecting those same people.

The relevance of this for today's debate is that only the recognizably scientific nature of anthropological expertise lends our advice credibility: the fact that it is indeed based upon 'observation and experiment, critically tested, systematized and brought under general principles'. If we admit that all we are doing is contemplating our own navels, no one will take us seriously. I am not advocating that we should claim to be doing science merely for strategic reasons, even when we know the claim to be bogus. My contention, to the contrary, is that it is not bogus at all.

The motion is not that anthropology is *only* generalizing, but that generalizing science is an essential element of the discipline. It allows for the possibility that there is more to anthropology than that, which is indeed so. But personally, I find it both more important and more interesting to learn about other societies than about the emotional responses to them of a single colleague.

Anthropology, then, is a rational, empirical discipline, or it is nothing. It is more than a mere literary genre, and certainly more than psychobabble. As Michael Carrithers wrote recently: 'it is difficult to see [ethnography] as achieving more than . . . good writing if it is not grounded in some thought about what is generally true of humans'.[12]

If social anthropology is only reflexive, if it is only autobiographical (heaven help us, not even biographical, but *auto*biographical!), if it is only a form of psycho-therapy for jaded aesthetes, then it is not worth doing.

It may be that as a consequence of doing anthropology we learn more about ourselves, but this is not and should not be its primary purpose. If we wish to do anything to help those we study – concern for whose welfare we parade like stigmata in front of students, readers and the general public – then for both methodological and strategic reasons, we can only do so by regarding our activities as scientific, and convincing others that this is so.

AGAINST THE MOTION (2)

JUDITH OKELY

In opposing the motion, I suggest we substitute the word knowledge for 'generalizing science'. I therefore argue that anthropology is knowledge or it is nothing. The word science is now culture bound, misleading and impoverished. It comes from the classical Greek which means knowledge. By the eighteenth century the meaning of the word was more specific, it included the search for underlying laws.

But even that more precise sense has been debased and confined today. We should consider the current meaning of the word science; it is far from the Enlightenment ideal and even further from the original idea of knowledge. Anthropology risks being unscientific in the original wider sense if it is defined only as science, and as a generalizing one at that. The current meaning of 'science' as proffered to social scientists is little more than scientism. It is still contaminated by positivism. Positivism may have been discredited in principle, but it operates in practice. One implication of this motion, you may feel, is that if you oppose it, anthropology is nothing. My arguments offer you more than that, indeed more than scientism. In opposing the motion you do not have to believe that anthropology has no claim to science.

Alternatively, you may think that by opposing the motion you are defining anthropology as mere literature, or – to use a much maligned word – as fiction. It is not my intention to argue that anthropology is fiction. However, in passing, I will clarify a common misunderstanding. The post-modernist use of the term fiction does not mean mere invention, all made up, fairy tale or fantasy. The post-modern definition is closer to 'social construction'. You may also be misled even about the classical notion of fiction. For example, the nineteenth-century writers of fiction such as Balzac, Tolstoy and Eliot did not sit at empty desks with virgin paper and write from the top of their heads. Balzac conducted painstaking historical and contemporary research into every ethnographic detail of his novels. When setting events in a specific year he made sure the appropriate characters wore the fashion of that season, down to the very shape of the sleeves. Far from inventing characters from thin air, he created them from meticulous first-hand or participant observation. The difference between his characters and individuals for anthropologists is that Balzac's were composites. Balzac, in *La Comédie Humaine*, even expanded on scientific theories of his time, believing that humanity could be classified into specific character types. Each type had its own temperament and physiognomy. Balzac's discredited theories were no more absurd than those of Lombroso, the criminologist, who made explicit claims to be a scientist. This is not to forget some fundamental distinctions between literature and anthropological ethnography. Artistic licence may, indeed must, encourage creative transformations.

Social realism, the seemingly exact replication of life in art, has its limitations. Eisenstein, the Russian film maker, in wanting to convey the moment and meaning of the October Revolution, incorporated imagery from symbolist poetry in defiance of his Stalinist patrons. Professed realism may prove less real in its outcome. By contrast, anthropologists aim at minimum, if not maximum, realism. They make their own distortions for ethical, political and technical reasons. Names are changed, anecdotes edited and disguised. A village may be a composite. Such distortions are not sufficient to call an ethnography literary fiction. In contrast to any novel, we would discredit a field monograph by an anthropologist who had only pretended to have been there. But as we look closer at the development from first ideas to fieldwork, note-taking and monograph, there are value judgements and choices. The necessary selectivity, the omissions, the accretions and theoretical paradigms lead us to acknowledge that the monograph is also a product and construct of the anthropologist's academic and historical time. The same could be said of Darwin's *The Origin of Species*, but we do not say that biology ceases to be a science. In unravelling the conscious or unconscious constructions in a monograph, we do not simply falsify and discredit the monograph as some might fear, we acquire knowledge into how a representative of one culture, usually the dominant imperial one, represents and explains another. The very selectivity of the content can also inform the reader as to what the people themselves chose to reveal to an outsider. To read a monograph as a historical construct enlarges our knowledge and raises the potential in a truly scientific enterprise.

Part of the selectivity of the monograph may depend on the age and sex of the anthropologist, as well as the theoretical paradigm.[13] It is obvious that one individual cannot hope to grasp the totality. The monograph gives us a very specific knowledge, but one with which others can engage. The specificity of the fieldworker should not discredit the knowledge acquired. Yet if we followed the positivists' tenets to the letter this knowledge would be devalued. One such tenet is the interchangeability of observers. Here anthropology has too readily allowed itself to be intimidated by scientism. The specificity of the fieldworker should be explored, not repressed. The extent to which observers are *not* always interchangeable should be a subject for scientific study.

Traditionally, social anthropology has permitted what it believes to be science to colour its own claims to science. The danger is that scientism, not science as knowledge, sets the agenda. We listen to scientists through keyholes. In practice, discoveries in the so-called hard sciences often occur in ways which are more familiar to the humanities. The difference is that social scientists pretend in print that their discoveries do not happen that way, whereas scientists and mathematicians have the hegemonic power to talk of their experiences without being discredited. It is said that the inspiration for relativity theory came to Einstein when he imagined a man moving so fast in space he could not see his reflection in the mirror he was holding. Thus the ideas were crystallized through the power of metaphor, and a Lacanian one at that. Contrast this imaginative freedom in 'real' science with the straitjacket of positivism. It retains its grip, especially on those who would define anthropology as a science or nothing.

One of the tenets of positivism is the unity of scientific method amidst the diversity of subject matter. In another, the natural sciences, more especially mathematical physics, set a methodological ideal for all the sciences, including the social sciences and the humanities.[14] Popper and the neo-Popperians, Jarvie and Horton[15] would hold with this, despite their alleged break with positivism. These neo-positivists likewise reduce epistemology to methodology. They assert that one objective method is suitable for both the natural and the social sciences. 'The concept of theory as method reduces a traditional role of theory as critique to the criticism of hypotheses.'[16] The Popperian concept of theory envisages the participant observer as laboratory technician, testing hypotheses and recording facts.

You may ridicule this analogy. The majority of social anthropologists might be reluctant to define themselves as technicians, positivist or Popperian. Why then do we still use the positivist's language as we go about our work? It is a web from which we should free ourselves. Too often, postgraduates are asked 'What hypotheses are you testing?' This is the kiss of death. Yet it is printed in research grant application forms, which postgraduates and we have to address. We continue to collude in the use of the word 'training', which reduces our research to a set of techniques. It sets the theoretical agenda. We react rather than initiate. Why do we not ask of others, 'Why do you bother with hypotheses?' Hypotheses limit the scope of knowledge. We know our research thrives on what we cannot begin to hypothesize. Agar has responded with 'the funnel method'.[17] This is an inappropriately mechanical metaphor for the creative experience of research.

Anthropologists still struggle defensively with the positivistic ideal of the objective observer, when our unique approach calls for a confrontation with self-awareness. Here reflexivity has magnificent potential in fieldwork practice away from the desk or laboratory bench. A limited science regards the interests of an ego with personal and cultural history as potentially contaminating. We should see it instead as contributing to the meaning of scientific practice.[18] Participant observation could be pondered, interpreted and explained. We hesitate to explore how it works, because we are intimidated by the phantom of detachment.

Let us examine the tradition that too often gives us the exact and natural sciences to mimic. Granted that we are still unflustered by any quantification ideal, the metaphor of precise measurement still leaks into our fictive hypotheses. Again, the practitioners whom we are supposed to imitate do not act in the way we imagine. A leading mathematician was asked how he went about solving difficult problems. His answer? *Think vaguely.* Would we dare write that in a research proposal?

The positivist precision is only one form, for we and those in the humanities also have precise standards. Today we appreciate the metaphorical and narrative style of Malinowski. It was only incidentally learned that part of that productive process came from reading Conrad and from a self-confessed 'shameful' obsession with novels in the field. We have rejected Malinowski's scientific theory of basic needs, meanwhile the ungeneralized anecdotes leave us knowledge. Science, in contrast, defines the anecdotal as pejorative.

A final characteristic of scientific explanation is that it is causal and subsumes individual cases under assumed general laws of nature; something Evans-Pritchard so severely contested. By contrast, a Marxist such as Maurice Godelier would sympathize and, were he here, would probably support the motion. But the Godeliers among you should recognize that in doing so, you are also voting with and for scientism. For a few, this would be no dilemma. A contributor to *Critique of Anthropology* has called for the end of fieldwork.[19] Once freed from what he called this 'straitjacket', the discipline could become truly 'scientific'. Thus the detachment of the observer from human contamination is accomplished at the expense of knowledge and in the name of science. For a more convincing Marxist anthropology, I would suggest the word scientific be replaced by materialist.

To conclude, we have been bewitched, bothered and bewildered by a limited definition of science, even within its Western history. Until we can redefine and extend the meaning of science, we should vote for anthropology as knowledge, global and unconfined.

Part II The debate

MICHAEL ROWLANDS   As the presentations of the four speakers fully confirm, the phrasing of the motion forces a rather stark polarization between 'hard' and 'soft' notions of science, and between generalization and understanding or interpretation. This takes our attention away from two issues which are much more important: first, the nature of comparison; and second, the formation of concepts. Both of these cut across the simplistic dichotomy between science and non-science.

RAY ABRAHAMS   I share this view. Had I been asked to propose a motion on this sort of issue, it would have been something like 'anthropology is a *chimera* or it is nothing'. For it is the attempt both to generalize and at the same time to take on board the intensity of the fieldwork experience that is at the heart of anthropology, and of the anthropological monograph. The latter, too, can be neither wholly one thing nor the other. Like a Zande witch-doctor, I feel that although the monographs I have written are not as good as I would like, somewhere or other there are people who have been able to write them properly. There is, in my view, a middle ground which is not just a compromise, and which is absolutely central to the subject.

TIM INGOLD   Can we compromise? On a number of issues the speakers have put forward directly contradictory points of view: one side argues that generalization is of the essence of what we do, although it is not *all* that we do; the other side argues that generalization is unprofitable. Should we aim for a compromise, or should we go for one argument or the other?

ELIZABETH TONKIN   One cannot avoid generalizing. It is a condition of talk that we use agreed terms and categories. But what anthropologists are really trying to do is to consider specific conditions and to ask whether they can be systematically related in any way. Rather than producing a set of generalizations or a set of individuated portraits, we try to discover what conditions will lead to something else, what kinds of conditions yield certain types of solution.

PNINA WERBNER   My concern is with the kind of relativism advocated by opponents of the motion, with its focus on the individual as interpreter, and its rejection of generalization. What they reject seems to be a sort of *cultural* generalization, which is not the true aim of anthropology as a generalizing science. I endorse the view that our objective is to analyse the structure of a society, with regard to its division of labour and its relations of power and dominance, and to understand how these are expressed in cultural terms. It is possible, then, to make cross-cultural comparisons without having to resort to stereotypical cultural generalizations. The latter, in my view, are almost racist constructs. *They*, it is said, are different from *us*; so different from us that we cannot compare them with ourselves. One has to be very careful with statements of this kind.

LYNN BRYDON   Most of us would agree, I am sure, that science cannot be simply identified with positivism. Yet as soon as one begins to talk about generalization one is forced back to the tools of positivism. I have yet to see any literature which shows how generalization can be undertaken in a non-positivist way.

NICHOLAS FIDDES   Referring to Anthony Good's hierarchy of the sciences, which places social anthropology at the summit, I wonder how it should be distinguished from sociology? Might it be that sociology tends towards generalization and social anthropology towards particularization?

KEITH HART   This is not an accidental question. The distinction between social anthropology and sociology is crucial. The confusion between them arose when social anthropology began to present itself as a 'sociology of the primitive' and to take on Durkheim's project as its own – allegedly for export rather than home consumption. Since that notion has been eroded, the problem has become more acute. I argue that the academic division of labour is itself in dire need of reform, and that to allow social anthropology's confusion with sociology to persist will be to the detriment of our subject. The only thing which can truly distinguish anthropology from the rest of social science is that it addresses human nature *plus* culture *plus* society. The fragmentation of nature, culture and society in the British version of the anthropological endeavour is at the root of the problem. To make the differentiation of sociology from social anthropology hinge on the general versus the particular is to fracture the dialectic on which all knowledge rests. Every kind of understanding requires us to postulate what is the same and what is different. The dialectic between the general and the particular is inevitable, and I cannot imagine how branches of knowledge could be divided on these grounds. But I would suggest that social anthropology in Britain has a very weak sense of its differentiation from sociology, and may indeed be undermined by that weakness.

ANTHONY COHEN   I do not have any sense of a weak differentiation between social anthropology and sociology. Despite eight years in a department of sociology, I have never been able to understand what sociology, or what *a* sociology, is about. If there *is* a distinction, it lies in the greater sense of plurality and diversity within departments of sociology than is found even within our own malaise-torn discipline of social anthropology.

MARILYN STRATHERN   When we set things up in terms of polarities, it often seems that the obvious solution is to compromise. In fact, both sides colonized the best points of the other, converting them into points of their own. But however much we may wish to borrow terms from one another, to compromise, to find middle ways, to imagine that we are doing bits and pieces of everything, we actually live in a social world which – looking in on us – asks the question posed by the motion. We are in a social situation where people use these dichotomies in relation to us: hard versus soft, general versus particular, scientific versus non-scientific. Should we, then, respond to our social environment, and if we do, should our response be couched in terms of these same dichotomies? Or should we escape? Two escape routes have been offered. The proposer offers an escape into the fantasy of some unknown future synthesis (and the trouble with immediate future syntheses is that all we do know is that they will be displaced in their turn). The opposition offers an alternative fantasy, into the imaginations of particular individuals.

MICHAEL ROWLANDS   Rather than trying to escape, one alternative is to understand and criticize the conditions that leave us having to respond to these polarities in the first place.

MALCOLM CHAPMAN   I believe the intellectual public is positivist in its overall outlook: it *likes* generalizing science. If anthropology pretends to be a generalizing science in these terms it is bound to fail. And what it will look like after that is precisely 'nothing'.

WIM VAN BINSBERGEN   In much of what has been said on both sides, I detect an enormous idealism, as if our main purpose in the pursuit of anthropology is to 'be there' and help other peoples, or to construct a universal edifice of knowledge. Taking a relative view, it is clear that our professional language, comprising the concepts and symbols we use, is grounded in specific material and social conditions. The production of anthropological knowledge is thus but one instance of the kind of process that we study among other peoples all over the world. Much of what governs our debate is therefore artificial, for science is a social process of production of knowledge, and in every case such processes contain contradictions that cannot be resolved, and indeed are not supposed to be resolved. Anthropology, likewise, is not one thing or the other: its internal contradictions are what keep it going, making it a living, social and (at times) a reflexive enterprise.

KEITH HART   Since I have been accused of presenting a fantasy as my solution to the problem posed, I should say that my aim was to give a historical account of the social production of knowledge over the last three centuries, and to situate anthropology within that account as something which has not existed eternally and simply allowed its practitioners to get on with their job, but which has specific historical conditions of emergence. And the evidence, I believe, suggests that at this juncture the anthropological project is in serious danger of eclipse. Though I do not know what form a future synthesis might take, I do think that the synthesis on which we have been working for the last hundred years is showing signs of senility.

ANNE FINK   The whole debate seems to resolve ultimately around the pursuit of truth: either truth in the sense that the positivists sought, or truth of the kind that Judith Okely suggests might lie in interpretation. Kolakowski,[20] in his book on Husserl's critique of positivism, points out that for all human beings who seek after truth, knowledge or science, it is the actual task that is important. Kolakowski's conclusion is that although we shall never get there, life is only worthwhile if we keep on trying. The point of our debate is to ask, 'How can we go about finding out about things better than we are now doing?' And I sense on both sides a desire for this ultimate goal.

MARILYN STRATHERN   When I used the term 'fantasy', I meant it in the sense of an imaginative solution to a real-life dilemma; I did not mean it in the sense of something a-historical. We have to consider whether we wish to situate ourselves within the currently dominant discourse, or whether – as anthropologists with access to the thought of peoples whose premises are not the same as our own – we can adopt a critical perspective on the kind of 'bureaucracy-speak' that informs (for example) the policy statements of government and research councils, and whose metaphors infiltrate the very way we think about our subject.

WENDY JAMES   I should like to take up Keith Hart's point that our central concern with human nature differentiates anthropology from other disciplines. Surely it is also characterized by a desire to get things right, to produce better ethnography. One sign of that better ethnography is the kind of concern with individuality that Anthony Cohen was talking about. Other disciplines actually produce rather bad accounts of peoples and cultures about whom we have a solid basis of knowledge in anthropological literature. Let me give you an example. I recently came across an account, coming from a philosophy department in Sweden, of the Nuer living in Ethiopia, otherwise known as the Nipnip. The book is called *Beyond morals? Experiences of living the life of the Ethiopian Nuer.*[21] The account does proceed from a contrast between this group and the Sudanese Nuer, who have become famous through the writings of Evans-Pritchard. However, the author ascribes the major differences between them to an overemphasis, in Evans-Pritchard's work, on the existence of moral ideas and norms among the Nuer. Her main finding is that the Nipnip have nothing which could be called moral ideas or norms. She claims that 'in contrast to most anthropologists', she has 'lived and worked with the people as one of them. . . . In order to turn myself into one of the Nuer people, I took off all my clothes'. That is her statement about her fieldwork, which lasted a full four months! She also claims that 'Religion and magic have no great importance in the life of the Nipnip'. Evans-Pritchard, of course, wrote a substantial book on the subject of Nuer religion. Though the author of this account is familiar with the anthropological literature on the Nuer, she does not seem to have understood its meaning. I am sure everyone here would agree that her's is an *inferior* account, which indirectly confirms the scientific validity of our own anthropological project – taking science in the broader and more old-fashioned sense invoked by Keith Hart.

UNIDENTIFIED SPEAKER   I am unclear from both sides of the debate about what they feel is the purpose of anthropology. Keith Hart wants to build a science of social behaviour. The other side advocates a reflexive stance, which tends towards a neo-colonialist endeavour of finding out more about ourselves by going to study other peoples. I wonder what they think the whole subject is for?

KEITH HART   We cannot afford to forget the objectives of anthropology. Part of the problem is that modern science has become remote, authoritarian and bureaucratic, subservient to the military and industrial complex. Scientists themselves have lost a guiding, humanistic conception of what they do. They can avoid thinking about the human consequences of what they do because it is so successful, and because governments and businesses pay them to do it. As a result, many humanists are thoroughly disgusted with, and alienated from, science. But science was once part of the general human endeavour to create by rational means democratic societies fit for human beings to live in. I argue that it still ought to be that, and that we anthropologists could be part of such a project if it were posed in this way. However, this view has serious ethical, political and intellectual consequences. I believe that anthropology *is* an endangered fragment of an Enlightenment enterprise which risks extinction. It would be good for us to recognize that, and to proclaim it with more vision and vigour than we do at present.

PREVIOUS SPEAKER   The main purpose of anthropology is to improve the circumstances of people by means of a better understanding between cultures. The limitation of anthropology to an academic discipline, and the retreat into the reflexive, do not appear to help that at all. There seems to be no attempt to find a compromise.

ANTHONY COHEN   Nobody here has pleaded for a 'retreat into the reflexive'. Moreover, the issue of compromise is getting a very good airing. What you are hearing are answers to your question 'What is anthropology *for*?', and these are easy to formulate. The *execution* of the answers is impossibly difficult; had we managed to find a way of executing them, this debate would be redundant. The object of anthropology is to understand, and through the approach we advocate we do feel, as Wendy James remarked, that we reach a degree and a depth of understanding that evades other disciplines. But we do not do this simply in order to reveal the anthropological self. Our object is not to get to know ourselves better by undergoing all the traumas of fieldwork and coming to terms with another people. Quite the opposite: by going through a process of introspection in struggling to make sense of what we see – and the process *is* an introspective one – we reach a quality of understanding of the peoples among whom we are living which is not accessible to other disciplines and through other methods.

WIM VAN BINSBERGEN   Most of us are not qualified to propound really meaningful models of the natural sciences. But to set the parameters for an adequate anthropology one has to consider not only natural science but also history. The models and paradigms of historians are much closer to ours, and they have more successfully negotiated the tension between generalization, subjectivity, reflexivity and so on. The debate cannot be complete without comparing anthropology to history in the same way as it has been compared to natural science. In particular, the awareness of the production of historical knowledge as something fully rooted in our society, but which nevertheless yields meaningful statements about other societies, is very instructive for us. The extreme emphasis on generalization across the whole board of human experience and action is not something to which historical comparison leads us.

JUDITH OKELY   In opposing the motion, we have been accused of 'navel-gazing'. I cannot see why, since none of us have suggested it. I carefully avoided any plea for the use of autobiography in this discussion, and certainly did not represent anthropology as a neo-colonial exercise. In fact, both I and Anthony Cohen have carried out studies in our *own* societies. These included 'studying up', looking at the powerful as well as the powerless. Moreover, being reflective is a political act. Someone who was truly reflective would consider the implications, for the people studied, of different ways of promulgating the results of research. One can write accessible reports or popular articles, or appear in the media, or become involved in political actions in which one's knowledge is made available to interested parties. One can also write for an intellectual readership. I am angered by the notion that anything associated with literary sensibility is self-indulgent. Why should we cut out one side of our brains in order to be intellectuals?

JOY HENDRY   I used to be a scientist, but am now quite confused about what science is, which is refreshing. However, I have a practical suggestion. There is, in the 'outside world', a strong view that science should be supported. Like Wendy James, I have read a great deal of bad work about the people I study, written by authors who are regarded as scientists and who can lay claim to a lot more money than can anthropologists. But if we at least *pretend*, to the outside world, that anthropology is a generalizing science, we might avoid the other outcome, that – through lack of support – it will become nothing.

ANTHONY GOOD   This reflects a point raised by a previous speaker [Malcolm Chapman] that if we claim to practise science we would surely be 'found out', and would inevitably fail. But unless we claim to practise science, no one will give us a *chance* to fail. In order that anthropologists should be taken seriously enough to be employed on development programmes, or for their advice to be heeded, they have to claim to be 'scientific'. For reasons I have given, I believe this claim is justified. But it has a strategic value as well. People who organize or have authority over development projects operate on the basis of a scientific model. Fortunately, we can legitimately claim to be scientists, and we should stress the fact that we are.

ANNE FINK   I have been most fortunate in having received a substantial grant to study a subject in social anthropology by a committee of biological scientists. They did admit that they had never given money to a person like me before. But I did not have to offer them a hypothesis. I had to offer an area that I thought needed social observation in order to resolve a problem about which biologists were arguing. They were quite prepared to accept the need for social inquiry, and to give me funds to further my social observations. It is very important to distinguish real scientists from 'pseudo-scientists'. Pseudo-scientific inquiry is positivism in its worst form, and has nothing to do with the work of those scientists whom I am accustomed to meet, and who are very open-minded.

JUDITH OKELY   Anne Fink's example proves my point: scientists have imaginations; they are open to creative ideas. But social scientists are so terrified about *not* being considered scientists that they clamp half their brains.

LYNN BRYDON   We do not have problems with scientists. I do not think anyone would dispute that scientists are open-minded and imaginative. Nor do we have problems in justifying ourselves before historians, literary critics or whatever. The 'clamp' comes when presenting ourselves to bureaucrats and managers. This new breed is to be found not only in the civil service and university administration, but also as successful entrepreneurs in university departments. These are the people we are up against now.

SUSAN DRUCKER-BROWN   Whether we call it science or not, there is general agreement that anthropology involves the observation of the outside social world, however the interpretation and analysis proceed after that. And there is an inevitable tension between the particularities of that world and the analysis one is going to make of it. Surely proper scientists (as opposed to pseudo-scientists) appreciate the different ways in which an external reality can be apprehended, and the difficulties of so doing?

RAY ABRAHAMS I wonder why the term 'science' was selected for inclusion in the motion, since it seems to generate a good deal of mutual misunderstanding. Would the debate have been any different had the motion been proposed that 'social anthropology is a generalizing *discipline* or it is nothing'?

TIM INGOLD The idea behind introducing the term 'science' was to raise precisely the problems and queries that have been discussed here: namely that those who both advocate and oppose 'science' in social research may be working with a view of science that scientists themselves have long ago discarded. If we were to adopt the kind of idea that contemporary scientists have of what they are doing, we might arrive at a new conception – indeed, a new synthesis – of what an anthropology of the future might look like.

ELINOR KELLY I should like to give an example of something based on generalized science, and which – for a number of reasons – had very deleterious consequences. It was the so-called 'Rickets Campaign'. The campaign was liberally funded by bureaucratic agencies, and received much favourable publicity as doing something good for Asian immigrants. Doctors have published numerous articles that add up to an impressive body of material about the seriousness of rickets among Asians in Britain. Their findings are presented in the classic form of statistical generalizations, as percentage figures. But when we looked at the number of cases of rickets that had actually been reported, and at the numbers of individuals included in each sample, we found that the latter varied between seven and twenty-three! I mention this example because if we are talking about generalizing science and its relation to the power and financial structures of our society, we should be cautious. We may have an important role to play in discrediting the 'scientific' premises of social or welfare policy.

MALCOLM CHAPMAN One should not overestimate the extent to which 'proper scientists' are friendly towards the kind of enterprise in which anthropologists are engaged. The overwhelming attitude in science is still a positivistic one. In my view social anthropology has an important job in opposing positivism, which is still virtually a religion in natural and social science, in welfare, and in ministries of intervention. One must, therefore, surely oppose the motion. I detect, however, a mood of 'transcendent abstention'.

TIM INGOLD   I hope there will be no 'transcendent abstention', since the two sides have presented arguments which cannot logically be endorsed at one and the same time. If people find themselves on one side or the other, they should come out and say so. My own experience with scientists is that they have very short memories. I remember hearing a talk by a distinguished geneticist who said he had just read *The Origin of Species* and was amazed to find how much of modern genetics was prefigured by what Darwin wrote in 1859. He had only just come to read work that was instrumental in laying the foundations for his own subject. In anthropology, by contrast, we are always referring back to the work of 'founding fathers' such as Durkheim, Weber and Marx. This sometimes leads outsiders to think that we have made no progress. But much 'progress' in science is achieved by leaving the underlying premisses of the enterprise unattended, thus freeing the hands and mind for more detailed and empirical work. Scientists, then, are apt to forget why they are doing what they do, whereas anthropologists are so busy remembering that they become paralysed when it comes to the doing.

KEITH HART   Looking at anthropology since the Second World War, there is no doubt that most of the big new ideas have come out of the humanities (including linguistics). Many have come from France, and we tend to represent them as anti-scientific because they are not empiricist in the British style. Yet the proponents of these ideas regard them as scientific, and regard themselves as practitioners of *science humaine*. Of course *science* does not mean exactly the same in French as science does in English, or *Wissenschaft* in German. My point is not to draw a rigid dichotomy between 'hard' science and the 'humanities'; it is rather that science is too important an idea to be left to the natural scientists. That is why I insisted upon the political context of whatever knowledge we produce, by drawing the link between science and democracy. If scientists support bureaucratic oppression or promote religious mysticism, we should seek to reform them in the name of science, not to oppose them in the name of anti-science. We should not reject science just because its practitioners are not what we would like them to be. The position I am articulating is *idealism*. It is a position based as much upon belief as upon knowledge. What I am emphatically *not* suggesting is that we should embrace empiricism, the appeal to normal experience which is the bread and butter of British social anthropology. Few social anthropologists are not, in their souls, empiricists. This is what underlies our current intellectual and political passivity, and I argue against it in the name of *science*, if not science.

UNIDENTIFIED SPEAKER The opposition between idealism and empiricism is a problem for me. How far can we go in generalizing a human science in order to escape from this opposition?

MARY SEARLE-CHATTERJEE Several people, including Anthony Cohen, have argued that the role of anthropology is to adopt a critical stance towards generalization. Yet even someone as positivist as Popper puts his stress on falsifying rather than verifying, as part of the systematic process of trying to uncover knowledge. So you could hold the view that the role of anthropology is primarily critical, and still support the motion.

JAMES WOODBURN I believe that anthropology *should* be a generalizing science. I am not sure that it *is*, or is likely to be in the near future. For one thing, the extent to which we still argue *ad hominem* is extraordinary: one declares oneself to be, for example, 'a supporter of Fortes' or 'an opponent of Fortes'. There is a tendency to accept or reject a person's entire work rather than to look in it for particular ideas one can use. Another tendency that we have as anthropologists, especially if you consider those who are now senior in the subject, is to devote the greater part of our lives defending ideas and theories based on material gathered at the very outset of our careers. We might wish that our ideas would develop as we build on new experience, but this does not happen very effectively.

MICHAEL ROWLANDS Judging by the sense of dualism underlying this debate, the notion of science that Keith Hart is advocating is not generally understood. Given an outline of the social history of knowledge from the Enlightenment to now, of the kind that Keith Hart produced, the other side could produce an *alternative* history in which Vico would be opposed to Descartes, Hegel to Comte, all the way through to Husserl and the phenomenologists. That dualism has been fundamental, as a contradiction, to the generation of certain kinds of discourses, or of knowledges. Is Keith Hart saying that there is no way of being scientific without being caught in this kind of dilemma?

KEITH HART   I argue that the notion of science, like other key words
in our civilization – economy, nature, city and so forth – *moves* all
the time. If we are not explicitly historical in this debate, if we do
not indicate where the word 'science' is now, or to which part of its
history we refer, we end up talking past one another. The debate
about science should not be an in-house debate about scientific
method, rather it should be about the modern historical context
that would give unity to the notion of science as a human project –
one suitable for anthropologists to adopt as their standard. There
are many practices, within the existing bodies of natural and social
science and the humanities, which could be enlisted in this project. I
would follow Foucault, or for that matter Saussure, in suggesting
that words like 'science' are best understood in relation to the
synchronic sets of which they are part at particular moments in
history. Thus, there was more in common between, let us say,
natural scientists and humanists in 1780s' Paris than between the
natural scientists of 1780s' Paris and the natural scientists of 1980s'
Los Angeles. Our problems in this debate stem from unspecific
reference to the words we are using, and to the sets of which they are
part. Up to a century ago, and in some parts of the world even now,
the opposition formed by science was with *religion*. Our debate is
essentially about the location of anthropology within a proliferating academic division of labour which is presently under extreme
pressure, and which has to some extent lost its way because
specialist practitioners have long ago given up justifying to
themselves why they do what they do, and why society should
support them in it. I suggest that if anthropologists pause to
reconsider their objective social enterprise, it could usefully be seen
as 'science'. I do not seek an empiricist justification for this use of
'science'. I agree with the deconstructionists that 'science' is largely
a rhetorical element of modern political discourse. If we are to be
part of that discourse, we would be unwise to abandon it.

ANTHONY COHEN   I have two points to make. The first is that I do
not recognize anthropology, as presented in Keith Hart's account,
as passive, depleted and demoralized. To the contrary: there are
respects in which it is more vigorous and exciting now than it has
been for a long time. There are no more theoretical monoliths, no
shibboleths. We are not now struggling to understand other
peoples for the sake of our own scholarly gratification or to build
schools of thought. We do it so that others might be better
informed. My second point is that this motion is not about

whether anthropology is a science. It is about whether it is a science that accomplishes its object by *generalization*. In addressing this question, speakers have taken one side or the other, or argued for a merging of both. Ray Abrahams and Wim van Binsbergen, in his first contribution, argued that we need both. According to Malcolm Chapman, if we try to generalize, we fail. Pnina Werbner says we have to be aware of the dangers of exaggerated relativism. I do not think that we can produce accounts of the societies we study which are both one thing and the other. We can be suggestive and we can be comparative, indeed, we all are, but we cannot – to borrow Judith Okely's telling metaphor – successively clamp one side of the brain and unclamp the other, and do a bit with both. We would become intellectually schizophrenic. What we do is to formulate a view, by experience, of the proper way to go anthropologically. And we have to go that way, else we shall end by doing nothing.

ANTHONY GOOD   The motion does not state that anthropology is *only* a generalizing science, but merely that science is an essential *prerequisite* for anthropology, and that was the argument I was proposing. Some of the discussion has fallen into the common trap of confusing science and scient*ists*. For example, stories of how bad scientists did bad science are not really relevant to the debate. We are concerned here with an ideal view of good science. In practice, natural scientists are as much prone as anthropologists to the faults mentioned by James Woodburn. They too indulge in *ad hominem* arguments; they too start out with notions which they spend the rest of their careers trying to defend. The idea that practising scientists, unlike ourselves, somehow follow an 'onward and upward' career path, progressively redefining or demolishing their earlier views or refining them in the light of experiment, is not really true. But the way they actually behave is not the point at issue. We are talking about how science, done properly, *could* be. We should not be confused by stories of bad scientists and bad anthropologists behaving badly.

JUDITH OKELY   I would also like to refer to James Woodburn's complaint that anthropologists are still looking through the mouse-droppings of their youthful fieldnotes. *They* have been guilty of 'navel-gazing', and should have been more reflective about their privilege and their intellectual practice. Had they been so, they would have moved on. Returning to the motion, I would still argue that what anthropologists take to be the meaning of science is what we hear through keyholes, and is a very impoverished view. That is why I oppose the motion.

NOTES

1   J. L. Peacock, *The anthropological lens: harsh light, soft focus*, Cambridge, Cambridge University Press, 1986, p. 83.

2   B. Kapferer, *Legends of people, myths of state: violence, intolerance and political culture in Sri Lanka and Australia*, Washington, Smithsonian Institution Press, 1988, *passim.*

3   A. Good, 'The culture of kinship', *Edinburgh Anthropology* 1, ed. M. Noble, 1987, p. 77.

4   L. Holy (ed.), *Comparative anthropology*, Oxford, Blackwell, 1987.

5   C. Geertz, *The interpretation of cultures*, New York, Basic Books, 1973, p. 5; D. Parkin, 'Comparison as the search for continuity', in *Comparative anthropology*, ed. L. Holy, Oxford, Blackwell, 1987, pp. 52–69.

6   J. Friedman, 'Comment on Keesing, anthropology as interpretive quest', *Current Anthropology* 28, 1987, pp. 170–1.

7   W. R. James, *The listening ebony: moral knowledge, religion and power among the Uduk of Sudan*, Oxford, Clarendon Press, 1988.

8   R. Keesing, 'Anthropology as interpretive quest', *Current Anthropology* 28, 1987, pp. 161–76.

9   L. Holy and M. Stuchlik, *Actions, norms and representations: foundations of anthropological inquiry*, Cambridge, Cambridge University Press, 1983.

10   K. R. Popper, *The logic of scientific discovery*, London, Hutchinson, 1968.

11   M. D. Sahlins, *Stone age economics*, London, Tavistock, 1972, pp. 1–39.

12   M. Carrithers, 'The anthropologist as author: Geertz's "Works and Lives"'. *Anthropology Today* 4(4), 1988, p. 22.

13   J. Okely and H. Callaway (eds), *Anthropology and autobiography*, London Routledge, 1992.

14   G. H. von Wright, *Explanation and understanding*, Ithaca, Cornell University Press, 1971.

15   For a detailed critique of Jarvie and Horton, see R. Ulin, *Understanding cultures*, Austin, University of Texas Press, 1984, pp. 42–70.

16   R. Ulin, *ibid.*, p. 66.

17   M. Agar, *The professional stranger*, London, Academic Press, 1981.

18   J. Okely, 'The self and scientism', *Journal of the Anthropological Society of Oxford*, 1975; R. Ulin, *Understanding cultures*, Austin, University of Texas Press, 1984.

19   J. Llobera, 'Fieldwork in southwestern Europe. Anthropological panacea or epistemological straitjacket?', *Critique of Anthropology* 6(2), 1986, pp. 25–33.

20   L. Kolakowski, *Husserl and the search for certitude*, New Haven, Yale University Press, 1975.

21   A. Akalu, *Beyond morals? Experiences of living the life of the Ethiopian Nuer*, Lund, 1985.

1989 debate

The concept of society is theoretically obsolete

Introduction

Tim Ingold

No term is more pivotal to the identity of social anthropology than that of 'society' itself, yet none is more contestable. The problems are several, and are indeed the central problems of the discipline. One is that, far from having devised the notion for its own theoretical purposes, social anthropology is itself a relatively recent *product* of a certain way of imagining and thinking about society which has a long pedigree in the history of Western thought. The challenge and the promise of anthropology is to bring ourselves to 'think society' in other ways, yet to do so is to undercut the very foundations of the discipline. No wonder, then, that anthropologists seem to live perilously on an intellectual knife-edge! Another problem, equally pressing, is that our own activity in thinking and writing is situated within a milieu in which 'society' is in common and everyday use, carrying powerful rhetorical overtones in the moral and political discourse of citizens as well as in the academic discourse of social scientists (who are of course citizens as well). There may well be debate about whether such a thing as society actually exists 'out there', but there can be no doubting the fact that there are people out there who regularly talk about it, and therefore that discourse on society is just as much a part of the reality we study as it is of our way of studying it, if indeed these two can be separated at all.

More than any other recent anthropologist, it was Edmund Leach who contrived to place the status of 'society' at the top of the theoretical agenda, at a time when – for most of his colleagues – the existence of societies 'on the ground' was a simple fact of life that required no further justification. The motion for the second in this series of debates was chosen to honour his memory, and at the same time to highlight the issues he raised in a way that speaks to pressing contemporary concerns.

In moving that 'the concept of society is theoretically obsolete', Marilyn Strathern and Christina Toren have in mind the specific sense of 'society' that has long been dominant in social anthropology, namely as a bounded totality or whole that is formed of the sum of its parts. Their objections lie not so much in the concept itself as in the other concepts it has engendered, notably 'the individual' as a pre-formed, natural entity and the idea of socialization whereby such entities are said to be moulded in the image of a collective ideal. Their plea is for an alternative conceptual vocabulary, anchored on the concept of 'sociality', that would enable us to express the way in which particular persons both come into being through relationships and forge them anew, without relegating both personhood and relationship to a domain of reified abstraction – epitomized by the concept of society – which, in a certain strand of contemporary political rhetoric, is but a prelude to their dismissal as illusory. While Strathern points to the disastrous consequences of such dismissal, Toren shows how a focus on sociality not only allows us to treat the developing child as an active subject at the centre of his or her own social world (rather than as a passive being on the margins of society), but also dissolves the conventional disciplinary boundary between social anthropology and psychology, allowing topics such as child development, once reserved for psychological study, to become legitimate areas of social anthropological investigation.

Opposing the motion, John Peel and Jonathan Spencer focus more on the word than the concept, stressing the plurality of connotations that – in different contexts – have adhered to 'society'. While not denying the force of the proposers' objections to orthodox social anthropological usage, their approach is first to go back into history for alternative senses of society, perhaps much closer to what is now claimed for 'sociality', and then to follow these senses forward to the present day along intellectual trajectories *other* than the particular route which engendered the discipline of social anthropology. Thus their appeal is to a much broader and more diverse tradition of social thought, and for an anthropology that would be eclectic in its search for theoretical inspiration. 'Society' for them is not a tool of analysis with a single, precise meaning, but the name for a problem space variably and flexibly defined by the co-presence in the same semantic field of other terms such as culture, community, nation and state. Nor can the analytic usage of the term be divorced from its political and rhetorical resonance. If, in some contexts, 'society' is called upon to represent the claim of the state upon its citizens, in others it may be mobilized to empower individuals or communities in their opposition to the state. As long as such struggles go on, argue Peel and Spencer, 'society' is a term that we are bound to go on using. Not to do so would imply that our theorizing could be somehow detached from the political realities of the world in which we live.

Contributors to the debate, as well as the four speakers themselves, are broadly agreed on two things: first, that the Durkheimian dichotomy between society and individual has become more of a liability than an asset to social theory; second, that theorizing about society is itself a social activity which takes its cue from a particular moment in history and intervenes in its course. The disagreements principally concern what theories and concepts are *for*. Should we, for example, strive for theoretical consistency and coherence across the discipline, regardless of ethnographic application, or are theories and concepts so inextricably tied to ethnographic experience that a common language is impossible – even undesirable? Is the concept of society applicable to some societies and not to others? The obvious paradox in the latter question leads to the further issue, already foreshadowed in the previous debate: if societies cannot be objectively defined as units of comparison, then what units do we compare? Or is comparative anthropology at a dead end?

Another, but connected, set of questions concerns the relations between theory and paradigm and the nature of advance within the discipline. For some, the paradigm is a kind of storehouse of theoretical concepts, for others it is the barely articulated ground from which they grow. The notion of 'theoretical obsolescence' suggests the passing of a paradigm, whose concepts no longer have a place in the new order of thought, yet it is doubtful whether paradigms succeed one another in an orderly, stage-by-stage series. If, by contrast, they course through history 'in parallel', then the possibility always exists to switch track, or for ideas to rebound repeatedly back and forth from one paradigm to another, becoming ever transformed in the process. Such, indeed, appears to have been the fate of the concept of society.

Behind the overt concern with 'society', however, the debate has a hidden agenda, always present but scarcely raised explicitly. This concerns the status of the very notion of 'theory'. I conclude with one observation in this regard, which is that there appears to be a formal analogy between the way in which 'theory' has been constituted in social science through its opposition to 'data', and the constitution of 'society' through its opposition to 'individuals'. In both cases, relationships are disembedded from the world and inscribed in imaginative constructs that have an existence apart, leaving a material residue in the form of populations of discrete, pre-constituted entities or events. Thus, to do away with the dichotomy between society and individuals is simultaneously to do away with that between theory and data. If we are to recast our concepts of the social to obviate the dichotomy, we must also recast our idea of the nature of anthropological theory. The following exchanges, perhaps, represent a step in that direction.

Part I The presentations

FOR THE MOTION (1)

MARILYN STRATHERN

At issue before us is an abstract idea, an object of thought. Clearly, it cannot be with abstraction itself that we disagree. We all make abstractions in order to extend our thinking. But it matters very much for *how* we extend our thoughts *what* abstractions we make. And the principal problem with abstracting 'society' as a concept lies in the other concepts it engenders.

An anthropological debate must appeal to anthropological reason, and theoretical positions have therefore to be understood in their cultural context. Whatever control we think we have over the development of our theories, they are also inevitably shot through with general habits of thought. Thus, in arguing that the concept of society is obsolete as far as anthropological theory is concerned, I am also arguing about a salient cultural artefact. Indeed, we are all living the disastrous outcome of a long cultural investment in the idea of 'society' as an entity.

This debate honours the memory of Edmund Leach. He was fond of pointing up the habits of thought that vitiated the theories of his colleagues, for example, the habit of dichotomous thinking. His 1961 critique[1] attacked the then fashionable dichotomies such as ecology versus social structure, locality versus lineage, village versus social group. There is, he argued, no autonomous realm of social existence to be pitted *against* the material facts of property or locality. Rather, such material facts are represented in and manipulated by social relations.

What gave the dichotomies a superficial realism was an overarching opposition between economy and society, and this in turn rested on the specific way in which the concept of 'society' was made into an abstract object of thought, on the form it was given. It was treated as though it were a thing. So it was possible to see this thing opposed to or in relation with *other* 'things', as in this case economy. But society, Leach declares, is not a thing: it is a way of ordering experience.[2] Such was the (cultural) tenacity of our habits of thought that Leach found it necessary to reiterate his view in the context of a strenuous objection to the way anthropologists talk of societies in the plural.[3]

The points I address are the same. To think of society as a thing is to think of it as a discrete entity. The theoretical task then becomes one of elucidating 'the relationship' between it and other entities. This is a mathematic, if you will, that sees the world as inherently divided into units. The significant corollary of this view is that relationships appear as extrinsic to such units: they appear as secondary ways of connecting things up.

This was not quite how Leach put it, and indeed he could not have put it so. The maturation of these mid-century ideas provides us with our present position. It makes us realize the damage that the concept of 'society' has done. For it is not, I repeat, any old abstraction that we are debating. It is a particular one, and one that carries a specific set of consequences for the way we shape others.

Let me pause on the fact that to make abstractions seem real we routinely give them concrete form, and offer a brief review of the form taken by various ideas in British social anthropology at the time of Leach's critiques.

First, as we have seen, 'society' was reified as an individual thing, set up as an entity in antithesis to entities of a similar conceptual order: society versus economy, the material world, even biology or nature. Although these could be seen as conceptual domains carved out of human life, thought of as 'things' they appeared to have an identity prior to their being brought into relation. In this company, 'society' referred generally to consociation. Any *particular* society then appeared as an individual manifestation of society in this general sense. This introduced a new concreteness.

Second, then, society was personified as a *population* among similar populations. Considered together, they appeared to resemble a collection of persons, except that as most societies were not in communication, the connections between them could only be typological. What were typed were the differences and similarities between discrete units. In the same way as one could count individual persons, it was thought one could also enumerate individual societies.

Third, each population could in turn be regarded as a collectivity of individual human beings who appeared as members of the 'society', as parts of a whole. Whether society was conceived as the sum of individual interactions or as an entity regulating the conduct of individuals, the point was the same.[4] In so far as 'society' constructed the set of relationships between its members, the individuality of the latter was taken to be logically prior. Individual human beings thus appeared as primary phenomena of life, relationships as secondary. Another dichotomy surfaced, here, between society and the people who composed it, so that when thought of as individuals, the latter were seen to have a separate existence.

The theoretical defects of these positions are well known. Once again we encounter problems raised by the initial concept.

Consider first the dichotomies between domains of study. The nurture/nature debate has run aground; the idea of society as being somehow opposed to biology has stranded anthropology at a distance from other fields of the human sciences;[5] while the exaggeration of society as an autonomous phenomenon has led us to discard whole areas of human competence as uninteresting 'material culture'.

Second, as my opponent will surely agree,[6] comparative anthropology is at an impasse. One impasse derives from our mathematics of whole numbers, the tendency to count in ones. A marriage rule in twenty societies becomes twenty instances of the marriage rule! We knew there was a problem with thinking of societies as bounded units, in that we cannot really count them up. But this second absurdity was compounded with the first. Society is either half a phenomenon (of which the other half is everything else to be studied about human life); or else a whole phenomenon divided into parts – systems, institutions, sets of rules. Parts appear like individual components that can also be enumerated. Hence we enumerate phenomena across societies, so that a rule or prescription can also appear as an instance of something with a certain rate of occurrence.

Finally, the idea of society as a whole beyond the (individual) humans who make it up has lured us to another concretization, to elaborate on the idea of individuals as somehow *members* of it. This led, for instance, to a fatal equation of 'society' with 'group'.[7] Group solidarity was interpreted as societal solidarity. It was fatal because it produced an internal canker of problems, such as 'women' who, because they did not belong to groups, seemed not to belong to society. Or it led to the bizarre idea that people everywhere represented society to themselves as an external object, enshrined in ritual cohesion or legal orders. The one abstraction proliferated others – religion represented society, law represented society – alike in being set against the individual who had to be 'socialized' into appreciating the power of this external entity. In short, what the anthropologist made into an abstract object of thought in the ordering of material had to be made visible as the object of other people's representations. Hence the years of what now seems a futile search for social order.

Clearly, our theories have exhausted themselves. You have the evidence – endorsing a very simple point about the nature of scientific revolutions. Theories rest on paradigms. A paradigm becomes visible at the point of exhaustion. No longer a taken-for-granted way for organizing the world, it appears in retrospect as a set of tricks of analogy and metaphor. In particular, observe the analogies for the concept of relationship: we have relations between separate domains of study (relating society to other things), between discrete societies (cross-societal correlations) and finally between individual human beings, where the external nature of relations is hypostasized in the concept of society itself.

The reifications, personifications and number games that we play with this concept, now in the singular, now in the plural, now related to other entities, now the sum of relationships, are exposed as rhetoric. Once understood as rhetoric, the concept of society cannot be reclaimed for theory.

The ground on which we move its obsolescence is simply that it is a calamitous 'has been'.[8] I comment on one theoretical calamity.

I have pointed out that a problem with the concept of 'society' is the other concepts it produces. And the most problematic for anthropology has been that of 'the individual'. The two have operated as the poles of a pendulum between which twentieth-century theories have swung.[9]

When 'society' encapsulated the further concepts of organization and rules, it drew attention to regularities in social life. But it then appeared as an order *against which* the individual actor constructed ambition or experience. So we are also familiar with the counterweight that came to be given to transactions in social analysis. Instead of a regulative 'group', society became concretized as an interactive 'market place'. Similarly, when society was imagined as an object of people's representations, it drew attention to the significance of symbolic activity, gave us a point of mutual comprehension: as 'we' imagine society as an external presence so must 'they'. But representations were then seen to mystify forms of domination, as in gender relations, as though certain persons were acting 'on behalf of' or 'in the name of' society. Instead, interest groups came into view like so many contestants.

For as long as the pendulum was in motion, the concept of society was a useful resting place. But the pendulum has virtually come to a stop. Having swung from social morphologies to individual transaction, from collective representations to the ideologies of interest groups, late twentieth-century anthropology has landed in the morass of social constructionism. This is a kind of collapsed, imploded version of the society–individual dichotomy, in so far as the model takes inspiration from the idea of external forces impinging on the individual and the individual asserting personal experience against society.

My point is straightforward. The pendulum *has been* useful, it has provided creative positions and constituted much of the internal dynamic of the discipline. And for as long as the concept of 'society' served as a focus for thinking about social organization, collective life and relationships, it served a purpose. Indeed, it has afforded useful derivatives – the epithet 'social', the concept of 'sociality' as the relational matrix which constitutes the life of persons, and even 'societies' as a shorthand pluralism for populations with distinctive organizations. To none of these do we object, for all refer to the significance of the relations within which persons exist. Our objection is to the distortion that arises when the concept of society ceases to signal these relational facts and instead obliterates them. Instead of sociality being seen as intrinsic to the definition of personhood, 'society' is set against 'the individual'. And because of the concreteness of individuals in our cultural worldview, it has been hard to shake off the assumption that the individual has a logically prior existence. Indeed, the priority accorded to the concept of individual is such that it has been applied to society itself: 'societ*ies*' take on the character of discrete holistic units.

The concept of society has thus existed in anthropological accounts as a rhetorical device – as a closure on ethnographic narrative,[10] fitting together parts of the analysis as though the social structure fitted together; as the possibility of theoretical integration made concrete in the encompassment of all social phenomena. Perhaps this may strike you as innocuous. In retrospect, however, rhetoric rarely turns out to have been neutral. I turn now to evidence from a different domain, one that forms the background to our present theorizing. It plays explicitly on the dichotomy between society and individual. It is, in fact, a terrible parody, a literalization of that theoretical pendulum, bashing us over the head with one of its poles.

When Leach said that society is not a thing, he meant that social practices are a medium of human behaviour and cannot be set against it. He was anticipating the pit into which our present mistress of self-fulfilling prophecies was to fall. I refer, of course, to the infamous declaration issued by Prime Minister Margaret Thatcher:

> *There is no such thing as society. There are individual men and women and there are families.*

The statement shows us what has gone disastrously *wrong* with making an abstract entity out of the particular concept under debate. Listen to the consequences.

First, individual motivations appear the only reality. Today we live under a political regime that has tried to sweep away the collectivities that intervene between state and 'citizen', and organizations that promote specific interests. And it is the same assault on social diversity that has encouraged both the privatization of previously nationalized industries and increasing control over the social services. Diverse modes of social organization offend. Corporations must be moulded into one model; tolerated only if conceivable as individuals.

Second, we live under a cultural regime that defines the individual in a specific way – as financially self-sufficient. All enterprises – industrial, educational, artistic – have to behave like such individuals, enterprises of independent means who attend to their own needs, and who are therefore socially alike in the way they keep their books, achieve performance targets, and so on. They interact only as 'customers' of one another, social action becoming a question of the individual's capacity to mobilize services.

Third, then, we live under a regime that would like to render invisible any form of social relationship that cannot be modelled on interactions between individuals and for which the market-place can serve as a metaphor.

Intolerance for diversity of social forms, individuals defined as consumers and providers of services, relationships rendered invisible – we see here the outcome of a long-established habit of abstracting society as an object of thought. It is *because* the concept of society had been bandied around as though it were some autonomous entity that it becomes possible to throw it all away and 'reveal' the seemingly concrete individuals underneath. For what Prime Minister Thatcher has done is a little obviation analysis on that concept – realizing that society is not after all a concrete thing but an abstraction. So, off with its head! The 'real world' consists of consuming bodies, rising from the table from time to time to check the share figures. Abstractions do not belong to this world; only individuals do. You see what has happened.

In one fell swoop Thatcherism could gather up all kinds of collectivities and organizations with a social presence, and in dumping the idea of society, dump them. They no longer derive legitimacy from their *social* nature because society no longer exists. Then what is substituted for the false 'thing', society, is the real 'thing', the individual. The form that the concept takes here allows this. Because society is reified it is also possible to reify the individual in antithesis. It is a sad cultural fact that the one always seems to precipitate the other.

Here is the absurdity, indeed tragedy, of operationalizing one pole of a dichotomy. Where the individual is thus produced 'in opposition to' society, the move conceals social formations and power relations. This is a prescriptive individualism that, among other things, makes invisible the massive commercial and military interests of multinationals, since all we 'see' is the extent to which the customer is the recipient of services. Moreover, it fosters the ecologically tragic promotion of consumer gratification. At this point one might argue for restoring the concept of society itself, for that would restore a balance. The cultural likelihood, however, is that it would not: it would only recreate its antithesis.

The motion that I put to you is that we do not need the concept of society precisely because we do not need the concept of the individual in contradistinction to it. As anthropologists, 'we' certainly have no business peddling that dichotomy. For what is calamitous for the nation at the end of the twentieth century is actually rather sad for us. In its early twentieth-century conceptualization of society as an object of study, anthropology started out with such good intentions. But I have shown the cracks that were already evident in Leach's criticisms. We have now reached the point of having to tell ourselves over again that if we are to produce adequate theories of social reality, then the first step is to apprehend persons as simultaneously containing the potential for relationships and always embedded in a matrix of relations with others. Christina Toren will elaborate on what we mean.

Meanwhile, I can only take the following stand. Certainly we need an obviation analysis on the concept, but not in order to deny abstraction. We need to recover the original intention of the abstraction, which was to convey the significance of relationships in human life and thought.

Social relations are intrinsic to human existence, not extrinsic. As objects of anthropological study, one cannot therefore conceive of persons as individual entities. Sadly, it is our very idea of society that has been the culprit. The unfortunate outcome of conceiving of society itself as an entity has actually been to make relationships seem secondary and not primary to human existence. Quite simply, then, we have reached the theoretical point of recognizing that as a concept 'society' has come to interfere too much with our apprehension of sociality. I move that it be despatched as obsolete.

AGAINST THE MOTION (1)

J. D. Y. PEEL

'Society' is a highly complex and many-sided notion. We can only debate its value realistically, giving due recognition to what people are actually doing with the concept, if we recognize the variety of its uses. We must refrain from defining it in a singular, particular way so that our view of whether it is a useful or outmoded concept becomes true almost by definition. Yet this is what Marilyn Strathern has just done. She has focused her attack on a particularly reified concept of society – one that has been influential enough in social anthropology – and has fairly criticized its 'thinginess'. But matters are much more complicated.

Several of the senses of 'society' are seen most clearly in relation to a particular antithesis: society versus the individual, versus culture, versus community, or, most pertinently, versus the State. We will proceed most appropriately if we treat 'society' as denoting a field of enquiry defined by the relations between all these senses.

Since what we are debating is whether to take away the very subject matter of sociology, let us turn – for a definition of 'society' that is reasonably uncontentious – to one of the leading sociological theorists of our day, Anthony Giddens. In his *The constitution of society* he distinguishes two primary senses of the concept:

1 'The generalized connotation of social association or interaction', i.e. patterns of relations between social actors.
2 A relatively bounded unity of social relations, a social system, contrasted to other surrounding societies.[11]

The distinction, in other words, is between society in general and any particular society. The classical social theorists vary in their emphasis: Spencer and Durkheim chiefly mean the latter, Simmel and Weber the former. The contrast recurs in closely related forms: 'grid' versus 'group', for example.

When applied concretely, the two main senses differ in their reference. Sense 1 may be applied to a generic kind of society: capitalist society, industrial society, colonial society, plural society, Muslim society. The label designates some key integrating or constitutive principle. In Sense 2, if the reference is to a modern or large-scale society, there is the strong presumption that it means the system of social relations corresponding to a state: for example, Japanese society, modern British society, society and democracy in Germany. The usage is similar for the smaller units customarily specified in ethnographic study: Tiv society, Kayapo society, Melpa society. But at this level, as we all know, things are more problematic. The Tiv may be exceptionally bounded, but many peoples, as Leach showed in *Political systems of Highland Burma*, are not.[12] These ethnographic units may (or may not) be so defined by their members, and rarely coincide with a state. Typically, the limits of linguistic intelligibility are taken to provide the boundary – and so 'society' here comes close to being a synonym of culture.

Each sense of society can, of course, be more abstractly theorized – and this is indeed the central project of social theory. As regards Sense 1, what Giddens calls his 'theory of structuration' aims to reformulate the antithesis of society and individual as 'the duality of structure and agency'. Ingold comes, by a different and more anthropological route, to a similar formulation in his *Evolution and social life*.[13] In Sense 2, society has been theorized in two main ways: in terms of 'system needs', as with Parsons's functionalism; and in an architectural or layer-cake image, as with the three 'instances of the social formation' of the French Marxists.

Such, then, are some of the main ways in which the concept of society is *actually* used. But a motion which proposes that society is an *obsolete* concept invites us to view it historically. And a little intellectual history *is* illuminating.

In English, 'society' – initially in Sense 1 – was first used in the sixteenth century. We find Hobbes using this sense in the famous passage in *Leviathan* where he sees 'no account of time; no Arts; no Letters; no Society; and the life of man, solitary, poor, nasty, brutish and short'.[14] This passage also looks forward to Sense 2, since it makes society's existence depend on the existence of a state: *Leviathan* is, of course, an argument to justify the absolutist state. In this empirical fusion (though conceptual distinction) of state and society, Hobbes looks back as well as forward – back to the Greeks in fact, who had no distinct term for 'society'. Famously, they subsumed 'society' under their political form, the *polis*. (The Yoruba, I note in passing, do the same with their term *ilu*, and for some similar reasons.) It was not that other forms of society (as we would say) went unrecognized – the kin-based *ethne* of the northern barbarians, or the *basileia*, the Persian imperial order – but only under the conditions of the *polis* was real human fulfilment, social life in the fullest sense, possible.

What happened in Europe, in the century after Hobbes, was that society further detached itself from the state, yet remained unavoidably but problematically linked with it. Now political forms were seen to be conditioned by the forms of 'civil society'. Society came first, not the

state. Ferguson's *Essay on the History of Civil Society* of 1767 was a
classic statement. Why did this development occur? For three reasons:

(a) There was the emergence of the capitalist economy, which formally
freed men as units of labour and revealed patterns of class relations
more clearly for what they were.

(b) There was a new freedom of association, eventually leading towards
democratic movements. Their greatest publicist, Tom Paine, gave a
fine expression to the society/state contrast: 'Society and government are different in themselves and have different origins. Society is
produced by our wants and government by our wickedness. Society
is in every state a blessing; government even in its best state but a
necessary evil.' Tocqueville would later go on to argue that political
democracy is vitally dependent on 'society' in the sense of social
institutions interstitial between individuals and the State.

(c) There was the rise of nationalism. A nation is a society in its cultural
aspect, and now it was argued with growing force that states *ought* to
correspond to nations, that they work best when attached to sets of
shared cultural understandings derived from a people's past.

Thus modern social theory emerged in the nineteenth century, with its
two linked senses of 'society': as patterns of association and as that
bounded entity which problematically connects with the state.

Now there are two essential worries which, to my mind, a social
anthropologist might fairly have about a concept such as 'society', on
account of its origin in a particular cultural milieu and a particular
historical epoch. I believe these worries to be ultimately unfounded, but
they need to be addressed.

The first worry concerns the cultural source of our concepts. To judge
from her recent book[15] and her contribution to this debate, Marilyn
Strathern feels keenly that so-called 'Western' concepts distort the
analysis of non-Western (in her case Melanesian) concepts and practices,
particularly as regards the cultural constitution of persons and individual–society relations. It is not possible here to go into this in proper
detail. Suffice it to make a few observations. The problem is to develop
concepts which allow the unprejudiced analysis of as wide a range of
different societies as possible. In general, it is no more than to be expected
that the social theory developed in large-scale, relatively heterogeneous
and differentiated societies should have some capacity to embrace the
realities of simpler and smaller-scale ones. Marx was right to consider
that political economy – whose own claims to supra-historical transcendence he of course rejected – nevertheless yielded a superior account of
earlier and/or simpler economic forms than was possible in the categories

of societies where the economy was (in Polanyi's terms) 'embedded'. Beyond this, though, we should be wary of treating 'Western thought' as if it expressed a single, simple view of society, whether in itself or in relation to individual or state. When we read that, say, an antinomy between society and the individual is alien to the Melanesian view, but by implication typical of the Western view, we have to ask whether Adam Ferguson was not, after all, a Westerner. To make the argument by a sort of 'reversed orientalism' only confuses the issue.

The second worry is more substantial. It is that our concept of a society – here in Sense 2, as a bounded entity in which economic, political and cultural unities are superimposed – may be too removed from the salient empirical realities which social anthropologists now have to tackle. This concern is well expressed in Michael Mann's *The sources of social power*,[16] which comes close to abandoning that concept of society, talking instead about 'multiple overlapping and intersecting . . . networks of power', which are variously economic, military, ideological and political. Anthropologists have often documented multiethnic social settings where there intersect such different spheres as, say, a national administration that speaks one language, local peasant communities where another is spoken, and traders belonging to an international diaspora who speak yet another. What need do we have of the concept of a 'society' here?

But to draw such an inference is misconceived, since it presumes that concepts are *meant* to be shadows or replicas of social realities. In fact they stand in a much more dynamic relationship to reality – pertinent to it, certainly, but selective from it, according to principles of theoretical relevance. Even in the nineteenth century, the first heyday of European nationalism, the concept of 'society' was highly ideal in relation to much of the reality. It presented a model of coincident cultural, economic and political spheres at a time when, for example, much economic activity was still locally organized, while in other sectors international or transnational economic networks were coming into being. In the same way, while a given religion was often an important component of a society's culture and a key source of national identity, minority enclaves and religious dissent within, and the formation (through migration and mission) of transnational religious solidarities, made it plain just how 'ideal' the notion of a national society often was.

But none of this invalidates the *concept* of a 'society'. It remains a crucial reference point or bench-mark, just as does the ideal type of bureaucracy in relation to some chaotic and corrupt civil service. It remains the case that states and, if they are large enough, cultures, may be powerful tractive forces, with a potential to organize social and economic relations around themselves. And I hardly need to point out that, despite some countervailing trends, the idea of a homogeneous national society retains a powerful appeal to millions of people around the world. That makes 'society' a cultural reality, and therefore also a social one, that we cannot ignore.

A debate on this motion, at this time (October 1989), cannot fail to address the much-reported intervention of the Prime Minister in social theory. The proposer of the motion has bravely taken the bull by the horns, and sought – though unconvincingly – to neutralize the effect of what must be highly unwelcome support. 'There is no such thing as society,' Mrs Thatcher declared. 'There are individual men and women and there are families.' What does it mean, this radical denial of society?

The family, one is to presume, is abandoned to the sphere of nature. The interaction of individuals through the market is extended; and that too is essentially justified because it is supposed to be 'natural'. But most significantly, to achieve this, the state is used against society, so that individuals confront a reduced yet more active state more directly than before. Its harsh liberalism invokes 'Victorian values' but diverges from them in major respects. Whereas Tocqueville grounded liberty and democracy in a vital civil society – that is, in collectivities or institutions that mediate between the citizen and the state – Prime Minister Thatcher relentlessly undercuts and devalues all such institutions: local government, trade unions, universities, churches, the BBC, even (in fact, though not in theory) the family. What is not privatized is subject to much tighter state control. Here the Thatcherite outlook differs from even that most sweeping of nineteenth-century *laissez-faire* tracts, Spencer's *The Man vs. the State* (1884). For Spencer deeply disliked nationalist politics, jingoistic wars, and the whole idea of the state as the instrument of a transhistorical abstraction such as 'the British people'. Above all, he would have thought it monstrous that the state should entertain a project of radically changing the people's culture, such as Thatcher's promotion of 'entrepreneurialism'.

For us, as social scientists, a most pertinent token of the practical drift of Thatcherite social theory has surfaced very recently. I refer to protests made at the Government's manipulation of the work of the Central Statistical Office and at official proposals that its activities should be both reduced in scale and confined more closely to government objectives. A pressure group set up to challenge this, led by Sir Claus Moser, has made the essential point that the CSO should be seen as serving, not only government's needs, but those of *society* at large. Those who would set society in opposition to the individual, or represent this as 'the Western view', are simply allowing Thatcherism to set the terms of argument; and when society goes, the individual is left confronting the state. Yet there is another, continuous strand in our tradition, which sees society as enabling, not as repressive, of individuals; and that often *against* the state.

We should not exaggerate the erosion of society in this country. But the relevance of the concept of society is seen even more strikingly outside Western Europe, where popular movements are directed against statist regimes of the Left. It is in the name of society that Poles, Hungarians and Czechs have overthrown ossified state structures, and here at least it is realized how much individual formation and fulfilment has society as its precondition, not as its antithesis.

The most telling and poignant case, however, lies even further afield, namely in China. Here we saw popular struggles for a democracy which the Chinese have never known, involving precisely a plea to their rulers that the state hearken to society. This phrasing was explicit in the Declaration made at the end of the Tiananmen Square occupation, one of whose four authors was a sociologist. What might especially instruct any anthropologist worried about the applicability of 'Western' concepts outside the West, is the symbolism adopted by the movement. Its very icon was the 'Goddess of Democracy', freely modelled on the Statue of Liberty, which points us directly back to the age of Paine and Tocqueville when the problematic of state and society was first formulated.

The motion invites you to deem the concept of society 'obsolete'. I put it to you that, if the task of anthropology is to engage with human actuality, it is hard to think of a concept which is *less* obsolete.

FOR THE MOTION (2)

CHRISTINA TOREN

Marilyn Strathern has shown us how the notion of 'society' carries with it the idea of the 'individual' and how, in doing away with the idea of society, we can finally dispense too with the idea of the asocial individual. In seconding the motion I shall concentrate on a particular theoretical domain. In essence, my case is this: given that meaning is – of its nature – inherent in social relations, given that we cannot even conceive of meaning unless we taken sociality for granted, we have inevitably to accept that the twinned notions of 'society' and the 'individual' (who is 'socialized' by society) are theoretically obsolete.

I ask you to consider a child, any child, a baby. Even before birth, it is in social relations with others in so far as others are implicated in and concerned about its expected arrival. At birth, it is immediately the object of other people's attentions and its mode of being in the world is mediated by others – what it is fed and how often, how it is clothed, handled, allowed to sleep or wake, carried about, left to lie and so on. We think of the child as simply *acted upon*. Indeed, our notion of socialization – which emerged in the nineteenth century and which is present in virtually all twentieth-century European models of child-rearing from Freud to Skinner – builds on and transforms that Christian notion of the later Middle Ages that the child was to be moulded like putty or clay. However, as any parent knows, children cannot be so moulded, and in recent years even the less coercive and more benign notion of socialization has come to be seen as inadequate.

This is because the notion of socialization cannot account, even in theory, for the microhistorical processes by which that new baby comes to be, say, a Chinese People's Republic doctor and leader of a women's association, a Fijian retired primary school teacher now paramount chief, an Iban longhouse leader and manager of a copra co-operative, a Hawaiian champion of Japanese *sumō* wrestling, or an Australian middle-class anthropologist mother of one. If society is to be the source of such material possibilities, then it has to be materially located somewhere – but it cannot be located in individuals for they are by definition the antithesis of society, so it has to be outside and above individuals, a system that is greater than the sum of its parts, an abstraction. From this theoretical perspective we are forever in a dilemma that we can never resolve. We have no choice but to change the terms in which our questions are framed.

Over the past fifteen to twenty years, it has become increasingly clear to psychologists concerned with children's earliest cognitions, that babies are born with cognitive abilities that are at once more extensive and more specific than had previously been acknowledged. For instance, in one experiment, pre-speech infants (6–8 months old) were shown pictures of objects and played a number of sounds; when they heard the drum beat twice they spontaneously looked at a picture of two objects and when they heard it three times they switched their gaze to a picture showing three objects. In other words, infants seem to have a basic ability for the sort of cross-model matching that underlies counting. Other experiments demonstrate that – well before they are speaking – babies are able, effortlessly, to form what are called 'basic level' categories – such as bird, dog, apple, doll, etc. Indeed, newborn babies can distinguish between living kinds and non-living kinds, and within living kinds, they can distinguish humans from other animals.

Now, most psychologists and even anthropologists have taken these findings to suggest that because they are innate, these cognitions are 'non-social'. This is, of course, an artefact of our notion of 'society' as something that is above and outside the individual. But it is surely absurd to call these cognitions non-social, for what the psychological findings demonstrate is that we are innately disposed to *attend* to the world, a world that is characterized by a number of invariant properties. It is a world where gravity keeps us all on the ground, where water runs downhill, where there is a regular cycle of night and day and of seasons, where objects are stable rather than unpredictably made and unmade, and where there are always, for any and all of us, other humans. If we are biologically social animals – as everyone seems prepared to accept – then our cognitive activity is rooted in sociality. For however remarkable may be the cognitive abilities with which babies are born, they are as yet incomplete. Human babies are well adapted to knowing the world, but they do not yet know the world in its historical specificity.

One can only come to know the world in and through relations with others, but babies are not merely the objects of others' attentions, nor is the world impressed upon them such that they become mere imitators or reflections of those around them. The psychological studies have made it quite plain that even the new-born baby is inevitably the *subject* of its own behaviour, active in the social relations in and through which he or she is already a particular person with a particular history. Each one is inevitably an active subject, not only because it is in the nature of humans to make meaning out of whatever impinges on them, but because each one actively seeks out information on which the mind may act. However, one cannot do this independently of others; such meanings as one makes are inevitably mediated by the manifold social relations in which one is always enmeshed and in which meaning always inheres. Indeed, the very notion of consciousness is predicated on an awareness of others in relation to oneself and of oneself in relation to others.

One becomes especially aware of this when looking at how children's notions change over time; what one finds then is that in the process of making meaning out of their own experience children submit willy nilly to the meanings that others have made. I say children, but I mean 'people' – for this is as true for us as it is for a newborn child or a three-year-old. This shows how inappropriate is the notion of socialization, with 'society' as its source. Of course, as Marilyn Strathern has already pointed out, concepts of sociality and social relations are derived from the notion of 'society'. And, like 'society', they are also abstractions – but as abstractions they denote dynamic social processes in which any person is inevitably engaged, rather than a set of rules or customs or structures or even meanings that exists *as a system* independently of the individual who is to be socialized.

I remarked that, because meaning is inherent in social relations, one has, in making meaning, to submit to the meanings that others have made. By the same token, others stand in a similar relation to oneself. However, one cannot specify an end point to any domain of cognitive development, even while one may take such-and-such a construct to be 'mature' or 'adult'. Of its nature, cognitive activity is creative in that even while one makes meaning out of the meanings others have made, one cannot help but constitute those meanings anew – and in the process introduce differences that are subtle or wide-ranging or even, sometimes, highly orginal. This perspective on meaning is *inevitably historical* for it allows our analyses to accommodate the material nature of social relations and thus to handle simultaneously both continuity and change.

I am asking you to reconsider our model of the human being, to give up the idea of the newborn child as a *tabula rasa* on which some abstract and disembodied society inscribes itself. I am proposing an idea of the child as being, and as coming to be, a particular person with a particular history, as coming into consciousness in and through the social relations in which he or she is at once the subject of his or her own acts and the object of the acts of others. Indeed, we have to conceive of the child – as of any person – as being in a social relation with itself in that it is at once the object of its own regard and the subject of its own actions. The baby who lies in its cot watching its own little fingers waggling does not have to make its hand part of its body by dint of some learned cognitive effort – all we know of children's innate faculties suggests that what is fascinating about the waggling fingers is the embodied awareness that one makes it happen oneself. And this very relation to itself as at once the subject and the object of its own actions is, in any child, mediated by the social relations in which it is not only acted upon by others, but also always a subject – one whose own activity helps to constitute those very same social relations and the meanings that are made in them.

You will have realized, no doubt, that in talking about cognition, meaning, particular persons, consciousness and so on, I am arguing not only against the idea of society, but also against the idea of culture. This is inevitable, for the idea of society brings 'culture' in its train. But if in many, if not most, of our analyses we have taken for granted the psychological processes by which one might be supposed to become a particular person with a particular history, we have in so doing also taken for granted the psychological processes by which people might be supposed to constitute meaning. We have left that problem to psychologists and, if we bothered to think about it at all, have simply assumed that the reified 'system of meanings' which emerges from our theoretical analyses is – at least in part – transmitted, as it were, 'ready made' to each member of the group we have characterized as part of a 'society'.

However, once we cease to use the individual–society dichotomy, once we realize that persons are not merely products of social and cultural processes but also, at the very same time, inevitably shaping those same processes, then we see that our analytical problems are problems of psychology as much as of social or cultural anthropology. I am not arguing that we have all to change the focus of our studies, but only that we have to be very aware of the model of the human being that our studies imply. The concept of society is theoretically obsolete, so is the concept of the individual. Let us take a new perspective – one where, at the heart of our studies, we locate persons who, as active historical subjects and the objects of others' actions, are at once both products and producers of infinitely variable but not arbitrary meanings. Meanings are variable because they are made by human subjects, but they are never arbitrary because, inevitably, they are made in social relations, and thus always in reference to the meanings that others have made and are making. There is no society and there are no individuals – only the social relations in and through which we become who we are in play, in work, in eating together, in conversation, in war, in ritual, in love, and in debate.

You who sit here today as listeners to the arguments put forward by Marilyn Strathern and myself – I ask you all, as persons who are at once the active subjects of your own lives even while you are acted upon by others, to take our meaning and make it your own. You will have to support the motion.

AGAINST THE MOTION (2)

JONATHAN SPENCER

Many years ago, at a seminar at the University of Edinburgh, my teacher James Littlejohn commented that in order to attempt the task of anthropological comparison we should aspire to 'become coeval with our own history'. I shall take this as the motto of my contribution. Those who demand a radical break between the present of anthropology and its past must first be clear exactly about what that past contains.

The wording of this motion suggests a very odd idea of the nature and shape of anthropological theory. It conjures up a vision of the white heat of theoretical progress, in which bad ideas are exposed and discarded and new ones take their place overnight. In practice, as we all know, there are few ideas in the theoretical toolbag so bad that no one uses them, and obsolescence can only be judged by long years of utter silence, not by the presence of polemic and debate. At a guess, I would say that 'primitive promiscuity' is some way past its sell-by date, while it is some time since I heard anything really new on the topic of 'animism'.

I would also ask you to remember that the proposers of this motion have set themselves by far the harder of our two tasks. While they are required to demonstrate that, always and everywhere, the employment of the concept of society will lead to confusion and error, we are simply required to suggest that in some contexts and in some uses we could imagine it providing some new insight. Not, please note, that everyone is required to use it; just that some may find it helpful some of the time.

I refer to contexts and uses in the plural because there is no simple unitary concept of society. Rather, it is one of those polysemic words – like culture or class – which have played a crucial role in the self-understanding of industrial society. Obviously, we must be wary of unproblematically transferring a word forged in such a specific context into another radically different context. But we should be just as wary of treating one contingent meaning of a word as historically transcendent.

Marilyn Strathern specifically objects to the concept of 'society' because it predicates an ethnocentric opposition between society and individual. Historically this assertion can be clearly shown to be untrue; whether or not it is true in the present is a matter for debate, and much, crucially, depends on how we view the tradition of European social thought from Marx onwards. Is this tradition first and foremost 'European', trapped within the narrow self-understandings of European societies as Strathern suggests, or is it, at least some of the time, oppositional, a tradition of critical thinking which has been pitched directly against the grain of dominant self-understandings? In the last analysis, I believe it is social theory's internal critique of industrial society which has opened up the space for the more radical critique which Strathern offers. Her work would be impossible without the earlier arguments of those like Mauss and Marx, who wrote at once about the nature of modern society and about imaginable alternatives to it, and whose greatest writings were simultaneously analyses and interventions.

I shall have more to say about anthropology and social theory towards the end of my argument. First I need to dispose of the alleged necessary link between 'society' and 'individual'. The original *Oxford English Dictionary* entry for 'society' divides its senses into four primary groups with thirty or so sub-senses; only one of these sub-senses employs the word 'individual' in its definition. If one searches through all the two million quotations in the OED one finds about a thousand occurrences each of the words 'society' and 'individual', but only eleven quotations in which both words are used together. The earliest of these is from

Blackstone in 1765, followed in historical succession by passages from Thomas Jefferson, Coleridge, Macaulay, Mill, Emerson, and Spencer.[17] But the earliest of these passages do not counterpose society and individual as separate and opposed things; for that we have to wait for the mid-Victorian period and particularly the writings of Mill. The opposition comes into very sharp and specific focus in the late 1840s and early 1850s. The word 'society' itself is several hundred years older than any of these examples, and its earliest uses incline more to the sense of companionship – which is the main sense of its Latin etymon *societas* – or association, senses which we can still just about discern when we talk of 'enjoying someone's society'. These senses are in fact much closer to Strathern's approved notion of 'sociality' than to her understanding of 'society'; the latter in fact represents one specific response to nineteenth-century history.

But of course it is not the only one. Mill's talk of a 'despotism of society over the individual'[18] can be contrasted with Marx's assertion that 'The human essence is no abstraction inherent in each single individual. In its reality it is the ensemble of social relations.'[19] In the terms favoured by the proposer of this motion, it looks as if Mill was a Westerner, whereas the young Marx (like his mentor Hegel) was probably a Melanesian.

I now want to turn away from the negative part of my case and to attempt to put forward some more positive reason for continuing to talk about society. Even if Strathern's fictional 'Western thought' only acknowledges one of several meanings of society, we still need some indication of new and potentially fruitful uses of the term. John Peel has already pointed out that society can be opposed to a number of different antonyms – society versus individual, society versus community, society versus the State. And these different senses have their own histories and historical preconditions. (In passing we might ask what exactly is wrong with dichotomies. Our opponents seem to think that the very fact that something is part of a dichotomy is sufficient reason to dismiss it as worthless; nevertheless some dichotomies – black and white, yes and no, p and not-p – really do signify important differences.)

In the Sinhala language there is a word *samajaya* which appears neatly to coincide in meaning with our own 'society'. So, for example, I would explain away my research to the curious by saying I was studying *samaja vidyava* – sociology or the study of society – while one of the oldest Sri Lankan political parties was called the Lanka Sama Samaja Paksaya – the equal society or socialist party. (In my experience the nearest word to individual, *paudgalayek*, is much less commonly employed and more restricted in both sense and context than its English equivalent.) Of course, the presence or absence of a word for 'society' is a matter of ethnographic interest, but in itself it is of no necessary theoretical consequence.

But let me contrast two Sri Lankan political representations, one involving this word for society and one not. In the 1860s a British civil servant got hold of a palm-leaf manuscript called *Dharmarajapota*, 'the book of the righteous king', which had been circulating in the Sri Lankan countryside. It foretold of the coming of a righteous king from across the water who would drive out the British and restore the old pre-colonial kingship.[20] In 1977 the main opposition party, the UNP, won a landslide electoral victory over the incumbent government with a campaign promising the building of a *dharmista samajaya* – a society in the spirit of the *dharma*, the Buddha's teaching. In both cases the ideal of the *dharma* was at the heart of the promised political order, but in the nineteenth century this was to be realized in the person of the king, whereas in the twentieth century it had given way to the building of a society.

This is, of course, only the beginning of a much more complex story. The commonest word used for government or state in Sinhala is still *rajaya* (thus the king *is* the polity and vice versa), and the attempted separation of society and state implied in the 1970s' slogan has itself been overtaken by events. But what I want this example to show is that political action in the 1970s was being imagined in a different way, and one index of that difference is the emergence of 'society', *samajaya*, as a self-conscious element of political representation. An obvious reason why people should have become more aware of a gap between state and society in a country like Sri Lanka is the fact that a distinction of this sort lay at the very heart of colonial practice which, as in India, was based on the ideal of orderly government without active reform of local society; the area of custom and customary law, in particular and with a few famous exceptions, was to be left untouched by government action. But in indigenous formulations order was guaranteed and instantiated through the person of the king; the idea of a government quite separate from local society was deeply problematic and the promised return of the king was an attempt to deal with that problem.

A century and a half of colonial rule may have established the possibility of differentiating state and society, and this possibility is clearly acknowledged in the slogan of the *dharmista samajaya*, but actual differentiation of state and society is, if anything, even more problematic today than it has ever been. Since the 1950s politics and political alignments have infused the texture of everyday life in Sinhala villages to a frightening degree; in the last few years political violence has escalated to terrifying proportions. As the Sri Lankan anthropologist Valentine Daniel has very recently put it, 'state and civil society... have been brought into active, even if explosive, engagement'.[21] Daniel's characteristically provocative formulation is not an answer to the mystery of Sri Lanka's political implosion, but it does indicate an area where we might start to look for such an answer, on the disputed boundary between state and civil society.

The example is obviously specific to Sri Lanka, and I do not claim that the problematic relation of state and civil society is going to be universally encountered. I think, though, that it will be manifest in virtually all colonial and post-colonial societies, and it is also quite easy to see areas of life in industrial society – the new social movements (including the women's movement) for example – which can be analysed in these terms. The area of enquiry I have sketched also promises the possibility of obtaining an ethnographic purchase on politics in complex societies, and thus of rejuvenating the moribund subdiscipline of political anthropology.

Do we really need the word 'society' for this? I doubt if it is essential. Language is creative and, forbidden one word, we can easily put together a substitute to serve the same purpose. Classical Greek poets composed tricksy stanzas which avoided common letters like sigma, George Orwell wrote a whole novel without any semi-colons, and Gramsci, whose influence should be obvious in the above discussion, was forced to recast his prison notebooks in safe non-Marxist euphemisms. At the same time, I feel no threat from anyone who chooses to ignore the word, or who prefers to take her ideas from other areas like psychology, literary criticism, or wherever. Anthropology tends to be theoretically promiscuous, and I am far more interested in illuminating accounts of what it might mean to be human in some very different circumstances than in the arid task of policing 'correct' theoretical language.

But let me suggest some reasons why we should think twice before discarding the word 'society'. First, history teaches that the road to theoretical heaven is not, on the whole, paved with circumlocutions, and it is surely more important to concentrate on the quality of the argument than on the precise vocabulary in which it is expressed. Only a very lazy critic would believe that the presence or absence of the word 'society' might signify good or bad anthropology.

Second, sometimes social facts *are* things. In some contexts it is important to remember the thinginess of society, the strength of the collective. 'Sociality against the State' somehow lacks the clout of Clastres's original title[22] and, to me at least, conjures up Leonard Bernstein's famous radical chic cocktail party for the Black Panthers in the late 1960s. Politics, resistances, involve more than dispositions (like sociality), they also involve aggregates or collectivities (like society). Any new political anthropology must necessarily question received ideas of power and the political, for example through Hannah Arendt's idea of power as collective action rather than individual domination,[23] and this in turn requires a recognition of the existence of human collectivities.

This points to a final consideration: the question of intervention. The groups which have been in the forefront of the intellectual struggle against racism and violence in Sri Lanka have names like the Movement for Inter-Racial Justice and Equality, the Social Scientists' Association, and the Campaign for Rational Development. Justice, equality, social science, rationality: we have here a formidable list of what self-styled post-modern critics would deride as the outmoded clichés of a defunct modernism. But I have no intention of telling the people involved with this work that they are the victims of theoretical misapprehension, trapped within Western categories that are theoretically obsolete. Instead I applaud their efforts to use whatever intellectual tools seem appropriate in order to understand the problems of their society.

I have deliberately drawn my examples from social theory rather than anthropological theory, and I have drawn them in order to illustrate this final point. As Cornelius Castoriadis puts it, 'Here the idea of pure theory is an incoherent fiction . . . Every thought of society and of history itself belongs to society and to history.'[24] My objection to this motion is the illusion it offers of an anthropology liberated from the social–historical circumstances of its own production. I suggest instead that we confront those circumstances, learn from them and, if we object to them, join together to change them. I suspect that our opponents in this debate might share this aspiration too.

In fact I suspect we are divided more than anything by the secondary ethnocentrism which derives from different regional traditions. Anyone who has worked in South Asia would wonder at Strathern's account of prevailing anthropological assumptions; this is because of the enormous influence exerted on South Asian ethnography by Louis Dumont. I have talked overmuch of tradition, and compounded my fogeydom by starting this argument with a tribute to my first teacher. Let me close with Dumont's tribute to his teacher: 'A fellow-student, who was not going to make ethnology his career, told me that a strange thing had happened to him. He said something like this: "The other day, while I was standing on the platform of a bus, I suddenly realized that I was not looking at my fellow-passengers in the manner I used to; something had changed. There was no longer 'myself and the others'; I was one of them. For a while I wondered what the reason was for this strange and sudden transformation. All at once I realized: it was Mauss's teaching." The individual of yesterday had become aware of himself as a social being...This is the essential humanist aspect of the teaching of anthropology.'[25] Today, this aspect of our work remains as true and as necessary as ever. I therefore call on you to reject this motion.

Part II The debate

SUSAN DRUCKER-BROWN   What would Marilyn Strathern do with the notion of culture? The antithesis between culture and society is what I find most central. Is 'culture' also obsolete as a concept?

MARILYN STRATHERN   We have to be very careful about the forms into which we put our ideas. I am not throwing out 'social' in the sense of sociality or social relations, nor would I reject the notion of ideas as having a cultural source. My objection to 'culture' would be on precisely the same grounds as my objection to 'society', arising at that point at which we begin to manipulate it as an imaginary entity.

SUSAN DRUCKER-BROWN   Yet even if sociality, in your sense, implies no contrast between the individual and a larger collectivity, it is still antithetical to culture.

CHRIS HANN   On the point of their objection to thinking of society as a unitary entity, I have much sympathy with the proposers of this motion. Yet on most other matters I am more in sympathy with the opposition, to whom I should like to address a comment concerning the problematic nature of the dichotomy between state and civil society. You cited events in China and Sri Lanka, and I can think of many examples from Eastern Europe, where intellectuals have put themselves forward as representatives of civil society wanting to sweep away authoritarian states. This sort of discourse is extremely common among intellectuals, although it does not really correspond to folk concepts. If we retain the concept of society for this reason, then we need to look very carefully at the relations between intellectuals who are using the rhetoric of state and society, and what is actually going on *outside* such intellectual circles in the countries concerned. I would argue a rather different case for keeping the concept of society, particularly in the light of experience from Eastern Europe, in terms of the changes that socialist governments have imposed from above. This imposition has many crude and oppressive features, but in a sense (that ties in closely with nationalist ideas which socialist governments have not been slow to draw upon for legitimation), you could nevertheless speak of – say – Hungarian 'society', in that the villagers whom I studied there actually feel themselves to be part of a society. This is not the same sense as that invoked by intellectuals when they argue for civil society pushing back the state. In other words, the folk concept of society in those countries now is one that *includes* what we are labelling as the state. It includes all that has been done by these regimes from above.

Returning to the theorists cited by both speakers for the opposition, it is worth noting that Tocqueville does not set up a simple opposition between state and civil society; he rather introduces a third area which he calls 'political society'. So long as we realize that the relations between civil society and the state cannot be simplified in the way that sympathetic elites are simplifying them in many parts of the world, and provided that we explore the notion of political society a good deal further, there might be a way forward. And we can retain the term 'society' in Tocqueville's sense.

JOHN PEEL   I said that the relation between state and society is problematic because there is certainly no one-to-one correspondence between them. Certainly, too, they exert a mutual influence on one another. Ernest Gellner[26] has written very astutely about the role that intellectuals play at a certain stage in the development of nationalism, in giving consciousness to peasant populations that had never hitherto thought of themselves as constituting – say – Hungarian or Czech society. Somewhat similar things have happened in Africa, but very often the society that African intellectuals have called into existence has been ethnic in character rather than one that has corresponded to a nation. The relation between state and society is also problematic because there are cases where the difficulties faced by an already existing state, and that can render it ineffective, lie in the absence of a society to which it might correspond. This is the case in many multi-ethnic national states in Africa, arbitrarily bequeathed by colonial politics, and in which intellectuals are asking themselves whether they can possibly bring a civil society into existence. Though the problem is expressed in terms of creating national consciousness, there are many other kinds of ways in which society and state can mutually influence one another. To call this relationship problematic is simply to draw attention to the whole field of issues entailed in it.

JONATHAN SPENCER   Further to what John Peel has just said, I hope nobody took me to suggest that in a brief sketch I could explain all that has gone wrong in Sri Lankan politics. I was merely trying to indicate that an exploration of the different uses that people have made of the concept of 'society' is a particularly effective way of making ethnographic contact with the politics of complex societies. Another reason why we should investigate this usage is that, like any other term of social theory, the concept of 'society' serves at once to describe a given institution and – as Charles Taylor puts it – to *constitute* social reality.[27] The ways in which people actually use the idea of society create what that society comes to look like in the long run. We cannot, as I fear the proposers of the motion are suggesting, divorce our anthropological representations from the potential applications and interventions of politics.

CHRISTINA TOREN   It was precisely my point that we are always implicated by our notions and theoretical assumptions. We, like our opponents, are equally concerned to investigate how these notions are understood. The burden of my contribution was to show that the only way to understand the rhetorical usage of 'society' is by comprehending the nature of the social relations constituted by such usage. These relations may indeed be divisive, repressive, and so on.

RICHARD FARDON   Just to clarify matters, could I ask each of the four speakers to say what is the single thing they most disagree with in the position of the other side?

MARILYN STRATHERN   I shall simply respond to one question put by the opposition: What is wrong with dichotomies? Prime Minister Thatcher's implementation of a dichotomy, stripped of one of its poles, shows exactly what is wrong.

JOHN PEEL   I disagree with hardly anything of what Christina Toren has said. But the idea she proposed, of individuals as both products and producers of social relations, resonates with a large tradition of nineteenth-century sociology which says just that. Weber, Simmel and the early Marx say it over and over again. Only by reducing the concept of society to a narrow, artificial construct can any plausibility be given to the motion at all. This is the single thing that I disagree with most.

JONATHAN SPENCER   Marilyn Strathern's recent comment exemplifies my objection, which is to the tendency to generalize from a single instance. That one dichotomy can be used in one particular set of political or historical circumstances in a particular way does not mean that all dichotomous thinking is necessarily bad. Likewise, that society has been posited against the individual by some people in some circumstances does not mean that 'society' has some magical power about it, or that it has some *mana* that will always result in its being used in that way.

MARILYN STRATHERN   Yet the single instance of enterprise culture is poured over our heads through every conceivable orifice!

CHRISTINA TOREN   Of course we are not saying that all dichotomous thinking is dreadful. Our concern is with the *theoretical* utility of the concept of society, and it is this that we argue against. Everything I said was indeed informed by nineteenth- and twentieth-century theories: material theories about social relations. To make these theories operationally more useful, I suggest that we move away from the individual–society dichotomy.

ALAN ABRAMSON   The proponents of the motion were ready to perpetuate the notion of sociality, so that the question really turns on whether there can be sociality without society. For the proposers, this possibility must exist. But if sociality involves communication, then it surely entails a common language. A constituency defined by common language would seem to be a precondition for the kind of sociality that the proposers are talking about. Can one, then, have such a constituency without a society in some sense? The answer, I think, is 'no'. Sociality thus seems to require some constituency reproducing verisimilitude in language, otherwise there could be no communication. So the question is: what reproduces common language? Though we may not have the answer yet, though the mechanism may remain ill-defined, we can still designate it by the term 'society'. That we still lack a correct specification of society does not mean that the concept is obsolete, merely that other traditions – the Durkheimian tradition in particular – have the wrong answers. But the Durkheimian question remains absolutely valid. Why have common language? Why do languages exist?

LADISLAV HOLY   I should like to return to the question of dichotomies. I would come down on the side of Jonathan Spencer, because without some dichotomy in mind it would be impossible to formulate, let alone to debate, the issue of the usefulness of the concept of society. That issue is itself the product of a certain kind of dichotomous thinking – for example society versus community, or society versus individual. Without these dichotomies we could not ask ourselves the question that we are asking today. The distinction we should draw is between use and misuse, rather than between utility and obsolescence. If the concept of society were abandoned as obsolete, then I wonder what other dichotomy we would come up with. We cannot escape dichotomy if we are ever to formulate any questions.

RONALD FRANKENBERG   I agree that we cannot manage without dichotomies. However, dichotomous terms may be linked together rather than just opposites: for example whilst good is usually seen as the opposite of evil it can also be seen as coupled with evil but with the possibility of transcending it.

TIM INGOLD   Two crucial issues have been put before us. The first concerns dichotomies, and it is clear that in our debate we have encountered two ways of thinking about them. On the one hand, we have been presented with such dichotomies as person–sociality or person–relationships, in which the paired terms signify mutually constitutive aspects of a single phenomenal field; on the other hand, we have dichotomies referring to a division between two independently constituted domains which may then be supposed to interact with one another. This latter view gives rise to the classic problem of dualistic thinking, namely, how is interaction possible between entities that belong to substantially separate domains, for example, of mind and matter? It is similarly hard to conceive, in Durkheimian terms, of an interaction between individual and society. From a purely neutral stance, there seems to be a dichotomy between two dichotomies: between a kind of relational thinking and a kind of entity thinking. Both ways of thinking entail dichotomies, but of different kinds.

The second issue concerns language. If I might put a question to the proposers of the motion: do they think that because the concept of society is, in their view, theoretically obsolete, the same applies to the concept of language? I particularly have in mind the concept of language that has entered the anthropological vocabulary in the sense of Saussure.

CHRISTINA TOREN   The answer to that is 'yes'. My own view of language is much influenced by the Russian school of Bakhtin and Voloshinov,[28] according to which we have to get away from the polarities of structure–process or *langue–parole* precisely because there is no point at which you can actually locate structure (*langue*). It can only ever be understood as an abstraction, because in reality language is a constant process of becoming. My view is thus radically contrary to that of Saussure.

ELIZABETH TONKIN   If the concept of society forms part of a theory, we have still to address the question of whether different theories work more or less well in their application, in practice, to different bodies of ethnographic material. There are clearly certain empirical cases where it makes sense to speak of society as a causative agent, but in other cases this gives us a very poor model of what is going on. This may depend on whether one is up against such well-formed objects as a state apparatus, or concerned with more loosely articulated fields of relationships.

JOHN PEEL   Though the concept of society is not exactly pre-theoretical, it is nevertheless somewhat trans-theoretical in the sense that one finds it used in the context of various and often opposed theoretical positions. In the early eighteenth century, 'society' was defined in terms of classes or productive relationships, with the state playing the role of mediator or counterbalance towards conflicts generated in civil society. On the other hand, 'society' has been seen, above all by nationalists, chiefly as a normative construct, and the state as dominating rather than reconciling conflicts. To take up the theme of language in another way: clearly the reification of language was part of the nationalist project, with the creation of literary standards and the promulgation of the idea that the language of the people is natural and appropriate for expressing particular thoughts. It is a social fact that languages, as we observe them in their patterns of use, vary a good deal in the extent to which they have been effectively reified, in how much they are given in advance so as to facilitate state formation, or how much they are things that established states help to create. All of these processes are going on, and entail different and often opposing theories. That is why I would see 'society', as I suggested early on, as a medley of issues rather than as a concept wedded to a particular theory (for example, Maussian or Durkheimian).

MARILYN STRATHERN   I would like to respond to Elizabeth Tonkin and also to Alan Abramson's earlier comment. The sense of variability and multiplicity in the meanings of 'society', that our opponents are putting forward, belongs to the heightened self-consciousness of late twentieth-century anthropology, which is beginning to look back and reflect on the rhetorical uses of the term. It is precisely this self-consciousness that makes us aware of how the term has meant different things in different historical epochs. I put it to you that this self-consciousness is also a symptom of the passing of the paradigm. Now, if nothing more were entailed than the replacement of one social theory by another, we could indeed regard the successor theory as providing a more refined or 'better' concept of society. We argue, however, that the concept is obsolete because we have to change in a much more radical way.

Let me briefly exemplify the problems to which we are led by theorizing on the notion of society. I refer to the way in which we produce abstract concepts, in the language of anthropological discourse, for the analysis of what have come to be known as initiation rituals. In the ethnographic context of the Papua New Guinea Highlands, these have been routinely understood in terms of processes of socialization. This is quite easy as long as one is dealing with boys' initiation because boys can clearly be socialized into society, but it becomes rather problematic when looking at girls' rituals as the argument has to be hedged around with all sorts of qualifications. Now what happens when the paradigm begins to become visible, and its potential exhausted, is that the theoretical puzzles to which the underlying concepts give rise accumulate to a point at which they outweigh the positive contribution of the concepts themselves. We are not, I think, required to spell out what kind of theory should be put in place of the old one, but I would venture one observation for your consideration, which is that I have found it far more helpful to think of initiation practices as ways by which people make known to themselves the fact that they can draw the capacity to make relationships out of persons. Boys, or girls, are put into a variety of situations in which what is demonstrated are the relationships that compose them and the relationships that they, in turn, can make. This perspective has proved useful to me.

JONATHAN SPENCER　The example that Marilyn Strathern has just outlined is extremely interesting, but the fact of her using a different language and different terms does not present a problem for me. For I am not arguing that she or anyone else is *obliged* to talk about the individual, society and socialization. As Elizabeth Tonkin rightly pointed out, it is intuitively obvious that some ideas work better in some contexts than in others. All we are saying is that we can imagine certain contexts in which it would still be appropriate to use some idea of society.

PETER GOW   In my own anthropological practice I am presented with the problem of how to deal with Amazonian cultures, and in this I have found the work of Marilyn Strathern extremely useful. But I fully accept that in drawing on it, I have started to write in a way that others might find virtually incomprehensible! I think it is dangerous to take the view that in one context the term 'society' is applicable and in another it is not. To say that the concept is useful in particular types of situations (such as Eastern Europe or post-colonial states in Africa) but not in others (such as Melanesia or Amazonia) is to invoke a sense of descriptive apartheid. And this raises the very serious issue of whether anthropology is liable to fragment into particular approaches to particular types of problems or whether it can remain as a single discipline with a shared theoretical language and a common arena of debate.

CHRIS FULLER   The argument advanced by Marilyn Strathern appears to depend on the notion that we are engaged in a kind of anthropology that can be understood in terms of Kuhnian paradigm shifts, that there is some kind of paradigm that is now demonstrably cracking, and that we can now move on to another. This, of course, is precisely analogous to the Thatcherite notion that there exists some kind of statist view of the world which has finally been shown to be bankrupt and must be replaced. Both notions are equally fantastical. In the real world, as in the discipline of anthropology – or indeed any other contemporary intellectual discipline – such radical paradigm shifts simply do not occur. Things evolve, terms are recycled and reused. The premiss, that there is some new dawn over there to which we could move by ridding ourselves of the tainted concept, 'society', is sheer fantasy.

PAUL HENLEY   The proposers of the motion proved their point about the divisiveness of dichotomies quite convincingly, but in so doing they completely undermined their own argument. For this depended on their setting up a false dichotomy between their view and that advocated by the opposition, by seeking to establish that there has been a long tradition in anthropology of dividing the individual from society. But as the opposition speakers demonstrated, the more subtle theoreticians – even in the nineteenth century – were well aware that individual and society are inseparable. I only began to understand the relevance of what Marilyn Strathern is proposing when she spoke about initiation rituals. Her point seems to be that we should be free to formulate finely textured explanations of what social institutions are all about. So the issue concerns the kind of interpretation or understanding that we are looking for in anthropology.

In this sense I think we should allow ourselves to be completely promiscuous in looking around the world, and around our own intellectual traditions, for whatever ideas suit our particular needs. It may be that certain paradigms are appropriate for certain kinds of problems, and that other paradigms are more appropriate for different sets of problems in different contexts and regions of the world. In one of his last papers, Meyer Fortes – referring to A. J. Ayer – distinguished between pundits and journeymen. Pundits are those who bring down theoretical tablets from the mountains, and try to impose them on the population; journeymen are workaday anthropologists who travel around the world buying their theories from a barrow according to their needs. I think the latter characterization better depicts our current situation. We should be free to delve into our historical traditions and use whatever theories are relevant to our needs. In this sense Marilyn Strathern is right: we have reached a point where there is no established paradigm. Instead we can mix ideas from diverse sources into a particular pastiche for dealing with the problem at hand.

TIM INGOLD   We seem to be at cross purposes, since the proposers of the motion are really concerned with an anthropology that tries to understand, in some general way, the condition of human beings living in relationships, whereas the opposition is looking around for terms suitable to describe, interpret and understand specific historical situations which are going to be different, depending on whether they are in Melanesia, Sri Lanka, West Africa or Britain. Part of the division lies in the question of anthropological objectives. Do we seek limited understandings of particular historical circumstances in one continent or another at particular periods of time, raiding our theoretical baggage for whatever comes in handy for saying what we feel we need to say; or are we trying to discover something about what being human entails, which transcends the particularities of historical, geographical and regional circumstance?

JOHN PEEL   While I accept Tim Ingold's characterization of the dominant interests of the two sides, I rather take against Paul Henley's celebration of pastiche. To draw on a theoretical tradition that runs back two or three hundred years (and I would certainly want to take it back beyond the nineteenth century) does not amount to pastiche. There was recently an exhibition at the Museum of Mankind by Eduardo Paolozzi, consisting of artworks from the ethnographic collections combined in various assemblages, which was shot through with the idea of pastiche. I felt it to be profoundly offensive precisely because it rested on the assumption that things could be wrenched from their specific spatial and temporal contexts in order to achieve an aesthetic effect. Considering Marilyn Strathern's account of how she would view initiation rituals in Melanesia, and the very different interpretations that have been made of initiation rituals in West Africa, I wonder to what extent these differences are due to locally prevailing cultural practices, and to what extent they are due to the various theoretical predilections of anthropologists. It may be, of course, that Melanesia is just made for the post-modern phase of anthropology, but I am doubtful, and in any case the issue can only be clarified by returning to systematic, comparative exercises in which one would ask , for example, 'Can Marilyn Strathern's conceptual framework be applied to initiation ceremonies in West Africa, Amazonia or wherever and, if not, why not?' Ultimately, if we are to remain faithful to the ethnographic enterprise, we must come back to such comparative questions, asking ourselves 'Why is it different in these different regions?' And the answer that we are almost bound to come up with is: 'Because this is the way Melanesian or West African or Amazonian cultures or societies tend to be.' This is potentially a much more interesting finding than that the differences are all due to the theoretical tastes of this or that anthropologist.

PAUL BAXTER   It may be that the term 'initiation rite' is such a category of art that to compare what we denote by this term in West Africa (or East Africa, which is my own area of interest) and Melanesia is to compare totally unlike phenomena. Whilst that may be so, if we proceed too far in this direction, anthropology will become completely fractionalized and we could almost assemble our monographs in a random fashion. I am very concerned about this trend.

DANIEL MILLER   I came to this debate with the dichotomy between society and culture, rather than that between society and individual (which was stressed by the proposers of the motion), at the forefront of my mind. I thought it a pity that the proposers concentrated so narrowly on 'society', since in my view it is society as it leads to various other notions such as social relations, sociability, social structure, kinship and so on – notions that are all very tightly connected – that constitutes the core of current anthropological practice, and that is potentially under challenge at this moment. It might, then, be more honest to widen the remit of the debate, and to ask whether a more fundamental paradigm shift is under way, and if so, what kinds of concepts would take their place in the discipline that social anthropology might eventually evolve into. Only if it can be shown that there are things which can be done with these new concepts that the traditional concept of 'society' – with its attendant emphases and reifications – will *not* allow us to do, can we decide that the latter is obsolete. This, of course, entails a larger debate. However, we can reach this level of debate, not through simplification but only through gradual complication, through the incorporation of a more subtle appreciation of relationships, and through an awareness that the phenomena we aim to understand are more complex than hitherto recognized.

TIM INGOLD   I have a further point relating to comparison. Traditionally, it was always assumed that societies are what one compares. Now we are being told that in some poles of the comparison, 'society' might be the appropriate term to use, whereas in others it might not be so apt. In that case, what are we actually comparing? I wonder whether the answer could be 'qualities of relatedness'. Perhaps the term 'society' connotes a certain quality of relatedness which is not encountered in those situations where ethnographers who have attempted to use the term find that it fails to capture the essence of what they are trying to convey. Thus we could retain the concept of society, so long as we are able to specify the particular kind of relatedness to which it refers, and so long as we recognize that this is not the *only* possible kind.

PENNY HARVEY   How is it that some societies come to constitute themselves *as* societies whereas others apparently do not? The proposers of the motion seem to offer a way of dealing with cases of the latter kind, where people do not constitute themselves as a society. The opposition, by contrast, seems unable to countenance such cases.

PETER WADE   I should like to ask a question about paradigms. In what sense can we speak of a paradigm shift when the kinds of ideas that Marilyn Strathern and Christina Toren have been talking about, such as the mutual constitution of persons and social relations, can certainly be traced back to the young Marx?

MARILYN STRATHERN   We are obviously agreed, the four of us, that we have a common enemy in the form of Thatcherite philosophy. The debate is about the best way to combat the enemy, and I think there is no disagreement on the necessity to do so. The political example I used, however, is but an example of the tragic way in which the concept of society has led to a proliferation of other, more dangerous notions. It is a red herring to argue that there is more to 'society' than the particular aspect I have chosen to criticize. The fact that this aspect is what trips us up from time to time is sufficient reason to dispatch the concept.

However the debate, and I *have* interpreted it narrowly, is about the concept's *theoretical* obsolescence. Now, as both opponents of the motion have observed, the history of theory is a delicate matter, sensitive to time and context. I am quite unmoved by the fact that 'society' has been used, in the past, in senses much closer to what I would call 'sociality'. I am unmoved by references to Marx and Mauss, and did indeed bring along my own quotation from the *1844 Manuscripts*,[29] which I shall inflict upon you:

> Above all we must avoid postulating 'Society' again as an abstraction vis-à-vis the individual. The individual *is the social being*. His life, even if it may not appear in the direct form of a *communal* life in association with others, is therefore an expression and confirmation of *social life*.

I am unmoved by the attempt to snare my precise argument with the claim that I was speaking for all of Western society at all periods. Indeed, my plea is for a return to the pretensions from which we started out at the beginning of this century, pretensions which are enshrined, for example, in Durkheim's manifesto. Durkheim said almost all the right things: that society is prior, that social life is prior, that persons are already embedded in relations. But the method by which social phenomena were to be thought of as things, the prioritization of society as an entity, endorsed the very individualism against which he argued, and (the whole history of Western society notwithstanding) we are heirs to the very specific devolution of those particular ideas.

I am unmoved, then, by general references to what happened in the 1860s here, there and everywhere; I *am* very interested in what happened in the 1960s because that has produced the generation of ideas which has brought us to our present pass in 1989. Of course I do not believe in a new dawn; I do not see anthropology as marching down a road either to a new dawn or into the sunset. Anthropology is a set of practices which is responsive to the particular situations in which it finds itself. We cannot, therefore, deliberately invent new paradigms; the point is that paradigms constitute the taken-for-granted grounds of our knowledge. It is impossible therefore to be specific about the paradigms upon which we are presently operating; however, we *are* required, as active, thinking persons, to remain active and to think about our current situation and specifically about the consequences of the political endorsement of what we as anthropologists have long held, very properly and very preciously, as a theoretical concept.

You will probably have heard from this debate that openness is being claimed both for and against both sides. Openness, or pluralism, is just a bit too easy to advocate. I actually have a problem with it, and that is with where the idea of pluralism comes from. Earlier I referred to mathematics, because there is a dimension I did not bring into the main point: sensitivity to the *present* world also requires new ways of conceptualizing relations for which the individualistic and totalizing parameters of our concept of 'society' are inadequate.

These days there seems too much movement, mobility, a kind of creolization, everything a part-culture or part-society. Transposed styles of life or ways of relating seem 'out of context', parts taken from some 'society' elsewhere. Yet we know that for the living of lives, the derivative, borrowed nature of people's circumstances seem as 'whole' to them as anything. One cannot attach holism to some supra-level such as society when people migrate with their lives on their backs. Then we resort to self-pitying metaphors of fragmentation – when it is quite clear that lives have always been made up of such parts and bits. Our part–whole metaphors seem inadequate. So, we also know that there is something awry with our approach to representations. We are cautious of global accounts, wary of claims to authentic representations, and then look back in despair at the plethora we have created. There seems too much of everything – everything in pieces: 'societies' devastated by political or ecological regimes; multiple voices and the mushrooming of different perspectives one *could* take on this or that, by ethnicity, gender or whatever. In short: pluralism.

The point is that any totalizing approach that tries to reinstate some transcendent concept such as 'society' will only reinvent this as plethora – a sense of society cut up, diffracted into its individual parts. We need some other way of thinking relations.

For our perceptions have shifted, and we cannot undo this fact. We *know* that we live in a world system and in an intensely parochial one; that we travel and stay in the same place; migrate and meet migrants at home; consume the world's products and contaminate our own resources. We see persons as parts of one another's economies, biospheres, even bodies if one thinks of organ transplants, and certainly we speak with one another's voices. With Leach's dictum in mind, late twentieth-century anthropology could do with a new mathematic. Not a mathematic of units and a plurality of units, whole societies and individual persons; perhaps something closer to the mechanics of the 'butterfly effect' – the notion that a butterfly stirring the air today in Peking can transform storm systems next month in New York.

JOHN PEEL   In the course of this debate, even speakers who seemed to support the motion nevertheless, in making their points, spoke of societies *as* societies. This is a term that people *do* use and that they will certainly continue to use. That tells us something about the sort of concept that 'society' really is. Theoretically, it is not a very committed notion. Rather than being tied to particular theoretical effects, on account of which Marilyn Strathern would move its abandonment, the concept of society is in our view deployed in a series of linked antitheses which together define a field of debate. The proposers of the motion have deliberately ignored the diversity of traditions in social theory. It is not a random chaos, and it does not reveal to us a succession of paradigms, each of which secures near universal assent before being replaced by the next. Thus at any one time, we have available to us a range of concepts of society. The essential question, I contend, is this: Will it be possible to talk intelligibly about situations and contexts and how they differ from one another, that is, to talk about them *comparatively*, without using some overarching concept such as 'society'? I think not. It was suggested at one point that we should compare 'qualities of relatedness' in context, but what then are those contexts – if not societies? We all know that 'society' is a concept that we shall continue to employ; we find it useful, indeed unavoidable, precisely because of the structured diversity of the tradition whose heirs we are.

CHRISTINA TOREN   John Peel is basically right. People undoubtedly (and unfortunately) will continue to use the term 'society'. Our point is not that paradigm shifts are so obviously apparent, or that general shifts in theoretical thinking are easily accomplished. As Marilyn Strathern has made very plain, one paradigm is not simply and neatly replaced by another. Since the paradigm is the taken-for-granted ground from which one works, it cannot readily be made conscious to oneself.

However, we are arguing that, *theoretically*, the concept of society is obsolete. I agree (with Peter Gow) that we should strive for the kind of theoretical vocabulary that enables us to speak to one another. This is crucially important for me, since my interest in being an anthropologist is to understand what makes human beings who they are, and how they come to be the people they are. The only way in which I can conceivably begin to understand this is by focusing on some very particular and historically specific set of circumstances. Now, if you look at the processes by which people come to be who they are, you are looking at the 'how' of something, rather than at the 'what'. And it is in looking at the 'how', the historical processes by which persons, through their mutual relations, come to be social beings, that we can realize the possibility of comparison.

JONATHAN SPENCER   The central question that has emerged in the course of this debate concerns what theory actually is. There are radically different views on this. However, pluralism is something we have to live with, it is around us all the time and cannot be wished away by some desire for unity. We have to think of ways of coping with this. Peter Gow spoke of the danger of proliferating incommensurable theoretical languages. But this notion of in-commensurability locks straight into the notion of paradigm, for we speak of people using different paradigms as talking incom-mensurable languages. However, our use of language is creative, and we can employ the same terms to mean different things. Whatever else may have emerged from this debate, it has proved that even if we differ in our conclusions, we can agree on what we are arguing about. The essential point, surely, is that we should keep on arguing.

NOTES

1 E. R. Leach, *Pul Eliya: a village in Ceylon*, Cambridge, Cambridge University Press, 1961.

2   *Ibid.*, pp. 304–5.
3   Recapitulated in E. R. Leach, 'Glimpses of the unmentionable in the history of British social anthropology', *Annual Review of Anthropology* 13, 1984, pp. 1–23.
4   Many of these points are discussed in detail in T. Ingold, *Evolution and social life*, Cambridge, Cambridge University Press, 1986.
5   T. Ingold, 'An anthropologist looks at biology', *Man* (N.S.) 25, 1990, pp. 208–29.
6   J. D. Y. Peel, 'History, culture and the comparative method: a West African puzzle', in *Comparative anthropology*, ed. L. Holy, Oxford, Blackwell, 1987.
7   For a recent critique, see D. J. J. Brown, 'Unity in opposition in the New Guinea Highlands', *Social Analysis* 23, 1988, pp. 89–105.
8   E. Wolf, 'Inventing society', *American Ethnologist* 15, 1988, pp. 752–61. 'The concept,' Wolf writes, 'has... become an obstacle.'
9   For a longer view, see T. Ingold, *Evolution and social life*, Cambridge, Cambridge University Press, 1986.
10 R. J. Thornton, 'The rhetoric of ethnographic holism', *Cultural Anthropology* 3, 1988, pp. 285–303.
11 A. Giddens, *The constitution of society*, Cambridge, Polity Press, 1986.
12 E. R. Leach, *Political systems of Highland Burma*, London, Athlone Press, 1954.
13 T. Ingold, *Evolution and social life*, Cambridge, Cambridge University Press, 1986.
14 Thomas Hobbes, *Leviathan*, 1651, Pt. 1 Ch. 13.
15 M. Strathern, *The gender of the gift*, Berkeley, University of California Press, 1988.
16 M. Mann, *The sources of social power*, vol. 1, Cambridge, Cambridge University Press, 1986.
17 The search was conducted on the Oxford University Press CD-ROM version of the First Edition of the *Oxford English Dictionary*.
18 J. S. Mill, *Essay on Liberty*, 1859, p. 29.
19 K. Marx, *Theses on Feuerbach VI*, in *The German Ideology* by K. Marx and F. Engels, ed. C. J. Arthur, London, Lawrence and Wishart, 1977, p. 122.
20 K. Malalgoda, 'Millennialism in relation to Buddhism', *Comparative Studies in Society and History* 12, 1970, pp. 424–41.
21 E. V. Daniel, 'Afterword: sacred places, violent spaces', in *Sri Lanka: history and the roots of crisis*, ed. J. Spencer, London, Routledge, 1990.
22 P. Clastres, *Society against the State*, Oxford, Blackwell, 1977.
23 H. Arendt, *On violence*, New York, Harcourt, Brace and World, 1970.
24 C. Castoriadis, *The imaginary institution of society*, Oxford, Polity Press, 1987, p. 3.
25 L. Dumont, *Homo hierarchicus*, Chicago, University of Chicago Press, 1970, p. 42.
26 E. Gellner, *Nations and nationalism*, Oxford, Blackwell, 1983.
27 C. Taylor, 'Social theory as practice', in *Philosophy and the human sciences: philosophical papers*, vol. 2, Cambridge, Cambridge University Press, 1985.
28 V. N. Voloshinov, *Marxism and the philosophy of language*, trans. L. Matejka and I. R. Titunik, New York, Seminar Press, 1973.
29 K. Marx, *The economic and political manuscripts of 1844*, trans. M. Milligan, ed. D. J. Struik. New York, International Publishers, 1964, pp. 137–8.

1990 debate

Human worlds are culturally constructed

Introduction

Roy Ellen

It is one of the aims of these debates that they address issues which are central to (and even constitutive of) anthropological theory, issues which – though they may enter into the deliberations of other disciplines – are seldom understood as their defining problematic. It is also one of their aims that anthropology should make some attempt to recapture its traditional ground, on the one hand, from encroachers and borrowers representing other academic disciplines and, on the other, from those who, while they describe themselves as anthropologists, nevertheless take an increasingly narrow definition of what the enterprise entails: I have in mind the extremes of biographical ethnography, textualism and neo-Darwinism.

This, the third debate in the series, amply fulfils these aims. It provides an opportunity to explicate the concepts of 'human worlds', 'culture' (of course), 'organism' and, perhaps more innovatively, 'construction'. Much hinges on the meanings attached to these key terms, on varying metaphorical styles and on the demolition and re-creation of those dichotomies which we inevitably live by. Some insight into the raw co-ordinates of the debate may be gained by picking out some of the threads under three headings: organism, culture and construction.

The motion, as put, contains an implicit counter-suggestion: that if human worlds are not culturally constructed then they must, presumably, be genetically constructed. None of the contributors, as it happens, take this line, but all are aware of the trap, and their respective positions are evident from the ways in which they use the term 'organism'. Wendy James is happy to concede that there are biological influences on human behaviour, but is steadfastly opposed to the *reduction* of humans to mere organisms, at least partly because in figurative language 'organism' carries derogatory (and deterministic) connotations which serve neither our understanding of humans nor of other animals. Far better, she avers, to conceptualize *Homo sapiens* as 'body plus'. Similarly, Tim Ingold scrupulously avoids the possibility that he be mistaken for a closet sociobiologist, or even a fellow-traveller; but he does take great exception to the description of non-human animals as 'mere organisms'. For him, part of the problem is that many contemporary biologists have abandoned the organism in favour of DNA, and with it the self-evidently correct notion that organisms develop interactively with others of their kind and with other constituents of the environment, making them anything but 'mere'. By the same token, 'body plus' implies for Ingold the idea that culture is somehow 'added on' to nature, thereby maintaining a pernicious opposition with its consequent oversimplification of the notions of both organism, environment and culture. No doubt, had there been clandestine sociobiologists lurking in the woodwork of the debating chamber, some at least might have accepted the idea of 'body plus', whilst pointing out that whatever we decide to call the extended human phenotype, it will nevertheless have selective implications for the genome.

While Tim Ingold and Paul Richards go out of their way to deny any affinity with militant sociobiology, Wendy James and Roland Littlewood are anxious to defend themselves against the charge that they might be new wave post-modernists. What James, at least, does assert is her implacable opposition to the notion of culture as a 'thing', advancing the view that what is really distinctive about *human* culture is the ability to be reflexive (in other words, to 'know what you know'), and stressing the 'irreducibly cultural character' of the way in which individuals, in a very real sense, *create* their worlds (that is, their 'environments') through sight, sound, touch and smell. Culture enters into the most trivial and obvious practical activity, including the sense of bodily presence and the way organic structures and sensations are translated by interacting wilful subjects. She suggests that in the contemporary uses of 'discourse', 'practice' and 'habitus' we find attempts to capture that pragmatic corporeal character of culture. As Littlewood puts it, our knowledge of the world only takes shape *as* culture, that is as our instruments or procedures for knowing (such as professional biology); we cannot experience the world out there as it *really* is, only in terms of what we bring to it, and that includes values. In this Ingold seems to find much with which to agree, and he is even prepared to claim that humans *do* differ from other animals in being able to make 'imagined' worlds. But he is not convinced that humans are uniquely privileged in their possession of a reflexive faculty.[1] Moreover, he objects indignantly to the notion that humans are somehow 'suspended' and act within some predetermined framework of meaning, and likewise to the idea that 'real' reality exists independently of the acting and perceiving subject.

If the discussion of organism and culture has a certain air of *déjà vu*, then the discussion of *construction* provided something altogether more original. Again, both proponents and opponents claim to share a common starting point, vigorously rejecting the outmoded stereotypes going back to Berger and Luckmann's *The social construction of reality*.[2] Littlewood reminds us that for many the notion of social construction has become a convenient orthodoxy, emblematic of a special expertise which anthropologists (amongst others) are thought to cultivate. He begins by mocking and caricaturing the excesses of constructionism, and parodies the ludicrous irrelevance of asking what it might mean to speak of the 'cultural construction' of a child dying of AIDS. But this is by way of an apology. Though we may reject a passive interpretation of construction in favour of an interactive one, the idea is so compelling that it cannot easily be dispensed with. Tiresome it may be, but we must retain it. Both Ingold and Richards object in principle to constructionist logic, with its implication of building to a blueprint, and to the 'arrogance' implicit in the idea that 'people make themselves'. In Ingold's terms, perception is rather a mode of engagement with the world, not a means of constructing it; hence his preference for 'dwelling' rather than 'building'. The world in which people dwell comes into being as we act in it, and 'persons' are constituted in turn by our engagement in that world, neither 'given' nature nor constructed culture. Richards prefers the active metaphor of performance – particularly musical performance – to both the sedentary sense of 'dwelling' and the mechanical sense of construction. We act as social agents, make mistakes, recover from both these and random disturbances and generally 'cope' in a world full of surprises. Plant breeding, for example, is not a branch of the cultural construction industry, but an intelligent awareness of Mendelian principles by people who dwell with plants. Social life is always provisional, 'work-in-progress', never completed and therefore not constructed in any ultimate way.

What strikes me about the debate, though it is characteristic of the genre and indeed of academic discourse more widely, is the extent to which divergences and agreements hinge upon the use of particular words and tropes, and on the dialectical invention, rejection and re-invention of analytic dichotomies. Assent and dissent in the realm of ideas depend not only on shared and contrasting metaphors, but also – and perhaps more revealingly – on shared words with different meta-phoric extensions, and on the degree to which we emphasize or qualify in the oral mode what we italicize or place within inverted commas in written texts. The word 'construction', for example, as first used by Berger and Luckmann, had no conscious antonym other than, perhaps, 'destruction'; but in a world where 'deconstruction' has a technical meaning, 'construction' is inevitably redefined; while in the hands of Ingold it has – as a synonym of 'build' – come to be opposed to 'dwell' in the sense earlier employed by Heidegger. There are numerous apologies for the inadequacies of ruling dichotomies: as between etic and emic, given and constructed, nature and culture, organism and environment, sensation and intellection, animality and humanity. Neither side agrees with a particular version of cultural constructionism, though all versions are clearly perpetuated through an antithesis with an equally unsatisfactory 'biogenetic determinism'. But beyond this we also find hostility to the conceptual paradigms in which we are forced to choose between such dichotomies. Ingold is all for transcending dichotomies – for example, by favouring the idea that persons and environments are reciprocally constituted. Littlewood concurs that there is an important sense in which everything is simultaneously natural and social, where 'natural' and 'social' are not different places but different maps. You do not have to deny the existence of the 'natural' map to be a social or cultural constructionist, or to use the notion of construction in a particular way.

What I find intriguing is the extent to which we can participate in that cultural event we call a 'debate' simply because it is assumed that we share a common lexicon and procedural know-how, only to discover that we are actually using words in subtly different ways which have very radical implications. This is a risk we run in any linguistic encounter, and unless we are persistent and repetitive we are inclined to interpret the utterance (we always interpret the utterance, rather than the message) in the form that is, for us, most easily comprehensible. This is what we call, when we recognize it, 'talking at cross-purposes', which is in effect to trivialize an inherent quality of human communication with dramatic and largely unexamined consequences. No doubt we have here plenty of grist for the textualist mill once it is through with ethnography; and I suspect that there is a fair probability that we may in ten years' time be hotly debating the use of 'resonance' as an analogy, or protesting that we should transcend the false polarization between 'natural' and 'cultural' maps, or complaining that 'dwelling' is an entirely inadequate word with which to grasp the truly interactive qualities of the way in which our minds organize environmental knowledge. Such predictions only appear cynical if it is believed that arguing over words does not advance learning. It might not, of course, but anyone even slightly acquainted with the history of science will know that such disputes are never far removed from the frontiers of understanding. Long may they continue to be so.

Part I The presentations

FOR THE MOTION (1)

WENDY JAMES

To find oneself invited to propose what on the surface looks like a harmless orthodoxy, a matter of general consensus – which could be read as a modest claim that people differ from other animals – is not easy. The real proposition will no doubt be sprung by our opponents; indeed some may suspect that this debate has been designed back to front, and that we innocent defenders of the established tradition have been set up for an ambush. It seems likely that we shall be confronted with a substantive, if negative, counter-proposition: that human worlds are *not* culturally constructed, that they are rather given in the genetic inheritance and organically founded consciousness which we share with other animals, and that this truth is concealed from conventional anthropologists by their dominant concern with social and cultural phenomena. Those who advocate a more 'biological' approach in anthropology may well hope that we will take a well-trodden path in defending some of the older orthodoxies and tired paradigms of culture as *system*. We, however, prefer to take a fresh path in proposing the motion, seeking to focus not upon the abstract external form of cultural phenomena, but upon the human being as a cultural agent and as the culturally formed subject of experience.

Allow us immediately to concede that human beings are indeed organisms shaped by genetic transmission, with bodily systems and nervous structures comparable to those of some other creatures. In many ways the activities of human beings appear to parallel those of other organisms: especially in the co-operative patterns seen in the nurturing of young, the search for food and shelter, the establishment of control over territory and groups, and in the context of grooming, mating, communication through signalling and other forms of 'consociality'. Like other creatures we are affected by the availability of water or food, by the intensity of heat or cold, and by the impact of disease – I do not need to extend this list; Roland Littlewood will elaborate later on questions of disease and pain. Let us also concede straight away the immense interest and potential importance of modern work on animal behaviour, and of the new philosophical writings on animals.

May we further clarify our position on 'culture'. In the previous debate, the notion of 'society' as denoting a concrete entity which could carry a plural sense was rejected. Let us dispose immediately of the corresponding nominal form of 'culture' which, in the reified sense of a thing that can be possessed, as a whole, by you or me and made a mark of contrast with some faraway tribe, seems to be creeping back into anthropological discourse. In asking you to support the motion, we would point out that it is built not around the nominal form of 'culture', but rather its adverbial form, which is a very different matter. Acceptance of our arguments does not mean having to admit to any vulgarly positive notion of culture as a tangible object; rather the contrary, as that idea may well turn out to form part of the old-fashioned rationalism of some recent advocates of a more 'biological' approach.

Our emphasis is rather upon the irreducibly cultural character of the way in which human life is lived. By human we refer basically to aspects of the species *Homo sapiens*, even in this Latin scientific technicality, 'wise'. As a limiting and ambivalent case, we would accept not the sociality of the bees or the birds, but the striking evidence that flowers, offerings and red ochre were used in Neanderthal burial rites.[3] At least since that time, we would argue, there has been a culturally constituted aspect or quality to all human action and experience. This aspect or quality, which inheres in any human world, cannot be separated out. The very notion of a 'world' implies some sort of coherence, if not as a simple integrated whole, then at least as an ensemble within which the possibility of cross-linkages of interpretation can be imagined; if the cultural element were withdrawn, separated or denied, the ensemble of fragmentary action and experience would fall apart.

Though the operations performed with hands, tools and eyes in the task of digging a hole may appear the same for an organism, whether that hole is for concealing treasure or for burying a child, the physical execution cannot be reasonably interpreted apart from a consideration of the purpose of the hole, which can only be understood culturally. And the purely behavioural observation of emotion, such as an account of the trembling and welling up of tears at a death, cannot distinguish between an actual event of death and an event pictured on the cinema screen.

Creatures other than human beings may well be seen to 'grieve' over a death, but *only* for us can such a reaction be triggered by what Wordsworth called that 'inward eye' as it contemplates non-events in memory, imagination and expectation while secretly weeping in the back row of the cinema. Consider the simpler case of hunger: the organic reaction of 'mouth-watering' is certainly set off in us with the smell of cooking or at the sight of food, but it is also, more complexly, triggered by the imagination and memory of food. More complexly still, perhaps, for the connoisseur – and we are all connoisseurs in a culturally constructed sense of the delights of the cuisines familiar to us – mouths water on reading a recipe for apple pie rather than one for a concoction of witchetty grubs, or vice versa.

I admit that my knowledge of modern biology comes largely from those of my students following an interdisciplinary course in human sciences. One told me recently that individuals of the human species have 98 per cent of their genes in common with chimpanzees, and that it thus follows that we are only 2 per cent human! It is no wonder that we find the new chimpanzee studies so fascinating; there is nothing like a twinge of self-recognition to make science, or history or myth for that matter, really gripping. For all that chimpanzees may be people too, I do wonder which small part or parts (maybe 2 per cent?) of the motion before us would *not* translate into any known chimpanzee tongue. Conceivably, given patient teachers, there would be little difficulty with a good part of it, even its casting in the dialectical form of a proposition to be questioned. 'Non-chimp-fella build toy-globe?' might plausibly be managed; but what of 'culturally'? The tiny element finally resisting translation could turn out to be the adverbial ending of this word: indicating not a visible element or action strung with the others, but a quality and a key relation, hierarchically encompassing and giving sense to the whole.

Perhaps the 2 per cent divergence in our genes is not as trivial in significance as its proportion might suggest. The crucial capacity that it confers presumably lies behind our ability to grasp, remarkably early, the principles of grammar and syntax virtually as used by adults, in spoken or in sign language, not to mention the possibilities for education in metaphor, make believe, ambivalence, deception, double meaning, jokes and so on. From the earliest stages in the development of the child, perception and learning are matched by the development of imagination and memory. Work by Russian scientists on teaching children who are deaf-blind has shown that if this condition sets in very early, before tuition has started, a child will have no 'memory' on which to build; such children have therefore to be taught finger techniques as far as possible before they may become needed. Of one such child, the teachers explained that they were helping him 'to construct his world' by this educative preparation. Otherwise, it was implied, it would be too late for him to learn how to communicate with others.

Here we come to the nub of what is a 'human' world: there are other people in it, from whom we learn, and with whom meanings have to be negotiated. Robinson Crusoe was in some senses alone before he found his companion, but even so, he brought with him a full range of culturally generated possibilities for dealing with his environment, derived from previous dialectics of give and take with (now absent) others; and when he found his companion, he gave him a name which provisionally defined the way they would together begin to construct a new social world. No person faces nature raw and cultureless. Even the geologist, chipping away at the mountain, brings with her complex cultural tools beyond her hammer. The new information she seeks derives its significance from scholarly questions previously posed; she does not face the mountain alone. You might elect to imagine, for scientific purposes, a human world constructed from scratch, between linguistic and moral *tabulae rasae*; this, however, is not science, hard or soft, but undoubtedly would be fiction and thus legitimately part of culture by anybody's definition!

Current social and cultural anthropology does not rely on a discrete conception of culture as an exclusively mental abstraction: recent writers have been able to find plenty of terms, some new and some refashioned from older usage, which draw 'culture' into the very heart of organic life, as it is lived by real people. Consider first the notion of *discourse*, which need not be limited to verbal exchanges, but can include non-verbal gesture and expression and even the communication of feelings; in its most serious sense it touches deeper levels of the circulation of systematically linked ideas about bodily life which would not necessarily be captured on a visitor's tape recorder. Consider further the related notion of *practice*, which never loses touch with the pragmatic bodily life of action, but at the same time – in current usage – carries a deeply cultural sense of transmitted significance. *Habitus* too, a particular formulation offered by Bourdieu,[4] is a concept rooted in both ecology and bodily activity, but it identifies the forms of these organic modes of action and interaction as the loci of intellectual and symbolic signification. The transmission of complex and symbolically loaded forms of discourse or practice, at all levels of human activity, requires the systematic and sophisticated training of the body, as well as the cultivation of psychological and moral dispositions. This is especially clear in the case of some of the more abstract cultural arts such as music, dance and painting, for which long physical practice in the older, literal sense is absolutely necessary. Talal Asad has argued, moreover, for the primacy of sheer *practice* in the cultivation of a pious disposition by the medieval monk.[5] But even the humblest of human actions, as Mauss pointed out half a century ago in his essay on techniques of the body,[6] result from the body's education and training: there is no culture-free mode of greeting, of eating, of making love, or even of the attainment of physical shape and size. Uduk villagers with whom I worked in the Sudan thought I had the hands and feet and teeth of a child, as I could not walk barefoot or weed the fields or crunch dry corn as they could. They thought me much younger than I was; twenty years of academic training was not evident to them.

Even more than one's outward appearance, one's inner consciousness of being an organism, I suggest, is not a given datum of nature, nor necessarily is it everywhere the same. It is of course a common human experience to become aware of one's body, and of its sensations. But the sense of bodily presence is itself shaped by education, by training, language, and expectation; as well as by the continual discursive processes through which we interact with others. A person can scarcely conceive of him- or herself as possessing a warm heart, a hard head and a clear mind, except in a community of others understood as having similar potential. In the case of the Uduk, the loosely corresponding notions might be a cool liver or a full and therefore contented stomach from which to make calm decisions, and an alertness to various aspects of reality through dreams.[7] There is a growing anthropological sensitivity to the cultural constructions of persons themselves, in their social interaction, and we are beginning to learn more of the ways in which organic structures and sensations are understood and of how this understanding may shape experience – or at least discourse about experience – among peoples like the Ilongot as described by the Rosaldos, the Chewong as described by Signe Howell or the Avatip as described by Simon Harrison.[8] These ethnographers, like Marilyn Strathern in her comparative studies of New Guinea,[9] no longer find the person to be a detachable and unitary given element, an indivisible organism. There are internal and external divisions and connections, not simply unfolding from some general biological programme, but definitively specified through the educational transmission and re-enactment of culturally significant and variable forms.

The community life of other animals, I suggest, *could* be (and may well have been) described in terms of discourse, practice and habitus, but only at the expense of devaluing these terms as they are used of human life – in the same way that the term 'culture' itself has been devalued by similar applications. I remember attending a panel discussion, years ago, on the subject of ritual, which was intended to facilitate a meeting of minds on this topic between zoologists and anthropologists.[10] It was quite easy to find agreement on various definitions: Julian Huxley, Konrad Lorenz and Victor Turner were able to bracket the courtship dances of a wonderful variety of birds and animals together with Ndembu rites of passage, under some broad conception of 'ritual' as the marking of important relationships through the stylized repetition of formal non-utilitarian behaviour. So much agreement seemed possible, because so many terms had already slipped between the social sciences and animal ethology that the problem had almost appeared to vanish. (Students used to read out essays about human bonding pairs, and about swans getting married.) Language, for the participants in the panel discussion, did not clarify but rather cloaked the difficulty. There seemed at that time to be a dearth of words to bring out the strongly sensed difference in quality between non-human and human ritual, and I believe we are facing a similar problem today. If you dwell on the organic aspect of human activity, while applying the notion of culture to the behaviour of other animals, you have achieved the illusion of uniformity through linguistic sleight of hand; and you have created the need for further terminological revisions to keep the problem in focus.

I can only touch briefly on the vital matter of institutional and collective organization: on questions of political economy, of kings, states and armies, of the law, of wages and prices – all 'culturally constructed' aspects of the world impinging on and motivating any human organism-person. I can easily think of myself at times as a gatherer and collector of fruits and nuts, as though I were still wandering around the African forest, as I once used to do, learning to recognize and harvest various leaves, pods and roots, and on occasion limes and pawpaws. But in the supermarket every item has a price, every single head of lettuce is disfigured with a mechanically imprinted number restricting my choice – even more disappointingly so in the case of the limes and pawpaws. Food gathering as a direct encounter with what is offered, or 'afforded', by the environment, may be one thing; what I myself can afford in the environment of my food gathering is an entirely different matter. I do not confront it as a consuming organism, but as a paid employee, a very different type of consumer. If I pocketed a pineapple I might end up in court. Can any human beings, even if untouched by the state and capitalism, and even if living largely as hunter-gatherers, seriously be held by modern anthropology to be totally unconstrained by forms of social and political economy? Even egalitarian sharing is a hard system, and one that is no less collectively ordered and culturally inscribed than any other. It is a romantic and naïve illusion, if one with a long genealogy, to suppose that groups of real hunter-gatherers are simply free-floating individuals working out their relations with trees, armadillos and each other from first principles at each encounter.

Organic life does not create persons: they have to be *specified* in language, in symbol and in law. The fact that the definition of personhood is so universally open to challenge merely confirms the essentially cultural character of the concept. The historical record is full of contested claims to personhood in one form or another, because the notion of personhood is itself inseparable from the notion of moral agency and legal rights. An element of *ought* rather than *is* always enters in. No rights are given in organisms: rights are culturally constructed before they can be extended to organisms of any kind whatsoever. Moral, jural, medical and divine arguments are adduced in pursuit of claims over personhood, and in the political struggle to impose one definition over another. When does a person begin in time, or end? When is a person merely a vegetable? Is a slave a person; or a child, a woman, a foreigner, members of another race? In a world based on the pragmatics of organic life alone, would the rights of biologically damaged beings be recognized? What of the rights of the unborn, and of the dead for that matter? What agreements about these matters could be made in the absence of writing or other culturally constructed forms of authorization, of verbal or ritual contract, pledge or promise? And yet, though we are organisms and our unique genes are so few, the greater part of our waking time, and even of our dreams, is taken up with worries about such matters, bearing on the rights and wrongs that we feel have touched our sense of personhood.

In a recent paper, Tim Ingold has launched a rearguard action against the biologists who, in their pursuit of hard science, have so stressed the determination of behaviour by genes or DNA as to have virtually abandoned the 'organism'.[11] We are entirely in sympathy with him in wishing to recapture for a broader anthropology those other creatures, especially the intelligent and furry ones like dogs and chimpanzees whom we have made our own in many respects (even reconstructing them culturally in our own image). Ingold may well deplore the reduction of the organism to its genes, on the grounds that the character of the whole, being more than the sum of the genes, is lost; but similarly *we* deplore the seductive language games of those who might wish to reduce us to mere organisms. Following a happy formulation of Steven Collins,[12] let us rather accept that while we are nothing if not embodied, we human beings have scarcely ever been able to define ourselves as mere body without a further completing element. In folk conceptions, as well as in philosophical, theological and socio-legal thought, there has always been a variable 'something', other than the organic, to make up a person;

persons in general are completely definable only as '*body-plus...*' – and anthropology cannot ignore this.

In asking you to support the motion, that human worlds are culturally constructed, we do not rule real people out of anthropology. On the contrary, we insist that real people are included *as such*, as '*body-plus...*' beings, not stripped of education, memory and imagination to the nakedness of the mere organism, the human being *manqué*. Only pseudo-science could set up such a bogus figure as the '*person-minus...*', and construct an explanatory anthropological system around it. But then elements of pseudo-science, and pseudo-history, are built into all known human worlds; eventually rejected as myth, they come to be seen for what they are – cultural constructions.

AGAINST THE MOTION (1)

TIM INGOLD

The motion for this debate invites comment on all four of its key terms, and I intend to focus on each in turn. First, what is implied about the condition of being human? Second, what does it take for there to be one world, or many worlds? Third, what role, if any, does culture play in the process of world formation? And finally, what is meant by speaking of this process as one of construction? I should make it clear from the start that my objections are not so much to the proposition in itself as they are to the kind of question to which it represents one possible answer. Thus the arguments I shall adduce could serve equally well to oppose the contrary thesis that 'humans inhabit a given world of nature'. What I reject is the very conceptual paradigm that forces us, in answering the questions it sets, to choose between animality and humanity, between one world and many worlds, between nature and culture, and between the given and the constructed. As I shall show, these four dichotomies are linked by a common, cognitivist orientation that contrives to disembed individual human beings from the relational matrix of their existence in the world, only to re-embed this world inside their individual heads. Having exposed the root assumptions of this orientation, I shall proceed to put forward an alternative view which restores people to where they belong, in an active practical engagement with constituents of the real world.

Although the motion does not explicitly say so, it carries the very strong implication – which I am sure most of its supporters would take for granted – that *non*-human worlds are *not* culturally constructed. In other words, the cultural construction of reality is supposed to be *uniquely* human, a fundamental aspect of the human condition as opposed to that of the animal. What, then, can we say about animal worlds? What are they like? It is commonly assumed, by zoologists as much as by anthropologists, that non-human animals live enclosed in a purely *physical* world. As beings of that world they are themselves physical objects. Each animal, population or species, according to a well-worn ecological metaphor, occupies a *niche*, a little corner of the world set up in advance, to which it has fitted itself through a process of evolutionary adaptation.

But this description of the animal in its niche, like that of the statue tastefully situated in an alcove in the wall, is couched in the language and from the point of view of the disinterested observer, presumed human. The statue, of course, does not have a point of view: the world does not exist for *it*; rather, both the statue and the alcove are components of a world that exists for *me*. By the same token, an account of the animal in its niche denies the active, perceptual engagement of that animal with its environment. Though I can describe the environment *of* the animal as it is presented to me (just as I can describe the animal itself), there can be no environment, indeed no world, *for* the animal. What I can do, that the animal supposedly cannot, is to take a step back from the physical dimension of existence, and to witness life in this dimension as a spectacle. It is to this spectacle, as presented to a subject disengaged from it, that we commonly refer by the concept of 'nature'. Indeed, a world can only be 'nature' for a being that does not belong there.

If the concept of nature thus implies a disengagement from the world, then the possibility of disengagement, in turn, is taken to be the hallmark of the condition of humanity. Human uniqueness is supposed to lie in precisely this: that whereas the differences among animal species are differences *in* nature, humans are different in being half in nature, half out. We are *in* nature to the extent that we are organisms with bodies, which depend on a throughput of materials and energy for their maintenance and reproduction. We are *out of* nature to the extent that we are persons with minds, with which we are able to reflect upon and represent the circumstances of our bodily experience. This reflexive process, according to conventional anthropological wisdom, is one of investing experience with meaning, and the source of all meaning is culture. As Geertz would have it, culture consists in 'the imposition of an arbitrary framework of symbolic meaning upon reality'.[13] What does this view of culture, and of the human condition, suggest about the world (or worlds) we live in?

There is, apparently, a real world out there, for it is upon this that our cultural meanings are said to be imposed. Yet this world, prior to its ordering through cultural categories, is mere flux, devoid of form and significance. To grasp its essence is the objective of the physical sciences, for which 'real' reality is that which exists independently of the acting and perceiving subject. This is not, however, the world that people see and know (and I shall leave aside here the implied question of how it is that physical scientists can nevertheless be people). For it is supposed that keyed into every human community is a particular symbolic schema, encoded in language and validated by verbal agreement, in terms of which the flux of raw sensory experience is organized into the enduring shapes and patterns that subjects claim to perceive in the world around them. Since different communities share different schemas, the members of each will perceive different things, even though the physical reality with which they are confronted may be one and the same. Thus it is that upon the one, universal world of nature are superimposed the many, particular worlds of culture. Human beings, it seems, live a split-level existence, with their bodies on one level and their minds on another. Anthropological literature reveals a fair crop of different terms that have been used to signal this dichotomy, among them 'real' versus 'perceived', 'operational' versus 'cognized' and, perhaps most notoriously, 'etic' versus 'emic'.[14]

What all of these conceptual oppositions have in common is the idea that whereas the first term pertains to a *given* world, the second pertains to a world that is *constructed*. I want you to pay attention to this notion of construction. It implies the working up of some raw material into a finished product, an imposition of form on to substance. More particularly, it implies that the form is programmed *in advance* of the creative process it directs, and by which it is simply *revealed* in the material. This metaphor of construction plays a crucial and often unacknowledged part in our thought, and not only in anthropology. In biology, for example, it is clearly evident in the notion of genes as forming a programme which directs the 'construction' of the organism. In anthropology, culture has tended to play the role that the DNA is made to play in biology, but the constructionist logic is just the same. The raw material consists of sensations, registered by our receptor organs by virtue of our bodily immersion in the physical world. Once picked up, these sensations are despatched to the brain where something rather remarkable happens, for the mind evidently gets to work on them, arranging them into some kind of configuration, such that the owner of the mind can claim to see a world of clearly recognizable and distinguishable objects. Thus the sensory input is *constructed* by the mind into images, or percepts, and it is culture, of course, that provides the template or building plan. In short, nature furnishes the substance, culture the form.

I have shown how the proposition that 'human worlds are culturally constructed' divides every human being into two parts, of which one is object to the other as subject, how it divides subjectively imagined worlds from an objectively given reality, form from substance, culture from nature. In turning now to the positive part of my contribution, which is to put in place an alternative perspective that would transcend these dichotomies, I intend to proceed in reverse order, disposing first of the dichotomy between the given and the constructed, and going on to do the same for those between nature and culture, between the one world and the many, and between the human and the animal.

Consider what happens in perception. For the cognitivist the human body, immersed in its physical surroundings, is but a passive register for the sensory stimuli with which it is continually bombarded. Hence the only activity in perception is mental activity, the building of raw sense data into structures. I reject this Cartesian distinction between sensation and intellection. Perception, I hold, involves the *whole person*, in an active engagement with his or her environment.[15] We perceive the world by moving around in it and exploring its possibilities. Seeing, hearing and touching, far from being passive reactions of the organism, are ways of actively and intentionally *attending* to the world – they are what people *do*. Perception, then, is a process of action; moreover, it is a process that is continually going on. There are no end-states in the form of images or percepts. If we ask 'What is the product of perception?', the answer can only be 'the perceiver'. In rather the same way, the product of consumption is the consumer. Like consumption, perception is a mode of *engagement* with the world, not a mode of construction of it.

This contrast between construction and engagement might be more simply represented as one between building and dwelling. It is by being dwelt-in, not by being constructed, that some portion of the real world becomes an environment for people. In opposing the motion, I want therefore to replace the building perspective of cultural constructionism with what might be called a 'dwelling perspective'. I do not of course mean to deny that humans build. We do indeed construct designs and impose them upon the world. My contention, however, is that *building is encompassed within dwelling rather than vice versa*. In other words, far from dwelling within a built world, we build within a dwelt-in world.[16] Indeed, how could it be otherwise? If all human life were circumscribed within the parameters of one or another cultural project, whence comes each project? Only the conventions of fiction and ethnographic texts afford the illusion of such closure. Real life has no authors save the persons who are living it, and these persons, if they would build, must *already* dwell. Thus every act of building is but a moment in a continuous process of dwelling. This process, as I shall now show, is one through which persons and their environments are reciprocally constituted, each in relation to the other.

Imagine a house. It is, from one point of view, a feature of the physical world, constructed to a design that is perhaps standard for a particular community. In that sense, it may be regarded as a building. But that is not how it is experienced by the people who live therein, and for whom it represents the most familiar part of their everyday environment. For them, it is not just a house, it is *home*; not just a building but a dwelling. So how does a house become a home? Not, I argue, by assimilating its physical features to a symbolic representational blueprint for the organization of domestic space, but rather by incorporating those features – walls, doors, windows, fixed furnishings and so on – into a characteristic pattern of day-to-day activities. Thus it is the very engagement of persons with the objects of their domestic surroundings, in the course of their life activities, that turns the house into a home. As the embodiment of these activities, the home environment is forever evolving along with the lives of its inhabitants. It is, if you will, a kind of monument to their endeavours, though with the proviso that it is never complete. Like the life of persons, the formation of the environment is always in the nature of 'work in progress'.

Though I have chosen, as an example, something that we normally think of as an artefact, all that I have said could apply equally well to some part of the physical landscape occupied – say – by a group of hunters and gatherers who have not sought to modify it to any significant extent. Indeed, the distinction we tend to draw between the natural and the artificial, between those parts of the physical world that have not and those that have been modified through the imposition of cultural design, is relevant only within the framework of the building perspective. Again, it is through *dwelling* in a landscape, through the incorporation of its features into a pattern of everyday activities, that it becomes home to hunters and gatherers. As such, the landscape is visible and durable testimony to the lives of previous generations of people who, in traversing it, have in a sense inscribed themselves into it. It follows that to sever the links that bind people to their environment is to cut them off from the historical past that has made them who they are. Yet this is precisely what orthodox culture theory has done, in giving recognition to the historical quality of human works only by attributing them to projects of cultural construction opposed to, and merely superimposed upon, an ahistorical nature.

The world in which we dwell, then, is a world which comes into being as we act in it, and in which *we* come into being as, acting in it, we also perceive it. It is not a given world of nature, nor is it a constructed world of culture, it is rather what I wish to call an *environment*. In so doing, I mean to establish a clear distinction between the environment and the physical world (or 'nature'). The latter, as I have already shown, can only be apparent to the detached, indifferent observer. We may speak of it as 'reality *of*'. The environment, by contrast, is 'reality *for*' – the real world constituted in *relation* to the organism or person whose environment it is. This is the world that we perceive, through our active engagement with it. The separation of nature and culture, as domains respectively of matter and mind that humans in their activities must perforce seek to bridge, far from existing *ab initio*, is a *consequence* of disengagement, of the turning of attention, in thought, reflexively inwards on the self rather than outwards on the world. Now although humans are undoubtedly capable of adopting such a contemplative stance from time to time, no one – not even a monk or a philosopher – can permanently live like that. As Whitehead (himself a philosopher) once remarked, 'from the moment of birth we are immersed in action, and can only fitfully guide it by taking thought'.[17] Or to reiterate my earlier point, he who would rebuild the world in his imagination must already dwell in it, and in the dwelling the world is no longer nature but an environment.

This point brings me to the question of the one world and the many. From the perspective of dwelling, the dichotomy is meaningless. For the dwelt-in world is a continuous field of relationships, unfolding through time. We could think of it as an unbroken landscape of variation. To be sure, different positions in the landscape will afford different views. But in the cognitivist perspective of cultural constructionism, the real world is treated as a thing that people look *at*, rather than a field that they live *in*. The world view is no longer a view *in* the world but a view *of* the world. Difference, then, ceases to be a function of positioning within a total relational field, and is attributed instead to arbitrary variations in the 'building plan' that individuals bring with them to the task of reconstructing the one given world inside their multiple heads. It is this inversion, by which the relational context of being-in-the-world is, as it were, turned 'outside in' to become a cognitive attribute of mind, that has given us the logic of the universal and the particular, the one and the many. For reduced to mere substance in the service of projects of cultural construction, the real world becomes 'all the same', indifferent to the manifold forms that our minds are supposed to impose upon it.

Finally, I return to the point from which I began: the dichotomy between the human and the animal. I have already shown that if the existence of a world *for* some living being depends upon an act of cultural construction, and if humans are uniquely capable of such acts, then there can be no world *for* the animal. However, by thinking of perception in the way I have just outlined it is easy to see that non-human animals can constitute their environments, just as humans can, through the very fact of their dwelling in the world. There is no fundamental difference here. It is in their capacity to construct *imagined* worlds that humans surely differ from other animal species, and in this both language and culture are directly implicated. But before you rush to interpret this remark as a total capitulation, let me remind you that such imagining is not a necessary prelude to our contact with reality, but rather an epilogue, and an optional one at that. We do not have to think the world in order to live in it, but we *do* have to live in the world in order to think it.

This leads me to wonder what kind of world those of you who support the motion think you are living in. Is it a world of the gods who, dwelling in the firmament, are constructing worlds for us humans to live in, and who – unlike ordinary mortals whose worlds are circumscribed by those constructions – can see the ground of nature beneath our feet? The proposers of this motion, I conclude, are either divine or incoherent. Perhaps they are both. On the grounds that a vote for divinity is a vote for incoherence, I urge you to reject the motion.

FOR THE MOTION (2)

ROLAND LITTLEWOOD

It seems that the motion I am seconding has insidiously come to be seen as the *status quo* of anthropology, our point of definition against vulgar materialists, biologists and applied anthropologists. The very notion of 'cultural construction' – or 'constructionism' as my psychologist colleagues disdainfully call it – seems to have become our official emblem, the popular orthodoxy that justifies our discipline to others. Undergraduates and students of social work are fed on a diet of (to take some titles from my shelves) 'The social construction of sexuality', 'The social construction of *homo*sexuality', 'The social construction of illness', and so forth. The very tiresomeness of it all has, I trust, impelled all right thinking people to align themselves *against* the motion, against this apparent orthodoxy.

Now, beyond its sheer tedium, there are indeed some problems with the construction industry, particularly the practical or vocational. One anthropologist I know landed a plum job at a prestigious medical institute to study patients' conceptualizations of illness, in order that medical services might be delivered more effectively. She caused serious problems on her first day by affirming that the doctors' own nosological systems were just as culturally given as those of their patients, just as arbitrary from the point of view of the phenomena in question. Similarly, were a medical anthropologist to arrive at a World Health Organization project on children with AIDS, he would be unlikely to enhance his utility by proclaiming that AIDS is a 'cultural construction'.

No surprise here. If everything becomes culturally constructed, surely we would find this world rather vapid, aetiolated, one in which we as individuals have no firm point for practical action, in which we merely strut around in a series of historically given tropes, doubtless of some intellectual elegance yet missing that immediacy of pain, of struggle, of interaction, the raw material of lived experience. If sex simply becomes gender, can I still connect? The buzz has gone. That sense of revelation which we experienced when we realized that our taken-for-granted little worlds were actually the representation of things much more interesting (a sense of revelation which I would argue, in a rather old-fashioned way, is still the source of the emotive power of social anthropology), has now become dissipated into an insipid 'official version'.

Are we fossilized in some position which seems not so much 'cultural' as one of 'high culture' – something metropolitan and Oxbridge, of the Senior Common Room where some apparently have the leisure to contemplate an elegant assemblage of recursive signifiers? It is perhaps time to descend to the market-place of ultimate reality, to some demotic world of dirt and mess, of accident and happenstance, of creolizing confusions, fluctuations and upsets, of societies in disintegration, of pain and arbitrary terror, of the abuse of children, and women, and men. Where are your settled societies of yesteryear fresh from colonial pacification? Where their neat correspondence between individual experience and the social order?

If I have caricatured the debate, some practical dissatisfaction with what is a particular conception of anthropological orthodoxy does indeed urge us to make contact with tackier, earthier areas: ecology, biology, sickness, something (if I may dare to say so) more 'natural', real, experiential, messy, elemental, innocent. Perhaps we should even be reaching out to some *Gemeinschaft*, effervescence, communitas or whatever. As in Dr Johnson's attempted refutation of Berkeley, we might wonder just how 'culturally constructed' is the experience of the child dying of AIDS. The very emphasis on 'culture' seems like a betrayal. The area of my own entry into anthropology, transcultural psychiatry, became moribund precisely because of this emphasis on the culture of

Black people, rather than on the culture of interaction, on its creation through conflict.

Take this word 'construction'. Construction is not invention or creation *ex nihilo*. Its resonances are clearly those of building. The bricks are there as bricks: they are not yet a house. The house 'is' bricks, not just 'of' bricks. The bricks are 'made into' a house but they are still bricks. Houses and bricks are clearly not things of quite the same order. If we take the figuration like this, we are of course potentially in trouble, for what then are these bricks? They are given already in experience. Or are they?

I think we have to distinguish between the child opening up the box of bricks already given, and the process by which societies develop bricks and houses in tandem. For the former, the bricks are given in experience. They are 'real'. They are 'there'. All you can do, all you have to do, is to decide to build a Georgian house, or a Victorian Gothic house, or a Dutch-gabled house (though it helps to have the curvy bits to build a Dutch house, you can do without). This is a model house: an anthropological model, and one which Tim Ingold demolishes as 'culturally constructed'. For actual builders in history, there are, of course, no such givens, except in as much as they take up in society the notion of bricks as a potential house – or as walls, roads, projectiles, pillows or conceptual art. To try to study from the outside how bricks and houses come into being is conjectural, an instance of the historical fallacy; every time we try to model it we ourselves end up using a child's set of bricks. If human worlds are culturally constructed in some more meaningful way, then this simplistic model is not one of cultural construction.

It is easy to dismiss, perhaps, because we are not ourselves bricks. Bricks are already a social given. Let us try something messier – physical experience, our lives as embodied selves, pain, rhythm, excretion, sex, sickness, death. These are the bodily experiences through which by empathy and action I am embedded in myself, and embedded in another way through my daily work as a doctor. Surely the way our bodies are 'constructed', the way they respond to perturbations, the very growth of cancer cells, are not dependent on human knowledge? And this *is* our world. To say of something which is lived-in that it is *not* culturally constructed is to say that it takes the same pattern for us independently of our apperception of it. It just goes on there, somewhere, in an uncertainly knowable natural world; if we cause it to happen without directly conceiving of it (say contracting AIDS through unfortunate sexual activity), then we cannot say we 'constructed' it, any more than a brick we accidently dislodged and then feel on our heads is a house, or even at that moment (for us) a brick.

Now, doctors have a term for these physically understood goings-on, a word that places them firmly in the biological world, a world which we too inhabit – though not just by virtue of being human. It would be difficult to disagree with Tim Ingold when he tells us[18] that this capacity to be human is itself part of our life as sensate organisms. And it would be equally hard to quarrel with the position that our very knowledge of the world, of the type we call 'biological' or 'natural', only takes shape *as* cultural institutions such as biological science, ecology, anthropology, *as* our particular instruments. Note that I say 'as' particular instruments, not 'through' particular instruments. Ingold argues that our dualistic vision prevents us from seeing the interaction between ourselves and our environment. I would rather argue that the very distinction between ourselves and our environment is already arbitrary. This is not idealism: obviously everything is natural, and everything is social. These are not additive qualities, not types of stuff. They are procedures, types of knowledge, embedded in certain very definite historical contexts.[19] The natural world and the social world are not different places but different maps.

One map, however, claims a greater transparency: that of the natural sciences. Because it examines our guts and pains and crops, because it claims these to be 'there', it conceives of itself as what it studies. And I think this is also true of Ingold's notion of direct perception, in which we discover, we do not invent.[20]

The word doctors use for the perturbations in our bodily selves is *disease*. Disease, they say, is real. It is there, visible or not, like it or not. It is to illness as bricks are to houses, a given script out of which we may attempt to construct personal life with the bits to hand. It is not a periodic table or a star map, but the elements and planets themselves. The fact that we use this term 'disease' in an extended sense to talk of social pathology, diseased societies and so on, does no more than demonstrate its powerful, everyday, experiential reality.

There are some problems here. Such an extended notion of disease is really no more (or less) unreasonable, or rhetorical, than the restricted use of it. Both are grounded alike in our assumptions as embodied social beings. Since the seventeenth century, Western thought has employed a now classical distinction between a human world of agency and a natural world of causal necessity.[21] 'Pathology' in the strong sense *is* supposedly out there in the natural world as 'disease', independently of our apperception of it. It is experientially manifest to us through a constructed 'illness', depending on our bodily states, values, expectations and the possibility of action, but it can be directly observed through the procedures of natural science, including ecology.

Yet disease is nevertheless some sort of *undesirable* state of affairs in the natural world, even if possibly independent of any necessary human apperception. How is this undesirability conceived? We have a variety of choices between entities and processes, between functional balance, anatomical change, evolutionary and developmental processes, or even deviations from ideal norms of health or autonomy. The conceptualizations themselves are not of course given by the subject matter but are selected within a social context. A particular pathology may be understood as all of them. The majority of these conceptualizations return us to the personal experience of illness, to pain and disability. Such experiences are themselves constructed in that pain, for instance, is not necessarily experienced as an illness or indeed as an unalloyed evil.

Where does the notion of 'disease' (in either a strong or a weak sense) get us? Does it entail some practical constraints on the limits of the phenomenon we could study and alter, defining 'it' as a phenomenon? Certainly. Does it entail some notion that the phenomenon is ultimately 'there'? This hardly seems necessary unless we feel unable to act without assuming our therapeutic procedures must have the power of controverting some almost inevitable, natural order of things. Through identification and extension we recognize 'pathology' in animals akin to ourselves (a recognition essential to veterinary medicine), but the limits of our sympathy fade when applied to unicellular organisms. Are phages the diseases of sick bacteria? In what environment can the tapeworm develop most fruitfully? An old medical adage goes that 'it may be a disease for you; for the tapeworm it is a problem of ecology.' The moral is that our idea of disease is radically rooted in our human world, in our embodied social being. There are no diseases out there, only perceived processes, some of which we feel we like (health), some of which we do not (disease). The choice is not given by the data. It is arbitrary. It is, if I may venture to say so, socially constructed. Disease is not there, like it or not; it is there because we do not like it. Contrawise, we *are* disease, not just in the sense that we share certain nucleotide sequences with bacteria, but also in that we are descended from among the limited and selected survivors of innumerable epidemics in which survival was determined by antigenic complementarity with bacteria or other micro-organisms. We are ourselves because we are diseases.

To reduce the notion of cultural construction to playing around with a set of toy bricks (a straw hut?[22]) is absurd. Any intelligent reading of our human actions affirms that we create the bricks as well as the house. To deny cultural construction is to suggest that we can really experience the world out there *as it is*. Some hope. We determine only in part what we call our environment, but we determine our experience of it, our human world. 'It' determines us, we 'are' it, but this 'it' is only an 'it' through human procedures, shared with our fellows. And these procedures are never innocent.

If the dualistic distinction between organism and environment, between the self's illness and its disease, between the human and the world, is an arbitrary cultural product, then so is any idea that they can interact. To take up Wendy James's culinary idiom, we are not only cutting up the cake in various ways, we are also doing the cooking. I am not sure that I can ever know what the environment is, but I think I can know how Tim Ingold constructs it.

AGAINST THE MOTION (2)

PAUL RICHARDS

When I was young my ambition was to master the intricacies of the great fugue at the heart of Bach's sonata in A minor for solo violin. Thirty years later I am still struggling with the piece. Not much culture has been constructed as a result, but instead I have acquired a comprehensive knowledge of the thought-provoking world of errors and mistakes. This leads me to wonder whether social life is as routinely impregnated with clumsiness as my violin playing. If it is, then it seems to me that we should pay as much attention to the question of how life 'flows' – of how social agents recover from mistakes and random disturbances and lurch onwards without their whole performance grinding to a halt – as to the notion of cultural construction. My problem with cultural construction is that it implies building according to a plan, as if each and every social performance were a skilled realization of an underlying text, score or structural blueprint. My fear is that in our enthusiasm for the Samuel Smiles's self-build philosophy of social life we will fail to think enough about improvisation. Cultural construction may be fine for professional anthropologists, who make a living by having something to de-construct. But how does it help in contexts – societies wrecked by war or famine, for example – where folk need to move on, where dextrous improvisation must be the order of the day?

From my perspective, this debate is taking place at cross-purposes, in that our opponents seem to think that to query their constructive approach to culture is necessarily to advance the claims, as an alternative, of some kind of genetic or environmental determinism. That is not my intention. What troubles me about cultural construction is the under-lying notion that human worlds are arrived at by stepping out of time and out of our bodies, and that we can in such a condition self-consciously *build* something – as if 'by taking thought' we *could* 'add one inch to our stature'. The reality seems to me very different – we do not construct, we perform. And in order to perform efficiently, or even to perform at all, we have to live within our limitations. We have to come to terms with our bodies. Hence my enthusiasm for Tim Ingold's notion that the word 'dwelling' rather than 'construction' better captures the sense of life-as-lived that he and I are anxious to defend, and my distaste for the appalling arrogance (or so it seems to me) of the notion that, as Berger and Luckmann have it, 'people make themselves'.[23] Incidentally, in re-examining their classic text, *The social construction of reality*, I was intrigued to find that they devote considerable effort to defining and discussing the terms 'social' and 'reality', but are much more vague about what they mean by 'construction', and how it is supposed to work. (Their book is altogether a characteristic 1960s' text: material constraints are firmly features of the past, and the human world is a *tabula rasa* for cultural transaction. In this context they may have felt no need to give the notion of 'construction' a very sharp analytical cutting edge.) Perhaps it will be objected that we are overly concerned about what, after all, is only a loose metaphor. My answer would be that loose metaphors are often the most powerfully problematic notions of all, since they are indiscriminate in what they block out of our field of vision.

In recent years, I have spent some time studying agricultural research institutions and trying to understand, in particular, how plant breeders arrive at their decisions. They face a series of dilemmas not unrelated to the issue at the heart of the present debate. Outside observers (at the outset myself included) tend to assume that plant breeders 'construct' improved plant types according to a blueprint supplied by Mendelian genetics – that in effect, having taken apart existing plants to discover how they work, they are free to imagine and build a better plant than any already existing. Only at this point (according to this 'de-constructive' account) does the breeder slip back into the mainstream of agrarian reality to carry out tests to confirm the value of the new variety in question.

The assumption that breeders are free to 'engineer' plants according to genetic blueprints – the root of a number of complaints by social scientists, perhaps misled by the wilder prophets of bio-technology, about the Green Revolution – is wrong on at least two major counts. First 'a great deal of biological variation is not discontinuous and not amenable to any simple particulate interpretation'[24] of a Mendelian kind. Plant breeders work as much with polygenic material as with major genes. Only in the latter case is 'classification by reliably expressed phenotypic effect' feasible. Second, at least as far as in-breeding plants such as barley and rice are concerned, it is logistically very difficult to set up a sufficiently broad-based statistical test of (say) all crosses of F_5 lines so as reliably to identify all promising lines (however 'promise' be defined). Impossibly large amounts of replication at different sites and over different seasons would be needed to identify all significant genotype–environment (GE) interactions, for example. This leads Simmonds[25] to an 'inescapable' if 'rather discouraging conclusion' that 'in practice, breeders discard as many families as they dare on general field characters and *are guided by general experience, instinct and "eye"* in effecting some kind of reasonable balance between numbers of surviving families and intensity of exploitation of each' (my emphasis). He adds that 'most breeders would agree, I think, that selection is often little better than random and none would care to bet that he had never thrown away an excellent family or line'. (Ethnographers working within reach of plant breeding stations sometimes have stories to recount of the corollary – of a judicious 'theft' of material discarded by breeders that later reappears as a successful local selection.) In short, then, plant breeders live with and shape germplasm as best they can – in Tim Ingold's terms they 'dwell' with it – but they are not 'in charge'. Plant breeding is an intelligent awareness of evolutionary principles, not a biological branch of the cultural construction industry.

That anthropologists and other social scientists should suppose otherwise – as clearly they do in their writings on the Green Revolution – is an example of a characteristic tendency to overestimate the extent to which human environments (behavioural, material–cultural and geographical) can be 'engineered' as distinct from 'shaped'. This is the nub of the distinction we wish to draw between the notion of 'constructing' human worlds, and that of 'dwelling' therein. But if Tim Ingold and I are considered to be flirting with old-style environmental determinism at this point, the deflationary references of our opponents to environment as an also-ran of human existence suggest that they share something in common with the heroic self-build world view espoused by the prophets of muscular bio-technology – an odd position for those supposedly fearful of a tendency towards biological reductionism.

I understand the seductive attractions of the cultural construction approach. As self-appointed interpreters of human worlds, anthropologists want to be in a position plausibly to *de*-construct: to show how the system functions, to reveal the inner logic of symbols, to show how the performance was 'put together'. But if social life (as distinct from its tropes – ritual set pieces, and the like) is work-in-progress, how can we pretend to exhume the blueprint upon which, supposedly, it is based? How could we ever know that human worlds were culturally constructed, if there is no grand design, and if human worlds never approach completion? One of the reasons Nietzsche thought music was such a poignant expression of life was that it helps to reconcile us to the absence of teleology. Manifestly, the purpose of a piece of music is not to arrive at the end! Life moves from where we find ourselves, from where we pick up the beat. The issue is how to move on from here. For many people, perhaps for most of the time, 'decoding' plans is an implausible or unhelpful source of ideas about where to move next, and about how to make such moves. (The difficulty is a bit like trying to provide a text-book account of how to ride a bicycle, or to fly a kite – the stream in which human worlds are carried is no more 'constructed' than the breeze!) But where might we turn for better, more helpful metaphors? Perhaps that currently fashionable word 'trope' (an interpolation in plainsong) serves to point us in the right direction, by reminding us of the value of music as a source of fruitful analogies through which to begin to grasp the flow of cultural phenomena.

A fine example of how anthropology might benefit from a more 'musical' approach to theory is to be found in a recent paper by Jane Guyer[26] on the division of labour and the rhythms of household life. Here she develops an extended musical metaphor, based on notions of polyrhythm and polymetre, to cope with the way in which lives within the same household can be highly differentiated but at the same time not necessarily in open conflict or disarray (men and women dancing to different beats). Her paper represents a striking and potentially very productive convergence of interest, apparent in recent work by anthropologists and ethnomusicologists, concerning the issue of the relationship of musical experience to social and ecological time. One of the most stimulating of these contributions from the musicological side is Chernoff's book on West African musical sensibilities: 'a drum in an African ensemble derives its power and becomes meaningful not only as it cuts and focuses the other drums but also as it is cut and called into focus by them ... rhythm is interesting in terms of its potential to be affected by other rhythms'.[27] Waterman, in his ethnography of *juju* music, sees this musicological observation as a key to understanding Yoruba social philosophy: 'In Yoruba thought, power (*agbara*) is also a gestalt process generated through relationships. A person becomes powerful only if he or she can maintain a broad network of willing supporters.' In Waterman's account Yoruba social life depends crucially on 'drumming up support' (in a quite literal sense). '*Juju* performance does not merely represent society: good *juju* is good social order'[28] – 'sweet life', as they say in many parts of West Africa.

Here, however, I need to make clear that in calling for a more sustained 'musical' approach to the study of human worlds, I draw a sharp distinction between the metaphoric usages of 'musicians' such as Guyer, and the recourse to formalistic analytic devices by the 'music critics' among the anthropologists, as for example in the work of Lévi-Strauss[29] – from my standpoint a case of 'constructivism' at its most arid! In place of 'cultural construction' I would call for what the economist Jacques Attali – in an audacious essay on the political economy of music – calls 'composition', which he regards as the 'negation of the division of roles and labour as constructed by the old codes'. For him 'composition is not the same as the [old] material abundance, that petit-bourgeois vision of an atrophied communism having no other goal than the extension of the bourgeois spectacle to all of the proletariat. It is the individual's conquest of his own body and potential.'[30]

I should make it clear that my appeal for a more 'musical' anthropology does not entail a return to the approach of Bourdieu, despite his frequent reversion to musical metaphor – 'conductorless orchestration' – and his claims to have dissolved the false opposition of rule and improvisation. Wrapped in the sticky webs of collapsed signification – habitus – Bourdieu's human agents are reduced to the status of Bayesian operators whose development has been arrested. The sphere of 'scientific probabilities' is counterposed to the social world in which there is 'the propensity to privilege early experiences'. This is a world in which there are no real surprises (and no scope for musicality) – 'the conditioned and conditional freedom habitus secures is as remote from a creation of unpredictable novelty as it is from a simple mechanical reproduction of the initial conditioning'.[31] But why then, we might ask, is the world such a surprising place?

I can think of no better way to conclude than to quote from a poem – 'The Hedger' – by the gassed-mad poet-musician Ivor Gurney. Written in the City of London Mental Hospital, Stone House, Dartford, some time during the 1920s, the poem is dedicated to the skills of the hedgers Gurney knew in his troubled wanderings in Gloucestershire after the First World War, and celebrates the 'musical' skills through which we all must learn to dwell in a world not of our making. Gurney pictures 'this gap-mender, of quiet courage unhastening' coping with his task by picking up the rhythm and pulse of the task in hand:

> . . . his quick moving
> Was never broken by any danger, his loving
> Use of the bill or scythe was most deft, and clear –
> Had my piano-playing or counterpoint
> Been so without fear

Then indeed fame had been mine of most bright outshining;
But never had I known singer or piano player
So quick and sure in movement as this hedge-layer
This gap-mender, of quiet courage unhastening.[32]

No score is needed, no loss of nerve or memory lapse disrupts the even flow of this virtuoso performance. Here is a craftsman enviably secure in his movements because he is at home in his body.

Postscript

Roland Littlewood and I agreed after the debate that the concept of 'resonance' might in many contexts usefully replace that of 'construction', since it moves us away from the troublesome notion of cultural action as the implementation of a blueprint or programme, and encourages the thought that much of what we do when we attempt to make the world is to 'tune in' to processes already in motion.

Part II The debate

EDWARD SCHIEFFELIN   It appears to me that both the proponents
and the opponents of the motion were vigorously attempting to
reject a now outmoded stereotype of the social construction of
reality, one that is characterized by a strong element of cognitivism
and Cartesian dualism. In its place we heard a call for the centrality
of the notions of environment, of participation, of action as
creative of the world in which we live. So how do the two sides
differ in this debate?

NIGEL RAPPORT   I agree that there was no great difference between
the sides. I felt that the opposers of the motion were constructing a
false dichotomy that does not really relate to the concept of culture
that was being put forward by the proposers. For example, the
distinction crucial to Tim Ingold's argument, between construction and engagement, is an invalid one. No one would argue for a
passive, non-interactive notion of construction. Or consider Paul
Richards' starting point, the supposed 'appalling arrogance' of
assuming the existence of blueprints situated outside time. No one
would really argue for a construction thus detached from time and
change. Indeed, the arguments of the opposition could be taken as
prime instantiations of the notion, which Geertz borrowed from
Weber, that we are suspended in webs of significance of our own
construction. I therefore support the motion.

TAMARA DRAGADZE   I think the argument is not so much about the
notion of culture as it is about determinism. Can we in anthropology espouse cultural determinism or any other kind of determinism? Or can there be no determinism? The debate has more to
do with these questions than with the actual concepts – nature,
culture, human worlds and so on.

TIM INGOLD   There is a real difference between what I and Wendy

James were proposing. She referred on several occasions to 'mere organisms', and to human beings as 'body plus' – as though their personhood somehow existed outside, over and above, or beyond their organic being. This is a view that I would reject, as I believe it is founded on a very inadequate notion (though one that is prevalent in social anthropology) of what an organism, human or otherwise, actually is. This misconception is shared by many biologists too: the very idea that cultural or social experience is something that can be 'added on' implies the reduction of the organism to (putting it crudely) that which we are 'born with', thus sidestepping the whole biological process of development. I, for one, do not think we can regard persons as in any way 'above' organisms, and would suggest that the phrase 'mere organism' is what signals the real difference between Wendy James's view and my own. As for Geertz and his 'webs of significance', this also reinforces the point that there really is a difference between us. I find this idea of human beings being suspended in webs of significance quite unacceptable because it puts us humans in a kind of free-floating world in which we are ascribing significance to things 'out there'. Behind this notion is the premiss that meaning is actually disembodied. For if that were not the case, then meaning would become coterminous with reality itself. And if meaning is coterminous with reality, then the concept of meaning itself becomes redundant.

ROLAND LITTLEWOOD   I also think that there are significant differences between the two sides, and I would like to ask Tim Ingold a question. He keeps making a distinction between the individual or the organism and the environment: what, then, is the quality of the knowledge of that distinction? Where is the distinction located? It seems to me that he is attacking the 'children's building blocks' model of construction, as though we had been claiming that it amounts to an assembly, into some kind of structure, of blocks that pre-exist in reality. But we were claiming nothing of the sort, for there are still problems with the nature of these blocks. Indeed, Tim Ingold's position seems very close to ours, so perhaps we could push him a little further. Where is the distinction between these things that are supposed to be interacting: organism and environment? What sort of distinction is it? Is it, as I was arguing, a distinction in human knowledge? It sounded to me as though, for Ingold, it is a distinction that exists 'out there', independently of our apperception.

TIM INGOLD   I am thinking about the relationship between the organism and the environment in a dialectical way such that each constitutes the other: that is to say, the coming-into-being or development of the organism is itself the development of an environment for that organism. Thus I am rejecting the idea, which is embodied in a good deal of ecological discourse (in the notion of evolutionary adaptation, for example), that environments can actually be specified independently of the organisms filling them, which then have to adapt to those given environmental constraints. On the contrary, it seems to me that organisms, through their development and through their activities, *constitute* their environments; but in a sense environments constitute organisms too because, the organism (or human being, as one kind of organism) through its development embodies its own perceptual experience of involvement with the world. Hence, the developing interaction across the interface between organism and environment is part of the process by which the organism, the human being, becomes constituted as the kind of organism or human being it is. I am thinking in terms of a dialectical relationship rather than a fixed dualism in which organism and environment can be independently specified and then set to work to interact.

EDWARD SCHIEFFELIN   I can see two perfect agreements with that: one is the point that Geertz makes in his article on 'The impact of the concept of culture on the concept of man'[33]; the other is exactly the sort of process that Peter Berger discusses in the first three chapters of *The sacred canopy*.[34] We have no argument with either of these.

MARILYN STRATHERN   It is quite clear that as a metaphor, 'construction' has had its day. No one appreciates the metaphor of a building or a house. Indeed, if the two sides were to be said to agree on anything, it is that each has exposed the other's argument as a construction; and from that follows a question. I was rather inspired by Paul Richards' reference to the skill or clumsiness with which one moves. Whether skilfully or clumsily, however, one does still move; whether in comfort or discomfort, one still dwells. The question I would like to put to the opposition is this: in what sense do they move *with* or dwell *with* the proposal?

PAUL RICHARDS   I think we could write music together if we tried! What I found inspiring in Jane Guyer's article (see Note 26) was the idea that opposition does not always have to be oppositional; it can also be syncopational – different levels of reality can move *with* each other, overlapping in complex ways, and out of that can come a sense of well-being. Perhaps we are just reinventing a kind of functionalism here. But what most outrages me about culture theory in modern anthropology is its inability to grasp music and dance. I have recently been reading the work of Lévi-Strauss, and this, to me, represents all that is wrong with the 'symbolic decoding' approach to musical or choreographic material. It is exactly the opposite of what Gurney tries to do in his poetry, which is to convey the sense that the meaning in music comes out of the doing. It is difficult to capture that sense within the format of a debate, because the very terms in which any debate is set up are timeless and oppositional.

MARILYN STRATHERN   But music is never in error. In what sense do you find the arguments that you are opposing to be *in error*?

PAUL RICHARDS   What I object to in the idea of human worlds being culturally constructed is that it does not allow space for inquiry into the *flow* of dwelling, of the life of persons – human organisms – in their environment. There is something deflationary about the way we use the terms 'organism' and 'environment', these terms come to us in a tainted form, as if to show any great enthusiasm for them is already halfway to advocating a vulgar genetic or environmental determinism. We need to find a way of getting into this kind of material that still holds the gains of modern culture theory. Guyer, however, has taken us in the right direction by speaking of the sense of well-being that comes out of improvisation when people are doing their own things in their own ways and yet all hanging together. We never really know why some things *do* hang together whilst other things are such an appalling mess. But there are now beginning to be ethnographies of performance that grasp some of these issues – an example in the musicological literature is Ruth Stone's book on Kpelle music performance, *Let the inside be sweet*,[35] in which Kpelle musicians themselves show how they achieve this sense of well-being when things hold together and make sense, and also how things can go so badly wrong that one can only stop and start all over again. But the reason why I quoted from Gurney is simply that he is so good at conveying the sense of well-being that comes from hard physical work: recall how he admired the hedger as being a greater musician than himself because he was not *hurried*, he worked – as a fine musician plays – with balance and poise. If only we could achieve that same balance in our own theoretical debates!

RICHARD FARDON   Both sides, I presume, share problems with the idea of worlds, and also with the idea of construction, but let us put these to one side for the moment. The thesis before us is that 'Human worlds are culturally constructed'. One problem is to know exactly how the humans and the cultures are supposed to relate to one another in that formulation. If I were to turn it around and say, 'cultural worlds are constructed by humans', would anybody on either side have any problem?

WENDY JAMES   We would have no problem. But I would like to address a specific question about music to Paul Richards. He has given us a very vivid and moving picture of the rhythmic aspects of performance in which we should immerse ourselves in our ethnography. What I miss, however, both in his presentation and in that of Tim Ingold, is substantive ethnographic material. A person from Brazil surely does not automatically enjoy the rhythms of Japanese music. If that is so, how can one dispense with the notion that there are culturally constructed musical traditions, as for example between Brazil and Japan?

TIM INGOLD   I have no problem with the idea that people from different backgrounds resonate to different kinds of music, but I do have a problem with the idea that this has something to do with 'culture', if that 'culture' is *opposed* to anything else. In other words, developing some kind of dance technique, or learning to play the piano, or responding to one kind of music rather than another, comes by way of experience in an environment. Obviously children learn as they grow up. The problem comes when we start thinking of that learning process not as one through which experienced relationships are incorporated into the person's very being, into his or her self (which is how I think musical sensibilities are acquired), but as one in which layers are *added on* from above. I want to think of the development of the human being as a process in which, right from the start, the child is immersed in a world, in a set of experiences which, through perception, are enfolded into his or her own person.

WENDY JAMES   We have some idea of how you want to see the development of the child. But let us take the question of music a little further. Paul Richards was describing his efforts, over thirty years, to practise Bach. Now you do not simply develop *into* the music of Bach, into its rhythm. You have it before you on a sheet of printed paper which has been replicated over several centuries. Without that 'high culture' tradition of music, without the 'construction' of Bach's own music that has been passed on historically and which you learn not by immersion but by accepting the guidance of a teacher, you would not enjoy Bach. My point is that there is an educational element in learning as it takes place. Children do not simply *absorb* learning. They are *taught* to pick up forms which are highly structured and sophisticated – the structuring has taken place outside them and is handed down to them historically. I would have thought it very difficult to present what is going on here as a mutually constitutive process between organism and environment. To see it in such terms would indeed amount to a new kind of functionalism, in which there is no starting point, no ending point, and no problem; everything appears to affect everything else in an unproblematic way. To me, learning Bach is a highly problematic matter for a child.

PAUL RICHARDS   But you do not learn Bach by decoding the notes on paper and then reconstructing them into the musical performance. The notes are presumably a representation of what Bach heard in his inner ear, and you can only start to play Bach when you have sufficiently absorbed the notes to be able to begin to get the music out of the violin. And that involves an interaction between the player and the musical instrument.

WENDY JAMES   That may be true of the performance. But 'Bach' exists outside the succession of individual performances.

PAUL RICHARDS   This is my problem with the notion of construction. We could find other words, like *doing*, with which I have no problem, and if Richard Fardon would rephrase the proposition to state that cultural worlds are humanly *done*, then I would raise no objection. But the term 'construction' seems to me to privilege the blueprint, or the piece of music as it is represented by notation on the printed sheet. This is then prioritized as if it had an existence outside time and is then brought into time through performance. That is the metaphor – and I am not talking *specifically* about music.

WENDY JAMES   But whose metaphor? We are having metaphors put into our mouths that we did not originate, and which represent an obsolete sociology with which we have never been associated. We do not write in that way, we do not teach in that way, nor have we invoked the idea of a timeless blueprint in anything we have said in this debate.

PAUL RICHARDS   Do you admit that there is no blueprint, that no symbolic decoding is going on?

WENDY JAMES   There are specific blueprints, of course, not just of individual pieces of music but of entire musical traditions. But such blueprints certainly do not stand out of time, they are produced within historical time.

ALISON NEWBY   I would like to respond to Wendy James's claim that 'Bach' exists on paper, in a fixed form that is handed down over the centuries. Now there are many different traditions of how to play a piece of Bach, or indeed of any other composer. The performance of a piece by a Russian composer, for example, will not be the same in Russia as it is in this country. There is a certain sense in which people's interactions with their environments *do* affect the way they play. Someone may teach you to play a piece in a particular way, but even within particular cultures there are differences in the manner in which the music is heard. Thus we do not know how Bach heard his own music, or what was important for him in his environment and his setting, but a glance at the history of performance reveals everything from Leopold Stokowski's use of a huge orchestra, that he clearly felt to be appropriate in *his* environment, to those who insist on the authenticity of using original instruments. So one cannot simply conclude that what is written down on the page is what you hear: the relation is much more complex than that. The way you play, and the way you feel the music, will be rooted in your own experience, your own interaction with the environment. I think this leads to the point Paul Richards was making.

WENDY JAMES   We would not deny the truth of what you say. But we are anxious not to forget that the differences in this musical tradition in place and time, which represent local variations and re-creations, are historical phenomena that are nevertheless under-written by a more fundamental continuity. The child, in school, is actually *taught* not only about such-and-such a piece of music and how it is to be played now, but also about how it might have been played in the past. You are able to *know* about the variations in the performance of a given piece of music around the world, because this is what you have learned. And such learning forms part of an educational tradition within which you have been brought up.

ALISON NEWBY   I only know how people play in other parts of the world because there has been a kind of explosion, in recent times, in ways of knowing about other people. I agree that it is nowadays more difficult to separate what people do of themselves from what they do because it has been taught to them. But anyone with experience of musical performance knows that every performance is unique in some way, albeit framed within the parameters of a cultural tradition.

EDWARD SCHIEFFELIN   The peculiarity of performance derives from its emergent qualities. With every culture, every orchestra, every occasion, the performance is a little different because it involves the emergence of qualities which are, in some respects, above and beyond what is on the written page or in the taught tradition; but these qualities of the performance, in turn, *become* part of that tradition and feed into it. That is how the tradition remains alive. Some traditions attempt to restrict or limit performance, but if the tradition ever remains alive it is because the performances themselves, in some important, non-trivial way, feed back into the way this is carried on. You cannot easily learn to play music from reading a book: you need a teacher, and you have to get the feel of an instrument. The whole process of playing Bach is exceptionally complex; what goes on in your head, what is on the printed page, your knowledge of history (that Bach wore a wig, had twenty-one children and so on) – all of this may indeed contribute to how you play the music. But the music that comes out, as performance, is neither separable from the tradition of which it forms a part nor wholly reducible to it either. This is a crucial point about performance that is easily forgotten: it not only continues but also *builds* the tradition.

ANDREW HOLDING   We seem to be obsessed at the moment with what *we* (as anthropologists) want, and unconcerned about what people might say *they* want. Speakers on both sides of this debate have used metaphors from *here* to bring out what they want to say, but I would be interested to find out how the people themselves, whose world or worlds we are talking about, would deal with the issue. Let me go back to the metaphor, drawn by Tim Ingold, of the hunter-gatherer and the house. I wonder how the hunter-gatherer would describe the house. Would he go about it in the same way that the speakers have done, in trying to give meaning to the title of this debate? If there is a similarity here, and given the practical impossibility of spelling out the whole process on every occasion, would it not be simpler to use the term 'culture' to describe the way in which meaning is made in the world?

TIM INGOLD   I believe that there are basic similarities in the ways people experience their environments. Nevertheless, a distinction is habitually made between the natural and the artificial environment, and it is often said that we, urban dwellers live in an environment that is largely artificial or 'built', whereas the hunter-gatherer lives in an environment that is largely natural or 'unbuilt', and that this fundamentally affects the way the world is perceived.[36] Now in a built environment people live in houses, which we generally class as artefacts, and an artefact – as defined within the tradition of Western thought – is a portion of the physical world that has been modified through the imposition of cultural design. This definition of the artefact, however, only makes sense as long as we think of the world as an external, physical reality that can be modified or transformed in this way. But that is not how the world, or portions of it, becomes an environment for people. Whether we are talking about houses, shops and streets for the urban dweller or features of the landscape in which the hunter-gatherer regularly moves around in the course of normal subsistence activities, it is through their incorporation into patterns of everyday practical activity that they become components of an experienced environment. In a sense, these features become drawn into the people themselves, just as the latter, in their activities, inscribe themselves into the objects of their surroundings. There is therefore no complete separation of person and environment; and in this respect it makes no difference whether we are dealing with something that is supposedly artificial or something that is supposedly natural. The natural–artificial distinction has no purchase when we think of relations between people and their environments in these terms. The difficulty is that for us, caught up as we are in so-called 'Western discourse', this way of experiencing the environment is hard to describe. We lack the terms for it. Perhaps you will then say: 'If that is indeed the way people experience the world, and granted that experience differs for people in different times and places, why should we not just call this way of experiencing "culture"?' One reason why I find this difficult to accept is that culture is an 'entity' term. Anthropologists still tend to speak of *this* culture as against *that* culture...

WENDY JAMES   No they do not!

TIM INGOLD   But they *do*, and as long as they do, they are tying culture up into entities and giving it a closure which is quite inappropriate when what we are in fact dealing with is continuous process.

ROLAND LITTLEWOOD   I feel that our opponents are paying less and less attention to what we have argued. They have reified culture, despite our insistence that the motion in no way demands a notion of culture as an entity, or even as an area. We are rather talking about *procedures*. This gives me an opportunity to come back to a question that I have already asked of Tim Ingold, but which I do not think he has adequately answered. It concerns the distinction between the individual and the environment. He said earlier that they dialectically constitute one another, and he has now gone on to explain that the individual is somehow 'comprehended' in the environment. This is the individual whom we presumably identify with ourselves as being human. My original question, which I would like to ask again, is this: where is the distinction between the individual and the environment located? How can it be located anywhere except in our words and in our perceptions? One moment it is said that the two 'constitute' one another, the next moment they are spoken of as separate entities. Surely, this is a cultural construction. If not, what?

PNINA WERBNER   Tim Ingold's argument focuses on the individual, and indeed depends on this focus. The environment can be anything: cultural, historical, biological, physical. Everything is environment, the continual focus remains on the individual as interactor. So of course, under the circumstances, the distinctions between culture and nature, and its corollaries, become nonsensical. But once the environment is seen to be constraining in a cultural sense, once we see teaching in a cultural sense, moving in a historical sense, then what becomes of the individual? Maybe culture is reified, but this does not mean that the individual exists on his own.

ELIZABETH TONKIN   Let me go back to Wendy James's point that people are taught, and learn, to play Bach through a kind of transmission process. Many of us are teachers and we have all had the experience of being taught, and we know that what is problematic about teaching – contrary to the notions that either people are receptacles into which information can simply be poured or that if you hit them hard enough it will somehow sink in – is that something happens, about which we know and understand very little, whereby people either do or do not 'click'. It is almost impossible to forecast whether people will click, or how they will do it. The process is a very complex one and has to do with (for want of a better term) cognition. But somewhere along the line there has to be an active cognitive processor which either does something with what comes in by way of socially mediated experience, or does not. It is cultural if you will, but clearly in another fundamental sense it is material.

ROY ELLEN   There has been some dispute between the two sides of this debate, at least between Wendy James and Paul Richards, concerning the meaning of 'construction'. Paul Richards referred, in his talk, to the title of the book (by Berger and Luckmann), *The social construction of reality.* Tim Ingold has, in his earlier writing, strongly criticized the use of conceptual hybrids such as 'socio-cultural', and has insisted on maintaining a clear conceptual separation between the social and the cultural. I wonder, therefore, whether the *social* construction of reality is quite the same as its *cultural* construction.

PAUL RICHARDS   I am not concerned about how the term 'construction' is qualified, it was to the term itself that I was objecting. My problem is epitomized in the simple question: how do you teach someone to ride a bicycle? How, when a performance has gone wrong, do you encourage people, enable people, empower people to put it back together again? How do *they* put it back together again? This is the central dilemma for those of us who have tried to carry out ethnographic work in, say, contemporary Africa, where life is disrupted by drought, famine and war. My fear is that 'construction' is not really helpful in these contexts. We do *not* know how people click, nor how they learn. We do not know how to create the conditions for that sense of well-being that allows the dance to move forward, for life to proceed in a healthy, syncopated way. Perhaps it is impossible to know these things; perhaps anthropology has nothing to contribute in this direction. However, it does seem to me that we have rather neglected these kinds of questions. My emphasis on music was not intended to make the perfect musical performance into a metaphor for social life. What I am interested in, and what I have learned from music, is the crucial importance of *mistakes.* When you are practising the violin in the privacy of your own home, you can stop as many times as you like and sort out the mistakes. But when you are in the midst of a performance, as every musician knows, you have to keep going – you have to develop techniques for *coping* when the performance goes wrong. It seems to me that the notion of cultural construction tends to emphasize what happens when things are going right, according to the programme, the notes, or the blueprint, however much we may want to situate the latter in history. That explains things when they are working well; what we do not know enough about is how people cope and pull through when things fall apart.

TIM INGOLD   Let me first make it clear that in focusing on human–environment relations, I do not consider the human being to be a self-contained, individual isolate which then *interacts* with his or her surroundings. On the contrary, to the extent that humans are persons, caught up from the start in an intersubjective, meaningful world of involvement with other people, they are also social beings. What I do reject, however, is the idea that the level of this involvement, whether it be called social or cultural, can be separated out from, and placed hierarchically above, the level on which human beings, as organisms, relate to other, non-human components of their environments. The only way in which that kind of separation can be established is by drawing a line between humanity and the rest of the animal kingdom, which is itself founded on an assumption of human uniqueness that is essentially Cartesian and that cannot, I think, be sustained. Of course, the real villains in this debate, in opposition to whom both sides find common cause, and with whom we have been careful to avoid any hint of collusion, are – let us say – certain biologists. You could call them sociobiologists, except that when you try to argue with them, they are inclined to adopt the same tactics as those used by the proposers of the motion for this debate, claiming to have long since discarded (if indeed they ever held) the premisses and presumptions that opponents attribute to them, even when those premisses and presumptions are constitutive of the very intellectual tradition to which they claim allegiance. It has been observed – in the context of the previous debate on the concept of society – that the classic attempt of Durkheim to capture the essence of what it means to be human, in a field of relationships with other humans, eventually backfired, on account of the fact that at the time of writing, he found it imperative to set up his theory as a counter to the individualism of such liberal philosophers of society as Herbert Spencer. In opposition to the aggregate of self-contained individuals, Durkheim posited the collective consciousness formed through their interpenetration, 'society-as-a-whole', and so on. We now find that this very opposition, between individual and society, prevents us from getting a proper grip on the nature of relatedness. We have something of the same problem here, because 'out there' are some sociobiologists (whether or not they have disowned this label) who have an extremely impoverished view of

what an organism is, and who are using quite blatant constructionist metaphors (such as that of the 'genetic programme') to
describe the nature of organic existence. In the oppositional
context of anthropology's stance against sociobiology (just as in
the context of Durkheim's stance against Spencerian individualism), the conception of cultural construction against which Paul
Richards and I have been arguing is itself reproduced.[37] In other
words, a version of cultural constructionism with which neither
side in this debate would agree is being perpetuated through its
opposition to an equally unsatisfactory biogenetic determinism.
This brings me back to a question that one speaker [Tamara
Dragadze] raised some time ago: is not the real issue one about
determinism? If there is one point that I really want to stress, it is
that the world is not a determined state of affairs but a 'going on',
which is constantly being furthered by agents within it. And these
agents are not only human, but include other organisms as well.
The world is not 'there', for us or anybody else to represent or to fail
to represent; the world is coming into being through our activities.
Of course other people are part of our world, just as much as is the
non-human environment; but we cannot exclusively privilege us
human beings with this world-producing effort – for the world is
coming into being through the activities of *all* living agencies. At
the root of the argument, then, is a question about our understanding of human uniqueness. And I think there really *is*, on that
ground, a difference between what I and Paul Richards have been
saying, and the arguments of the proposers.

WENDY JAMES   I think it will be clear that there is a great deal of
sympathy underlying our exchanges. We would fully accept Tim
Ingold's suggestion that our focus of study should include the
person as a centre of experience, and as an agent. Likewise, we are
unanimous in rejecting a rather rigid and artificial notion of
culture as a thing, *a* culture, going into the plural, which in my
opening remarks I did suggest we should drop. There are other
points of sympathetic contact as well, such as the concern with
music, with the development of the physical capacities of the
person, with the kinds of questions that arise if we ask how people
can learn to do things like ride bicycles (when they have already,
presumably, invented the wheel). I particularly sympathize, too,
with what Paul Richards had to say about the failure of older
anthropological models and paradigms to deal with current crises
such as are being experienced in Africa, with famine, disease, war

and death, on a scale with which it seems almost impossible to deal analytically. Of course there are many students in the field at this moment, trying to cope as researchers with the problems of making sense of these situations, and to come up with interpretations and analyses that could be of humane use and practical help. In the situation of a refugee camp or a settlement scheme, or a front-line relief centre such as those run by Medecins sans Frontières in the middle of a war in Africa, I would have thought that the notion of construction could be of some help, and I would like to argue for its retention.

There are several levels on which we can hold on to it. At the lowest level we may be dealing with an assortment of people who have lost their motives, their money and their connection with a homeland, people who are actually trying to rebuild a new community, sometimes physically, carrying building materials to construct their houses. The notion of the reconstruction of community is one which would resonate not only with what is in the minds of the researcher, the relief agency and the government of the country concerned, but also with what the people themselves think they are doing. They may see themselves as rebuilding their families, their homeland, and so on. Here the idea of rebuilding resonates with the actions that people themselves are actually engaged in. At higher levels, too, the notion of construction is surely relevant. It operates at a collective level on which this debate has scarcely touched. In my opening remarks I did mention the level of the state, which constructs (for example) economic policy, roads, legal and political institutions, and prisons. A notion of cultural construction, if taken seriously, should be carried through to this collective level. The model proposed by Tim Ingold in particular, of the evolving relations between the human being *qua* organism and the environment, clearly does have its centre of gravity in the single being rather than on the collective level of – for example – the state, town council, university, or even household. Now it is perfectly true that, perhaps in the way anthropology has been taught, many assumptions have become fossilized about the solidity and autonomy of collective phenomena. These have possibly weighed too heavily on us and obscured areas in which this debate could move forward. Nevertheless, the collective level exists, there are ways of talking about the state and of collective cultural phenomena, such as musical or dance traditions, which do not rest on naïve notions of *the* culture, conceived as an entity, somehow detached from lived reality, lived experience.

Tim Ingold has accused me of being too scornful in my reference to 'mere organisms'. But I have heard women complain, after being in the maternity hospital, 'I was treated just like an organism'; they have felt that their very personhood has been abused or insulted. And of course this has now become a collective cry, that women should be allowed to give birth at home, in a more human and personal environment, and not reduced to mere bodies on hospital beds. This brings me back to another point that I made in my initial remarks: that an organism does not, in itself, have *rights*. In a sense, that is what lies behind the complaint of women who say that they had been treated as mere organisms in the context of giving birth, when they were not even ill. Their rights and their self-respect, as persons, have been infringed, neglected. Thus the notion of person*hood*, as I suggested, is not self-evident. It has to be defined. And in very many cases, that definition has to be struggled for. This reminds us about the making of boundaries. Our opponents *have* been rather keen on setting up dichotomous boundaries and attributing them in some cases to us, but in other cases setting them up for the purposes of their own argument: for example between the social and the cultural, and between perception and imagination. Boundaries of this kind do not seem to be regarded by our opponents as at all problematic. But as Roland Littlewood has asked, where *is* the boundary between the person-organism and the environment? You will recall his opening remarks, in which he suggested that we are ourselves because we are descended from the survivors of previous epidemics; we are *artefacts*, in that sense, rather than agents – artefacts of crises external to us.

I would like to conclude by picking up on the point raised in the debate by Andrew Holding: he asked, with reference to the hunter-gatherer and the house: what does the *hunter-gatherer* say? Though I have listened carefully, I have missed, in the presentations of the opposition, any reference to *specific* symbolic or other formulations from any particular hunter-gatherer group. I, too, would like to know where the boundary between person and nature, home and bush, might be placed, and where we should locate the interaction between the two. I would like to know the fit, or lack of fit, between a representation like that of Ingold, with *his* hunter-gatherer facing the environment, and the representation you might actually find in a real human community. Let us by all means return to real human communities. The picture that Ingold gives us of the isolated hunter-gatherer in the environment is in my view a myth, one that sanctions (to use an old-fashioned term which is not part

of my normal vocabulary) a new kind of functionalism that
pervades both his writings and his remarks in this debate. Let us
ask that hunter-gatherer. Now, I have carried out fieldwork in an
area where the hunting idiom is still very prevalent even though
opportunities for hunting are, from the point of view of local
people, unfortunately very rare. The corresponding myth would
not envisage a male hunter with his spear facing the environment,
looking out from the door of his hut or the entrance to his cave. It
would portray a woman in her hut whilst the man is out in the
forest, in the domain of nature. Unless one tries to engage with *real*
ethnography, with actual representations of this kind, originally
couched in another language, it is difficult to prevent a debate like
this from becoming a ritual game of words. And surely, in dealing
with these representations, we are concerned with the processes
and products of cultural construction.

NOTES

1 There is mounting evidence to support the view that at least some non-
human species possess a reflexive capacity. See, for example, D. L. and R. M.
Seyfarth, *How monkeys see the world: inside the mind of another species*,
Chicago, University of Chicago Press, 1990.
2 P. Berger and T. Luckmann, *The social construction of reality*, Harmonds-
worth, Penguin, 1966.
3 J. Gowlett, *Ascent to civilization: the archaeology of early man*, London,
Collins, 1984, pp. 106–7.
4 See, in particular, P. Bourdieu, *Outline of a theory of practice*, trans. R. Nice,
Cambridge, Cambridge University Press, 1977.
5 T. Asad, 'Towards a genealogy of the concept of ritual', in *Vernacular
Christianity: essays in the social anthropology of religion presented to Godfrey
Lienhardt*, eds W. James and D.H. Johnson, Oxford/New York, JASO/Lilian
Barber Press, 1988.
6 M. Mauss, 'Body techniques' [1934], Part IV of *Sociology and psychology:
essays by Marcel Mauss*, trans. B. Brewster, London, Routledge & Kegan
Paul, 1979.
7 W. James, *The listening ebony: moral knowledge, religion and power among
the Uduk of Sudan*, Oxford, Clarendon Press, 1988, esp. pp. 68–83.
8 M. Z. Rosaldo, *Knowledge and passion: Ilongot notions of self and social life*,
Cambridge, Cambridge University Press, 1980; S. Harrison, 'Concepts of
the person in Avatip religious thought', *Man* (N.S.) 20, 1985, pp. 115–30;
Signe Howell, *Society and cosmos: Chewong of Peninsular Malaysia*, Oxford,
Oxford University Press, 1984, esp. pp. 127–74.
9 M. Strathern, *The gender of the gift: problems with women and problems
with society in Melanesia*, Berkeley, University of California Press,
1988.

10 Symposium on 'Ritualization of behaviour in animals and man', *Philosophical transactions of the Royal Society of London*, no. 772, volume 251, Series B, 1966.

11 T. Ingold, 'An anthropologist looks at biology', *Man* (N.S.) 25, 1990, pp. 208–29.

12 S. Collins, 'Categories, concepts or predicaments? Remarks on Mauss's use of philosophical terminology', in *The category of the person: anthropology, philosophy, history*, eds M. Carrithers, S. Collins and S. Lukes, Cambridge, Cambridge University Press, 1985, pp. 46–82.

13 C. Geertz, 'The transition to humanity', in *Horizons of anthropology*, ed. S. Tax, Chicago, Aldine, 1964, p. 39.

14 See, for example, H. C. Brookfield, 'On the environment as perceived', *Progress in geography* 1, 1969, pp. 51–80; R. A. Rappaport, *Pigs for the ancestors*, New Haven, Yale University Press, 1968, pp. 237–41; R. F. Ellen, *Environment, subsistence and system*, Cambridge, Cambridge University Press, 1982, Ch. 9.

15 This account of perception follows the approach of 'ecological psychology', pioneered by J. J. Gibson in *The ecological approach to visual perception*, Boston, Houghton Mifflin, 1979; see also E. S. Reed, 'James Gibson's ecological approach to cognition', in *Cognitive psychology in question*, eds A. Costall and A. Still, Brighton, Harvester Press, 1987.

16 See Martin Heidegger's celebrated essay, 'Building dwelling thinking', in his *Poetry, language and thought*, New York, Harper & Row, 1971, pp. 145–61.

17 A. N. Whitehead, *Science and the modern world*, Harmondsworth, Penguin, 1938 [1926], p.217.

18 T. Ingold, 'An anthropologist looks at biology', *Man* (N.S.) 25, 1990, pp. 208–29.

19 R. Littlewood, 'From categories to contexts: a decade of the new cross-cultural psychiatry', *British Journal of Psychiatry* 156, 1990, pp. 308–27.

20 T. Ingold, 'Culture and the perception of the environment', in *Bush base: forest farm. Culture, environment and development*, eds D. Parkin and E. Croll, London, Routledge, 1991, pp. 39–56.

21 R. Littlewood, *op. cit.*

22 Cf. 'The three little pigs', in I. and P. Opie, *The classic fairy tales*, Oxford, Oxford University Press, 1974, p. 94; B. Bettelheim, 'The three little pigs: pleasure principle versus reality principle', in his *The uses of enchantment: the meaning and importance of fairy tales*, Harmondsworth, Penguin, 1978, pp. 41–5: 'Since the three little pigs represent stages in the development of man, the disappearance of the first two little pigs is not traumatic ... '(p. 44).

23 P. Berger and T. Luckmann, *The social construction of reality*, Harmondsworth, Penguin, 1966.

24 N. Simmonds, *Principles of crop improvement*, London, Longmans, 1979, p. 82.

25 *Ibid.*, p. 132.

26 J. Guyer, 'The multiplication of labor: gender and agricultural change in modern Africa', *Current Anthropology* 29, 1988, pp. 247–72.

27 J. M. Chernoff, *African rhythm and African sensibility: aesthetics and social action in African musical idioms*, Chicago, University of Chicago Press, 1979, pp. 59–60.

28   C. A. Waterman, *Juju: a social history and ethnography of an African popular music*, Chicago, University of Chicago Press, 1990, p. 220.

29   C. Lévi-Strauss, *The naked man: introduction to a science of mythology*, 4, New York, Harper & Row, 1970.

30   J. Attali, *Noise: the political economy of music*, trans. B. Maasumi, Manchester, Manchester University Press, 1985, p. 135.

31   P. Bourdieu, *Outline of a theory of practice*, trans. R. Nice, Cambridge, Cambridge University Press, 1977.

32   From *Collected poems of Ivor Gurney*, ed. P. J. Kavanagh, Oxford, Oxford University Press, 1982, p. 161. Reproduced by permission of Oxford University Press.

33   C. Geertz, 'The impact of the concept of culture on the concept of man', in *New views of man*, ed. J. R. Platt, Chicago, University of Chicago Press, 1965.

34   P. Berger, *The sacred canopy*, New York, Doubleday, 1964.

35   R. Stone, *Let the inside be sweet: the interpretation of music event among the Kpelle of Liberia*, Bloomington, Indiana University Press, 1982.

36   This view is very well argued in P. J. Wilson, *The domestication of the human species*, New Haven, Yale University Press, 1988.

37   See, for example, M. D. Sahlins, *The use and abuse of biology*, London, Tavistock, 1976. Sahlins counters the claims of the sociobiologists with a vigorous assertion that human worlds of meaning are engineered in accordance with imposed, symbolic blueprints. Culture, he writes (p. 13), is a 'meaningful system of the world and human experience that was already in existence before any of the current human participants were born, and that from birth engages their natural dispositions as the instruments of a symbolic project'.

1991 debate

Language is the essence of culture

Introduction

Tim Ingold

Not so long ago, it would have been considered self-evidently true, by the vast majority of anthropologists, that human cultures owe their very existence to language. This assumption, which made of language the indispensable tool of anthropological inquiry, also served to remove it, and its role in cultural processes, from the field of investigation. Nowadays we are no longer so sure, and by the same token the use of language both by the peoples among whom we study, and in our own research and writing, has become a focus of critical attention. That many today would doubt that language is the essence of culture, or at least regard this as a matter calling for justification, is eloquent testimony to the extent to which anthropology has cut itself loose from past certainties. We have begun to question whether, or in what sense, things like 'culture' (or cultures) and 'language' (or languages) can be said to exist at all, whilst talk of essences immediately sparks off charges of unwarranted reification. What is left of the old maxim that 'to under-stand the culture you must first understand the language', when verbal discourse seems to generate as much misunderstanding as understand-ing, and when a large part of what goes on in everyday life appears to be independent of – and even resistant to – linguistic articulation? It was to address questions of this kind that the proposition, 'language is the essence of culture', was adopted as the motion for the fourth in this series of debates.

Ostensibly, the argument is about whether language calls into being the cultural worlds in which people live, or whether these worlds are given form and meaning by virtue of a cognitive engagement that precedes language, and to which language gives no more than superficial and incomplete expression. David Parkin, proposing the motion, and Brian Moeran, seconding, both take the view that even those objects of cultural experience that might at first glance appear to have nothing to do with language – such as paintings or smells – only exist for us *as* paintings, smells or whatever by virtue of activities of classification, interpretation and judgement. These activities are social, and require a medium of symbolic communication. That medium is language. Thus it is within verbal discourse that those meanings are constituted, and held in place, which give form to the raw material of sensory experience. Against this, in opposing the motion, Alfred Gell argues that culture consists of concepts rather than verbally constituted meanings, and that these concepts are established in the course of a direct, practical involvement with other persons and things in one's surroundings, an involvement which need not (and for small children manifestly does not) entail fully-fledged verbal discourse. And James Weiner, seconding the opposition, makes the parallel point that speech, far from serving to represent in words what people already know on the basis of their practical experience, is but part and parcel of an overall current of skilled activity, that includes all kinds of everyday non-linguistic practices as well.

Paradoxically, this brings Weiner's position closely into line with that of the motion's proposer, Parkin. Both refuse to draw any absolute line of demarcation between speech and such non-verbal forms of communication as manual gesture or facial expression, or between these and other kinds of cultural conduct. For Parkin, the proposition 'language is the essence of culture' implies that the two are simply indissoluble one from another: any attempt to draw them apart would lead to the absurdities of culturally decontextualized language and linguistically decontextualized culture. Weiner's opposition to the motion, on the other hand, is targeted on the very possibility of 'essence', on the idea that there is such a thing as language which may or may not be the essence of culture, or conversely that there is such a thing as culture, of which language may or may not be the essence. Thus to argue that language is *not* the essence of culture is not necessarily to imply that something else, such as dance or pantomime, *is*, although one participant in the debate – Chris Knight – does indeed mount an argument to this effect.

Gell's view, however, is quite different. He does not hesitate to speak of a 'capacity for language', with a clearly defined neurophysiological substrate in all human brains, and he puts up a robust defence of the distinction between verbal speech and non-verbal communication whilst recognizing, of course, that the latter is the normal accompaniment of the former. But this language capacity, he argues, is not what enables culture to come into being; it rather serves to convert into discourse what has already been brought about through the work of 'cognition and sociality'. And although Moeran disagrees, arguing strongly that cultural forms (including even those for which a non-linguistic essence is claimed) exist only thanks to language, he appears to share with Gell the underlying assumption – which both Parkin and Weiner reject – that language is critically distinct from non-verbal behaviour. His is an argument for grounding the non-verbal in the verbal, not for dissolving the distinction between them.

To unravel the complexities of this debate it is important to realize that underlying the argument about the role of language in the constitution of cultural worlds is a more fundamental issue, which precisely crosscuts the first, about the ontological status of language itself. This issue arose in connection with three interlocking themes concerning, first, the distinction between language and music, second, the relation between words and concepts and, third, the emergence of language in ontogeny and phylogeny. What follows is a brief introduction to these themes, and the questions they raise.

Studies in neurophysiology have provided us with apparently incontrovertible evidence that linguistic comprehension and musical appreciation involve the functioning of neural circuitry in different regions of the brain. Does this not prove that music is, at base, independent of language, and hence that language alone cannot be the essence of culture? For where would culture be without music, or for that matter without mathematics, or art, or dance? Yet for the neurophysiologist who puts the question, 'Which parts of the brain are involved in language and which in music?', and who seeks to answer it from studies of the disabilities of patients suffering from various kinds of brain damage, the distinction between language and music is already presupposed. It is embodied in the very questions he asks of the data at his disposal. But on what grounds is the distinction drawn? How do we draw the line between, say, speech and song? Both, surely, involve the expressive use of the same bodily organ, the human voice. Challenged to identify the source of a song's meaning, we might agree that it is brought forth in the very act of singing, and is inseparable from the sounds themselves. Why, then, should we be led to believe that understanding the meaning of a spoken utterance differs in any fundamental way from understanding the meaning of a melodic line of song?

The answer is that this belief is founded on the axiom that words refer to concepts. As Gell remarks, in the course of this debate: 'Who, after all, ever *said* anything in music?' The premiss behind this admittedly rhetorical question is that unlike the sounds of music, the words of language draw their meanings from a source outside themselves – namely from concepts already installed in the several minds of the members of a community of speakers. Language, it is argued, makes it possible for ideas to be *shared* within the community, though such sharing clearly requires that a set of conventions be already in place, mapping words on to their (more or less arbitrarily assigned) conceptual referents. Yet to argue thus is to assume, at the base of language, an ontological dualism between mind and world, such that speech serves to give 'outer' expression to 'inner' mental states or beliefs or ideas *about* the world. Weiner, for his part, explicitly sets out to expose and subvert the propositional attitude entailed in this view. In a revealing exchange with Knight, each accuses the other of introducing an unacceptable distinction between word and gesture. To appreciate what is at stake in this exchange, it is important to clear up what was a source of some confusion in the debate, namely the slippage from 'vocal' to 'verbal'. To communicate by gesture, in so far as this does *not* involve the use of the voice, is not in itself to communicate without words, for there are systems of manual signs – such as those in use in communities of the deaf – that have all the properties of verbal language. If, with Knight, we take the defining characteristic of language to be that the signs of which it consists refer to shared concepts, to a set of collective representations, then it makes no fundamental difference whether these signs take the form of pantomimic gestures or of verbal utterances. For Weiner, too, the manual gesture is not fundamentally different from the spoken word, *not*, however, because both refer to concepts, but because with both, the meanings they convey are inseparable from the bodily activity of their production. In his view, words no more derive their meanings from an external attachment to concepts than do gestures!

To claim this is at once to dissolve the foundations for the conventional distinction between language and music, and between speech and song. Indeed, Weiner's position recalls that of Merleau-Ponty, who maintained that if we could only liberate language from the efforts of the grammarians to determine its 'correct' forms, in terms of the rational application of rules, we would find that 'the words, vowels and phonemes [of language] are so many ways of "singing" the world'.[1] Thus the meaning of speech, like that of song, lies in the circumstances of the speaker's *engagement* with the world; it is not something that precedes that engagement, and which it serves to deliver. Now Parkin, too, rejects the absolute opposition between verbal and non-verbal communication, regarding the very category of language, constituted by that opposition, as an analytic fiction. Words may have conventional meanings, but these conventions are not given *a priori* but have to be worked at: each is the product of a historical struggle, and each a site of ongoing contestation. Compressed into the meaning of every word is a history of past usage, embedded in specific contexts of relationship between speakers and hearers.

This leads finally to the issues surrounding the emergence of language in ontogeny and phylogeny. Gell, who introduces these issues into the debate, argues that the achievement of linguistic proficiency is an *end-product* not only of the developmental process of cognitive growth in the child, but also of the evolutionary process of hominization that led to the emergence of (so-called) anatomically modern *Homo sapiens*, 'people like us'. The implication, however, is that every infant member of the species comes already equipped with an evolved 'capacity for language', whose realization depends upon subsequent ontogenetic development in an environment that includes speaking caregivers. On what grounds, however, can one presume the pre-existence of such a capacity? Is it not to commit the fallacy of positing language in advance of the processes that give rise to it? And if the category of language is itself an analytic fiction, a historical product of the modern imagination, and one moreover that is purveyed primarily by adults, what justification is there for treating language as a human universal that has underwritten the work of the imagination ever since, as they say, 'history began'? And how can we any longer regard language as something whose evolution or development we can attempt to describe or explain? Indeed, we would have to conclude that the whole debate on language origins, which has recently gained so much momentum, is seriously misconceived.

The debate that follows does not resolve these issues. On the contrary, it opens up a Pandora's box of doubts and queries that are crying out for attention. When it comes to language and culture, it seems that anthropology will have to go back to the drawing board. To sort out all the issues raised in this debate will keep us occupied for many years to come.

Part I The presentations

FOR THE MOTION (1)

DAVID PARKIN

Considerable confusion surrounds the word 'essence'. It is much
maligned and sometimes seen as necessarily linked to essentialism, that
constraining mode of thinking that reifies, concretizes and fixes
artificially the infinite flexibility of what we say and do. But the
fundamental sense of essence is much more innocent: it has to do with
presence, with existing or, simply, being.

Thus a gloss on the proposition before us today – language is the
essence of culture – is that language is the way of being of culture. If
language is the way of being of culture, then the reverse applies, and
culture is the way of being of language. In other words, the two are
indissolubly part of each other. That, then, is my starting-point, and I
would further insist that anyone who argues for the analytic separation
of language and culture, as distinct fields of study, reproduces the folly
that led linguists, on the one hand, to study languages as though they
could be divorced from the contexts of social life, and anthropologists,
on the other hand, to report their observations of cultural practices
without adequate reference to what the people themselves had to say.

One aspect of the combined essence of language and culture lies in
their operation as systems of communication. It was not for nothing that
Lévi-Strauss[2] grouped together marriage alliance, the exchange of goods
and services and mythology as the culture of communication. As
anthropology has moved further from structuralism and semiology,
the idea that language and culture are indissolubly part of each other has
been strengthened even more. In place of the structuralist view of
meaning as already given in events and sayings, and as grounded in
fundamental properties of the human mind, we have come to look at the

myriad ways in which people construct and work at their social worlds through continual improvisation and interpretation. This point is critical. For it is through their interpretations of events that people make judgements, sometimes accepting them but as often contesting them. We might call this a workaday hermeneutics or perhaps hermeneutic bricolage.

One of the great past mistakes of anthropology was to define and think of language as though it were isolated from other forms of human activity. Those who would argue that language is not the essence of culture, that culture need not include language as part of its essence, and that therefore culture can exist independently of language, commit the error of imagining language to exist in a vacuum.

It is perfectly true that much theoretical linguistics depends, for its data, on the fiction of the socially decontextualized speech event: it focuses on strings of grammatically acceptable sentences that are supposed to have truth values, but completely omits any reference to the vital paralinguistic properties of gesture, mood and sentiment, and to differences of status, hierarchy and power between speakers and listeners. Even the culturally abhorrent may appear to be grammatically acceptable, if treated as governed by hermetically sealed rules standing outside of culture.

The anthropological corollary would be the absurd claim that there exists a linguistically decontextualized culture, one that operates without language and that can be studied as such. I find such an idea preposterous, as I do the idea of separating out verbal language from non-verbal communication. Indeed, the category of the verbal, set up by such separation, is itself an analytic fiction. The constitutive essence of verbal language is the same as that of non-verbal activities. To that extent we may speak of the indispensable role of language in human culture: for that which constitutes language is also that which constitutes what we more broadly call culture.

Having recognized the mutual indissolubility of language and culture, I should like to move on from the idea of each as purely semiological, and to view them rather as partaking of various semantic fields.

Semiology is not, of course, the same as semantics. Semiology is based on the idea that signs have meaning in relation to each other, such that a whole society is made up of relationally held meanings. But semantic fields do not stand in relations of opposition to each other, nor do they derive their distinctiveness in this way, nor indeed are they securely bounded at all. Rather, semantic fields are constantly flowing into each other. I may define a field of religion, but it soon becomes that of ethnic identity and then of politics and selfhood, and so on. In the very act of specifying semantic fields, people engage in an act of closure whereby they become conscious of what they have excluded and what they must therefore include.

Here I return to my claim that we should see both culture and language as having to do with communication. Of course, culture is not *only* about communication. We make things, create objects of art and spin a web of complex understandings, not all of which may be intended as ways of communicating messages. But I would insist that they are at least expressive, and to that extent open to interpretation by other people.

Semiology's mistake was to assume that the piece of wood someone has whittled into a particular shape communicates a meaning. It may have been so intended, but in many cases it results simply from an aesthetically satisfying activity. On the other hand, meaning is commonly attributed to objects and activities by people, who may then go on to insist that this is what the artist or author intended. That they may be wrong or inconsistent in their attributions is irrelevant to the fact that such interpretations occur and so set up chains of judgements. For all his brilliance in other respects, Collingwood may have been wrong to argue that an individual's *artistic* imaginings can remain outside of language. As Wollheim counters,[3] art, as a concept, only makes sense in terms of our social relationships and communications with others.

In other words, in dealing with society and culture as total entities, we do not and cannot stop short at whittled pieces of wood or the apparently random products of people's private imaginings. Rather, we find ourselves at some point examining the public, social and cultural uses to which objects and activities are put and the ways in which people classify them. The imperative of language is itself that of the cultural, and while mental excursions may well be made into non-verbal otherness, these are in the end interludes, often highly creative, which are organized over time in terms of the dispositions and orientations of linguistic–cultural communication.

It is unfortunate that the anthropological sub-field of ethno-classification essentializes people's taxonomies by claiming that these folk classifications denote central cultural truths, when in fact they are rarely clear-cut, consistent, or separable from practical activities. Of course, that persons in society do classify, albeit only provisionally and for certain purposes, is undeniable. As we well know, it is the human intellect that works to create mytho-poetic culture and science, and this is only possible thanks to the human capacity for language.

If we were to imagine human culture with classification but without verbal language, it would still include the paralinguistics of communication. The prehistoric cave paintings at Lascaux, Les Eysizes and elsewhere may be powerfully moving, and the people who produced them clearly had culture, with perhaps limited verbal language. Yet they were able to hand on – that is, communicate – the technology and sentiments both of what we have come to regard as an art form and of the various uses to which it may have been put. Pre-verbal language was clearly there right from the start. As recent research has shown, language probably began as pantomime and not acoustically:[4] it is both verbal and non-verbal and can only be treated as such. That is to say, language in this complete sense was, and still is, inextricably implicated in human culture.

But even when we do emphasize its verbal component, we find language to be indispensable in constituting later human cultures, of the kind that anthropologists have been studying for the last seventy-five years. The point is that the verbal and non-verbal dimensions of language always stand in some kind of tension with each other. For instance, 'ritual' may seem to be based on physical actions, gestures and bodily divisions rather than on verbal language, with the emphasis on the ways in which participants stand, move and act in relation to each other and to their bodies through the phases that make up the ritual, rather than on the verbal commands that may accompany these phases. Yet it is only possible to classify that ritual event in relation to other events by setting them against a wider backdrop both of people's classifications and of their judgements *over time*.

This aspect of time is crucially important. While monuments, mementos, effigies, art objects and rituals may, over many generations, reproduce motifs and phases, their relational significance is always – in the last instance – open to wider verbal contestation and appeal. And the verbal is the final arbiter in contests to decide, rightly or wrongly, what is authentic and acceptable practice.

This lies at the heart of what we may call power in culture as distinct from power in society. Social power is exercised when groups fight each other. Cultural power is exercised when groups negotiate their respective boundaries. A society totally without a language of argument is not capable of converting power contests into the moral judgements that make up the persisting differences between cultures.

Let me expand on this point. The anthropological idea of human cultures clearly rests on the idea that there are differences between them. As observers, our views of such differences are based on indigenous versions, as peoples themselves argue with each other about what is proper Nuer or Dinka custom or about who is entitled to be called Nath or Jieng. But the very notions of 'proper custom' and of ethnic belonging and entitlement take us into questions of morality and law.

It is partly in this sense that Evans-Pritchard argued that social anthropology was the study of societies and cultures as systems of morality. Can we possibly envisage human culture without such moral and legal senses of boundedness, and without the forensic argumentation that this requires? Without moral and legal argumentation, humans would literally be cast into a world of actions without words in which, ultimately, questions of inclusion and exclusion could only be settled by brute force. It is precisely the potential in human cultures to argue a case verbally, whether on moral or legal grounds, that gives them their best hope for survival.

My argument, then, is that in the evolution of territorial and material interests, even the non-verbal in human culture can only be perpetuated through the kinds of verbal persuasion needed to settle moral and legal claims, with the result that a wide variety of rhetorical styles develop – a very essence of culture indeed. In recent years, intellectuals have castigated the logocentric bias of Western thinking, and have denounced the tyranny of verbal language as a determinant of our presuppositions and a prison-house of our creative impulses. We have, I believe rightly, come to accept such critical reflection as part of our methodology. But these deconstructive critiques have only been possible through the very medium which is questioned, and which is not therefore to be regarded as discredited but, on the contrary, as continually enriched by the questions asked of it. Alongside its potential for abuse and control, verbal language has this capacity for enrichment.

In this sense language is the forensic that makes the creative possible. It is a part of our cultural heritage that has become ever more central as the complexities of power and inequality multiply in a world in which cultures are brought into confrontation and collusion. The various media that bring about such often destructive closeness – that is to say, the sounds, visual images and modes of verbal persuasion – are all in various ways evocative. But it is of course verbal language which is by far the most effective in reciprocal argument. Can anyone therefore doubt that it is the essence of culture, hopefully for good, but also perhaps for bad?

AGAINST THE MOTION (1)

ALFRED GELL

The proposition that language is the essence of culture can be contested at two levels: first, at the level of general concepts and, second, at the level of empirical generalization. That is, one can object to the very notion that culture has an essence, and this is partly what my colleague, James Weiner, is going to do. I agree with him about essences, but I am not going to anticipate his arguments. Instead I shall convert the proposition, which I also believe is conceptually objectionable as it stands, into a number of other less objectionable assertions about human evolution and cognition. I intend to show that even if one sweeps away the cobwebs that must obscure any proposition which speaks of these hardly well-delineated entities, one is left with a collection of more accessible empirical propositions that are still demonstrably false.

Taking the most charitable view possible, the proposition can be recast as making three sets of claims: one concerning human phylogeny, a second concerning human ontogeny, and another set concerning phenomenology.

1 It is claimed that, phylogenetically, a capacity for language is the crucial trait which distinguishes our species from the great apes. The modification of the cognitive apparatus to accommodate language was the crucial step in hominization.
2 Ontogenetically, it is claimed that what permits the human infant to take its place in the social world of other human beings is culture, which is conditioned by language, which in turn arose through the special evolutionary trajectory envisaged in (1).
3 Phenomenologically, it is claimed that human cultural life consists in transactions which are either speech events or are derived from them (such as interior monologues, or 'thoughts'). Selfhood is linguistic self-awareness, or inner speech. The world is construed, in thought, through language-based conceptual categories, so that culture in general has the same cognitive basis as the associated natural language.

I hope that most people would agree both that the three claims just adduced correspond to the sense of the proposition we are debating and that, all things considered, I have formulated them in a way designed to exhibit the proposition in the best possible light. But even recast in the form of these reasonable-sounding paraphrases the motion is still false, and contrary to reasonable inference and practical experience, as I shall now demonstrate.

I am not a specialist in human evolution, but I do not believe that specialists in the subject would disagree with the obvious objections which I am going to raise against the first claim.

The pongid and hominid lineages separated long before there was the remotest possibility of ancestral hominids having had the ability to' speak. This separation was initially associated with the evolution of specialized hominid lower limbs and feet (for walking and running) and the concomitant freeing of the upper limbs and hands for holding, carrying, striking and throwing. The new limb and pelvic anatomy had implications in the domains not just of feeding behaviour, but also of reproduction and social behaviour. Hominid infants can be carried, unlike pongid infants who must often ride. And it is accepted that during this early (australopithecine) stage there took place the profound alterations in reproductive biology which distinguish humans from apes – that is, the development of the monthly cycle, the disappearance of external sexual swellings, and so on, all of which provide the biological basis for the distinctively human system of mating and child-rearing. While these momentous evolutionary changes were underway, there is no suggestion, in the form either of artefacts or of changes in the cranium, of any enhancement of cognitive capacity, let alone of linguistic ability.

Thus we can forget about the australopithecine stage altogether. But it might still be felt that the later stages of hominid evolution, leading up to the emergence of *Homo sapiens*, might be more relevant. Could it not be argued that the transition from the cognitively primitive australopithecines (who persisted for a long time whilst hardly changing at all) to their modern descendants has to be explained by the introduction of a new disturbing factor triggering an evolutionary leap forward? And would not language be a prime candidate for consideration as this factor?

This raises the problem of dating the 'origin of language'. Palaeontologists preside over the evidence bearing on this question, which is not to say that they agree on its interpretation. In fact, they are divided into two camps: those who suppose that *Homo erectus*, or even *Homo habilis*, had some form of language, as against those who think that, to the contrary, language was (and is) associated uniquely with *Homo sapiens* (with a question mark concerning the Neanderthals).[5]

The argument for an early origin rests on a somewhat circuitous base, since there is nothing in the actual remains or productions of *Homo habilis* or *Homo erectus* that unambiguously suggests language. The expansion of the brain may be connected with enhanced manipulative skill rather than with language as such, and there is certainly nothing at all 'symbolic' in the appearance of any of the artefacts these creatures left behind. The argument is not based, however, on direct evidence of symbolic–linguistic processes, but on the underlying assumption that the relatively rapid evolutionary changes affecting these hominids were associated with the development of distinctively 'human' complexity in the conduct of social relationships, and that this complexity is inconceivable without abstract language and the ability to deploy symbols.

In other words, the appeal is to principle, not evidence. But what would this principle be? It is, of course, none other than the very one we are presently debating – namely, that language is the basis of human life, life shaped by 'culture'. The proposition that *Homo erectus* or *Homo habilis* 'had language' is plausible only if the proposition 'language is the basis (essence) of human existence (culture)' is true, and it is asserted only by thinkers who make this particular assumption. But if our debating proposition figures as an assumption in the thesis of the supposed language-capacity of *Homo habilis* and *Homo erectus*, then it is plain that the language-capacity of these hominids cannot be adduced as 'evidence' (even tenuous evidence) that our debating proposition is valid. That would be too blatant an instance of *petitio principii*, and obviously a worthless argument.

An alternative possibility is that the evolutionary transition from *Homo erectus* to *Homo sapiens* was triggered by the appearance of language. At this point in prehistory we find distinct local traditions in artefacts, stylization, evidence of design in the sequencing of manufacturing operations, and so on. There are also bones with scratches on them which suggest tallies, and evidence of ritual activities, not to mention art. The idea that *Homo sapiens* was, from the start, language-using is based on direct evidence, not on principle, and is indisputable. Indeed, how could one dispute this conclusion? After all, *Homo sapiens* is us, and we certainly talk.

But precisely because *Homo sapiens* is us, phylogenetic arguments have no bearing on the truth of the motion before us. If language only evolved with *Homo sapiens*, then we might as well have been concentrating on modern hominids all along, without reference to earlier epochs of human evolution. Human evolution was practically over and done with before the appearance of any evidence for language use. Language cannot therefore be considered a prime mover in the process of hominization. Our species evolved *into* a language-using one, but it evolved *as* a non-language-using one. Thus there are no grounds, in hominid phylogeny, for supposing that it was because they evolved linguistic communication that hominids evolved all the other traits which set them apart from pongids. On the contrary, everything suggests that it was because the hominids departed from the pongids in other, non-linguistic ways that they eventually came to differ from them with respect to the capacity for language as well.

Now let me turn to ontogeny. Once again I cannot claim expertise, but I do not think that any child psychologist, of whatever theoretical persuasion, would suppose that infants only form social relationships once they have acquired command of language, or to the extent that they are in command of it. On the contrary, children initiate social relationships within weeks or even within hours of birth, and these relationships are complex and nuanced long before even the most primitive sentences are produced, during the second year of life.

Moreover, even the most ardent innatists do not believe that children learn to speak spontaneously. What infants may possibly do spontaneously is listen sufficiently attentively to the spoken language they encounter, so as to form mappings between utterances and features of the world that they are able to cognize in a non-linguistic way. Outside the West, where parents are often tormented by competitive anxiety as to the verbal proficiency of their offspring, parents have tolerably clear motives in encouraging the development of linguistic ability – namely, so that children can respond to instructions concerning their proper behaviour. Language is the gateway to culture in the imperative mood; 'do this, do that, hear and obey, child'. For this reason the Greeks concluded that monkeys did not speak because they did not wish to be enslaved and made to work. This myth accurately reflects the imposed nature of language. But why, then, are humans amenable and monkeys not? Why do infants eagerly embrace the meshes of language in which they must become entrapped? Is it because language as such (and culture-as-language) is their biological destiny? I do not think so. Language is just a means, one among many. What happens is that infants are drawn into language as a by-product of their intense cognitive engagement with the world, and their intense social engagement with other persons in whose company they experience the world. The mother's words are an enfolding, caressing presence, an auditory substitute for the womb. This auditory embrace has to be elicited, however, by constant counter-prestations of childish babblings, and woe betide the unspeaking child who will be uncomforted and spurned.[6] The child is obliged to evoke its surroundings in words – its companions, toys, pets, fantasies and discoveries – as the price of recognition in the speaking world. But when we come to examine the treasures which the child is obliged to produce and display in order to be recognized, we do not find that these consist of a language as such, because the language is always provided from the outside, and is not the child's own. What the child has to display is wit, invention, imagination and insight – that is, a much broader range of cognitive accomplishments than language itself. These accomplishments may culminate in the making of utterances (not necessarily, since infants can be witty in lots of other ways) but in any case they do not originate in the cognitive mechanisms which make utterances possible.

Thus, just as we saw that language marks the conclusion of the hominization process, but not the driving force behind it, so also we may say that the acquisition of adult language is an end-product of cognitive growth in the child, but not the process of growth itself, in that the child has to have the insight, the concept, the fantasy, before these can be turned into language and used as bargaining-chips in the process of social exchange. It may be that the motives which impel children to speak are social, but this is not to say that these social motives have been linguistically implanted and stem from the necessity of language. The child's need for love, solicitude and reward precedes the onset of language and develops independently of it. Deaf or otherwise unspeaking children have all these needs, for instance, but their fully human inner life manifestly does not take place in a code that we would recognize as linguistic.

Just as language is phylogenetically a late acquisition of our species, so also it seems to me that, ontogenetically speaking, it is a phenomenon of adulthood. Children can talk of course, but complete control of language, elaborate narrative, oratory, exposition and argument are confined to adults, and often to older ones at that. In effect, it is these gradually acquired, advanced language skills which, in literate and non-literate societies alike, are the true index of social adulthood, the measure of the extent to which a person has left childhood behind.

It follows that if we accept the motion that language is the essence of culture, we are obliged to adopt an adult-centred perspective because language means *adult* language, especially that kind of super-adulthood which goes with displays of discursive wisdom. But this would be to exclude a large proportion of the human population from culture, namely the mass of infants and immature children who have yet to master advanced discursive forms – if indeed they ever will. Many never do, for structural reasons stemming from gender, status, class, and so forth, quite apart from considerations of intellectual ability.

But these unaccomplished persons excluded from the charmed circle of discursive adulthood are indisputably human, social and cultural beings. And even the accomplished speakers were once like them, having to arrive at a complex social adjustment and a sophisticated cognitive level in the process of mastering language. But if we define 'culture' as what is made apparent in accomplished language, then we have no means of understanding how culture comes into being, because culture is already fully present in the accompanying discursive forms.

If culture has an 'essence', then this must surely be what enables culture to come about as a process. Yet culture is only converted into discourse once it has already come about; language finalizes what cognition and sociality have accomplished in advance. This is not to deny the importance of language in social life, in so far as social life consists in the communication of ideas. But language is not the originating factor. It is not the essence of culture, but its surface crust or shell, marking the point where the underlying processes shaping thought, action and behaviour halt and fragment into a cascade of words.

Finally, I consider the phenomenological proposition that culture is language-like, equivalent to a language, or just *is* language, nothing more. I reject these propositions on the grounds that culture consists of concepts, and concepts cannot be understood in terms of the associated linguistic code, or the mechanisms which interpret the meanings of particular words in particular sentences. These mechanisms are formidable, but they by no means exhaust the domain of cognition in general. Or, more generally, culture includes language, but consists of much more besides.

Concepts are prior to language in so far as they consist for the most part of networks of exemplary instances and practical routines connected with them – routines which include appropriate forms of utterance, but also mental imagery, action sequences, and so on. Concepts do not come from language learning, but from experience and practice, and they are not codified as dictionary entries, or as check-lists of features.

I derive these points from Bloch,[7] who has recently emphasized the non-linear nature of reasoning in practical situations. Bloch argues that the psychological processes of deciding 'what to do next' in practical situations (he cites car driving and chess playing as examples) involve far too many situational variables to be handled in linear fashion, and can only be explained in terms of a parallel-processing or network model. Marshalling ideas into a linear chain, the eternal problem of the prose writer, imposes a very special type of cognitive demand. Most thinking is not like this at all and is only peripherally linguistic. When I think, I watch mental television and comment on it in words, and when I draw, words cease. Musicians and mathematicians likewise engage in prolonged wordless reveries. But what is culture, minus music, art and mathematics? And if culture were all words, how laborious it would be –

like the famous philosophers' Cup Final in Monty Python, in which the ball was never kicked at all!

So much for the phenomenological point. I conclude that language is by no means the essence of culture, taking 'culture' to refer to the species-wide ability to think and act in an organized and distinctively human way. But before concluding, it occurs to me that there may be some people here who are unhappy with this global concept of Culture with a capital 'C', and who may still be inclined to think that, cognitive theory aside, culture with a small 'c' – i.e. English culture, French culture, Yanomami culture – is bound up with the specifics of the English, French or Yanomami language, each considered in its particulars. I cannot address this issue in detail but I would like to make two quick points.

Holland has given us many things: the earliest and best optical instruments, some fine music, and above all an incomparable, unprecedented treasury of images; as Alpers[8] has shown, it is to Holland that we owe the birth of the distinctive visual sensibility of the modern world. But I trust I shall cause no offence to Dutch people in remarking that the Dutch language is by all accounts a complete joke, despised even by those who speak it, a language in which nothing significant has ever been, or ever will be said. Now it would clearly be a travesty of culture-historical justice to identify Dutch culture, in any way, with the Dutch language. We all 'speak' the Dutch visual language, because the Dutch gave modern man his eyes; but the Dutch verbal language has nothing to do with anything important about Dutch culture and is, I believe, destined to be abandoned altogether in the none-too-distant future.

Conversely, English is indisputably a language in which a great many important utterances and discourses have been framed. But has this been by persons who have shared the same 'English' cultural premises? Far from it. English has been, and is, spoken by a spectrum of people from every modern historical epoch, social class, ethnic and national identity. The excellence of English is that it is a common code in which mandarins and anarchists, Indians, Nigerians, Poles, Americans, etc. can frame remarks which may be deeply offensive to other English speakers, who cannot avoid understanding what their linguistic compatriots have in mind to say. It is just because language does *not* determine culture, attitudes, and values, that cultures can engage, clash, and contend. And that is good. But if languages were coterminous with their associated cultural schemata, none of that could ever happen, because merely to speak the same language would be tantamount to sharing the same ideas. And in so far as this conflict demonstrably does occur, we have proof positive that language is not the essence of culture.

FOR THE MOTION (2)

BRIAN MOERAN

In supporting the proposition that 'language is the essence of culture', I do not intend to follow the example of the previous speaker, who sidestepped the issue before us by 'recasting the proposition' in terms of the origins of language and culture. Instead, I shall follow strictly the line of thought developed by David Parkin, who has already expounded on the indisputable facts that not only is language the essence of culture as we know it, but also that it already exists in what might be called '*pre*-verbal' societies. This means that language actually pre-empts culture and that – while bewaring the Durkheimian fallacy and taking account of the Saussurean distinction between *langue* and *parole* – there is a real sense in which language belongs to culture and society before it belongs to either you or me.[9] On the one hand, only where there is language is there 'world'; on the other, language always pre-exists the individual subject and is the very realm in which she or he unfolds. Language is therefore prior to all particular individuals, their being emerging only in language. Thus being – or 'essence' – itself becomes central, for it speaks through language (without necessarily becoming reified in the process).

On the other hand, there are some who would argue that there are certain cultural forms – for example olfactory sensations, or sexuality – which stand outside of language.[10] With such an intelligent and deeply sensitive audience as yourselves, it is probably not necessary for me to rebut such putrid arguments. But in case there are some among you who have been swayed by heady words designed to confuse otherwise well-ordered thoughts, I would like to consider further the argument that there are certain cultural forms which are non-linguistic and that language, therefore, is not to be reduced to culture.

At this very moment, as I speak (a word I would ask you to mark well), thirty fully grown men of various shapes and sizes are cavorting on a rectangle of neatly mown grass somewhere in the south-western suburbs of London. To some it may not be immediately clear as to precisely why these men, half of whom are all in white and the other half in a combination of orange and green, should be expending so much energy in pushing, shoving, jumping, running, kicking and throwing themselves at one another (with an occasional judicious punch and stamp to give flavour to the occasion) in such a manner as to invite injury to skin, muscle, organ and bone – all on the off chance that one of their number will secure possession of an oval ball and with great panache leap over a white line temporarily scarring each end of the splendid green sward on which they are – I quote – 'playing'.

The progress of this particular game of rugby – for that is what, in essence, I am describing – is being eagerly watched, not merely by a referee and two touch judges (let us now use the customary terminology), but by a whole crowd of people who are themselves of all shapes and sizes, lifestyles, classes, creeds and so on – people who at various moments during the game give vent to their pleasure, ecstasy, frustration, disappointment, even disbelief by shouting, whistling, singing, groaning, clapping hands, stamping feet, waving scarves, placards, flags and so on. Such basically non-verbal activities are also indulged in by the tens of millions of people around the world – in cultures as disparate as those of Canada and Hong Kong, of Samoa and France, of Zimbabwe and Japan – who will, thanks to the wonders of modern technology, be simultaneously viewing this World Cup final on their television sets in the privacy of their homes or in the communal atmosphere of their local pub, bar, café, tea-house or palm-thatched hut.[11] For one hour and twenty minutes, with a five-minute break for refreshment, a large part of the world, it seems, is at this very moment participating in a splendidly non-verbal cultural event.

But is this really so? Can we honestly say that a game of rugby (or of soccer, *sumō*, ice hockey, hurling, cricket, American or Australian rules football) has nothing to do with language? Of course we cannot. For a start, although the fifteen men on each team are involved in a heavily physical activity, they are continually shouting instructions to one another while play is in progress (as in the simple 'pass it, Nige!', or in the coded numbers for the line-out throw – '14–21–7–92'). For his part the referee not only gives linguistically predetermined signals to indicate a goal, offside, which side is to put the ball into the scrum and so on; he will frequently reinforce these signals with verbal comment. This is, indeed, his prerogative – witness the way in which he will further penalize an already penalized player for 'talking back'. Thus, although language *should* be absent in some respects from this cultural activity, we find that it is in fact very much a part of it, as the team makes use of a (usually timely and well-planned) injury or half-time to assess the game and plan further tactics. And of course, there is a very real sense in which the fact that a game of rugby does have tactics and rules makes it almost identical to that game of chess used by Saussure to illustrate his distinction between language and speaking.[12]

This brief, but crucially important, brush with language is also found off the pitch where the crowd will give vent to its joys and frustrations. For all we know, even now the spectators at Twickenham will be engaged in a vocal rendering of 'Swing low, sweet chariot!' – a song which gains its significance both from previous international games of rugby in England and, of course, from the way in which these games have been presented to members of the 'Great British' culture.

It is here that we come to another critical point about this 'essentially' non-linguistic cultural activity, for, as we are all too aware, this game is being televised, and because it is being televised, it is being talked about. Every game of this sort employs cultural experts who act as commentators, discussing the progress of the game itself, analysing it at selected moments, and providing prognoses about its eventual result. In the process of such commentary, these cultural experts call upon a whole range of connotations and meanings that make rugby in Great Britain, American football in the USA, or *sumō* in Japan not just a 'cultural' event with a small 'c', but part of a national Cultural identity. And language is absolutely integral to this process of creating what amounts to a cultural essence.[13] The rules, traditions, regulations, expectations, and moral and ethical codes that make up this particular cultural form ultimately rely on – and cannot exist apart from – language.

Let us move on. Realizing the quickness of the sand into which their arguments are being seen to sink, opponents of the motion might anxiously point out that, although language may be essential to *our* culture, it is not necessarily the case that the same importance is attached to it in *other* cultures. In other words, the proposition 'language is the essence of culture' is seen to reflect an underlying presupposition that 'language is the essence of *Western* culture'.

As anthropologists are all too often accused of cultural bias, we must commend such sentiments. But alas! There is here a linguistic slippage which simply will not do. As my example of the game of rugby has already shown, cultural events are *always* accompanied by words of one sort or another. But language does not merely accompany culture in this manner; it *defines* culture. The same is as true of olfactory sensations – smells, to you or me – as of such pursuits as Zen meditation in which the aim is to achieve a total oneness with the world by denying the differentiation between self and other, between mind and body and hence – in our definition of the problem – between language and silence.

Even here, the only way in which we *know* that, for example, smells exist *culturally* is because they are named. The only way in which a smell can evoke some *cultural*, as opposed to *individual*, experience is through the transmission of that evocation in language. In other words, by naming or otherwise describing smells, one brings the non-linguistic immediately into the realm of language. Similarly in Zen Buddhism, by talking of the overcoming of language and the striving after oneness with the world, one presupposes that the self, and the cultural world in which the self develops, are already premissed on language. By trying to overcome a posited opposition between self and language, the Zen Buddhist monk merely asserts that language *is* already the essence of culture, and that the only way in which it is possible to reach this non-linguistic state is by means of language. Hence the importance of the *mondo* form of question and answer between master and pupil in Zen Buddhist practice. Language is denied only through language, at which point the acolyte attains enlightenment – a void wherein there is neither culture nor language. From the non-linguistic state the return to culture can only be effected by resorting again to language. Thus even in this non-Western, anti-logocentric activity, language cannot exist apart from culture, nor culture apart from language.

This brings me to one final counter-argument that might possibly be put forward as a means of subverting what is, after all, an obvious fact: that language is, as I have shown, the essence of culture. It might be argued that there are certain cultural objects or events which have persisted for decades, even centuries, and which have, as a result, proved that they are beyond language, since they clearly contain within them some 'essence' which is over and above the linguistic essence proposed here.

An example of such a cultural object with an 'essence' of this nature might be a play by Shakespeare, a painting by da Vinci, a Ming celadon pot, a Benin mask, or the cave paintings of Lascaux mentioned by my colleague. Such objects – the counter-argument would continue – are readily apprehensible as objects of 'art' because they contain within them some dramatic or other aesthetic quality that can be recognized by *anyone* in *any* culture at *any* period in time. And how do we know this? The art objects themselves proclaim their aesthetic qualities as 'aesthetic facts'.[14] Language thus becomes totally inadequate and unnecessary to the appreciation of such forms of culture.

It is clear that, in coming to terms with such an argument, we are being obliged to deal with *belief*, as much as with any form of rational thought. Do you really believe that your reaction to *Hamlet*, the *Mona Lisa*, or other such art work stems from your immediate and unmediated experience with the object itself? Of course you cannot believe this, because it is not true. You gasp in wonder at an oil painting in the Louvre, because it is in the *Louvre*, set apart from other more or less similar paintings by special lighting and curtain effects, cordoned off from too close contact with humanity by a rope that is especially watched by one or more uniformed officials. You gasp because you have been conditioned to gasp (you are in a *museum*, in front of an *oil painting*, in the presence of *guards*, and so on), not because the painting itself has some innate, essential quality that moves you into the realm of paralinguistic ejaculation or any other form of climactic ecstasy.[15]

That is all very well, you may say. But how is it, then, that *Hamlet* or the *Mona Lisa* has *always* been seen as art? Does this not prove that it *must* have some innate quality, some essence, that is apart from language? I am sorry to disappoint you, but upon closer examination of this question, we discover, for one thing, that the works of Shakespeare, for example, have *not* always been seen to be 'art', and that there was a long period in English (and world) cultural history when our 'great' 'national' playwright was ignored. And even had one of his works – let us say *Hamlet* – been seen as 'art' in all cultures of the world during all the four hundred and more years since its writing and first performance, it is obvious that my account of what *Hamlet* might mean now in certain cultural conditions, or of what it might have meant in times past, is still *my* account, inescapably influenced by my own language and frames of cultural response, and that a sixteenth-century Elizabethan courtier's account of the same play would be equally so influenced. And the same would be just as true of an eighteenth-century Guatemalan peasant's account or a twentieth-century Japanese *sumō* wrestler's account of *Hamlet*. In other words, there is no proof that what each sees as 'art' is in any way the same. All we know is that people make certain claims and put forward certain opinions which are then culturally contested.

Thus we have no choice but to accept the fact that art – *even* art – depends for its very existence on language. Art becomes 'art' because of the activities of an art world,[16] and in particular of certain critics and educators who, with the consummate linguistic skills characteristic of such other cultural experts as rugby football commentators (or anthropologists in a debating hall), lead you by a concerted rhetorical effort to be persuaded that art is beyond language, even though the only way in which they are able to try to so persuade you is through language itself.

And since, as I have shown, cultural objects can never be untied from language, regardless of the culture or historical period in which they are found, it must be admitted that the proposition before you is in fact correct: that language is indeed the essence of culture, for – as Wittgenstein so rightly said – the limits of language are the limits of the world.[17]

AGAINST THE MOTION (2)

JAMES F. WEINER

I want to thank Brian Moeran for appealing to Ludwig Wittgenstein in his last sentence, for it is with Wittgenstein, whom Pierre Bourdieu once described as the thinker he most often turned to in times of difficulty,[18] that I begin. But my remarks are not, as were Brian Moeran's, directed towards the *Tractatus logico-philosophicus*, where Wittgenstein was concerned with reference, but towards *Philosophical investigations*, where he came to grips with the notion of meaning within which the whole issue of reference is embedded. To paraphrase: 'If the words "language", "culture" and "essence" have a use, it must be as humble a one as "chair", "table" and "floor".'[19] I want to examine each term of the proposition before us, and to ask whether there are in fact recognizable entities that we can label as 'language' and 'culture'. I also want to ask whether these are in fact the kinds of things that have essences – in other words, I shall question whether there are things called 'essences' at all.

The motion also confronts us, as David Parkin noted, with that age-old paradox of hermeneutic reflexivity: how can something, namely language, be at one and the same time both the object and the tool of inquiry? That is, to what extent is the phenomenon we are now engaged in a part of the question we are addressing? How can one engage in a *debate*, using all the rhetorical skills that one's language affords, to argue that language is *not* the essence of culture? The very fact that we are here doing precisely what we *are* doing is evidence enough that for us language is, at the very least, the essence of our craft. It is one of the 'tricks of the trade' that we academics learn: we, for whom language is the sea within which we swim, can nevertheless undermine the grounds of that medium without it affecting by one whit the naturalness, legitimacy or reality we ascribe to our discourse or academic life activity. If we were whimsical about this, we could call it, in the spirit of Weber, the *routinization of nihilism*. At any rate, the point is that both the affirmation and the denial of the thesis are proof of the counter-thesis, that language is not the essence of anything. We can only accept that the proposition is false within the context of a debate such as this, whereas it will resume being 'true' in the most spontaneous, 'natural', and practical way possible once the debate is over. (That is, the possibility of both the affirmation and the denial of the thesis is anticipated by the context of this particular language game in which we are now engaged, and so both have a literal meaning only within its confines.) Another way of putting this is to say that our conscious uses and deliberate objectifications of language presuppose what David Parkin described as a prior, spontaneous, non-cognitive practical engagement with and mastery of vocal activity; and the things we can say about the various forms of speech that are the products of a very special form of objectification – a debate, writing anthropology, a myth or ritual or poem – are restricted in their scope.

In other words – and I thank Brian Moeran for pointing it out – we engage in *language games* all the time, but language games are precisely not hypostatized languages as we are used to thinking of them, and to which we think we have been addressing ourselves so far. They are more like what Donald Davidson[20] calls 'passing theories' that we take up and discard as the situation merits; working hypotheses about what the world is like and what other people are referring to when they speak. In anthropological craft, a 'passing theory' is the set of glosses we come up with for rendering the utterances of our hosts into our own language. What we construct is not a translation from the language of the X into the English language but a passing theory about how we and they have come to agree on what certain utterances and other communicative acts mean in particular contexts.

Thus I doubt whether there is anything as reified or identifiable as culture or *a* culture, or language or *a* language. Questions about language as the essence of culture cannot be divorced from parallel considerations concerning the essence of language itself, or of thinking itself, all of which have been addressed in some way in the debate so far. The question of essences, then, has to go right through to the One Big Essence (or Meaning) of it All – spirit, or mind, or deep structure, or rationality, or what have you – the quest for which has been called, perhaps sardonically, 'ontotheology' by certain European philosophers.

One would have first to identify what it is about language that makes it the essence of culture. Is it its arbitrariness? Its rule-orderedness or systematicity? Its creativity? Its poetic quality? There are as many different 'fundamental' or 'essential' features of language as there are theories of why language is essential. Each of them reveals some feature of human social life that its proponent wants to single out as being particularly redolent of cultural or human essence: speech, rhetoric, myth, ritual, magic, song, poetry, art, exchange, production – all of which I think have been mentioned in this debate. But this covers virtually everything, and what we have done is not so much shown that language is the essence of culture as demonstrated that we have no idea of how practically to distinguish between the two. If language has no special properties apart from any other kind of activity, then how can it be the essence of anything?

The problem is not that we lack a good practical grasp of what speaking and communicating are all about. It is just that we too readily turn the contingency and strategizing that mark these activities into the abstract systematics so beloved of Enlightenment approaches to human life. The historical shift, in twentieth-century philosophy, from talking about the essences of objects or things to talking about the meanings of words did not of course leave anthropology untouched, and in fact it probably represents the point at which Malinowski's anthropology became ascendant over that of Radcliffe-Brown. But there are those who remain sceptical of the metaphysical claims behind this shift. Nelson Goodman, for example, reminds us that 'philosophers [and one could include social scientists too] sometimes mistake features of discourse for features of the subject of discourse. We seldom conclude that the world consists of words just because a true description of it does, but we sometimes suppose that the structure of the world is the same as the structure of the description.'[21] The problem with us anthropologists is that *we are inclined to confuse culture and language with its means of elicitation*, or to confuse meaning with the methods we have of making it apparent, of adducing it. Part of this *illusio* by which language is hypostasized involves maintaining that there is a difference between the elements of the speech one is describing and the labels or categories one is using to analyse them (i.e. between words and parts of speech, or between metaphors and their glosses, or – in ethnoscience – between semantic markers and semantic distinguishers). Or it involves maintaining that the activity of analysis, the use of analytic language, is itself somehow free of the value-ladenness of the object of analysis – i.e. natural language itself.

There are two functional arguments – three really – which have been made today about language or, let us say, about any bit of human behaviour we may care to isolate. All of these arguments are misleading in various degrees. The first is embedded in the structuralist theory of language and it claims that all expressive behaviour has the job of *representing* something – world view, culture, cosmology, the Mind (whether 'savage' or 'bourgeois'), that is, something essential – to its users. A lot of anthropologists who think they have rejected all or some of the structuralist methodology (such as the part about binary oppositions) nevertheless hold fast to this underlying functionalism. But my question is this: why is it thought necessary for a people to represent to themselves *what they already know*, or what they already perfectly practise? What myth or ritual – it is over such things in particular that many anthropological arguments about the nature of language are fought out, as this debate shows – would have any value at all for the people who tell it or practise it if it only 'modelled' how they think? In providing the gloss to a myth, in decoding a ritual, in giving an interpretation to a work of art, in finding underlying structures to speech, it is we who make of such underlying interpretations the 'surprise of origin', as Roy Wagner once described it. In writing it, we place over practice the mask of convention; in the hearing and the interpreting of speech, we put in the conventional spaces and intervals which make language into something linear, relational and representational.[22] But the trouble with seeing any behaviour as conventional *in its essence* is that its subversive, innovative, creative, extemporizing effects – all of the strategies of improvisation that make the conventional visible and tangible – are themselves routinized, compartmentalized and conventionalized.

Language-as-representational-system, then, is not the essence of anything. There are, however, two other senses in which it could be argued that language has some essential function. The first points to its communicative function as a vehicle for the exchange of information. The second, adopting the material sense of functionality, rests on the degree to which interaction-through-speaking – the actual practice of people flapping their jaws at each other – dominates human day-to-day activity. Let us take care to keep these two senses separate: it could very well be that a lot of jaw-flapping takes place without achieving any real exchange of information at all, especially given the extraordinary vagueness and polyvocality possessed by even the simplest and most unremarkable terms, leading one commentator to remark that 'the commonplaces which make communication possible are the same ones that make it practically ineffective'.[23] Nor does it help to give scientific credibility to this confusion between levels of functionality by calling one semantic and the other pragmatic, for that merely covers over the epistemological problem posed, and also allows the semantic function to colonize the pragmatic one, producing just another 'surprise of origin'. What is left is then the second part of this functional argument, one that is ultimately more Durkheimian, that the mere activity of jaw flapping as 'work' or *energeia* is socially integrative. But it is the fact that these last two functions can be separated that, interestingly, allows us to see Durkheim in a new light (with regard to his remarks on social density).

Left with the last functionalism, the material one, we are now led to consider whether some 'cultures' are more 'vocal' than others – a question that calls up such images as that of the taciturnity of the American Indians, like the Western Apache described by Keith Basso, who often 'give up on words'.[24] We are into comparative considerations of the sort that Hubert Dreyfus exemplified by contrasting the American baby, whose parents spend a lot of time talking to it and eliciting speech from it, with the Japanese child whose parents elicit 'presence' rather than vocalization.[25] If these directions strike one as ultimately leading to such absurd questions as whether there could be a 'culture' which made do with an absolute minimum of speaking (recall how early American pioneers, confronted with sign-language-using Plains Indians, concluded that they had no faculty of speech), it is only because of an excessive focus on the *function* of speech, with its emphasis on communicating measurable quanta of information at the expense of the *being* of speech – that is, all the things that the human symbolic capacity is enabled by. (I hope you realize by now that I am using the notion of being in a way quite different from that employed by David Parkin.) Moreover, we often insist that measuring information is the same thing as counting bodies in the world, stressing its symbolic representational properties at the expense of its literalness and materiality in itself.

Speech is a part of social interaction more generally, and is inextricable from a range of other behaviours whose communicative function we take as a prior assumption rather than as a hypothesis to be tested. In other words, we have to confront the question as one about the embeddedness of vocal and verbal behaviour within a whole range of other similarly elicited behaviours such as comportment, interpersonal affection and intimacy, the learning of interpersonal spacings (i.e. the proxemic sense), daily rhythms, tastes in food, toilet habits, aesthetic judgements and so on. The point is that we are talking about the reproduction of some total bodily *habitus* and not about culture in the sense of a code that is structured by a set of rules. Like Mauss, who found that to analyse magic he had to consider the total range of social meanings that were available to a magician, the search for the essence of language or communication is coterminous with the search for whatever makes possible the relational and the conventional in human life. As Wittgenstein suggested, we have to clarify how to ontologize that question before we can know how to proceed.

Part II The debate

CHRIS KNIGHT   In order to understand what language or culture is, we have to understand what it is not. This is very difficult for social anthropologists to do. Perhaps, because they themselves live in a linguistic and cultural milieu, it is well-nigh impossible for them to obtain an adequate perspective. We came closest to it when Alfred Gell spoke about palaeontology, and about whether the australopithecines or *Homo habilis* or *Homo erectus* did or did not have language. He was quite right to conclude that they did not. In order to get any scientific perspective on this, we have to look at the capacities of our nearest relatives, the non-human primates. Specialists are currently more or less agreed that non-human primates have the capacity to sign: they use call signs and they can label objects in their environments.[26] They also have concepts, but these are not *common* concepts. For example, one chimpanzee may imitate the movements of another in reaching for a banana: the first, in its movements, is not *really* getting a banana, but does so only symbolically. Its gesture is a pretence. It is, moreover, an individual one, it is not part of a common repertoire. Thus chimpanzees have signs, and they have concepts; what they do not have is signs *for* concepts. Chimpanzees can lie, but they cannot lie *collectively*. And the essence of human culture is the capacity, collectively, to lie – that is to enact the pantomime or fantasy, for example in dance, of being (say) kangaroos when the participants are not really kangaroos at all. If chimpanzees could do this, to pretend collectively to be what they are not, then they would be moving in the symbolic domain. To do it, they would not need verbal language. What is needed is a collective repertoire of gestures; it has to be collective in order for those gestures to be shared and for their meanings to be communicable.

What I have found disappointing in the presentations is the way the issue of the relation between language and culture has been presented as one that can only be approached philosophically rather than through objective scientific inquiry. Only one speaker, Gell, has addressed the issue scientifically. I should like, however, to respond to his point that there is nothing to be learned from the phylogenetic approach since to find out what anatomically modern humans can do we need only look at ourselves. This is not so. Archaeologists and palaeontologists have shown that anatomically modern humans were living 90,000 or 100,000 years ago – possibly even 130,000 years ago – without any evidence whatsoever of music, dance, ritual and symbolic culture. It looks as though it was not until some 60,000 years ago that the revolution of the Upper Palaeolithic – a revolution that was evidently both social, sexual and political – enabled anatomically modern humans, who were potentially *capable* of language, to establish the kind of collectivity in which language could actually be developed. Simply to have a capacity does not mean that it will be realized. No doubt human beings have had the capacity to type for many thousands of years, yet this capacity has only materialized in the last few decades. Thus it is not sufficient to talk about the capacity for language that anatomically modern humans doubtless possessed; we have also to consider the political decisions that, through their establishment of collectivity, made possible its realization. That is why I would support the view that language is *not* the essence of culture. It is indeed a *part* of culture, but the central essence of culture is the collective pantomime – the rituals and gestures which, once collectivized, could be invested with a common significance.

GEORGE WILMERS   It seems to me that the term 'language' is to be understood either in such a general sense as to mean any system of communication, whether verbal or non-verbal, in which case the motion is simply tautologous, or else in a more specific sense that would exclude certain major cultural forms. Two of the most striking exclusions are mathematics and music. As regards mathematics, though some sort of language is clearly necessary for its communication, very few mathematicians would argue that language has much to do with the essence of what mathematics is about. Now as regards music, it is of course self-evident that music does not require language for its immediate communication. You might, however, still believe that the real meaning of music is somehow bound up with language, or in other words that music *requires* language for its interpretation or for its appreciation by the individual. But so far as I know, this is contradicted by physiological evidence which indicates that music is handled by a different part of the brain from the part that deals with verbal language. It is known that lesions can occur in the non-dominant hemisphere of the brain which actually prevent the appreciation of music. They have the effect on the individual that music is registered simply as sound without meaning, yet the ability of patients to understand the meaning of ordinary verbal discourse remains unimpaired. At the same time, other kinds of lesions, affecting the dominant hemisphere of the brain, prevent the individual from understanding the sounds of ordinary speech even though he can hear them. The patient cannot understand speech but can still understand music. This seems to me to be quite overwhelming evidence in support of the view that, in reality, the structures involved in musical appreciation and in the appreciation of other significant forms are quite different.

IAN DUNMORE   We need to ask what is meant by language, and what is meant by communication. Are these the same or quite different things?

RICHARD WERBNER   There may be more disagreement between those who appear to be on the same side than between those who appear to be on different sides. This puzzles me more than the question of what is meant by language and communication. On the one hand, Alfred Gell was very strict. He wanted a clear definition of what language is and implied that as a phenomenon, it is quite distinct. And for that reason, he opposed David Parkin for letting language spill over into communication or, more generally, into culture. On the other hand, James Weiner was apparently for dissolving the essence of culture, language and everything else. By the end, I felt that Gell's main opponent was his seconder!

TIM INGOLD   Three significant questions have been raised so far. First, to put it baldly, there is the question of philosophy versus science. Can the issue of the relation between language and culture be resolved through scientific investigation, for example of the palaeontological evidence or of the behaviour of non-human primates, or are we really dealing with philosophical issues that must ultimately force the practitioners of natural science to rethink their epistemological assumptions?

Second, there is the question of how language stands in relation to mathematics and music, particularly music, and of the neurophysiological correlates of that relation. To what extent does the brain structure our patterns of thought, and to what extent is it rather the case that our patterns of thought structure our models of how the brain works? (In a recent article, a distinguished neuro-physiologist claimed, in all seriousness, that when people deliver well-formed propositional statements these issue from the neocortex, but that what the author rather primly called 'curse words or interjections' issue from a more primitive part of the brain, the limbic system.[27] It does sometimes seem that the conventional dichotomies of Western thought, between reason and emotion, and even between language and music, lie behind such models of the divided brain.)

Third, there is the question of how we should define language anyway, and of the relationship between language and commu-nication.

DAVID PARKIN   I believe Chris Knight falls into the same trap as Alfred Gell. He opposes the motion, yet it was I, in proposing it, who suggested (following Kendon) that language began as panto-mime. The underlying problem lies in the arbitrary separation of the verbal and non-verbal. When Knight or Gell speaks of the 'capacity for language', that separation, which is only evident from the way language appears to us in the present, is assumed as though it were there from the start. Similarly, when Gell refers to phylogenetic and ontogenetic processes, he is judging these by their end-products. But if you take a genuinely processual view, then it is clear that language must have been preceded by some-thing. It could not arise, of a sudden, *ex nihilo*. As Kendon shows, we are mistaken in assuming that language originated with acoustic communication. It did not. It originated with a whole range of kinds of communication. And when Gell speaks of the development of language in ontogenesis, he has in mind the socialized adult, the adult that is culturally complete and therefore linguistically complete. He refers to the child as a cultural entity but not a linguistic one. And yet linguistic competence is based upon socialization. Would this not apply to cultural competence as well? If it did, then by Gell's argument, the child would be without both culture and language. And this exactly makes our point.

ALFRED GELL   The question before us is not whether pantomime is the essence of culture, but whether *language* is. And this is not a question about origins. Thus I am not saying that palaeontology is irrelevant. I would only say that it is not relevant to the truth or falsity of the motion as proposed. Clearly, the study of the role of language in human evolution is interesting and worthwhile. But the reasoning tends always to work from the present to the past, as in ethnoarchaeology where a model derived from present observation is used to interpret some prehistoric site. Now, there is clearly a connection between linguistic theory and archaeology or pre-history, in that one can use linguistic theory to make various inferences about early man. However, having made such inferences on the basis of back-projection from contemporary language, what you cannot do is to put this in reverse, using these inferences to bolster whatever conclusions you might want to reach about the centrality or otherwise of language as a contemporary phenom-enon.

I should like to add a comment regarding language, music and the brain. Although the evidence suggesting that language and music involve different hemispheres of the brain would appear to support our case, this is in fact a double-edged sword since it is clear that the dominant hemisphere is the linguistic one. Popper and Eccles,[28] for example, have argued quite cogently that damage to the centres of verbal language – i.e. Broca's area and Wernicke's area – does lead to profound transformations in people's sense of self, since their actions are no longer accompanied by an interior monologue which, at least according to some interpretations, is consciousness itself. Eccles, for example, has quite explicitly identified consciousness with Wernicke's area. Now I would not go along with this. Hence, when it comes to the neurological arrangements, I find myself on rather difficult ground in that there does exist rather specialized circuitry for managing verbal acoustic language which develops in the early stages of ontogenesis and that has nothing directly to do with music. Thus, the neurological evidence could be adduced both to support and to oppose the proposition. What we are left with is the rather more difficult problem, so far as the brain is concerned, of understanding the integration of the whole rather than of locating particular func-tions of particular parts. People like Eccles, who are keen to localize particular functions, can do so to their satisfaction. But what nobody appears to be able to say, at present, is just how all the various parts are connected up.

JAMES WEINER   I should like to respond to Chris Knight, because while it might seem that he is arguing more for our case, I would not wish my position to be identified with his. In what sense can one distinguish between what Knight calls a gesture and what he calls verbal behaviour? What is the difference between a vocal gesture, which is a word, and which is, after all, produced through bodily exertion, and the kind of gesture to which he refers? Is it supposed that the former is more symbolic, more arbitrary, more representational?

As regards the issue of music: I would not wish to dispute the findings of neurophysiologists who claim that appreciation of musical structure is somehow localized in a different part of the brain from that involved in the appreciation of verbal or sentential structure, that is of speech. But the questions I should like to pose are these: First, why, and under what circumstances, are we led to take it for granted that a piece of music has one kind of meaning and that an utterance has another? Only because we draw a distinction between these two kinds of meaning are we led to look for its neurological correlate. And second, why, and under what circumstances, are we led to believe that the skills necessary to appreciate or perform music, and the ways we learn them, are any different from the skills of speaking, and the ways that *they* are learned?

TIM INGOLD   The resort to neurophysiological evidence entails a certain risk of circularity, since neurophysiologists, too, use metaphors to describe processes in the brain, and these metaphors tend to be drawn from the language of cultural representation. You cannot, then, turn this around to claim that these representations have an independent basis in neurophysiology. It also seems to me that the problems of delimiting music as a phenomenon in its own right are rather similar to the problems of delimiting the phenomenon of language. I wonder whether the dichotomy between language and music, which some neurophysiologists would say is inscribed in the division between the two hemispheres of the brain, is not one that is specific to our own tradition of thought, and whether such a dichotomy would be recognized by people elsewhere.

IAN KEEN   The debate has been largely about boundaries, or about trying to draw boundaries around the unboundable. Yet it seems to me that the notion of culture is only useful as long as it remains vague, and that once you try to define it too precisely you are in for a lot of trouble. Though the speakers have talked about the definition of language, they have not talked at all about the definition of culture, of how culture is to be bounded. Alfred Gell, for example, included social relationships and practical knowledge, of a kind that is presumably found in non-human species as well. In that case they, too, would have culture, which leaves me quite unclear about what the concept can possibly mean. But I think David Parkin comes to much the same conclusion, for if language can be non-verbal, then other species have language, and since Parkin equates language with culture, they must have culture too. But if both Gell and Parkin arrive at a rather similar point, it is only because, for both, the meaning of culture remains more or less implicit.

DAVID PIRIE   I am puzzled that we should still be debating whether there can be languages that are not verbal. I have assumed for some time that music and mathematics are handy examples of systems that work pretty much in the way that language does, not, however, by patterning words but rather by patterning signs or symbols of other kinds. Indeed, Alfred Gell confused me with his palaeontological lesson, when he argued that the key move towards the human was the development of the lower limbs and of manual dexterity – as if these had nothing to do with any development of language. But if language can include the smile and other facial gestures, which I think is relevant in view of what Gell had to say about infant development, and if it can also involve manual gestures, I wonder whether we can any more assume that the key communicative skills of human beings are so exclusively verbal. Even accomplished speakers still find it necessary to resort to using the kinds of facial and manual gestures that I take to represent forms of communication arising much earlier – in both ontogeny and phylogeny – than verbal language. It is worth noting that all four of today's speakers, each one a sophisticated master of verbal expression, have nevertheless made eloquent use of both facial and manual gesture: indeed, to pick up the various nuances of what has been going on in the debate one has been at some advantage in being able to look as well as just to listen.

ALFRED GELL   If you allow that language can be any system of communication involving manual gestures, smiles or other kinds of expressive bodily movement, then we would have to grant language not only to chimpanzees but also to dogs, lions, and any number of other creatures. At that point it seems to me that the whole argument must degenerate: once we start asking whether, say, the smile is the essence of culture, or the fear grin the essence of culture for chimpanzees, there are no longer any boundaries for the discussion at all. To my mind, it is quite clear what language is. It is what children are taught when they learn to speak, and it is the phenomenon which is of interest to linguists. That, it seems to me, means verbal language. It does *not* mean pantomime or gestures or doing cartwheels. It means talking. If we can't recognize language when we see it on a dark night, there's no hope at all. It is of course perfectly true that language always comes in association with other things. But the phenomenon which enables you to recognize that language is *there*, mixed up with all the pantomime, is the use of words and the characteristic employment of linguistic coding, grammatical devices, and all the other contrivances by which language creates references to itself. I cannot see how one can possibly pursue an argument along the lines that language is just any kind of communication, nor do I think that music is a language. Who, after all, ever *said* anything in music?

KAY RICHARDSON   If we suppose that patterning is the essence of language, and that *meaning* – rather than language – is the essence of culture, then the question of the relation between language and culture could be rephrased as one about how we can get from duality of patterning to meaning. Would anyone on the panel care to comment on this idea?

ALFRED GELL   I am not sure whether duality of patterning as such can be regarded as intrinsic to language, because there exist linguistic systems, for example manual sign languages, which are nevertheless heavily iconic. What *is* characteristic of language, though, is abstract reference. I am not saying that language has to be verbal, but I do think that it has to be other than totally embedded in a flow of ongoing bodily movement.

KAY RICHARDSON   In terms of the kinds of things that concern linguists, I am worried about privileging sign relations over structural relations in our characterization of the nature of language, and of ignoring questions of productivity.

ALFRED GELL   There would be no productivity of language unless people had a continuous flow of new ideas. When I go on speaking, for ever and ever, it is not because I have an inexhaustible supply of language, it is because I have an inexhaustible supply of ideas! That's the difference.

DAVID PARKIN   On that point, I would agree with the previous speaker. It seems to me that theoretical linguistics has been guilty of privileging words outside of their social context. This is a danger to anthropology and to a lot of the things we stand for, because it is so easy to take a word or a string of words – an event of speech – out of context and to fit it to any situation you like. The point about the origin of language, as I said before, is that you cannot arbitrarily establish your cut-off point, as Gell seems to be saying. The origins of the capacity for language, assuming that it is acceptable to speak of such a thing, remain unknown, but we seem reasonably confident that it would have begun with non-acoustic forms of communication. I don't think it is wrong to allow an elision of concerns with communication and concerns with language. These are labels. 'Language' is a label, it's a term, 'communication' is another term. Let's accept that, phenomenologically, language and communication merge: for the challenge is precisely to escape from these kinds of terminological dichotomies.

Perhaps I could take the opportunity here to attack the common identification of language with sequentiality. Consider the sentence, 'I saw the girls crossing the street'. In terms of the patterning of words, there is of course a sequence here. 'I' comes before 'saw', which comes before 'the girls crossing the street'. But whereas the words are rendered sequentially, the concepts to which they refer exist simultaneously. There is a tension between the sequentiality of speech and the simultaneity of the concepts which are expressed by means of speech. And that is also the tension between the non-verbal and the verbal. Thus language is but an aspect of some more general form of communication.

FRANK MAGNE   It seemed that Brian Moeran, in seconding the motion, was talking about language on the level of *langue* (in the sense of a shared system of signification). In proposing the motion, however, David Parkin seemed to be talking about language at the level of *parole*. It is important to know whether the proposers agree about what language is, or about the level on which they are talking about it. I address this comment more specifically to Parkin, since he dwelled on language in its rhetorical and discursive aspects. I believe that if we were to look at the language of everyday spoken discourse, then we would find that it is not shared. Thus the degree to which language is shared within a culture may be seen to be problematic. And the one thing you do *not* find in spoken rhetoric and discourse is an essence of culture. What you find, rather, are the fragmentations of indeterminacy. In that sense, spoken language does not create but rather problematizes culture. To put it another way, unspoken language is language taken-for-granted, spoken language is language problematized and – therefore – culture problematized.

DAVID PARKIN   I think I would be in close agreement with what has just been said. I would certainly not take a view of culture as homogeneous, bounded, fixed or constant. At an explicit level, the discourse of culture may have more to do with misunderstandings than with shared understandings. I would certainly not take a view that depended principally upon the assumption of shared understandings. What we may have, however, is a polythetic recognition of there being misunderstandings which are linked to each other by virtue of previous arguments, or in other words a kind of argumentative sequence in which each contribution bears some kind of family resemblance to those preceding it. So, yes, there are misunderstandings but there are also sufficient common grounds for people to recognize where misunderstandings occur. The common recognition of misunderstanding seems to me to be what makes discourse possible between people who know they are talking the same language, in both the literal and the metaphorical sense. This is tantamount to cultural reflexivity: to culture (if you will permit the reification for a moment) constantly reflecting upon its own boundaries, its own constancy and its own cohesiveness.

CHRIS KNIGHT   I referred earlier to Kendon's work. What he did was to find a basis for distinguishing between primate call systems and language. Vervet monkeys, for example, have labels for denoting things. They have one sound for an eagle, one sound for a snake, one sound for a leopard. Thus they can name things in advance, and they agree on these names. However, they can only make the sound for leopard if a leopard is actually there. Likewise they can only make the sound for snake if a snake is actually there.[29] Now when the primatologists who discovered this played back a recording of the vervets' sound for leopard, the monkeys looked in the forest for a leopard; and when they played back the sound for snake they all looked in the grass. If you think that this is all there is to language, then clearly, vervet monkeys have language. The crucial point, however, is that the words of human language are not labels for things, they are labels for concepts. And because concepts are independent of space and time, human language is able to create a symbolic domain which is – in a sense – immortal. How did that come about? Kendon's argument is that the concepts have to come first. There have to be concepts to label before you can label them. Now non-human primates have concepts; they àre not, however, shared, and are not communicable. Each individual invents its own concepts through direct experience of the world around it. But with the advent of verbal language these concepts, for the first time, could be communicated and shared. Now as Bickerton[30] points out, it is only to the extent that the expression of concepts becomes shared, as in pantomime, that you can begin to have labels for its constituent elements. To follow this argument through is to move to the conclusion that the essence of culture is – and I will tell you what I think it is – *dance.*

JAMES WEINER   You (Chris Knight) have still not answered my earlier question. To what extent do you think these pantomimic gestures are any less arbitrary or less representational than words?

CHRIS KNIGHT   I say they are exactly the same. I refuse to accept your distinction.

JAMES WEINER   So how can you make any kind of evolutionary or developmental sequence from gesture to language?

CHRIS KNIGHT   Archaeologists and palaeontologists are agreed that until you reach the symbolic domain of ritual and dance, then you certainly do not get language as we understand it! Alfred Gell is quite right on that point. It is indeed absurd to suggest that the australopithecines or *Homo erectus* could possibly have had language; we know they did not because they had no ritual and no dance – indeed there is no evidence for such things until around forty-five to fifty thousand years ago. But to support David Parkin, it is also clear from the record of the emergence of dance, pantomime, rituals and so on, that the symbolic domain arose as a *totality.* We have to treat that domain as a whole, rather than abstracting out its linguistic component.

IAN KEEN   The last speaker's argument relies on the notion of 'concept'. According to Johnson-Laird,[31] a concept is a mental representation. It seems to me that a vervet monkey must have a mental representation in order to recognize a snake in the grass. If that argument is correct, then Knight's notion of the concept is vacuous.

CHRIS KNIGHT   But we do not find vervet monkeys dancing around pretending to be kangaroos!

ANDREW HOLDING   If, in talking about language, we are pointing to something that is not in fact *there*, then this surely proves the point made by Chris Knight, that this is precisely what apes cannot do.

CHRIS KNIGHT   If you were to see chimpanzees imitating, say, a snake or an eagle, or some other animal, then they would be in a fantasy world, they would be lying collectively. Thus even if they were just dancing their activity would nevertheless be fully encompassed within the symbolic domain. It would be *as if* they had language. They would not need the verbal side of it, but once they had got that – and we are now talking about early hominids – their brains would be quite adequate to do the rest. The dimension of collectivism is thus crucial to the very existence of the symbolic domain.

CHRISTINA TOREN   True, the concepts come first, but what language allows you is recursiveness, the ability to make attributions about attributions. This, then, is responsible for the enormous explosion of words, for productivity.

CHRIS KNIGHT   Exactly. With language you can continually refer to your own doubts, and to those that are collectively felt.

TIM INGOLD   As I understand it, the crucial problem here is one about how words acquire meaning, and about whether the difference between the way in which words and other kinds of gesture acquire meaning is really one of degree or of kind. We might say of the gesture that, in a sense, it delineates its own meaning. The question is whether this is also true of words. Are words fundamentally expressive, in that sense, or is meaning something that is attached *externally* to words – as is assumed by linguists who speak of words being attached to concepts? Chris Knight's argument appears to envisage a quite basic difference in this respect: a quantum jump between the ways in which non-verbal gestures (such as the signs of non-human primates) acquire meaning and the ways in which the words of human language acquire meaning. Words, he tells us, are different because they are attached to concepts. Thus we are faced with a problem concerning the status of the concept itself, of the mental representation. Do we have to suppose that such representations are implicated in language at all? Do words actually take their meanings from their attachment to mental images that are mapped on to an otherwise meaningless world 'out there', or do they gather their meanings from the relational properties of the world itself, given the situational contexts of utterance and the histories of past usage?

JAMES WEINER   There is very little evidence to suggest that we can distinguish between the word and the concept. This was the basis of Emile Beneviste's[32] critique of Saussure. There is no objective way of showing that in the act of speech itself, we actually make any distinction between the word and the concept. For all practical purposes, the word *is* the concept. We learn about both at the same time, and as we do so, we have no way of practically distinguishing between them. It is only in retrospect, when we come to speculate on the nature of language itself, that we begin to separate word and concept and to theorize on the relationship between them.

The point that I made in my presentation was that it is only in the restricted context of what is going on among us here, in this room, that the various arguments that have been put forward can be judged true or false. Nothing that exists outside of this room is, in any practical sense, going to affect the outcome of the debate. Our appeals to theory or to particular 'facts' are speech acts whose sense is bound to the context of the here and now.

GEORGE WILMERS   But we are also bringing in various paraphernalia from the outside.

JAMES WEINER   Yes, and tomorrow we may bring in other things, or use the things we brought today in completely different ways.

CHRISTINA TOREN   Underlying this proposition is a concern about the way we anthropologists do our work, about what precisely we are doing when we attempt to analyse the practices of other people. For the proposition implies that culture can be analysed *as if it were* a language. Yet we have spent years showing that this is just what *cannot* be done. There are whole domains of human behaviour which, when you come to analyse them, clearly turn out *not* to be language-like. What is important is to look at the interplay between those aspects that do have language-like properties and those that do not.

Of course, one idea that has always been very important in American cultural anthropology, by contrast to the British social anthropological tradition, is precisely that culture is immanent in language, that it comes already packaged in linguistic forms. But we know this is not the case: neither is language ready-made, nor does culture come ready-made with language. Concepts are themselves the objects of description; they are things we work at, and whether in language or in any other medium, they have to be built up or constituted over time. In this connection, Alfred Gell's point about ontogeny is extraordinarily important. I strongly disagree with Brian Moeran and David Parkin, since both of them took an adult-centred perspective. If you try to understand how children come to acquire those notions that inform, say, the political economy or the rituals of the society in which they grow up, then you get a picture very different from the kind of seamless whole envisaged by the proposers. It is a picture full of shifts and discontinuities.

With respect to the neurophysiological arguments, I believe it is a mistake to infer, from looking at what people with lesions in particular areas of the brain can or cannot do, that each area is responsible for just that component of behaviour in which the sufferer experiences disability. The challenge is to understand what is happening in the whole brain, and indeed in the nervous system as it extends beyond the brain. The latest neurophysiological evidence suggests that even the simplest acts of perception involve the entire nervous system, from its most distal points across all regions of the cortex. So, for example, the registering of a smell does not happen in some particular, specialized 'bit' of olfactory cortex. It is rather the whole cortex that is activated. Moreover, for any individual the pattern of nerve firing changes over time.

What this means is that we are not only cultural but *biologically* cultural, and hence our prime task must be to understand the way in which history informs the processes of ontogenetic development whereby we come into being as cultural organisms. In this respect I am entirely in agreement with James Weiner when he says that he wants to break free from the terms of this debate. The proposition itself actually leads us astray.

GEORGE WILMERS I never meant to suggest that all brain functions are localized, and I am well aware that recent theories in neurophysiology hold that the entire brain is involved in many functions. This does not, however, allow you to ignore the evidence. If lesions in particular parts of the brain affect or have a tendency to affect the understanding and production of speech, and if lesions in other parts of the brain affect the understanding and appreciation of music, then this *is* evidence that the structures which enable one to understand music are inherently different from those which make possible the comprehension of speech.

CHRISTINA TOREN But you are leaving out ontogeny. Almost always, in studies of people with brain damage, the subjects are relatively mature. They are people who, before the damage occurred, had already acquired musical, linguistic and other abilities. This makes an enormous difference. Suppose instead that one were experimentally to take a batch of humans at birth, to damage different parts of their brains, and then to observe what happens. Then you might find out something interesting! Such an experiment is of course practically inconceivable; my point, however, is that from studies of people whose mature capacities have been impaired we cannot find the answers to our questions about how these capacities are formed in the first place.

DAVID PARKIN   Let me respond to Christina Toren's charge of adult-centredness. I think she has got it quite wrong. Of course we are taking an adult-centred view because, in addressing the proposition, we are dealing with some kind of relationship between language and culture. Now, if we were dealing *only* with, say, the possibilities of the emergence of adulthood, then that would be a different matter altogether. But our view is adult-centred because we are dealing with power, with authority, with the capacity of individuals who *have* reached adulthood to implant ideas about culture. Cultures are not self-generated.

CHRISTINA TOREN   But children are people, not implants. And they build up or constitute their notions over time in the light of their experience.

DAVID PARKIN   Do you then feel that adults are irrelevant to this process?

CHRISTINA TOREN   Of course not. But what you discover by looking at the process of ontogeny is precisely how adults, as it were, deceive themselves, or in Bourdieu's terms, how they become enchanted by their own practice.[33]

DAVID PARKIN   That's possible, but it doesn't show how they have the authority and the power to limit, prescribe and proscribe the directions which children take in their development of speech. And that's critical. The world is an adult world, based upon the uneven distribution of power. Whatever the possible influences on children's development may be, most of them are heavily weighted in favour of adults. This is a sad fact that bodes ill for the cause of children's liberation.

CHRISTINA TOREN   Of course they are weighted in favour of adults, but that doesn't permit you to say that culture is what adults do . . .

DAVID PARKIN   I never said that.

IAN KEEN   But your view is nevertheless a very Eurocentric one. Among the Yolngu, an Aboriginal people of Arnhem Land, Australia, children have their own autonomous culture and, within a certain age range, adults have very little control over it. From toddlers to pre-adolescents, these children are highly autonomous;

indeed, in many Yolngu settlements this autonomy has been the cause of all kinds of social problems. I agree that adults impose constraints and draw boundaries, but there is, nevertheless, a lot of autonomy there.

DAVID PARKIN   Surely, such autonomy may extend from the age of ten here, from the age of five there, from the age of one elsewhere. But there must be a limit.

MARYON MACDONALD   I work as an anthropologist in the European Community, and I find little difference between what I have just been studying in Brussels and what I now hear in this debate. We should remember that considerable public funds have been devoted to the support of languages in Europe because there are people 'out there' who, as a matter of common sense, *believe* that language is the essence of culture. Similarly, there are others who argue that dance is the essence of culture. I make this point because no one in this debate has attempted to view the motion as an object of *ethnographic* interest. I agree with many of the points that have been made, for example, that we cannot necessarily turn to neurophysiology as providing an innocent representation of the world, though some aspects are doubtless more resistant to deconstruction than others. And the same goes for palaeontology and primatology. But the motion as proposed is not in principle resistant to deconstruction, and I think we should go ahead and treat it as something of ethnographic interest, situated historically, and to go on from there to examine our own assumptions.

BRIAN MOERAN   I did in fact introduce an ethnographic example into my own presentation, referring to Japanese society and Zen Buddhism, where much emphasis is placed on the non-linguistic aspects of enlightenment. There is a great argument, the details of which need not detain us, concerning the question of whether Japanese people are – shall we say – 'non-linguistic'. The Japanese are inclined to set themselves off against 'logocentric' Westerners in these terms, yet at the same time they have major schools and educational institutions which rely totally on language and the use of the written word, and which are seen as laying the foundations for success in life. There is clearly a paradox here. Part of the problem is that the Japanese are trying, at one and the same time, both to set themselves off against Westerners, and yet to project themselves as belonging to an advanced industrialized society. So they put forward the notion that the essence of Japanese culture is non-linguistic as a kind of counter-Orientalism, in order to resist the Orientalism projected by the West. My point is just to show that the claim to a non-linguistic essence is grounded in a cultural discourse that is itself couched in the medium of language.

PAUL BAXTER   I would like to draw attention to the situation of people with severe hearing impairments. For centuries, certainly in Europe, such people have been culturally and socially marginalized. In the first decades of this century there was a strong movement, which actually began here in Manchester, to overcome this by teaching the deaf to speak, and thereby to promote their integration into society and culture. For many this worked. But in last twenty years or so, particularly in America, the deaf have been saying 'We do not want this; we have a language, which is a sign language but not a vocal language, and it has as much of a right to exist as any other. We have been culturally colonized and, as a sign now of our own cultural integrity, our language must be recognized as standing alongside and on a par with all other languages.' For these people, at least, the language itself has come to be the very essence of what they describe as their own culture.

IAN KEEN   Let me restate my point: that what is important about language has been lost because the debate has been so much about how to put boundaries around it. What, unfortunately, we have not discussed here is the importance of language in the constitution of praxis, although the matter was touched upon in relation to the question of mathematics and music.

DAVID PIRIE   One speaker (Alfred Gell) saw fit to say that Dutch painters were responsible for the way in which modern *man* sees the world, as though this was the only kind of vision that really matters. I wonder whether this is an example of how language can come before ways of conceptualizing.

TIM INGOLD   Your point, as I understand it, is that there may be a gender aspect to our comprehension of what language is.

VALRETER THOMPSON   I think it is important, too, to be aware of the way language has been used as an instrument of power in the field of education – for example, to disadvantage black people in schools and universities.

TIM INGOLD   The key terms, language and culture, are of course caught up in a system of power relations. We have heard about power relations between parents and children, between men and women and between educators and educated. Moreover, as we well know, the word 'culture' is situated in the nexus of power relations between Western nations and colonized peoples. It is important to recognize that both 'language' and 'culture' subsist within relations of this kind.

DAVID PARKIN   I want in summing up to make two main points. First, it is quite true that we have focused more on language than on culture. We tend to evade the question of the definition of culture because we are perpetually worried that if we examine it too closely it will slip away from us and we will be left without a subject matter. One of these days we will have to face this problem; meanwhile the concept of language calls up such a rich web of metaphoric connotations that however long we go on talking about it, we can be confident that it will never disappear. Now it seems that there are two general approaches to thinking about what language is. One takes a broad view of language as having to do with symbolic communication. Some concern was expressed about this, as though by broadening out our notion of language in this way we might lose sight of something essential, something so well refined by successive generations of linguists. I do not accept that concern: indeed, I think that as anthropologists we should be forever deconstructing and recasting our concepts, including that of language. The second view of language is the narrow one, 'language-as-we-conventionally-know-it', meaning by that, the kind of language I am using now but presumably without hands, without the smile, without the expressive modulations of voice and gesture. It is precisely this narrow view of language, as consisting of grammatically acceptable sentences totally divorced from the social context of utterance, that has caused so much confusion in theoretical linguistics, and it is surely antithetical to the spirit of anthropology.

My second general point is: why this motion? Indeed, we should situate ourselves historically in terms of our intellectual discipline, and I wonder whether the proposition, 'language is the essence of culture', is not really a polite or evasive rendering of an altogether different proposition, which is that language *essentializes* culture. This is often what is really at issue – the essentialization of a whole range of activities through the privileging of language which, for this reason, appears to become so important to us in modern society. I cannot dissociate the use of language from power; I cannot dissociate its evolution from the organization of human (or hominid) groups, and I cannot divorce it from the fact that all such groups have evolved through struggle. So to me language emerges from struggle even as cultures defend themselves, advance themselves, and achieve their distinctiveness. As I have said before, language and culture are indissolubly involved in each other, and I don't feel at all ashamed to advocate that broad proposition.

ALFRED GELL   I would like to return to Richard Werbner's point, that there seems to be some difference between James Weiner and myself on why the motion should be rejected. First of all, both logically correct and fallacious arguments can be adduced to support a conclusion which is none the less true. That is, true consequences can be derived from false premises as well as from true ones. So on its own, the mere fact that we might adduce different arguments to back up the same conclusion does not make the truth of our conclusion any less likely. But I do not in fact believe that there is such a profound difference between us. I do not see how anyone could defend the idea of anything, like language, being the essence of anything else, like culture. I agree entirely with what James Weiner said on these points, and I would have made them myself had I not known he was going to do so.

What I tried to do, however, was to look at the kinds of lower-level generalizations from which the idea of a language-essence might conceivably have been distilled, and to show that these generalizations do not stand up to critical scrutiny. I do not think that we can define language once and for all in the context of a debate such as this, nevertheless I see no reason to opt for the ultra-inclusive definition of language which has been advocated by some people here, simply because it encompasses everything. After all, humans really do produce verbal utterances, and there really are areas of the brain which are demonstrably involved in the production and comprehension of speech and which, if interfered with, cause various kinds of aphasia. Moreover, the asymmetry between the two hemispheres of the brain is not difficult to demonstrate experimentally, and has even been established cross-culturally – so we know it is not just members of our own culture who are subject to this particular pattern. Thus there is abundant evidence for the existence of something which, although we may not be able to define it precisely, is manifestly focused around sentential logic, the creation of discourse, and so forth. It is sufficiently readily observable not really to require much by way of further definition.

It is clear, too, that it does not constitute an essence – not, at least, an essence of culture. Let us say that the essence of Euclidean geometry is the logic of proof. Although this logic does not constitute a theorem in itself, its application in the process of proof is surely what geometry is all about – it's the whole purpose of the exercise. Now if language were an essence of human culture, then one should be able to identify it in the same sort of way: as providing a means for framing discourse in the form of logically connected sentences, and for the demonstration of propositions through reasoned verbal argument. And, as such, it would have to be an essence not just of what has been going on amongst us here, but of human life everywhere. Yet nobody could possibly imagine that our debate here is anything other than a highly specialized exercise in academic discourse. The idea that we should project the format of the academic debate as a model for what goes on generally in human life and experience seems to me utterly preposterous. Language may be the essence of academic debate, much as the logic of proof is the essence of geometry; but language is not the essence of *culture*.

BRIAN MOERAN   I am not sure that our positions are so different. To some extent the recasting of the motion in phylogenetic terms, in terms of language standing at the *origin* of culture, has sidestepped the issue. This is not what we were arguing at all. We were saying that language and culture are part and parcel of each other, and we tried to focus on social aspects of *language-in-culture*. As David Parkin said, the constraints of language are not fixed or given. There are forces that produce them, that modify them and that transform them in the course of actual communication. So language is not a monolithic system but a process that is continually going on. And this is the sense in which it may be said to constitute the essence of culture.

JAMES WEINER   My concern was to expose many of the ideas that remain implicit in our view of what language is, for example that it provides a vehicle for the external expression of internal mental states, that speaking is voluntary activity which is all the time under conscious control, that it is intrinsically creative, that it is some-thing that is always moving from the 'inside' to the 'outside'. And while we do nowadays make a point of stressing that the ultimate arbiter of language is always social, we nevertheless continue to read back into the individual the *source* of language. My argument, then, was against logocentrism. Logocentrism is not just a matter of seeing everything as a form of language or as a form of representation. It is rather a matter of seeing the individual, the knowing subject, as having independent access to a total picture of his or her world. But the fact is that whenever we focus our attention on something, something else drops out of the field of view. When the Yolngu of Arnhem Land (to whom Ian Keen referred in his comment) consciously assert that children are autonomous, by the same token they are rendering more problematic the fact of parental control over them. For all that I agree with much of what she said, to speak – as did Christina Toren – of children voluntaristically constituting their own world is only to make problematic the extent to which children are, in a very real sense, reproducing what they have learned from their parents.

And so we cannot talk about what is internal to the subject independently of that subject's positioning in a field of external relations: that is, we must consider the subject in a context of intersubjectivity. In much of what has been said today, there is still a discernible attempt to hold on to the notion that the subject is ontologically *prior* to his or her relations, allowing for a one-way movement from subject to knowledge to concept to expression. It is against that very logocentric (and Eurocentric) notion that I was arguing.

NOTES

1 M. Merleau-Ponty, *The phenomenology of perception*, trans. C. Smith, London, Routledge & Kegan Paul, 1962, p. 187.
2 C. Lévi-Strauss, *Structural anthropology*, Harmondsworth, Penguin, 1968, p. 83.
3 R. Wollheim, 'Art as a form of life', in *Philosophy as it is*, eds T. Honderich and M. Burnyeat, London, Allen Lane, 1979.
4 A. Kendon, 'Some considerations for a theory of language origins', *Man* (N.S.) 26, 1991, pp. 199–222, esp. p. 215.
5 W. Noble and I. Davidson, 'The evolutionary emergence of modern human behaviour: language and its archaeology', *Man* (N.S.) 26, 1991, pp. 223–54.
6 D. Anzieu, *The skin ego*, New Haven, Yale University Press, 1989.
7 M. Bloch, 'Language, anthropology and cognitive science', *Man* (N.S.) 26, 1991, pp. 183–98.
8 S. Alpers, *The art of describing: Dutch art in the seventeenth century*, Harmondsworth, Penguin, 1983.
9 See also T. Eagleton, *Literary theory*, Oxford, Blackwell, 1983, p. 71.
10 Even with such cultural forms as these, linguistic terms tend to pervade their description. Alfred Gell has himself referred elsewhere to 'the restricted language of smells', while Foucault calls smell 'a great sexual sermon'. See

A. Gell, 'Magic, perfume, dream', in *Symbols and sentiments: cross-cultural studies in symbolism*, ed. I. M. Lewis, London, Academic Press, 1977, p. 26; M. Foucault, *A history of sexuality, vol. 1: an introduction*, Harmondsworth, Penguin, 1981, p 7.

11   Readers dubious of the spread of television sets to native huts are referred to the Far Side cartoon, 'Anthropologists! Anthropologists!', by Gary Larsson.

12   F. de Saussure, *Course in general linguistics*, translated and annotated by R. Harris, London, Duckworth, 1983, pp. 87–9.

13   B. Moeran, 'Individual, group and *seishin*: Japan's internal cultural debate', *Man* (N.S.) 19, 1984, pp. 252–66.

14   See, among others, Benedetto Croce, *Aesthetic – as science of expression and general linguistic*, London, Macmillan, 1909.

15   See P. Bourdieu, *Distinction*, London, Routledge & Kegan Paul, 1984.

16   See H. Becker, *Art worlds*, Berkeley and Los Angeles, University of California Press, 1984.

17   L. Wittgenstein, *Tractatus logico-philosophicus*, London, Routledge & Kegan Paul, 1981.

18   P. Bourdieu, *In other words*, Oxford, Polity, 1989, p. 9.

19   L. Wittgenstein, *Philosophical investigations*, Oxford, Blackwell, 1953, No. 97.

20   D. Davidson, 'A nice derangement of epitaphs', in *Truth and interpretation*, ed. E. LePore, Oxford, Blackwell, 1984.

21   N. Goodman, *Problems and projects*, Indianapolis, Bobbs-Merrill, 1972, p. 24.

22   See J. Derrida, *Of grammatology*, Baltimore, Johns Hopkins University Press, 1976.

23   P. Bourdieu, 'The historical genesis of the pure aesthetic', in *Analytic aesthetics*, ed. R. Shusterman, Oxford, Blackwell, 1989, p.154.

24   K. Basso, '"To give up on words": silence in Western Apache culture', *Southwestern Journal of Anthropology* 26, 1970, pp. 213–30.

25   H. L. Dreyfus, *Being-in-the-world: a commentary on Heidegger's 'Being and Time, Division I'*, Cambridge, MA, MIT Press, 1991, pp. 17–18.

26   A. Kendon, 'Some considerations for a theory of language origins', *Man* (N.S.) 26, 1991, pp. 199–222.

27   R. E. Myers, 'Comparative neurology of vocalization and speech: proof of a dichotomy', in *Human evolution: biosocial perspectives*, eds S. L. Washburn and E. R. McCown, Menlo Park, CA, Benjamin Cummings, 1978.

28   K. R. Popper and J. C. Eccles, *The self and its brain*, Berlin, Springer International, 1977.

29   R. M. Seyfarth, D. L. Cheney and P. Marler, 'Monkey responses to three different alarm calls: evidence of predator classification and semantic communication', *Science* 210, 1980, pp. 801–3; D. L. Cheney, 'Category formation in vervet monkeys', in *The meaning of primate signals*, eds R. Harré and V. Reynolds, Cambridge, Cambridge University Press, 1984.

30   D. Bickerton, *Language and species*, Chicago, University of Chicago Press, 1990.

31   P. Johnson-Laird, *Mental models: towards a cognitive science of language, inference and consciousness*, Cambridge, Cambridge University Press, 1983.
32   E. Beneviste, *Problems in general linguistics*, Coral Gables, University of Miami Press, 1971.
33   P. Bourdieu, *Outline of a theory of practice*, Cambridge, Cambridge University Press, 1977, p. 167.

1992 debate
The past is a foreign country

Introduction

Tim Ingold

The past is a foreign country: they do things differently there.
L. P. Hartley, *The Go-Between*

The ethnographic present is dead, but we do not know with what to replace it. The trouble with the ethnographic present – that style of describing forms of life other than our own as though what people say and do now they have always said and done, and always will barring external intervention – is that it robs the life of these people of its intrinsic temporality, removing their society from the 'timestream of history in which ethnographers and their own societies exist'.[1] For the ethnographer there is life after fieldwork, and for the people, too, life goes on after the ethnographer's departure, just as it did before his or her arrival on the scene. The ethnographic encounter is, after all, but a moment in the historical unfolding of a field of relationships in which all parties are inevitably bound up. But to represent the people as existing forever within that moment, caught – as it were – in suspended animation, is to consign their lives to a time that, in the experience of the ethnographer, has already been left far behind. As with the dreamlike world of our childhood recollections, where time stood still, the ethnographic present is the projection, on to another place and another people, of our own past – a 'foreign country', where they 'do things differently'.

These memorable words, penned by L. P. Hartley in his novel *The Go-Between*, strike at the heart of the problem: that to replace the ethnographic present as a convention for describing the life of other peoples, we have to think again about the ways in which we understand the past in our own lives. And it was to address this problem that Hartley's phrase, 'The past is a foreign country', was adopted as the motion for the fifth debate in this series. As the exchanges recorded here reveal, the debate opens up a series of quite fundamental issues concerning the relation between past and present, the construal of difference, the awareness of time, and perhaps most importantly, the respective roles of history and memory as modes of apprehending the past or of bringing it to bear in the present. Indeed, the contrast between what could be called *historical* and *memorial* approaches to the past emerges as a key axis of division between the two sides of the debate. David Lowenthal, proposing the motion and the author of a book that bears Hartley's phrase as its title, is himself a historian; Gillian Feeley-Harnik, opposing, is an anthropologist, as are the two seconders, Penelope Harvey and Susanne Küchler. This is not primarily a debate, however, between the disciplinary orientations of history and anthropology. To the extent to which these orientations can be distinguished at all (a moot point), the issues addressed here are common to both.

Persons and events are not, of course, intrinsically of the past. They become so, as Harvey points out in the discussion, only in relation to the moving prospect of the present. But this observation immediately raises a dilemma. On the one hand the past, being by definition that which is not directly 'present' to consciousness, seems cut off from the world of our contemporary experience. In Lowenthal's words it is over, finished. Like our childhood we have left the past irrevocably behind. Yet on the other hand, have not the events of our childhood played a formative role in the development of our own capacities of awareness and response? If, as history, the past lies *behind* us, as memory it remains very much *with* us: in our bodies, in our dispositions and sensibilities, and in our skills of perception and action. In the first sense, the past seems *alien* to present experience, in the second it appears to be *generative* of that experience. Is the past, then, as the proposers of the motion would have it, a foreign country, or are we rather – to paraphrase Küchler's position in this debate – creatures of the past abroad in the present?

In this question lies the problem of the relation between history and memory. The problem is a formidable one, not least because remembering is a notion that can be interpreted in so many different ways. One sense refers to acts of recollection or commemoration, in which events which actually or supposedly took place in the past are represented (literally, made present again), whether in writing, oral narrative, monumental sculpture or dramatic performance. However much it may strain towards authenticity, such representation can never evoke the same response from readers, viewers or audience as did the events depicted from those who lived through them, if only because current perceptions are coloured by what came after, and because background features of an event, that may have gone unremarked by the original participants, are foregrounded in its representation as 'signs of the times'. For this reason authentic reconstruction, far from bringing the past to bear in the present, tends to highlight the disjunction between them. Indeed, as Weiner observes in an acute comment, it is the very fact of repetition – the going over again of past events that is always entailed in the production of history – that establishes the horizons of the present, dividing the witnessing of events from their commemoration, perception from recollection.

There is another sense, however, in which remembering is not so much something people do, as something that is implicated in all that they do, in that it underwrites their capacity to act effectively, and without accident, in their surroundings. This capacity is not, of course, unique to human beings; indeed, many other animals may be said to deploy memory in this sense, even though they presumably lack the linguistically grounded ability of humans to reflect upon, and to commemorate, past experience. Memory, here, refers to the way in which specific competencies are built into the bodily *modus operandi* through repeated trials. In human societies, this is the essence of learning by apprenticeship.[2] Our everyday lives call for the employment of countless skills, in moving about, using tools, speaking, writing, wayfinding and so on, most of which have been acquired through long and sometimes arduous practice. By and large, the work of memory in the performance of such tasks is concealed behind their smooth and successful accomplishment. Memorization is a problem for the novice, not for the experienced practitioner. It is when things go wrong, due to an insufficiency or deterioration of know-how, that our normal dependence on mnemonic processing becomes painfully evident.

There is an intimate relation between commemoration and memorization that has yet to be fully unravelled. Both involve repetition. The telling of stories, for example, may be regarded in two ways: from the point of view of the narrator, as a celebration of the characters and events of the tale, and from the point of view of the listeners, as part of an ongoing education of the senses. This duality is evident even in the meaning of the verb 'to tell'. This can, on the one hand, refer to the act of narration in recollecting events that took place long ago. But it can also refer to the discriminating judgement of the perceptually skilled practitioner, who can 'tell' – for instance – whether a note is out of tune or the whereabouts of an animal from its tracks. In the first sense – telling as narration – the past is set off as the object of an account told in the present; in the second sense – telling as perception – past experience provides the very foundation, through practice and training, for present skills. Thus the two meanings of telling correspond closely to the varieties of remembering outlined above, as well as to the contrary senses of the past – as behind us and as with us – that characterize the initial positions of the proposers and the opposers of the motion.

Overshadowing the entire debate, however, is the spectre of 'presentism', the doctrine – classically enunciated by Malinowski – that perceptions of the past, understood as facts of the present, are wholly responsive to current interests, unconstrained (in Peel's words) 'by the "otherness" of what the past really was'.[3] The case for the proposition lies largely in the need to recognize this otherness, and to quell the tendency towards presentism in our own thinking. We are all too inclined, Lowenthal observes, to populate the past with people like ourselves, pursuing the same aims and responding with similar feelings, albeit dressed up in different cultural costumes. A similar view of cultural diversity – that Marett once called a 'tissue of externalities'[4] – lies behind the commercially motivated attempts, described by Harvey, of the world's nation-states to put their traditions on display for the enjoyment of the universal tourist. Whether the concern is with people of the past or of the present, otherness is here reduced to the cosmetic variety of consumer choice.

But if the terms of the motion set it explicitly against presentism, the speakers for the opposition are equally concerned to show that their rejection of the motion is in no way based on presentist assumptions. It is of course true, as Feeley-Harnik recognizes, that we have no way of knowing people of the past save through our present selves. But the self is not to be identified with a free-floating intellect, detached from the conditions of human bodily existence in the physical world. It is rather a unity of mind and body, whose very placement in the world presupposes a history of past relationships. Enfolded in the consciousness of the self, as its memory, this past is active in the present. Implied here is a radical critique of the orthodox notion, in cognitive psychology, of memory as a *store*, a cabinet of images and recollections from which the mind can pull out whatever it needs for current purposes. This is the kind of memory that we attribute to computers, as measured by their information storage capacity. Yet for Feeley-Harnik, such memory is fundamentally *amemorial*, divorced as it is from the movement of consciousness, the passage of generations and the flow of real time. It is precisely this effacement of time, collapsing all lived experience – past, present and future – on to a single plane of virtual reality, that characterizes what Feeley-Harnik sees as the intense presentism of contemporary perspectives.

Much has been written on the relation between history and anthropology. Curiously, however, this literature makes little mention of memory. Perhaps this is because the study of memory was assumed to be exclusively a matter for psychologists. It is no wonder, then, that they came up with a concept of memory that was remarkably insensitive to both time and social context. Such a concept is no longer tenable. With this debate, remembering is at last returned to where it belongs, in the active and creative involvement of real people in a real world.

Part I The presentations

FOR THE MOTION (1)

DAVID LOWENTHAL

This proposition differs from others previously debated here in at least four ways. First, it is a quotation; second, it is the title of a book; third, it is a metaphor; fourth, its chosen champion is a non-anthropologist.

Let me address the quotation, which comes from L. P. Hartley's novel *The Go-Between*. Hartley's opening line, 'The past is a foreign country', is the title of my own book; my main theme is his next phrase, 'they do things differently there'.[5] Both lines are packed with meaning for life, life stories and history proper. The gulf between childhood and maturity echoes that between then and now, *historical* changes in English manners and mores. Ability or failure to heed such changes counterpoints *The Go-Between*'s private tales.

Significantly, the film-script of Hartley's book omits these lines and shuns their implications. The past is not foreign or different. The entire weight of the film rests on the shock of sexual revelation, the calamitous gulf between the world as seen by young Leo and by the adult lovers. History vanishes; change is simply life-cycle nostalgia. For film-makers and film-goers the past is *not* a foreign country.

In neglecting the novel's social and historical dimensions, *The Go-Between*'s film-script resembles many popular tales set in other times or bridging past and present. Beyond their costumes, docudrama characters differ only in age and gender or status; the same motives and mentalities are shown to animate mythical or medieval as modern folk. In stories stripped of specific place or context, elemental passions are enacted on a timeless stage.

The second departure is that our proposition derives from my book. Do not conclude that I have a vested interest in defending it. My use of the phrase did not mean that I believed the past *was* a foreign country. I chose it to reflect a profound shift in scholarly perceptions of the past since the late eighteenth century. But to show that the past is *viewed* as a foreign country is not to claim that it *is* one.

Third, the metaphor. No metaphor is strictly true, or it would not be a metaphor. Many metaphors are such common coin that we forget they are not literally true. That is not the case with 'the past is a foreign country' – at least not yet. Hence there are logical grounds for dismissing the motion straightaway. To avoid this trivial impasse, we must hold to metaphorical intent, not insist that the past be shown as *actually* foreign.

Fourth, I speak as a historian who sees the past as contingent and disorderly, patterned only by hindsight. Historians have spent two centuries sloughing off universal explanations; few now doubt that the past is foreign. Why should anthropologists? Perhaps your doubts reflect the discarding of the notion of a pre-contact ethnographic present, a once-foreign past now exposed as a flagrant fraud.[6] Perhaps, with Luisa Passerini, anthropologists who fault historians for neglecting unsung, anonymous lives are still seduced by the deceptive timelessness of many vernacular songs.[7] Perhaps the journal *History and Anthropology*, after four years of hibernation, is now reawakening to truly exotic medleys.

'The past' is too protean to parse here, but its doubleness demands one caveat. The past is both what has happened and how we view what has happened, knowing that we can never see it whole or unscreened by present goals and grammars. With time's arrow the actual past is gone forever; it is not just foreign but antipodal, beyond reach. The past is perceived through memory, with which it constantly interacts, and through historical texts, whose fixity distances us from them. Not the actual past, but this compage of recalled and chronicled pasts, should engage us here.

Now consider the 'foreign country', where 'they do things differently'. Whether visited in fact or in fancy, this foreign country induces culture shock. It is foreign because strange, mysterious, even incomprehensible. The present – our own country – is not easy to fathom either. But familiarity persuades us that we *do* or at least *should* know it. With Hartley, I view the perceived past as not merely different but foreign, inscrutable and alien to most travellers, even anthropologists.

Recent critics have refuted claims of ceaseless change, at least in Britain, where change is anathema anyway. Perhaps a while ago the past was foreign; but not now. 'Do I amaze the young with my unbelievable tales of Britain in the Fifties?' asks an observer. 'Blink, today, and you could *be* in the 1950s. My... Land Rover actually *is* from the 1950s. So is my dinner jacket.'[8]

As with luxuries, so with landscapes. A time traveller from the Great Exhibition of 1851 to the Festival of 1951 would be surprised how little had changed, and forty years on still more so. Unlike the Victorians, who replaced Britain's whole man-made environment within forty years, the twentieth century has left it largely untouched. 'Board a train anywhere in Britain's prosperous South-east and the odds are that the station has not changed since the 1870s.' Nor have the tunnels and cuttings, embankments and bridges, or the rows of backstreet terraces your train traverses.[9]

But a closer purview from another historical perspective yields a much more foreign view. In this light, 'even the nearby 1950s now seem a profoundly different and ... almost unimaginable time. [We simply] do not live in a world of push-buttons, delta-winged cars, asymmetrical ashtrays, and Tupperware sociality.' Are such things not too trivial to matter? It depends on the nature of the gaze. For many, 'this collection of objects gave off and took in the meanings of this now deeply alien period'.[10]

In pre-Enlightenment Europe, the past was domestic because human nature was thought universally the same. Circumstances and motives were constant over the entire sweep of mundane time, past and present wholly analogous. History taught lessons because the past kept repeating itself.

Two sets of discoveries made the past foreign: comparative scrutiny of datable texts showed how unlike our own were previous modes of thinking and feeling; and manifold contacts with exotic peoples dispelled belief in human uniformity. Loss of faith in a divinely ordained history and the acceleration of visible change made the past not just remote but fearsomely *different*. As history diversified it also grew ephemeral: views of the past were now always in flux. 'In the same town,' wrote Goethe, 'one will hear in the evening an account of a significant event different from that heard in the morning.'[11] The mere passage of time made the same past *look* different.

It is stunning to watch Goethe's contemporaries shift the paradigm. Thus Chateaubriand in 1797 tries to parallel old and new revolutions, reasoning from past to future in the customary way. But he was forced to realize that whatever he had written during the day was by night already overtaken by events; the French Revolution had no previous example.[12] From then through Henry Adams, the pace of change increasingly foreclosed resort to a past ever more foreign, hence ever less relevant.

Consciousness that the past was unlike the present, that people in other times and places did things differently, came to be central to progressive Western thought. The past became a cluster of distinctive realms, each with its own motives and mechanisms. And other mentalities seemed the more intriguing because so remote from our own. Even the social Darwinists' evolutionary resemblances are now gone; we no longer think of exotic 'others' as living fossils from our own ancestral past.

But these insights are not widely shared among other cultures, nor widely accepted even in our own. Even for academics, most of the time, the past is not a foreign country but our own, however filtered or sanitized. And the public continues to explain the past – their own or others – in terms of the present. Historical empathy, morally louche and mentally limp, is extolled by educators. Present-day aims and deeds are imputed to folk of earlier times. Heritage jettisons the past's cultural distance. Historic sites, museums, and costume romance cleave to the hoary dictum that human nature is constant, that people are essentially unchanged from age to age. The past is seen as another present.[13]

Even the best historians further this fallacy. The immediacy of *Montaillou* and *Martin Guerre* thrills many. But they yield little more than a voyeur's view of remote peasant lives. Their vivid intimacies promote empathy but limit understanding: they underscore the constancies of life, but obscure or ignore the historical trends that both *link* past and present and *differentiate* past *from* present. This is why the historian Natalie Zemon Davis rewrote her film script of *The Return of Martin Guerre* as a scholarly book. It troubled her that the film departed 'from the historical record . . . . These changes may have given the film the powerful simplicity that made the Martin Guerre story a legend in the first place.' But they weakened its contradictions, she felt, by glossing over sixteenth-century religious and social realities.[14]

The foreignness of the past precludes its desired domestication. We are too easily swayed by a spurious likeness, a seeming continuity. Take the word 'artificial'. Today it is a slur denoting the second-rate. But in 1610 a composer was praised as 'the most artificial and famous Alfonso Ferrabosco'. Time has reversed the meaning of artificial from 'full of deep skill and art' to 'shallow, contrived and almost worthless'. We should be wary of *anything* from the past that appears familiar.[15]

The pictures of Piero della Francesca 'are enclosed in a terrible carapace of false familiarity', notes Michael Baxandall, because we assume we know the biblical themes of Renaissance painting. Yet we do *not* understand them as folk did then: we lack *their* spontaneous and unselfconscious use of their own cultural conventions. And because *we* see Piero with eyes widened (or blinded) by Poussin and Picasso, we can never fully enter their perceptual world.[16]

Nothing replicates the past as it was for those who lived it as their present. We meticulously revive bygone times; but we do not engage with them as natives or re-create their original auras. When writing his books about the Edwardian period, a fictional historian marks each page 'with some pungent signal – a brand name, song, form of speech, public person or event in the news – to bring the odour of the period to life. Cheating, of course. Few people living in a period notice such things. Their real sense of their time is as unrecapturable as the momentary pose of a child.'[17]

The authentic early-music movement epitomizes the past's obstinate foreignness. It enhances what we know of and how we enjoy baroque music. But original intentions, original scores, original instruments, original ambiences all elude us. Unlike the A minor Fugue that Paul Richards invoked in a previous debate,[18] some of Bach's music was written *not* to be performed; his B minor Mass was presented to the Elector of Saxony as a promotional portfolio, thus 'the most "authentic" approach to [it] is not to perform it at all, but to read the score and consider Bach for the job of *maestro di capella* in your local church'.[19] Facsimile instruments do not guarantee facsimile sounds; the acoustics of modern concert halls depart from those of earlier locales; broad-band mechanical noise is now an all-pervasive background. We have no *castrati* to sing scores composed for them. And because boys' voices break much earlier than in the past, less-skilled youngsters today have to sing soprano parts meant for older boys who were more musically mature.[20]

The musical past stays foreign because we now grow up with other musical experiences, inhabit other acoustic worlds. The modern performer never wholly internalizes music of the past, feels it in his blood and bones like a native of the period. Nor can we shed our familiarity with *subsequent* music. Those who have heard Verdi are bound to hear Monteverdi differently. Similarly doomed is Sam Wanamaker's dream of performing the plays of Shakespeare as they were originally done, in the 'authentic' new Globe Theatre, whilst neo-Elizabethan audiences pelt the cast with Kentucky Fried Chicken.[21]

Modern museum visitors, no less than musical audiences, are ineluctably of their own epoch. What they make of what they see is shaped by creations and viewing habits that post-date the relics they observe. Time's erosions and accretions are bound to alter viewers' perceptual frameworks as well as the objects themselves. We cannot see the spinning wheel displayed as those who used it did. For us it is not a new tool, but a *former* tool, left stranded in the present by the tides of industrial change. Its proper role today is that of antique decor in some atavized locale. For people to see spinning wheels as they were once seen, the whole history of spinning jennies, Crompton mules and so forth would have to be unknown to them.[22]

But if the past is indeed a foreign country, is it not many lands rather than just one? Like any place abroad, each past is unique – as unlike others as it is unlike the present. Yet in two senses the whole past departs from the present, just as all alien lands are unlike our own. The sojourner in any foreign country remains an outsider never fully naturalized. Nor are we ever wholly at home in the past, however steeped we may be in its relics and memories and in sympathy with its denizens. Time travellers cannot escape the remembered experience of their own temporal prism. In the past, unlike its own people, they eternally engage the *un*familiar.

A second feature sets the past apart: bygone times lack the uncertainty of our own, because they are *over*. The past makes a better narrative than the present because it ends. Hindsight gives a clearer shape to history than to present raw experience. Hence historians endow the past with an ordered clarity contrasting with the chaos or imprecision of their own times. The view that the past has a pattern, evident in our much edited memories, is an illusion bred and bolstered by historians.[23]

It is the essence of nostalgia to yearn for a time when life was *different*. Not the past as it was or even as wished, but the condition of *having been*, with an integral completeness lacking in any present. No one ever experienced as 'present' what we now view as 'past'; selective oblivion, hindsight, and narrative necessity lend it anachronistic coherence. We recast the ongoing present as we live through it; we stand outside the past to view its more finished forms, including its *now* known consequences. Despite its strangeness, the past thus feels definitive and magisterial.

Because it is over, our own childhood is like this too: unlike later stages in our lives it is finished, completed, summed up. We may not come to terms with our childhood. But in memory, childhood feels unlike our present incoherent mess; its tale is framed by a timeless beginning and end. The saga of childhood has the shape of fable: 'once upon a time', it starts, and the story ends with 'living happily ever after'. Only in the past, we know, did things ever happen that way.[24]

The patterns we find in the past, personal or collective, are patterns rewoven by ourselves on old family fabrics. The past is a sanctuary for whatever versions of reality we seek to promote. And it goes against the grain to confess to ourselves that this precious legacy is a modern contrivance.

Twenty years ago *Punch* (remember *Punch*?) termed the past the 'foreign country with the healthiest tourist trade of all'.[25] Back then, 'healthy' meant what 'seriously' means today, as in 'seriously rich'. Back then, tourism was funny but not fatal. When you sold the past you lost your soul; but the past itself was safe. No more; that foreign country is now so fragile that heritage hucksters threaten to exhaust the resource. When no past remains but an Orwellian contrivance, we will have colonized and domesticated that foreign country.

AGAINST THE MOTION (1)

GILLIAN FEELEY-HARNIK

I argue against the motion – 'the past is a foreign country' – first because Hartley[26] coined the phrase ultimately to contradict it, and we should at least begin by addressing the participants' own views; second, on more general logical and phenomenological grounds, because all we know is here and now. Our knowledge of the 'past' is based on 'present' evidence, and at the deepest level of our being, this evidence is intensely spatial, mediated through our bodily movements. I shall argue that taking this approach does not condemn us to presentism. On the contrary, it may provide us with more precise ways of grasping the distinctiveness of people both in their face-to-face relations and in more global spatial and temporal contexts. And finally, having included 'us' among the participants, I want to move from these linked contrasts between foreignness and sameness, distance and proximity, past and present, to the questions of direction, of the meanings of human lifetimes and of human history, that they imply.

I begin with Hartley's own book, *The Go-Between*, from which the terms of our debate come, recalling the advice of Beruriah, Talmudic scholar from the second century of the Common Era (Palestine): 'Look to the end of the verse', before pronouncing impetuously on the significance of what is actually just a beginning. She gave this warning about methodology in a commentary on childbirth: Isaiah's vision of the birth of a 'people' from an ostensibly barren woman[27]. The narrator in *The Go-Between*, Leo Colston, states at the very outset: 'The past is a foreign country: they do things differently there.' But the central theme of his story is not the past as a foreign country, but how the past has come to seem that way, owing to energetic forgetting, desperate attempts to deaden feeling. And it is about the going-between from which new life comes.

Leo Colston's journey begins when he accidentally discovers the diary in his collar box, taking him back over the ground of his forgetting to himself as a child, innocent messenger of Marian and her lover Ted, for whose subsequent suicide, when their secret relationship was revealed, he feels responsible. As the author states at the end of the book,[28] Leo has returned to 'the world of the emotions' to which he has become a 'foreigner'. There he serves again as a 'go-between', now between the elderly Marian and her young grandson 'Edward (only don't call him that)', Ted's grandson and positional successor, as Africanists might say, who is concealed within Hugh Edward Winlove, 11th Viscount Trimingham. Freed of shame about his illegitimate past by Leo's new going-between, Hugh Edward may be able to marry and regenerate new viscounts. Even Leo may now be able to love again and create new life.

Hartley's book went through twelve reprints between 1953 and the 1974 impression I read, distributed in Britain, North America, and perhaps elsewhere. The book is still available in hardcover, paperback and large print editions. All this suggests that its theme has some enduring popularity. Given other great literature on this topic – including, if we follow Hyman's *The tangled bank*,[29] the dramatic metaphors of Darwin, Marx, Frazer, and Freud – it seems likely that European and North American scholars too are still preoccupied with long-standing eschatological concerns to *re*connect far and near events, which we see as critical to our own redemption and rebirth, our continuity through time.

If we really followed Hartley's logic, we would not oppose ourselves, but attend to the dynamics of connection, suppression and reconnection that he describes. And indeed this is the logic of David Lowenthal's book, as shown in his conclusion.[30] But for the sake of debate, I shall argue that these movements begin from our most immediate, proximate circumstances. We begin from the here and now. As Peel puts it, this is the 'ontological truism (that conceptions of the past are facts of the present)'.[31] We have no access to a 'past' that is not mediated through the 'present'. Or to rephrase this point in a way that does not abstract these processes of knowing from knowers: we have no knowledge of past *people* except through present *people*; we have no way of knowing others except through ourselves.

In different ways, Peel, Appadurai and Toren have pointed to fruitful ways of recognizing this dilemma, while avoiding presentist traps, by emphasizing, as Peel puts it, 'the mutual conditioning of past and present'.[32] Here I wish to consider research on history and memory. To some extent, this research reproduces earlier oppositions between historicism and presentism using the imagery of a genetically universal individualism. And in practice, work on memory alone seems to be bifurcating along the lines of a dichotomy between textuality and embodiment. But some of the literature deriving from psychologists' so-called 'ecological' approaches to memory, together with some ethnographic accounts, suggest ways of getting beyond these nested dichotomies.

They do so by focusing not on 'history turned into nature', as Bourdieu saw the *habitus* of memory,[33] or even on the hegemony achieved in 'naturalizing' social inequalities, based on the assumption that this process of naturalization somehow bypasses our critical faculties, stereotypically associated with speech. Rather, they show that remembering, which some scholars identify with consciousness, involves processes of our human being-in-the-world that cannot be severed along the lines of such distinctions as between mind and body, inside and outside, individual and society, or distant and near.

The orientation of the most fruitful research could be characterized in biologist Ruth Hubbard's terms as 'transformationism'. She is arguing against the separation of biology and culture, or at least against their simple connection. The relationship is neither determinative nor additive; it is interactive and transformative. This means that 'biological and environmental factors can change an organism so that it responds differently to other, concurrent or subsequent, biological or environmental changes than it would have done otherwise. Simultaneously the organism transforms the environment which, of course, includes other organisms.... There is no way to sort out the biological and social components.'[34] This also seems close to what Ingold calls the 'mutualism' or 'synergy' of persons and environments.[35] This is the perspective from which we could integrate recent work on the physiology of remembering in the brain with work by ethnographers, historians, psychologists, philosophers, poets and others that puts remembering back into the world, showing how we experience time through the immediacies of place.

Peculiarly – though perhaps explicably from an ethnographic point of view, taking into account explanatory metaphors linking mind-brain and globe – the major recent discovery in neurophysiology is that long-term, or declarative, memory is not coextensive with the whole brain, as most had assumed. It is localized in the medial temporal lobe: the hippocampus, together with adjacent anatomically related cortex (entorhinal, perirhinal and parahippocampal cortex). As two prominent practitioners put it, 'the ability to acquire new memories is a distinct cerebral function, separable from other perceptual and cognitive abilities' (otherwise described as 'regular, on-line functions').[36] Yet the key purpose of these local organs is to bind together or integrate the diverse elements of which memories are made by linking together the several sites all over the neocortex with which they are associated.

The hippocampus (with its related organs) is crucial in establishing these links at the time of first learning, and continues to strengthen the global connections in the brain until they eventually become 'independent' of the medial temporal lobe system.[37] In this state, any one element may call up all the others, leaving the medial temporal lobe system free to create new memories, new integrated systems.

The memories created through the localized medial temporal lobe system are called 'declarative' memories, defined as long-term 'information about facts and events... accessible to conscious recollection', in contrast to 'nondeclarative (implicit) memory includ[ing] several kinds of abilities, all of which are unconscious and expressed through performance'.[38] This contrast may actually have the effect of perpetuating mind–body, verbal–nonverbal, propositional–ritual distinctions. Yet even by the neurophysiologists' own accounts, the relationship between speech and other sounds, word images, and visual and other sensory imagery is much more complex, frustrating conventional dichotomies.

Furthermore, these same declarative memories have been found, especially by so-called ecological psychologists, to be highly 'state dependent', meaning that some details about the circumstances in which a person first learns or experiences something become inextricable from it, critical to recalling it years – even decades – later. Some of the most interesting examples of this research on the way memory 'goes between' distant and near experiences have to do with odours,[39] as the ethnography of Gell, Howes and Siegel might lead one to suspect, although their research does not have to do with memory or 'smellscapes' as such.[40] The spatial dimensions of experience turn out to be even more crucial. The place that held the experience together, like Combray in Proust's teacup, continues to hold together the several places in the brain, confirming the view of phenomenologists who argue that we experience temporality spatially in moving.[41]

Thus, our ways of characterizing the past, or past people, in spatially distant terms are likely to be secondary elaborations of the processes involved in objectifying or distancing others. The work of psychologists, even the ecologically inclined, has been limited to fitting people with beepers as they go about their daily rounds.[42] The ethnographic data on this issue are much richer, suggesting the existence of other phenomenological theories, comparable to those of Merleau-Ponty, Bachelard or Casey in Europe and North America. For example, Western Apache use place names and stories about places associated with persons to evaluate moral behaviour. Once heard, the stories are felt to 'stalk' people through their thoughts, 'piercing' them like arrows, and finally 're-placing' where and with whom they can 'live right'.[43] The weeping 'bird sound word' songs of Kaluli funerals and *gisalo* ceremonies evoke powerful images of landscapes, paths and places through which, as they 'harden' in the course of the singing, living people reconnect with their ancestors in seen and unseen worlds.[44]

Malagasy ethnography shows how these phenomenological connections between space-time and persons may be related to wider political–economic relations – in the capture of people in slavery and other states of servitude, which Malagasy see as a condition of being 'lost' to one's people and place. Malagasy data also show how the politics of history, divesting people of identity, of their presence in a contemporary world, is above all a politics of place – dispossession and reorientation, burial and exhumation.[45] It is more than ironic that so much recent scholarship on history, tradition, or even memory in anthropology, has focused on questions of time, when the most salient feature of relations between Europeans or North Americans and the 'non-Western' category of foreigners has been the appropriation of land, the places in and through which people create their times and beings, where memory and history are inextricable from political presence and political economy.

Once we recognize how our experiences of time are rooted in the immediacies of place we can no longer affirm that the past is a foreign country, except in so far as we have tried to distance the presence of people in our actual lives. Nevertheless, this view does not condemn us to the individualist prisons of presentism. In addition to contemporary ruins and reconstructions of past actions, including those 'substantial convictions' about the past[46] with which we continually reassess our present places, we may invoke Gadamer's 'historicity of reason',[47] which he developed in an argument against historicism, and examine the process of 'fusioning' along 'horizons' (curiously very fitting with phenomenological, psychological and ethnographic data on memory and place) as a continuing social process.

There is also the possibility that such phenomenological, sociological and political–economic understandings of the spatial historicity of reason, which ethnographic data suggest might be quite widespread, could find their way into linguistic semantic systems, not simply in the deictics of language, but perhaps also in widespread foundational metaphors of landscape as knowledge.[48]

I have been arguing about the placedness of time. The past is not a foreign or a distant country; it is the very ground on which, in which, with which we stand, move and otherwise interact; out of which we continually regenerate ourselves in relations with others, partly through distanciation. But if we ask whose problem is this and reconsider ourselves as participants, this still leaves unanswered the deeper questions about time's arrow, whether these places have any direction to them. I see no clear direction, no foreign country against which we might see or measure our redemptive nativity, as it were – our renewed becoming. The possibility that direction might be our main concern in distinguishing between foreign and native, past and present, was provoked for me, first, by Trautmann's recent article on 'the revolution in ethnological time' in the 1860s;[49] and second, by the very particular form that these questions about history and memory, past and present, have taken these days. Trautmann argues that the key event in the formation of anthropology alongside history in the 1860s was not Darwinism, but the prehistoric 'abyss of time' that suddenly opened up with the collapse of biblical chronology.

Progressive evolutionisms did seem to dominate during these years, but they did so alongside a keen awareness of countervailing movements in the work of scholars like Marx, Darwin, Frazer, and Freud, while their colleagues in physics were beginning to formulate the second law of thermodynamics concerning entropy. And it is clear from current debates in astrophysics and evolutionary biology that these questions about 'time's arrows' (Stephen Hawking includes 'psychological' as well as thermodynamic and cosmological arrows) – especially the question of whether these arrows have any direction – remain wide open. And scholars of human behaviour are surely brooding on the same questions, which is the basis of my second point.

For North Americans and Europeans, these are not remote questions; they are concretely embodied in people. The Holocaust now stands at the centre of the most significant controversy about our ability to claim that a 'past' exists at all, and about the strongest evidence on which we can base such claims – namely conventional historical data, like archival documents, and the 'substantial convictions' of people whose memories are indivisible from their flesh and blood. These controversies have existed since the 1940s, but have been intensifying since the late 1970s and early 1980s, finally provoking the President of the American Historical Society to make a formal response at the Society's annual meeting in autumn 1991, *declining* to affirm explicitly that the Holocaust had occurred, and instead calling on scholars 'to initiate plans now to encourage study of the significance of the Holocaust'.[50]

Since well before that moment, now elderly survivors had been provoked by these controversies to place their memories on record by means of videotape, a medium whose more intensely sensory nature was itself felt and seen as lending greater veracity and authenticity to their words.[51] This sense of the historicity of the immediate person was most graphically expressed in Spiegelman's subtitle to *Maus: a survivor's tale* – 'My father bleeds history'.[52] What these records document is the coexistence in the present, in themselves, of what one woman called 'these double lives. We can't cancel out. It just won't go away'. In his analysis of the videotapes in Yale's Fortunoff Video Archive, Langer (following Charlotte Delbo) distinguishes between 'common memory' – coherent, chronological images of the past detached from the present, and 'deep memory' – the intensely painful and chaotic reliving of irremediable losses. Yet these are continually interconnected in the actual testimonies. One of Langer's main themes is the survivors' own conviction that the past must be *made* into a foreign country within themselves, as a condition for their belief in humanity; connecting past and present would only reveal the fundamental *in*humanity of humans. Yet 'you won't understand' is invariably followed by 'you must understand', leading Langer himself to affirm the evidence of their very testifying, that this connection is and will continue to be made.[53]

It is striking that these controversies are focusing even now on redefinitions of a social category of people who, as Eilberg-Schwartz and Boyarin have argued, have long served as inner others, foreigners, or strangers within predominantly Christian regions and eventually nation-states.[54] These others exemplified in particular how Europeans sub-stantiated their past-to-present directional histories, associated with particular kinds of redemption in territorially defined states, by contrast to the ostensibly groundless chronologies of landless wanderers.

These events – as also logically these arguments I have made about the placedness of our times – raise further questions about the relation of our current concerns to our larger circumstances. These might include the outcomes of land transfers in global migration patterns associated with flexible accumulation; the development of electronic technologies con-necting these far-flung places, whose chief attribute, reckoning by differences in price, is 'memory', yet which are deeply amemorial in leaving no generational trace;[55] and the possibility, through our experiences of these phenomena, of new ways of rethinking the 'mind/bodies' through which we apprehend our regeneration in place-time.[56]

FOR THE MOTION (2)

PENELOPE HARVEY

It will by now have become obvious to you that we are not dealing with a motion of the same kind as those previously debated in this series, such as 'language is the essence of culture' or 'the concept of society is theoretically obsolete', but rather with a statement more along the lines of 'my grandfather is a tapir' – a proposition which may, when uttered in the context of ethnographic research, be worth attempting to take literally, but which is otherwise more likely to be interpreted metaphorically. What we are asking you to consider is the metaphoric potency of the statement 'the past is a foreign country'.

David Lowenthal has argued that although our view of the past is quite evidently an artefact of the present, it is nevertheless incommensurable with the present. I want to push the application of this metaphor – to contemporary popular culture and to non-Western contexts – by looking more closely at the nature of this incommensurability. How might the notion of the foreign country help us to grasp this sense of difference? And what are the effects of producing such a difference?

Perhaps I should start by pointing out that L. P. Hartley's use of the phrase in *The Go-Between*, 'The past is a foreign country: they do things differently there', is already a qualification of the motion that suggests a place distanced from ourselves, inhabited by people whose 'otherness' is constituted by the distinctiveness of their actions. I will return by several different routes to *this* notion of the foreign country, but would simply stress at this point that we are not debating the usage in *The Go-Between* and that there are ways in which we might conceive of the foreign country that do not concur with L. P. Hartley's formulation.

I start on familiar territory – the foreign countries which we visit with ever greater ease and frequency, on business and on holiday, as members of what James Clifford has called the 'traveling cultures'.[57] Some commentators on the post-modern have suggested that we have in such travels radically altered our senses of both the past and the foreign – in what David Harvey has referred to as the 'time–space compression' of the contemporary world.[58] I would argue that difference is still an important aspect of these experiences, but it is an anodyne difference, a difference that relies on the generation of massive variety and choice – but a choice in which everything is easily accessible because there is no hint of that difference which cannot be immediately assimilated and consumed.

Expo' 92, the Universal Exhibition which has just closed in Seville, raised interesting questions about the location of foreignness in the contemporary world. One of the striking things about the Expo was that despite the participation of 110 nations, each of which mounted an exhibit specifically designed to communicate an image of that nation to the world, none of the countries felt very foreign. All the pavilions displayed a very familiar brand of otherness – the familiar differences which we find on television, in travel brochures, in the shops, in public galleries and on foreign holidays. Cultural variety was consistently represented in terms of folkloric dances and songs, history was invariably portrayed as chronological narrative or an array of ancient artefacts. Difference was most evident in the form of the differential access to the technologies of hyper-reality through which visitors could experience the sensation of movement through space and time. There were some displacements involved: Spain, Canada and Venezuela emerged as the new world superpowers in the competition for sensation; the United States was embarrassed.

The Expo is one way in which we produce and consume foreign countries – not *the* European or Western way, but a significant one none the less, in which governments are prepared to invest considerable resources (the estimated cost of British participation was 54 million US dollars, Morocco spent 35 million just building its pavilion) to generate images that products people are anxious to consume (there were 40 million visits during the six months of the Exhibition).

Furthermore, it is a way of producing the foreign which has resonances in many other areas of popular culture. For example, in the film *1492: Conquest of Paradise*, Ridley Scott's latest multi-million dollar production, a thoroughly late twentieth-century Columbus 'goes in search of paradise'. The Costa Rican coastline is already amazingly familiar in its guise of the Caribbean island, and though Hollywood's 'savages' (no credits to know how they might identify themselves) are distanced by language, they are still quite familiar – we've seen them before in *The Mission*, *Fitzcarraldo*, and even *Emerald Forest*.

Foreign countries can thus be thought of as examples of the tasteful, sanitized, ubiquitous difference that we produce for ourselves, in the vicious circle of what has been called 'postplural nostalgia',[59] where the innovations and changes that produce variety have simultaneously destroyed tradition, convention and choice. My main point, of course, is that if the past is not foreign in a contemporary world, then neither are foreign countries.

But I can also bring to your attention other ethnographic cases in which the distance implied by temporal difference, while not rendering the past totally alien, nevertheless calls for its domestication. The past is foreign in the sense of indicating difference, but it is a difference across which interaction and communication are possible, and productive engagement can be achieved. In these ethnographic settings the concept of separation is important to the generation of continuity and tradition.

Susanne Küchler has documented the *Malangan* sculptures of New Ireland which, after they have been displayed and transacted in mortuary ceremonies, are disarticulated, distanced or physically removed: 'left to rot, burned or sold to European visitors'.[60] But they do not disappear, they maintain a presence in memory which makes possible their reproduction. Subsequent sculptures, although never exact replicas, are reminiscent of an object seen in the past and of the past relationships which that object entailed.[61] Separation is required conceptually in order that continuity and sameness can be made apparent. The past is thus brought into the present, but the process requires that its otherness be addressed.

I am also thinking of recent Amazonian studies which have noted the ways in which people conceptualize kinship as the memories of productive engagement. Here again, the incommensurability of the past is problematic, and its otherness has to be dealt with. Memories of prior actions and relationships are responsible for the concrete effects of engagement, which are felt in the present. Thus for the people of the Bajo Urubamba in the Peruvian Amazon, history *is* kinship, and self-identification is that of a 'mixed people'.[62] Not to remember someone is to do them violence, leaving them alone and segregated.

But these are not people for whom there are no foreigners. Their own immediate past can be prevented from becoming foreign, so long as memory operates to humanize it; however, this domestication of the past is vital in order to separate the domain of human relations from other temporal domains which are intensely foreign, times of which no human being has any memory.

Accounts of 'first contact' give us an opportunity to consider the dynamic between a remembered (actualized) past where people seek to overcome temporal distance in the production of human sociality, and a distant, inaccessible temporal space inhabited by non-human forces. Moments of first contact are strange and unusual because we are dealing here with extremes of foreignness, a degree of otherness which is, by definition, dangerous and unpredictable. The disconnection between parties to the interaction is such that the *relationship* has no past, and thus there is no memory through which to understand its nature.

Marilyn Strathern has argued that the significance of the appearance of the first White Australians in Mount Hagen centred on the Hageners' recognition of themselves in the outsiders.[63] Once the Hageners discovered that the outsiders were a source of pearl shells and could be engaged in productive relationships they could then be understood as operating in a human time dimension; their past was of this world. The encounter was no longer one of first contact, the Australians had simply emerged from those previous temporal engagements that constitute the present. The foreigners were neutralized. They could be domesticated in similar ways to other aspects of the past.

The Australians knew differently and arrived in Mount Hagen, armed with their cameras, to film the sensation which they expected to cause.

They knew that they were participating in a significant temporal event, believing that their presence was to have a transformative effect on the history of those with whom they came into contact. This was an interpretation totally at odds with that of the Hageners who seem to have decided that the Australians themselves *were* the effect, an effect which – I understand – they were pretty impressed with nevertheless.

Consider now the currently topical first encounters between Europeans and native Americans. Contemporary fifteenth-century commentators conceptualized the nature of these encounters through the evocation of extreme distance. Here we find accounts of absolute foreignness. The European response to the native Americans was one that concentrated on their difference – an otherness which was constituted through an appeal to temporal and spatial domains of which they knew, but had no memory. The authoritative texts of classical antiquity had informed them of the existence of the monstrous races, of people with heads on their chests, with ears that covered their bodies, the one-eyed cyclops, people who walked upside-down or whose feet pointed backwards – just some examples from the lengthy catalogue of inversions, suppressions and exaggerations of known human bodily features.[64] The perverted habits of the cannibals, the sodomists and the incestuous, who were also reported as inhabiting the New World, furnished further examples of difference as extreme distortions of the recognized limits of human bodily practice. The dilemma of how to produce a recognizable image of absolute otherness is of course impossible to overcome, and we find that even the monstrous races are therefore inevitably imaginative variations on familiar forms. The temporal connection between these monsters and the fifteenth-century Europeans was one of coexistence in radically demarcated spaces on the far edges of the world – the simultaneity was not one of time–space compression.

The native Americans seem to have had the opposite reaction, and considered the possibility that the Europeans were beings not so much from another space as from another time – returning ancestors, prefigured catalysts for the catastrophe that would destroy the world and produce a totally new social order. The complex preparations for the new age can be glimpsed in the millenarian movements that took place throughout the Americas in the sixteenth century. For them total otherness was expressed by temporal rather than spatial distance.

Finally we have the foreign country in the sense of the contingency and disorder of contemporary nation-states. When Eric Wolf argued, a decade ago, that anthropologists need to discover history, he stressed that he was not referring to 'Western history divided into separate nations... but the contacts, connections, linkages and interrelation-ships'.[65] He wanted to do away with 'the notion of the nation as internally homogeneous and externally segregated and work instead with a notion of "differently oriented accents... in a state of constant tension, of incessant interaction and conflict"'.

All governments seek to produce nation-states as discrete entities, with populations that, if not homogeneous, maintain at least a pluralism of mutual accommodation. Expo is the cosmetic version of this attempt, with its images of the desired end product. But the processes through which governments attempt to produce such nations are, as we can see in the world today, not just extremely violent but also perpetually unresolved. Government strategies for the production of the nation-state do not simply rely on the imposition of order, stability and structure but in many cases also operate through normative disorder, through secrecy, silence and paranoia.[66] However, the force of disorder is not a state monopoly. Official versions of state history can be produced, but the interpretations of such histories and the memories of those whose experiences are not articulated therein are not so easily controlled. Alternatives do not necessarily emerge as coherent narrative connections – indeed, they often carry more force or resistance if they remain in a state of disarticulation. Their forms may be totally unfamiliar and hard to fathom, as for example the Andean *ñaqaq* – slaughterers who ambush people at night, mesmerize them, slit their throats and extract their grease to run the economies of European nations.[67]

I have been working round to those depictions of the most alien of foreigners, which anthropologists have produced for us, in order to address finally what I think is an important issue implicit in the motion that the past is a foreign country. This is the question of 'time and the other' in contemporary anthropology.[68] Harris has noted that time 'fascinates both by its ubiquity and its invisibility. It is universal and yet it seems to offer the possibility of entering into "different worlds", so that it is a common means for expressing the exotic and cultural difference.'[69] My interest in this issue lies in this notion of cultural difference in contemporary anthropology.

I have tried to show that the foreign country is a vehicle for the expression of difference that can range from the anodyne difference of consumer variety to the empty space of the exotic, devoid of memory and thus of relationships, ready to be filled with fantasies, doubts and nightmares. I have pointed to the otherness of disarticulation which is often required for the ongoing generation of kinship and identity, and I have discussed the contested effects of memory in the constitution of contemporary nation-states.

How might anthropology engage with these possibilities? How do we deal with the dilemma posed by the apparent inevitability of reproducing either the distance of the exotic or the triviality of the anodyne difference? Anthropologists have tended to take one or other of two solutions: there are those who use anthropology rhetorically, to relativize our own cultural practices. They run the risk of generating self–other dualisms, the structures of distance which produce the exotic, and the homogeneity of a collective Western self which converts difference into privilege. Then there are those who use anthropology historically to look at the complex interactions through which the foreignness of others is produced, but who run the risk of denying the fact that our understandings of history and political economy are dependent on culturally specific concepts of persons, time and space.

I believe that it is vital for contemporary anthropology to be mindful of this contradiction without trying to iron it out. 'The past is a foreign country' is an admirable maxim for this endeavour as it encapsulates both the notions of incommensurability and the limits to knowledge, as well as referring to the process of differentiation and exclusion by which we produce our constructs of time and space.

The present always requires some concept of disarticulation from the past, and that disarticulation invariably connotes a degree of otherness. My argument, in essence, is that there is no way around the issues that this metaphor of the past as a foreign country evokes, and that whether we like it or not, we have to find a way to use it.

To speak of the past as a foreign country is to make a metaphorical statement about difference. That difference can itself take a range of forms, and this range is pertinent to the theoretical dilemmas of contemporary anthropology. The facts of the matter are that the foreign is no more (and no less) accessible than the past, and that we are always caught between the twin poles of anodyne difference and absolute otherness. Remaining mindful of these poles we must steer a course between them as best we can. To pretend that the differences highlighted by the metaphor are ephemeral is a delusion.

AGAINST THE MOTION (2)

SUSANNE KÜCHLER

The motion for this debate invites comment on all three of its key terms. First, to most people it would make more sense to say that it is the *present* which may be construed as foreign; the uncertainty over the past implied in the motion puts us in mind of Oliver Sacks's case stories of amnesia and multiple personality, which show how dependent commonsense behaviour and identity are upon the ability to live with one's past.[70] Second, the *foreign* character of the past may be asserted as an ideological statement that serves to make the present into an island that is isolated, defensive and incommunicado. Yet from another point of view, both cultural transmission and innovation involve acts of remembering which require that the past be rendered into a familiar thing that can be grasped intuitively.[71] Third, by saying that the past is a foreign *land*, distanced from the present, the past, and thus memory itself, is made into a passive repository from which certain valuable commodities may be selected to be used or traded in the present. The peculiar property of remembering, however, is the active role it plays in consciousness – only when seen from the mechanistic perspective of behavioural science does memory lose its interested and intentional facets as an embodied mode of understanding.[72]

If there is a key assumption underlying the motion it resides in the supposedly disembodied character of remembering; suggestively 'placed' where it can only be intellectually possessed, that is in a 'foreign country', the past is taken to be literally out of touch from those who produced it. Without stating the point explicitly, the motion implies that there is nothing about the past which is effective beyond the moment in which it was lived time. We are told to envision ourselves as though we were as distanced from the past as we are from the land of our dreams and adventures; to suppose that what we know about the past is, like a dream or a travelogue, but a mixture of truth and imagination – made up as we go along to fit our vision of what it must have been like. The transcendent quality that the motion attributes to the past is a romantic illusion, construed indeed by romanticism, and betrays a certain attitude carried forth by historians in their own project of colonizing the past. The motion fails, I argue, because it disregards the complexities created by the fact that we live with, and by virtue of having, a past which at one and the same time is shaped by memory, and also shapes our memory. The past may have its uses in the legitimation of the present, but is this all there is to it?

Having described the key assumptions of the proposition, I would now like to put forward an alternative view which restores the past to its active engagement in the present, not as a fictional by-product of that present, but as a constituent of the real world.

We know about the past, whether our own or that of our culture or of the cultures of others, through photographs and written documents, but more importantly, through our bodies and through artificial images – from landscape to architecture and painting. Body and image bear the traces not just of time, but of memory-work, that is of a process of remembering or the material acts of inscribing which reify cognition itself.[73] Bodily habit, as found in gestures or skills or simply in our ability to move about in the environment both predictably and without accident, testifies to the significance of relying on the presenting of the past in an unquestioning and indisputable way.[74] Man-made images similarly posit a remembrance. In order to consider images as embodying memory-work we have to revise the prevailing assumption that the mnemonic function ascribed to the image is to operate as an *aide mémoire*; this function is in fact historically specific, resulting from the displacement of a rhetorical mnemonic technique into the visual realm during the Italian Renaissance.[75] Image production, however, always involves mnemonic processing in the form of the artificing function of the hand, which consolidates and reifies cognition in the act of inscription upon the material. The trace left of mnemonic processing in the products of image-making is in no way unconsciously perceived, but is vital to the reception and transmission of the works themselves.[76]

The past, whether personal or cultural, is thus in no way uncontaminated by memory, but is already the product of memory-work, and only as such a product is the past present in consciousness. The belief in the purity of past experiences, of learning, and of their testimony which survives as relics, is an essential cornerstone of twentieth-century psychology, which has assumed that the past is carefully stored in the unconscious, to be brought into consciousness only through remembering. This notion, that memories of past experiences and learning – once rendered unconscious – are stored in the brain, has come under increasing attack during the last decade and now seems to be untenable. Conventional wisdom ignored the possibility that memories were part of the very structure of consciousness. Yet as Israel Rosenfield has argued, 'not only can there be no such thing as a memory without there being consciousness, but consciousness and memory are in a certain sense inseparable, and understanding one requires understanding the other'.[77] As an aspect of consciousness, human memory is thus relational, ever evolving, and ever changing, intrinsically dynamic and subjective. If we therefore have to discard the comforting and age-old belief that our knowledge is 'stored' somewhere in the brain, only waiting to be unlocked, we have also to do away with the idea, contained in the motion, that the past is 'stored' in a distant, 'foreign' place waiting to be opened up through selective recollection.

Memory in the sense used here is generative, as it allows for the generation of ever new versions of experience without deviating from the familiar. The presenting of the past in memory is relevant in the sense that it is self-relational and thus involved in the fashioning of identity, but this in itself forms a predisposition for certain aspects of the past to be incorporated within personal or cultural history. These aspects are ones which either occasion a remembrance or else are construed as doing so. Certain odours, as famously described by Marcel Proust, evoke extensive chains of remembering;[78] certain places evoke memories of the long past days of childhood;[79] architecture, artefact relics and poetics entice remembering because they are the products not of compulsive repetition of the past, but of a remembering which implies a mastering of the past through the transformation of material.[80]

I propose to get away from the model of cultural transmission which states the obvious, that is, that the present is in some manner governed by our perception of the past, and to move towards an understanding of the presenting of the past in consciousness and its effect upon the shaping of the future. Consciousness, as recently defined by Israel Rosenfield, is the dynamic synthesis of the past, present and ego in remembering without which a person would act like a character in one of Oliver Sacks's books – disoriented, helpless, alienated and lacking identity. In its immediacy, such synthesis in remembering is essential to habit formation and thus to skill, something usually associated with the repression of consciousness and the work of the unconscious. On the one hand, it can be a wholly subjective experience, such as when the developing infant gazes at a bright spot on the wall which is there every morning during waking hours; he does not have to selectively reproduce in his mind all the previous times in which he saw this bright spot – his memoryscape encompasses all past and present occurrences in an instant which is one step towards the development of the sense of self. On the other hand, the synthesis of past and present is essential to the formation of social memory in objectification; a *Malangan* sculpture, an Aboriginal bark painting or an engraving by the Dutch engraver Goltzius does not selectively reinterpret the past, but rather encompasses the past. Constancy and correctness are important attributes of these cultural images. Their forever reproduced form or underlying template testifies to the fact that they do not serve as *aide mémoires* for a contextual past, but are rather products of memory-work through which a culture may possess its past immediately, without hesitation or speculation.

Transmission at the personal and cultural level is not an activity involving choice. But nor is it a passive mechanism. It is not like a game of Chinese whispers, whereby changes in the message are brought about by successive mishearing. The non-problematic aspect of remembering, something Neisser has termed 'natural memory', and the active appropriation of the present involving consciousness in habitual action, have yet to be explained. We have not found a solution by claiming, as the motion does, that recall is inherently transformative and that it reappropriates the past in ever differing ways. This is because remembering has an organization which is likewise reproduced in every act of remembrance, the changes of which are still unaccounted for. We have, then, to acknowledge not only that remembering is active in transforming our versions of the past, but also that remembering has its own history.

Part II The debate

PAUL RICHARDS   I would like to ask all four speakers whether they think the *future* is a foreign country.

DAVID LOWENTHAL   In my view the future suffered the same fate as did the past, when people began to realize that the course of history was not uniform or predictable, that one could not learn from the past in order to predict the future. Thus the future has become unutterably foreign. We simply cannot know what it is going to be like, and in the meantime we solace ourselves with notions about the end of history.

GILLIAN FEELEY-HARNIK   I see the question as relating to time's arrow. Even to ask whether the future is a foreign country is to presuppose that there *is* an arrow. Following on from my earlier arguments, it seems to me that this kind of future is in the same category as the past, though conceptually it is like its opposite. In a sense it is just a mirror image of the past. In speaking about the future people do indeed take up the same kind of logic as they use to speak about the past. With regard to the way our ideas concerning time have been changing, we have in fact become increasingly presentist, even intensely so. And in this presentist perspective the future does appear like a foreign country – one that, compared to the present, has little reality.

PENELOPE HARVEY   The answer to the question will depend on what you think a foreign country is. In one sense the future is completely unknown; in another sense it is what we make of it now. Clearly, the images by which we can portray the future in the present can only be drawn from the contemporary context. This is why science fiction or futuristic films that may have been made no more than fifteen years ago nowadays look so dated. Thus a concept of anachronism that applies to ideas of the past can apply just as well to our changing ideas of the future. From this perspective, the future *is* a foreign country.

SUSANNE KÜCHLER   Going back to my argument about how, in the act of remembering, the past is immanent in the present, I would hold that the future is also immanent in the present – in so far as it can be foreseen. The future is always regarded as what is within our grasp, what is seen as effective. Whether the intended effects are actually realized is, of course, another matter.

GILLIAN FEELEY-HARNIK   I have been trying all along to anchor the questions raised by this debate to ethnography, to concrete circumstances that would help us to sort out these questions both substantively and theoretically. Now there is one point concerning the issue of the way we think about the future – and indeed about time generally – that ties in very closely with the argument I put forward about the presentism of contemporary perspectives. It is that the techniques and technologies of memory have changed so radically. I have referred to Carruthers' study of memory techniques, *The book of memory*.[81] Carruthers goes back to the Greeks and Romans and their 'Method of Loci', by which a collection of things may be committed to memory by visualizing each as though it were placed at one of a series of locations along a well-known path. She traces this method right up through the Middle Ages and the Renaissance, and then shows how it began to collapse with the invention of printing. The earliest books – all those beautiful illuminated manuscripts with their decorative initials and so on – still furnished mnemonic loci: they were not things of a bookish, textual nature, but rather offered a succession of visual images that would assist those who saw reading as a form of remembering. Yet to return to our own time, Carruthers could write her book thanks, in part, to a technology which – however reluctantly we may have embraced it – is so radically different from what has gone before that it has actually transformed us. And even though computers are priced in proportion to their memory, this electronic technology is, to my mind, deeply *amemorial*. Ironically, computers now have the capacity to erase any trace of generation. A striking example of this capacity is 'morphing', the technique whereby you can transform one picture into another, dot by dot, on the computer, with no way of knowing to which generation each belongs. Here, time and the future are obliterated. Our capacity to experience and perhaps even to think of the future is changing into something else altogether.

RICHARD FARDON   The phrase, 'the past is a foreign country', put me in mind of the country from which no one ever returns, and which we cannot therefore know anything about. I mean the land of the dead. And this led me to ask: Whither are we supposed to come back once we know about the past? There has been much talk of presentism, and some concern with the different ways in which memory – whether individual or to some degree shared – intervenes between the present and the past. But my question is: how does the past figure in the arguments we have heard? Are the four speakers talking about the same kind of past? And bearing in mind that I am already trying to remember what was said barely half an hour ago, how are we to understand the present?

TIM INGOLD   Richard Fardon has raised three separate issues. The first concerns how we are to think about death in relation to life as a past or future state. The second concerns the differences between the sort of past that is so far off that it seems beyond our experience altogether, a past that is bound up in our biographical experience, and a past that is very close – such as a few minutes ago – but which still leaves us trying to remember what happened at that time. Can we treat all these pasts together, or must they be kept distinct? The third issue follows from this question. What exactly *is* the status of the present? And do our speakers mean the same thing by it?

DAVID LOWENTHAL   Let me take up the question of death. It has been said that everything we know of the past exists in the present. This is certainly true – almost by definition. Yet we also have a profound sense of generation, albeit threatened by the electronic monsters to which Gillian Feeley-Harnik has referred. All of us have a deep knowledge of having come from somewhere, of having been generated. And most of us have the feeling of having generated someone or something that will survive us: children, ideals, functions or whatever. Considerable parts of the meanings of our lives are bound up with these senses of not existing only now, not being just in the present, but of having a past from which we have come, and a future to which we are presumably giving or lending something of ourselves, as well as what we have acquired from others. The question that has been asked about death is significant, for it bears on the issue of how we conceive of ourselves in a stream – if not necessarily in a time – of generation. These conceptions are constantly in flux. You may recall what Woody Allen had to say about immortality. When an interviewer pointed out to him how wonderful it was that he was leaving all his marvellous films to the future, his response was: 'I don't want to be immortal by leaving all these films to the future; I want to be immortal by living forever.' This is a paradigmatic response to the issue of the role of the individual in a world with a sense of time in which the notion of passing on a heritage or an inheritance has become more and more atrophied. Our sense of personal death thus seems to me to be bound up with the extent to which, and the ways in which, we feel we are part of both a personal, a familial and a social stream of time (if I may use the word 'time' without the arrow, for the moment).

GILLIAN FEELEY-HARNIK   There are, of course, some anthropologists who would seek to formulate universal theories on the basis of what people have to say about death. But in this instance I would be more of a relativist. It is quite obvious from ethnography that although death is a universal phenomenon, it evokes the most particular and diverse ideas concerning its significance. Understanding these ideas calls for further studies of memory, time and history of just the kind that Susanne Küchler has carried out. Turning to the question of what are pasts and what is the present, I have tried tentatively to explore, in a more general way, what seems to be an area of convergence between psychology, physiology, phenomenology and ethnography, concerning the manner in which we experience time in intensely spatial ways. When you look at ethnographic accounts of memory, you find that much of what people talk about does in fact have a common theme. One of the most striking of these themes is food. Malinowski noted that whereas Trobriand Islanders thought of consciousness and the intellect as being located in the larynx and in speech, they imagined their memories to have sunk deep into their bellies: thus the seat of memory was the stomach.

With reference to language, Joel Kuipers[82] has coined the term *entextualization* to denote the way in which particular strands of speech are taken up and become progressively generalized. In trying to imagine how people generalize their very particular experiences of time and place, it occurred to me that we might adopt an analogous notion of *ensomatization*. But some sort of universal foundation is necessary in order to be able to grasp how people coming from different vantage points can engage in the politics of history as effectively as they do.

PENELOPE HARVEY   On the question of how to draw a line between the past and the present, it is most important to realize that past and present are relational categories. Thus the past, and any significance that may be attributed to it, exists in *relation* to the perspective of the present. Clearly, understandings of death are ethnographically specific; however, for many people the distance involved in death does not prevent a deceased person from remaining in the present – indeed, considerable effort may be invested in keeping death and presence concurrent. But we need to bear in mind the way in which memory operates here. We may have to distinguish kinds of pasts in terms of kinds of memory. I am thinking in particular of Peter Gow's work on the people of the Bajo Urubamba,[83] though I am sure there are many other appropriate examples. Gow shows how these people distinguish kinds of relationships that are remembered from those of which they have no memory. The latter are assigned to a nasty, pre-human time when people didn't remember each other and when groups were far too specific and different, by contrast to the contemporary human world in which, so long as you can remember people, you can keep them with you in the sense of achieving some kind of sociality. But even if the argument is cast in terms of the operation of memory, we are still dealing with something that is grounded in ethnographic specificity.

SUSANNE KÜCHLER   So far as meaning is linked to understanding, some immediate synthesis of past and present is surely implied. In the ethnographic example just mentioned, the people construed as living before the time that could be remembered were presumably not capable of being understood: they could not be remembered, they could not be understood, they could not be known. If we accept the idea of a relationship between remembering and consciousness, then we cannot ask such questions as 'When does the past begin, and where does it end?', 'When does the present begin, and where does it end?', or 'When does it go into the future?' For it is precisely in the perception of familiarity that the act of remembering and the act of consciousness lies. I am thinking in relation to my own study of the *Malangan* sculptures of New Ireland.[84] When they see a sculpture, people do not call up the different kinds of images they have seen in the past, but rather interpret the present image in the light of the kinds of relationships that are actually in the process of being established. They are trying to influence the relationships that will exist in the immediate future; they are not speculating about other kinds of images that existed in the past. Thus in my view, the past is not something that can be regarded as having started at a particular point, or even as having

entailed certain kinds of events. But one can of course assume the
position of the historian who seeks to interpret the past in terms of
particular interrelations between specific events.

ALFRED GELL   It appears to me that there are, in fact, two distinguishable meanings that can be attributed to the past, and
depending on which meaning you adopt, you can support one
side or the other in this debate. When the subject of time is
discussed by philosophers, one device they use is to distinguish
between two kinds of temporal series. The first, known as the A-
series, is based on the ideas of ontological subjectivity and
linguistic tense, in which past and future are anchored in present
experience; the second – the B-series – consists of a spread of events
in abstract space–time, such that the relationship between events is
described as one of their coming 'before' or 'after' each other.[85] It
seems to me that from the perspective of the B-series, 'before' *is*
indeed a foreign country, situated in an inaccessible region of the
spatiotemporal continuum. It is by definition a foreign country, in
the same sense that Mongolia is a foreign country – that is, it takes
time to get there. Yet the sense in which the proposition has mainly
been taken has been in relation to the A-series, a sense which is
clearly subjective, based not on the past as a spread of events in
space–time, but on the past as a *map*, constructed and held in
people's heads, of relations between events which are salient today.
Since any such model or map of currently salient spatiotemporal
relationships emerges from a process of cognitive functioning that
is going on in the present, the past as construed within it cannot
possibly be described as foreign or alien. Thus to argue – as I think
Penelope Harvey did – that the past is a 'foreign' country (with
quotation marks around the word 'foreign') is actually to *oppose*
the motion rather than to support it. For it is to suggest that the
foreignness of the past exists only within the terms of people's
present-day cultural constructions. If, however, we adopt the B-
series notion of the past as a spread of events in space–time, then
the argument *for* the motion is perfectly reasonable. In that case we
can speak of the past as a foreign country without having to place
the word 'foreign' in quotes.

PENELOPE HARVEY   Alfred Gell suggests that I had put quotation
marks around the word 'foreign'. But I had not, rather they were
placed around the words 'foreign country'. I agree that in terms of
the space–time continuum of the B-series, the past is irrefutably
foreign. From a phenomenological perspective, on the other hand,

it is only so if you regard foreignness as tantamount to alienation and total otherness. My point, however, is that if you think about the past not as 'foreign' but as 'foreign country', then it no longer necessarily implies total and absolute difference. But this solution, however neat, still raises the question of how we come to terms with difference, and of how we are to deal with it. The positive value of thinking about the past as a foreign country lies in the way in which it opens out to a consideration of the various ways in which relational terms such as past and present can actually be treated. Moreover, we are brought face-to-face with the problem of incommensurability and the limits of knowledge, as well as with the fact that we can only represent these through our own particular constructs of time, space and person.

GILLIAN FEELEY-HARNIK   I too have been trying to sort out my position with regard to the two alternative views of time which Alfred Gell has outlined, and which could – so to speak – make either side in this debate right. That's why I became interested in the question of time's arrow. Why should philosophers have imagined there to be an arrow of time at all? Seeking an answer to this question led me to the second law of thermodynamics, and to the writings of physicists like Stephen Hawking who – with the philosophers – have been wrestling with the problem of the directionality of time. They think of at least three different kinds of directions: there is a psychological arrow, a thermodynamic arrow (in the direction of chaos), and a cosmic arrow (that is, the expansion of the universe). So long as the universe continues to expand, the cosmic arrow of time will continue in its present direction; but once the expansion has ceased and the universe begins to implode upon itself, the direction will be reversed. There has been much controversy about what will then happen to our time: will we live backwards or think backwards? Will time disappear? Hawking himself has recently reversed his own opinion on these matters; moreover, there have been further complications. Thus the second law of thermodynamics predicts a disintegration into chaos which, as Hawking points out, will be the end of us human beings as well; yet there are those such as Prigogine who have argued, to the contrary, that out of this increasing chaos has come life, and life's increasingly complex forms.[86]

What I ask myself as an ethnographer is: how is it that these physicists have come up with such ideas about time and time's arrow? There are many possible ways of formulating ideas about time and of grounding them in the events of the physical universe. So why are they thinking of time in these particular ways right now? It seems to me that this question has to be asked and answered in the context of current events. This is not an entirely presentist point of view. I am merely saying that as ethnographers and historians we have to ask such questions in relation to social life.

JAMES WEINER   Let me try to make the two sides of this debate collide more directly by suggesting that the proposers are more interested in the *writing* of the past, whereas the opposers are concerned with the past as it is remembered by those who actually experienced it. However, I would like also to focus on one particular point that Susanne Küchler made. She criticized the dualism that suggests that the perception of an event is different or separate from its recollection. I agree that there is no way, *prima facie*, in which we can distinguish between perception and recollection. I do not think, however, that this observation lends support to the phenomenological position that both Susanne Küchler and Gillian Feeley-Harnik have put forward. On the contrary, it offers more support to the position taken by Penelope Harvey. She is the only speaker in this debate to have acknowledged the idea of difference – of unrecoverable, undefinable difference. In the absence of such acknowledgement, the two speakers for the opposition are both advocating a form of presentism – in the sense that only what is *present* in consciousness is worthy of our attention. Penelope Harvey, by contrast, is trying to account for the things that *cannot* be present to our consciousness, but which nevertheless involve human endeavour, human behaviour. An important aspect of her argument is the idea that it is the writing of history that lends a semblance of reality to these things, such that history seems to be about real things in real time. Let me remind you of the point Freud made, which has been seized upon by so many writers involved in post-modernist debates, namely that the patient always begins his or her analysis with a repetition. We might say that the historian likewise always begins his or her treatment of a subject with a repetition. Thus the division between the original perception of an historical event and its recollection, its passing into memory, is something that can only be *imposed* by the form of writing.

GILLIAN FEELEY-HARNIK   It is not that Susanne Küchler or I failed to acknowledge the idea of difference. To take a more presentist position is not to deny difference, it is rather to ask the question:

'How *do* we apprehend those things that are not immediately present to our consciousness?' Whether our concern be with what Peel calls 'substantial convictions' that might even be written in texts, or with objects we encounter, or with monuments, or with other human beings (who are, after all, different from the human being that I am), the problem is to envision how these things are apprehended. And in tackling this problem, it seems to me, anthropologists can usefully join forces with psychologists, physiologists, ecologists and others, since what we are trying to do is to break out of the straitjacket of old dichotomies and to do justice to the intimacies of these processes of apprehension, as well as to their global extent. This requires more interdisciplinary work.

SUSANNE KÜCHLER   I would simply like to reinforce Gillian Feeley-Harnik's point, that we are not arguing for the impossibility of the conscious perception of difference in the present. Our concern is with how the different is actually assimilated into the present, into the familiar. Referring back to the case of first contact between the people of Mount Hagen and White Australians, were not the latter wrought upon by the Hageners themselves to produce images of their own making? Of course it is possible to perceive difference, but is it not at the same moment turned into something familiar – into another image that one has created for oneself? And if the different is thus familiarized, how can we any longer sustain the notion that there is some ultimate strangeness that absolutely resists assimilation?

ALEXANDER LOPASIC   It seems to me that both sides of the debate are perfectly compatible within the terms of anthropology as a discipline. If we need a definition of anthropology for the purposes of the current discussion, we could say that it is the study of distance and difference, or of 'otherness'. As such, it can be traced back at least to the time of Herodotus, who has been called the father of history and who may be regarded equally as the father of anthropology. Now at that time, difference and otherness were the concern of societies that were still largely illiterate. Such societies had their own interpretations of past, present and future, and in many cases they could move quite readily from one temporal domain to the other, backwards and forwards, through rituals and dreams and in many other ways. For them the idea, as we know it today, of a clear-cut historical, evolutionary and scientific divide between past and present scarcely existed. But when anthropologists (that is, students of difference) from illiterate societies move to literate ones, then of course the situation changes: they become aware that there is something called the *reconstruction* of the past, which is a very difficult problem. To do it properly, one has to go through a series of documents which must be verified, clarified, compared and contrasted, and so on, in the course of which a *certain* past is reconstructed.

DAVID LOWENTHAL   With regard to James Weiner's surmise that we (the proposers) are on the side of the writers or makers of history and they (the opposers) on the side of those who suffered from it: I think there is some merit in that argument. By having to take up these positions we have been forced into an emphasis, on the one hand, on a historical approach to the past, and on the other hand, on a memorial approach to the past. The arguments of Gillian Feeley-Harnik and Susanne Küchler have certainly emphasized the role of memory. They have also stressed the salience of a much more recent past than that with which we have been dealing. Thus in a sense, where their approach has been psychological, or even physiological, ours has been more historical. This does not mean, however, that we are on the side of historians *against* the sufferers, though I can see how such a misapprehension might easily arise, and I can also see how distinctions between oral memory and written memory, or between oral evidence and written evidence, may in this context take on a political significance. Indeed, the history of scholarship is replete with illustrations. Take the case of Herodotus, who was mentioned a moment ago. In the second century, Herodotus was denounced by Lucian as a liar. He must, said Lucian, be tormented in Hades more than anyone else,[87] for historians – unlike all other people who are inclined to lie whenever they get the opportunity – should never lie. Even today, the stock phrase 'he lies like an eye-witness' indicates how little credence we are prepared to attribute to ordinary, first-hand observation.

In many ways, then, the arguments used by our opponents in this debate have been concerned much more than have ours with memorial processes, with pasts that are not written down and not thereby preserved from alteration. It is certainly true that the arrival of print culture has made a huge difference, *even* in societies that remain oral societies – as all societies do to a considerable extent. We need to take into account the really extraordinary and important differences between things that endure relatively unchanged or can be checked for change, such as writing and (to some extent) relics, and the stuff of memory which is more difficult to check and more subject to the specific dynamics of individual interpretation. This is not just a matter of distinguishing between a distant and a more recent past; it is also a question of the kinds of evidence at our disposal and the kinds of understanding to which it gives rise. Thus in one particular sense you cannot deny my memory, because it is *my* memory. If I say I remember something, you could perhaps seek to verify it by checking it against certain kinds of evidence, but you cannot deny that it is *my* memory.

TIM INGOLD   Is not this thesis, that our own memories – in so far as they are part of us, of who we are – cannot be denied, the plank on which we tend to rest our claims to ethnographic authority? Thus, speaking as an ethnographer, I might claim that what I write about a certain people is authoritative because it is based on my own experience of fieldwork, of having 'been there'. I raise this matter only because there does seem to be a connection between current debates about ethnographic authority and the contrast that David Lowenthal has drawn between memorial and historical approaches.

GILLIAN FEELEY-HARNIK   Our basic problem is as follows: how do we apprehend a world that contains so many different and diverse things? How do we apprehend things that are *not* ourselves while recognizing that we have no way of doing this except *through* ourselves? How can we understand what they are, while acknowledging that it is *we* who are looking at *them*? For they *do* exist out there; they *can* be documented. I do not believe, therefore, that ethnographic authority rests solely on the authority of the ethnographer. For other people have their authorities; other objects have their qualities. Our task is to do justice to these others, and to our involvement with them, not to flood them with our own preconceptions. This is the essence of empirical responsibility.

We are dealing, of course, with a situation of plural knowledges. There are many co-existing ways of understanding time and space, whatever terms you may use for them. What Susanne Küchler and I have been trying to do is to excavate forms of consciousness, knowing, understanding and time that have been marginalized by what you could call the hegemony of the book. So effectively have they been marginalized, indeed, that we can only begin to grasp them now – in radically changed circumstances – through the work of scholars such as Carruthers, to which I have already referred.

ALFRED GELL   David Lowenthal argued that the past is a foreign country because you can never experience, say, early music as it would have been experienced by the people of the period in which it was originally written and performed. But I would seriously question whether it is the purpose of modern purveyors of early music to recreate that original experience. Consider Handel's *Coronation Anthem*. Apparently the official who was in charge of the coronation was thoroughly disgusted by the music: in his view it was all noise and disorder. For one thing, the musicians were unable to play it; for another, he didn't like it anyway. It would surely be impossible to reconstruct a performance of music that is both badly played and completely misunderstood (unless the audience was carefully selected to consist only of persons known to dislike it intensely). And indeed there would be little point in doing so! What the purveyors of early music want to do is furnish music for our enjoyment, not to provide us with some experience of early music *as if* one was there, say, at the Coronation itself. And this is a perfectly valid objective, so long as it is not confused with the realization of historical truth.

DAVID LOWENTHAL   In proposing the motion, I did bring up the now discredited notion of the ethnographic present. However, it has not otherwise figured in our debate. I wonder whether the anthropologists here would have more to say about it.

MARILYN STRATHERN   A brief response: the ethnographic present does not lie in debate, it lies in books. It has to be understood in the context of the way books are written.

It appears that the arguments on both sides of this debate collude in the assumption that the past is somehow subsumed under the present, regardless of the kind of past it is. But they disagree over the outcome. On the one hand, the past is portrayed as recollectable, as not *only* our past; on the other hand, it is portrayed as *non*-recollectable, remaining both intact and foreign. I would like to ask the speakers on each side to explain what they see as the dangers entailed in adopting the other side's point of view.

ANDREW HOLDING   And whichever way the debate goes, what are the implications of the different arguments for anthropological theory?

PENELOPE HARVEY   There is indeed a sense in which the proposition can accommodate both sides to this debate. If we agree, as Marilyn Strathern has just put it, that the past is subsumed under the present, then what are the dangers of concluding – with our opponents – that the past is *not* a foreign country? I see two problems. First, David Lowenthal has pointed out that we cannot re-enter the perceptual world of the past, for the ways we perceive are bound to be affected by what has happened since. How, then, if we take the point of view of the opposition, are we to understand the *experience* of anachronism? Second, how could we deal with *not* knowing: with things that cannot readily be incorporated into one's present?

GILLIAN FEELEY-HARNIK   Let me respond to Penelope Harvey's second question. Empirically, it seems that we are able to deal with unknown things, in part, because we do not come to them with a sense of complete not knowing. Rather, we attempt to grasp and apprehend them on the basis of what we have. This is where I found the work of Gadamer on the historicity of reason so enlightening.[88] Gadamer tries to grasp the exact process whereby we bring to bear a certain historicity of reason on persons and things we have never experienced before, such as in situations of first contact. But there is another side to this process, which has to do with the way we *forget* things or put them at a distance. We have not yet discussed this aspect so extensively, but it too could be understood from a more phenomenological viewpoint.

DAVID LOWENTHAL   With regard to the dangers inherent in adopting our opponents' position, let me first say that I am delighted by the reminder that it is a *country* we are dealing with. There is, after all, something to a country: we may not like other countries, but they do have certain aspects in common, some degree of comparability. We are not dealing with Hades, or even with the Antipodes, but with places that are to some degree known. Now it seems to me that to conclude that the past is *not* a foreign country is to run the risk of legitimating the efforts of those who would continually remake the past to be like the present, for whatever presentist purposes they have in mind: political, social, economic, polemical. I am worried by the extent to which people – especially those without a knowledge of history – are enabled, by the fact that the past is very vivid to them, to treat it continually as though it were just like the present. This can work at the expense, especially, of those who have been savaged by history, or who have been its sufferers in one way or another. I am thinking of minorities, or tribal groups – peoples with pasts that are different, pasts that we think of as group possessions. Many pasts are like this; that is to say, each is in the nature of a *heritage*. Each is exclusive to the group or country concerned, and must indeed remain so – incomparable, mysterious to outsiders. I have in mind the example of the Sacred Bundle of the Pawnee Indians, presented not long ago to a museum in the American Mid-West, with the specific injunction that it should not be opened. The Bundle was regarded as the embodiment of tribal memory, and would hold its significance for the tribe only so long as it remained unopened and thus unknown to others.[89] It is important to recognize that many pasts *must not be known* by others if they are to retain their power and significance for ourselves.

TIM INGOLD   We have discussed the relationship between history and memory at some length, but have yet to deal with the issue of forgetting, which Gillian Feeley-Harnik raised a moment ago. What, exactly, is involved in forgetting? Is it the simple opposite of remembering? If not, how should it be conceptualized? How are memories erased?

It seems that when we speak about forgetting, or about remembering, as something that people *do*, we run into similar contradictions to those surrounding the notion of trust. It has been said that you cannot build up a relationship of trust deliberately, or strategically, because the principle of strategic self-interest subverts the very basis on which the relationship is to be established.[90] Likewise, how can we regard forgetting as a deliberate, intentionally motivated activity, when the very formation of our intention entails calling to mind what we are supposed to forget?

GILLIAN FEELEY-HARNIK   I think we have a deeply held conviction that forgetting involves a loss. This is very clear, for example, in Hartley's book. Its message is that we need finally to be able to recover and reintegrate the forgotten past in order to become fully mature persons. But whether this conviction is specific to our own European or American background, or more widely held, I do not know.

DAVID LOWENTHAL   I should like to make a general plea for forgetting, on the grounds that to remember everything is to be an idiot. A man who cannot help but remember everything can never generalize. Life involves selective forgetting. If we could not forget most of what we knew or even remembered, we would not be able to organize the rest of our knowledge sufficiently even to survive. But there are other levels of forgetting, such as oblivion – which requires of one, as a condition of survival, to be able to forget enormously painful events, in order to avoid the regressions that would otherwise follow. I am mindful of the role this has played in

English history. Two 'acts of oblivion' were passed by Parliament in the seventeenth century, one in 1660 and the other in 1690, to 'forgive and forget' what was done by the opponents of the two kings of the immediately preceding period, in order to help reintegrate the country. This became a general principle of political philosophy with Hobbes, who emphasized, as have many others since, that in order to form a polity, or to be able to proceed as a collectivity, people must agree on what to forget and what to remember.[91]

GILLIAN FEELEY-HARNIK   I should like to conclude with two points on this business of forgetting. First, if we look at the ethnographic evidence, we find that the work put into forgetting is substantial. It may take the material form, say, of prohibitions on speech, and it needs to be organized so that people are *made* to forget. Particularly clear instances of this come from studies of Melanesian societies, and especially of activities surrounding funerals that very often involve the break-up of descent groups. We have scarcely begun to study the consequences of this kind of forgetting for people's sense of themselves, their identities and their well-being.

My second point is that forgetting, it seems to me, is a deep and central issue in our whole way of thinking about past, present and future. It has to do with the significance we give to lifetimes. There are some things, certainly, that we all have to forget: we all know Sherlock Holmes's dictum that you need to forget so as to rid your mind of inconsequentialities. But much of our sense of saving ourselves and of regenerating ourselves over time has to do with *not* forgetting, with reintegrating events from our very beginnings with events from our more recent past. This is an important phenomenon that could be analysed further in anthropological terms.

NOTES

1   R. Sanjek, 'The ethnographic present', *Man* (N.S.) 26, 1991, pp. 609–28, esp. p. 612.
2   E. N. Goody, 'Learning, apprenticeship and the division of labor', in *Apprenticeship: from theory to method and back again*, ed. M. W. Coy, Albany, State University of New York Press, 1989; J. Lave, 'The culture of acquisition and the practice of understanding', in *Cultural psychology: essays on comparative human development*, eds J. W. Stigler, R. A. Shweder and G. Herdt, Cambridge, Cambridge University Press, 1990; F. Sigaut,

'Learning, teaching and apprenticeship', *New Literary History* 24, 1993, pp. 105–14.

3   J. D. Y. Peel, 'Making history: the past in the Ijesha present', *Man* (N.S.) 19, 1984, pp. 111–32, esp. p. 112.

4   R. R. Marett, *Psychology and folklore*, London, Methuen, 1920, p. 11.

5   L. P. Hartley, *The Go-Between*, London, Hamish Hamilton, 1953; D. Lowenthal, *The past is a foreign country*, Cambridge, Cambridge University Press, 1985.

6   B. S. Cohn, 'Anthropology and history in the 1980s', *Journal of Interdisciplinary History* 12, 1981, pp. 227–52; E. R. Leach, 'Tribal ethnography: past, present, future', in *History and Ethnicity*, eds E. Tonkin, M. McDonald and M. Chapman, London, Routledge, 1989, pp. 34–47.

7   L. Passerini, *Fascism in popular memory: the cultural experience of the Turin working class*, Cambridge, Cambridge University Press, 1987, p. 3.

8   M. Parris, writing in *The Times*, 19 October 1992, p. 14.

9   'A survey of Britain', *The Economist*, 24 October 1992, p. 4.

10   G. McCracken, *Culture and consumption*, Bloomington, Indiana University Press, 1988, p. 132.

11   J. W. von Goethe, 'Schreiben an Ludwig I von Bayern vom. 17. Dez. 1829', *Gesamtausgabe* 24: 316, quoted in R. Koselleck, *Futures past: on the semantics of historical time*, Cambridge, MA, MIT Press, 1985, p. 216.

12   F. R. de Chateaubriand, *Essai historique, politique et moral sur les révolutions anciennes et modernes*, Paris, 1861, p. 249.

13   D. Lowenthal, 'The timeless past: some Anglo-American historical preconceptions', *Journal of American History* 75, 1989, pp. 1263–80.

14   N. Z. Davis, *The return of Martin Guerre*, Harmondsworth, Penguin, 1983, p. viii.

15   A. Rooley, *Performance: revealing the Orpheus within*, Shaftesbury, Dorset, Element Books, 1990, p. 5.

16   M. Baxandall, *Patterns of intention: on the historical explanation of pictures,*. New Haven, Yale University Press, 1985, pp. 111–15.

17   P. Dickinson, *Death of a unicorn*, New York, Pantheon, 1984, p. 25.

18   P. Richards, this volume p. 123.

19   H. Canning, 'Authenticity and Bach', in *Towards Bach* programme, South Bank Centre, London, 13–26 August 1989.

20   R. Taruskin, 'The pastness of the present and the presence of the past', in *Authenticity and early music*, ed. N. Kenyon, New York, Oxford University Press, 1988, p. 144; H. Haskell, *The early music revival: a history*, London, Thames & Hudson, 1988; and R. Leppard, *Authenticity in music*, London, Faber Music, 1988, give analogous views. On pre-industrial and modern soundscapes, see R. M. Schafer, *The tuning of the world*, Toronto, McClelland and Stewart, 1977.

21   S. Wanamaker, 'Shakespeare's Globe reborn', *Journal of the Royal Society of Arts* 133, 1989, pp. 25–34.

22   A. C. Danto, 'The problem of other periods', *Journal of Philosophy* 63, 1966, pp. 566–77.

23   A. Schlesinger, Jr., 'The historian as participant', *Daedalus* 100, 1971, pp. 339–57; W. W. Menninger, 'Say, it isn't so: when wishful thinking obscures historical reality', *History News* 40 (12), 1985, pp. 10–13; D. Lowenthal, *The*

past is a foreign country, Cambridge, Cambridge University Press, 1985, pp. 234–5.

24 J. R. Townsend and J. P. Walsh, eds, *Travellers in time: past, present, and to come*, Histon, Cambridge, Green Bay Publishers, 1990.

25 S. Morley, 'There's no business like old business', *Punch*, 29 November 1972, p. 777.

26 L. P. Hartley, *The Go-Between*, London, Hamish Hamilton, 1953, p. 9.

27 Commentary on Isaiah 54.1 in the Babylonian Talmud, Berakhot 10a.

28 L. P. Hartley, *The Go-Between*, London, Hamish Hamilton, 1953, p. 296.

29 S. E. Hyman, *The tangled bank: Darwin, Marx, Frazer, and Freud as imaginative writers*, New York, Atheneum, 1974.

30 D. Lowenthal, *The past is a foreign country*, Cambridge, Cambridge University Press, 1985, p. 412.

31 J. D. Y. Peel, 'Making history: the past in the Ijesha present', *Man* (N.S.) 19, 1984, pp. 111–32, esp. p. 112.

32 *Ibid.*, p. 113; A. Appadurai, 'The past as a scarce resource', *Man* (N.S.) 16, 1981, pp. 201–19; C. Toren, 'Making the present, revealing the past: the mutability and continuity of tradition as process', *Man* (N.S.) 23, 1988, pp. 696–717.

33 P. Bourdieu, *Outline of a theory of practice*, Cambridge, Cambridge University Press, 1977, p. 78.

34 R. Hubbard, *The politics of women's biology*, New Brunswick, NJ, Rutgers University Press, 1990, pp. 115–16.

35 T. Ingold, 'Culture and the perception of the environment', in *Bush base: forest farm. Culture, environment, and development*, eds E. Croll and D. Parkin, London, Routledge, 1992.

36 L. R. Squire and S. Zola-Morgan, 'The medial temporal lobe memory system', *Science* 253 [20 September], 1991, pp. 1380–6.

37 *Ibid.*, pp. 1380, 1385.

38 *Ibid.*, p. 1381.

39 For example, H. Ehrlichman and J. N. Halpern, 'Affect and memory: effects of pleasant and unpleasant odors on retrieval of happy and unhappy memories', *Journal of Personality and Social Psychology* 55, 1988, pp. 769–79; F. R. Schab, 'Odors and the remembrance of things past', *Journal of Experimental Psychology: Learning, Memory, and Cognition* 16, 1990, pp. 648–55.

40 A. Gell, 'Magic, perfume, dream', in *Symbols and sentiments*, ed. I. Lewis, London, Academic Press, 1977; J. Siegel, 'Images and odors in Javanese practices surrounding death', *Indonesia* 36, 1983, pp. 1–14; D. Howes, 'Olfaction and transition: an essay on the ritual uses of smell', *Revue Canadienne de Sociologie et Anthropologie* 24, 1987, pp. 398–416. The geographer D. W. Gade coined the term 'smellscape' to counter European and American geographers' lack of attention to the odours of places, which he associates in part with a general cultural bias against acknowledging odours; see his 'Redolence and land use on Nosy Be, Madagascar', *Journal of Cultural Geography* 4, 1984, pp. 29–40.

41 Most recently, E. S. Casey, *Remembering: a phenomenological study*, Bloomington, Indiana University Press, 1987, especially pp. 181–215.

246   *The past is a foreign country*

42   E.g., W. F. Brewer, in *Remembering reconsidered: ecological and traditional approaches to the study of memory*, eds U. Neisser and E. Winograd, New York, Cambridge University Press, 1988, pp. 21–90.
43   K. Basso, '"Stalking with stories": names, places and moral narrative among the Western Apache', in *Text, play and story: the construction and reconstruction of self and society*, ed. E. M. Bruner, Washington, DC, American Ethnological Society, 1984, pp. 19–55.
44   S. Feld, *Sound and sentiment: birds, weeping, poetics, and song in Kaluli expression*, Philadelphia, University of Pennsylvania Press, 1990.
45   G. Feeley-Harnik, *A green estate: restoring independence in Madagascar*, Washington, DC, Smithsonian Institution Press, 1991.
46   J. D. Y. Peel, 'Making history: the past in the Ijesha present', *Man* (N.S.) 19, 1984, pp. 111–32, esp. p. 112.
47   H-G. Gadamer, *Truth and method*, New York, Crossroad, 1982.
48   A. Salmond, 'Theoretical landscapes: on cross-cultural conceptions of knowledge', in *Semantic anthropology*, ed. D. Parkin, London, Academic Press, 1982; see G. Feeley-Harnik, *A green estate*, pp. 466–7.
49   T. R. Trautmann, 'The revolution in ethnological time', *Man* (N.S.) 27, 1992, pp. 379–97.
50   W. E. Leuchtenberg, cited in K. J. Winkler, 'How should scholars respond to assertions that the Holocaust never happened?', *The Chronicle of Higher Education*, 11 December 1991, pp. A8–A10.
51   S. Heller, 'Yale's "Archive of Conscience" provides scholars with videotaped accounts from Holocaust survivors', *The Chronicle of Higher Education*, 11 December 1991, pp. A9, A11.
52   A. Spiegelman, *Maus: a survivor's tale*, New York, Pantheon, 1986, p. 7.
53   Cited in L. L. Langer, *Holocaust testimonies: the ruins of memory*, New Haven, Yale University Press, 1991, pp. xiv, 7, 53.
54   H. Eilberg-Schwartz, *The savage in Judaism: an anthropology of Israelite religion and ancient Judaism*, Bloomington, Indiana University Press, 1990, Part I; J. Boyarin, *Storm from paradise: the politics of Jewish memory*, Minneapolis, University of Minnesota Press, 1992.
55   M. J. Carruthers shows the interconnections between new print technologies and changing ideas and practices concerning memory, reason, and moral regeneration; see *The book of memory: a study of memory in medieval culture*, Cambridge, Cambridge University Press, 1990.
56   Research on immunology and new reproductive technologies suggests radical changes in people's experiences of their bodily boundaries. See E. Martin, 'Toward an anthropology of immunology: the body as nation state', *Medical Anthropology Quarterly* 4, 1990, pp. 410–26; M. Strathern, *Reproducing the future: essays on anthropology, kinship and the new reproductive technologies*, New York, Routledge, 1992.
57   J. Clifford, 'Traveling cultures', in *Cultural studies*, eds L. Grossberg, C. Nelson and P. Treichler, London, Routledge, 1992.
58   D. Harvey, *The condition of postmodernity*, Oxford, Blackwell, 1989.
59   M. Strathern, *After nature: English kinship in the late twentieth century*, Cambridge, Cambridge University Press, 1992, p. 43.
60   S. Küchler, 'Malangan: art and memory in a Melanesian society', *Man* (N.S.) 22, 1987, pp. 238–55, esp. p. 238.

61 *Ibid.*, p. 241.
62 P. Gow, *Of mixed blood: kinship and history in Peruvian Amazonia*, Oxford, Clarendon Press, 1991.
63 M. Strathern, 'The decomposition of an event', *Cultural Anthropology* 7, 1992, pp. 244–55.
64 P. Mason, *Deconstructing America: representations of the other*, London, Routledge, 1990.
65 E. Wolf, *Europe and the people without history*, Berkeley, University of California Press, 1982, p. 4.
66 M. Taussig, *The nervous system*, London, Routledge, 1992.
67 P. Gose, 'Sacrifice and the commodity form in the Andes', *Man* (N.S.) 21, 1986, pp. 296–310.
68 J. Fabian, *Time and the other*, New York, Columbia University Press, 1983.
69 O. Harris, 'Time and difference in anthropological writing', in *Constructing knowledge: authority and critique in social science*, eds L. Nencel and P. Pels, London, Sage, 1991, p. 147.
70 O. Sacks, *The man who mistook his wife for a hat*, London, Duckworth, 1985.
71 I. Rosenfield, *The strange, the familiar and the forgotten: an anatomy of consciousness*, New York, Knopf, 1992.
72 B. Bridgeman, 'Intention itself will disappear when its mechanisms are known', *Behavioral and Brain Sciences* 13, 1990, pp. 598–9.
73 S. Küchler and W. Melion, *Images of memory: on remembering and representation*, Washington, DC, Smithsonian Institution Press, 1991, p. 10.
74 P. Connerton, *How societies remember*, Cambridge, Cambridge University Press, 1989; E. Casey, *Remembering*, Bloomington, Indiana University Press, 1987; M. Johnson, *The body in the mind*, Chicago, Chicago University Press, 1987.
75 F. Yates, *The art of memory*, Chicago, Chicago University Press, 1966.
76 See, for example, M. Baxandall, *Painting and experience in fifteenth century Italy*, Oxford, Oxford University Press, 1987; W. Melion, *Shaping the Netherlandish canon*, Chicago, Chicago University Press, 1992.
77 I. Rosenfield, *The strange, the familiar and the forgotten*, New York, Knopf, 1992, p. 3.
78 M. Proust, *Remembrance of things past*, Harmondsworth, Penguin, 1983 [original 1913–27].
79 G. Bachelard, *The poetics of space*, Boston, Beacon Press, 1964.
80 R. McDonald, *The burial places of memory: epic underworlds in Virgil, Dante and Milton*, Amherst, University of Massachusetts Press, 1987.
81 M.J. Carruthers, *The book of memory: a study of memory in medieval culture*, Cambridge, Cambridge University Press, 1990.
82 J. Kuipers, 'Place, names, and authority in Weyéwa ritual speech', *Language and Society* 13, 1984, pp. 455–66.
83 P. Gow, *Of mixed blood: kinship and history in Peruvian Amazonia*, Oxford, Clarendon Press, 1991.
84 S. Küchler, 'Malangan: art and memory in a Melanesian society', *Man* (N.S.) 22, 1987, pp. 238–55.
85 A. Gell, *The anthropology of time: cultural constructions of temporal maps and images*, Oxford, Berg, 1992, pp. 149–55.
86 S. W. Hawking, *A brief history of time: from the big bang to black holes*, London, Bantam Press, 1988; I. Prigogine, *From being to becoming: time and*

complexity in the physical sciences, San Francisco, W. H. Freeman, 1980; I. Prigogine and E. Stengers, *Order out of chaos: man's new dialogue with nature*, London, Heinemann, 1984.

87   Lucian of Samosata, 'The way to write history', in his *Works*, eds H.W. Fowler and F. G. Fowler, Oxford, Clarendon Press, 1905, pp. 109–36.

88   H-G. Gadamer, *Truth and method*, New York, Crossroad, 1982.

89   D. L. Good, 'Sacred bundles: history wrapped up in culture', *History News* 45(4), 1990, pp. 13–14, 27.

90   G. Hawthorn, 'Three ironies in trust', in *Trust: making and breaking co-operative relations*, ed. D. Gambetta, Oxford, Blackwell, 1988.

91   D. Lowenthal, 'Memory and oblivion', *Museum Management and Curatorship* 12, 1993, pp. 171–82.

1993 debate

Aesthetics is a cross-cultural category

Introduction

James F. Weiner

At one point in his initial argument for the motion 'aesthetics is a cross-cultural category', Jeremy Coote remarks on the spate of anthropological monographs that have appeared in the past few years with the word 'aesthetics' in their titles, and he wonders why this word so rarely appeared in such titles before, say, 1970. Undeniably, social science and anthropology have recently been seized by a concern with aesthetics (and also poetics). The reasons for this have to do, I think, with current theorizing about modernity and modernism, and the place of anthropology and of social theorizing in general, within late twentieth-century Western culture and society.

Broadly speaking, we can identify three connected phenomena of the late twentieth century. First, we have witnessed the emergence of mass, globalized media, particularly in their visual forms of television, video and film. Second, because instantaneous global communications are obliterating the temporal intervals between events and their communication and witnessing, we experience a suppression of time, a phenomenon made more pronounced by the ease with which artefacts, practices, languages and events from varying historical and temporal frames are now juxtaposed in our everyday life. Finally, as a consequence of this, we now commonly experience a suppression of space too, a virtualization of spatial perceptions and relationships, so that relations of proximity and remoteness have to be simulated through global media rather than appealed to in terms of absolute geographic distance.

The combination of this universalization of televised representations of the world with our dominant global political motif, nationalism, has powerfully enhanced the *aestheticization of politics* which has been such a key component of twentieth-century modernism in Europe and North America. Nationalism inevitably depends heavily on imagery – on myth, on visual icons and display, on state theatre and ceremonial, all of which make it intrinsically interesting to anthropology. Nationalism and culture are of course intimately connected, and appeals made in the interests of national identity often resemble the arguments with which anthropologists justify their identification of culture. In anthropology, the aestheticization of politics becomes the aestheticization of culture and indeed of the social itself.

Considered in terms of its practical effects on the conduct of our everyday lives, our dependence upon global media encourages us to make everything into an issue of representation and self-representation, and of image manipulation, management and achieved consensus. This transformation in our representational practices has also affected our anthropology, and has led many to consider culture and social life likewise in terms of representation and self-representation. And although this aestheticization does not, except perhaps tangentially in Alfred Gell's comments, enter into the present debate, it is well to set the debate in the context of these broad developments, for they are indicated all along the way.

Howard Morphy, proposing the motion, and Joanna Overing, opposing it, begin by almost perfectly characterizing Kant's two treatments of the concept of aesthetic in his First and Third Critiques respectively. Morphy maintains that aesthetics is about how the human sensory capacity construes and gives form to stimuli. Overing speaks of aesthetics as the judgement of beauty and of taste, of the 'pure' aesthetic as such, and regards it as a phenomenon of European modernism not automatically applicable to non-Western societies.

The two seconders maintain this contrast between the transcendental and the pure Kantian aesthetic, but in a way that reverses the respective positions of the proposers. For now we find Jeremy Coote, seconding the motion, arguing that if the Dinka and Yoruba people themselves appeal, in their own vocabulary (as do Overing's Piaroa), to ideas of beauty and grace, then this fact alone should convince us that aesthetic categories have cross-cultural applicability. This point was further emphasized during the discussion by Marcus Banks. He observes that all of the participants in the debate have carried out their ethnographic work in 'non-state societies' and that, had any of them worked in the complex societies of Asia (for example in India and China) where aesthetic discourse and theory are well developed and have a long history unaffected by anything modernist or European, then the motion would have appeared literally uncontestable.

However, Peter Gow, seconding the opposition to the motion, responds to Banks and in so doing draws the two Kantian notions of aesthetic into a closer relation by appealing, after Bourdieu, to the idea of distinction or discrimination. While, on the one hand, the categories of intuition and cognition combine to give human beings the capacity to make distinctions between objects, on the other hand, the history and theory of art and aesthetics provide people in the West with the practices and vocabulary by which to make the judgements that underlie and instaurate their social and class distinctions. *This* is what is distinctive about *our* aesthetic discourse. Gow concludes from this that our aesthetic practice is always to make such distinctions, to make *judgements*. To the extent that anthropology's whole rationale is to *avoid* making such judgements – the most salient in this context being the judging of a culture in terms of its capacity to produce beautiful things – then it must be anathema to anthropology.

I would like to depart here from the precedent of editorial impartiality, and take a stand myself. I think that in hindsight, Gow's was probably the argument that clinched victory for the opposers of the motion. For it drew attention away from what I believe was a snag in Overing's initial argument. This snag concerned an issue that seemed to weave its way through the entire debate: that of contextualization. Overing objects to the modernist aesthetic because it aspires to remove the art object from its situatedness in the world. Among the Piaroa, she observes, considerations of the beauty of objects are inseparable from questions about their utility and their everyday productive potency. But she maintains that the anthropology of art, still seeped in the modernist sensibility of the transcendence of the art object, finds 'the idea of the everyday utility of objects of art ... odious'.

During the debate, however, Sonia Greger made the important point that in the Third Critique, Kant was *not* talking about the autonomy of the aesthetic object in terms of those contemporary notions of judgement to which Bourdieu and Gow appeal. Kant believed that the art object had 'purposiveness without purpose'. He wanted to know precisely why the art object could *not* be an object of judgement in the normal sense. That is, he was addressing the issue of transcendence without which, as Gell's recent article on Trobriand art makes clear,[1] the work of art allows us no perspective at all on the everyday. And to return to my initial observations, it is only because, quite unlike the essentially *nineteenth-century* modernist aesthetic that Overing invokes as her straw man, our current *late twentieth-century* life has been so thoroughly aestheticized, that our sensitivity to what Baudrillard calls 'critical transcendence' – which he could only mean in this original Kantian sense – has disappeared. 'Art is dead ... because reality itself, entirely impregnated by an aesthetic which is inseparable from its own structure, has been confused with its own image.'[2] Overing's plea for contextualization would appear to have much the same image in mind. But in the pursuit of this, we lose any possibility of characterizing the power of art as transcendence, something which still needs to be debated within anthropology.

Part I The presentations

FOR THE MOTION (1)

HOWARD MORPHY

Let me begin by saying what this debate is not about. We will not be arguing for a universal aesthetic: that there are universal criteria for evaluating the aesthetic properties of works of art that operate cross-culturally – properties such as balance, relative proportion, symmetry and so on. We will not be arguing, as Firth and Forge have argued to some extent,[3] that the criteria for determining what is or is not good art exist independently of culture. We are simply concerned to establish that the concept of aesthetics is a useful one to apply in cross-cultural analysis. Far from commending our aesthetic judgements of other people's artefacts, we hold that the aesthetics of objects should be analysed in the context of the society that produces them: it is this use of the concept of aesthetics, to develop understanding of 'other' people's cultures, that gives it cross-cultural applicability. We will argue further that in failing to consider the aesthetics of cultures, anthropologists ignore a body of evidence that allows them a unique access to the sensual aspect of human experience: to how people feel in, and respond to, the world. We do not entirely exclude the possibility of certain universal features of human aesthetics, but we do not intend to explore them here.

First, what do we mean by a cross-cultural category? We see anthropology as a discipline that involves the translation of events and behaviours of one culture so that they can be understood by members of another in terms of the value that they have in the context of the originating culture. Anthropology so defined depends on the existence of implicit or explicit cross-cultural categories, which are used in this process of translation. Anthropology originated as a European discipline and the main goal of translation was to satisfy a European audience. The terminology and problematic of anthropology were biased towards European concerns and the categories of European systems of thought. But it became a discipline set up to eliminate its own biases. The history of anthropology has in part been the development of a conceptual vocabulary designed to understand culture in context. This weak form of cultural relativism, with its underlying objectivism, has guided anthropology through most of its history. The idea that there is something out there that can be understood in its own terms better by anthropologists than by non-anthropologists has long been the main justification of the discipline. Although such a perspective can be criticized for being part of the very process of constituting the 'other', of reifying culture, and of fixing the fluidity of human systems of meaning, I see such arguments more as cautions than as theoretically valid critiques.

The process of anthropology as cross-cultural translation has resulted in the development of a metalanguage for discourse. This metalanguage includes both substantive terms for institutions, groups, and objects that can be usefully applied across cultures, and certain analytic concepts that can be applied to understand socio-cultural processes. The former are exemplified by concepts such as lineage, moiety, spearthrower and pot; the latter by terms such as segmentation, alliance and symbol. The metalanguage is not as widely shared as those of many other disciplines such as structural linguistics, with its set of precise definitions of terms and its conventional epistemology. The vocabulary is that of a field of discourse which is shifting over time and in which many people disagree on the meaning of terms, often using them in fundamentally different ways without realizing it. Certain terms, such as 'patriliny', have a longer duration than others. Who still remembers what complementary filiation is?[4]

The vocabulary that develops is not a passive one. The enterprise of anthropology is a dialogue and one that inevitably results in change both in the subjects of its enquiry and in the discipline itself.[5] The terms of anthropological metalanguage become part of the way members of the cultures studied present themselves to the world. Yolngu people in Northeast Arnhem Land readily use the terminology of clans and moieties in talking to Europeans. However, it would be wrong to overemphasize the diffusion of anthropological terms relative to those of other disciplines. Yolngu use the linguistic terminology of verbs, nouns, relative clauses and retroflex consonants with a facility that would delight a Conservative minister of education. And the legalese of contracts and copyright has entered Yolngu everyday discourse: bark paintings are now 'title deeds',[6] and people are liable to ask for royalty agreements for the reproduction of photographs. The process, however, is a two-way one and concepts that develop and acquire a specific meaning through anthropological research can affect the way a particular topic is understood in Western society. The impact of anthropological analyses of witchcraft on studies of European history is a case in point: the historians have been freed from a contemporary, Eurocentric concept of witchcraft by Africanist research, enabling them to reach a better understanding of their own past.[7] Words in anthropological metalanguage are gradually distanced from their meaning in everyday language and acquire value from their use in anthropological discourse, which increasingly departs from Eurocentric preconceptions. In applying the terms to new contexts anthropologists must always be aware of the danger of imposing external meanings on the phenomenon in question; concepts must be used flexibly in the process of cultural translation.

Concepts which prove to be overly Eurocentric – such as 'civilization' and 'primitive' – are eventually discarded, while the meaning of others is modified. Certain terms remain, however, and their retention implies that the phenomena from different cultures included within their respective ranges of reference are in some way comparable. This has resulted, on the one hand, in the development of regional vocabularies that apply to such culture areas as Island Polynesia or the East African cattle belt and, on the other hand, in an increasing generality of anthropological language. Because the process of anthropology has been one of acknowledging cultural diversity, there has been a tendency to move towards general concepts such as 'exchange', 'gender' and 'identity'. The general concepts that survive say something about the capacities of human beings and the possible characteristics of human societies. It is in this context that we place the anthropological concept of 'aesthetics'.

Aesthetics has an established place in European philosophy, referring to a particular capacity for response and a form of action in the world that is as integral to our notion of what it takes to be a human being as is the capacity for thought. While anthropologists have learnt to take none of their universal categories for granted, in practice such categories are invaluable for comparative research even if they are eventually rejected. We argue that the proposition 'human beings have the capacity for aesthetic response' is no more or less challengeable than the proposition 'human beings have the capacity for thought'. Both are general propositions that result in a multiplicity of different enquiries.

I will not provide a simple definition of aesthetics, since it would be as difficult as trying to provide a one-line definition of human thought, and

I would be in danger of creating my own straw person. Rather, I will indicate the range of issues with which cross-cultural research into aesthetics is concerned.[8] Aesthetics is concerned with the qualitative effect of stimuli on the senses. The stimuli may be material in form, stemming from properties of the world that can be seen, felt or heard, or they may result from the apprehension of an idea. Such stimuli are integrated in many different ways with human cultural and behavioural systems, and can be interpreted on many different levels: a sound can be a component of speech, a light can be a warning, a pin prick can be medical therapy. An aesthetic response reflects the human capacity to value the properties of form independently of any particular function. Aesthetics involves the valuation of qualities along a range of dimensions including softness, hardness, lightness, heaviness, brightness, sharpness and so on.[9]

We do not argue that the stimuli are experienced quite independently of culture, and certainly the valuations are relative to cultural context. The stimuli have a relative autonomy in that an electric shock, a flashing light, a heavy object falling on the foot, or the smell of rotten eggs may have similar neurophysiological effects for everybody. But even so, pain thresholds vary individually and according to socialization, and at the extremes sensations often merge. People are socialized into a world of sensation which in turn affects the quality of an experience or the way an object is experienced; what some people find pleasurable others find repellent.

Aesthetics is concerned with the human capacity to assign qualitative values to properties of the material world. We do not assert that the particular attributions made are universal. The physical properties in themselves are not qualities but differences which form the basis for the distinctions that underlie the system of valuation. The physical properties have an effect on the senses, but it is the process of aesthetic transformation that gives a value to a property, a value which often becomes associated with an emotional response. We argue that the human capacity to transform physical properties into aesthetic valuations is integral to understanding human action and choice in both contemporary and evolutionary contexts. Without taking aesthetic factors into consideration, it is difficult to explain why in the Aurignacian period in Europe, some 30,000 years ago, beads were made from such a limited range of raw materials, all of which shared the characteristics of pastel colours and a soft soapy texture.[10]

Aesthetics is concerned with the whole process of socialization of the senses with the evaluation of the properties of things. However, such socialization takes place in the context of the process whereby qualities acquire connotations and are incorporated within systems of meaning.

This can happen at the general level of the qualities themselves, as Munn has shown in the case of heaviness and lightness in the Massim region of Papua New Guinea.[11] More specifically, qualities are organized in formal systems of art, music or design, to create forms which can be used for particular purposes or to create contexts for certain events. Thus music or sculpture may be intended for contemplation or to mark a royal celebration.

It is this interrelationship between the sensual and the semantic that makes aesthetics such an important focus for anthropological research, for just as the quality of a sensation can be interpreted as a meaningful sign, so too can an idea evoke an aesthetic response. Ideas can calm and excite the senses as much as objects can. The vocabulary of the senses provides a unique resource to approach the way in which people feel themselves to be in the world. Aesthetics gives access to the experience of spiritual power, to the feeling of being in the presence of authority, as well as, more mundanely, an understanding of why some people buy a particular brand of soap.

Anthropology has recently begun to emphasize the way in which social processes and values are objectified in a variety of forms ranging from the human body, through the house and basketry types, to the form of mortuary rituals. Such objectifications[12] become the locus for social and cultural reproduction, for socializing people into the routines and taken-for-granted dispositions that help sustain the familiar world in which they live. We would argue that in most cases these mediating forms are better approached through a broader perspective concerned with qualities of forms that transcend the particular and operate across contexts.[13] The anthropology of the body must be an anthropology of clothing and bodily adornment just as much as the anthropology of clothing requires an exploration of bodily concepts and cognitive constructions of the body. And the anthropology of clothing must be integrated within an anthropology of aesthetics which places the particular meanings, connotations and sensual effects of bodily appearance within a more general framework of qualities, their valuations and their cultural construction. We do not of course posit a uniform cultural aesthetic, nor do we intend to remove aesthetics from the arena of practice. Rather, we see aesthetics as a field of discourse that operates generally in human cultural systems, since like cognitive processes it can be applied to all aspects of human action.

It is partly through the transformation of physical properties into aesthetic qualities that people feel or sense their existence in the world. These qualities are important in influencing the kind of environment people create for themselves, the contexts in which they feel happy or anxious, the choices they make as to what to wear or which soap powder to buy. Aesthetics is thus integral to the study of consumption, of religious experience and of political authority, as well as more obviously in the areas of the anthropology of art and material culture.

AGAINST THE MOTION (1)

JOANNA OVERING

The proposition that aesthetics is a cross-cultural category can be contested for one very good reason: the category of aesthetics is specific to the modernist era. As such, it characterizes a *specific consciousness of art*. Technically, aesthetics refers to the philosophical study of art which had its origins in the late eighteenth century – it was Baumgarten who coined the term, in his *Reflections on poetry* of 1735.[14] Thus far from having universal appeal, the meaning of aesthetics is intrinsically historical. As Eagleton remarks,[15] the 'aesthetic' is a bourgeois and elitist concept in the most literal historical sense, hatched and nurtured in the rationalist Enlightenment.

Peter Gow and I will address two issues. First, we shall stress the peculiarity of the category, for the West is the odd man out in its consideration of beauty and artistic activity. Most peculiar is the idea of the autonomy of the arts, of something called the 'fine arts' as a distinctive area of activity separated out from all other domains of experience. For this we can thank the influence of Kant, who decreed aesthetic judgement to be essentially different from judgements of moral and scientific kinds. We have disengaged 'the arts' from the social, the practical, the moral, the cosmological, and have made artistic activity especially distinct from the technological, the everyday, and the productive. Second, our concern is to reveal the incongruity of such a cleansed notion of the art object, with its emphasis upon formality, unsullied by use or even desire, when set against other people's conceptualizations of the beautiful and of the production of it. Art and beauty are not so decontextualized in other societies. In Greek and Roman thought, for instance, art's value was tied to its perceived productive and social utility.

The argument, then, is that the category of aesthetics, which is inconceivable apart from modernist concerns, is one that more than anything else anthropologists must overcome. It brings hidden dangers to the task of understanding and translating other people's ideas about the beautiful because deeply embedded within it are categories peculiar to modernist thought.

To help elucidate the particularity of the category, I shall present ethnographic data first on the well-known *Zwázibo* peoples and their Cult of the Art Object, and then on the Piaroa of the Amazon. The aim is to contrast two peoples who are respectively exotic to each other on matters of art.

About three centuries ago, *Zwázibo* wise men of *Naeporúe* culture rebelled against their priests: they accused the priests of ignorance, and of proclaiming untruths about the cosmos. These wise men then declared themselves to have possession of the true secrets of the universe, because they had discovered the magic and potency of numbers: this they had done through the power of their own thought. It was through the contemplation of these numbers that the universe could be known and controlled, and all things materially good attained. It appeared that this was true, for their new magic turned out to be spectacularly successful. It was especially beneficial for the *Zwázibo* people, who became the most powerful and wealthy people of the *Naeporúe*. The priests were proven wrong, and their outmoded beliefs were discarded.

However, without gods, priests and cosmology, life became very drab. Life needed more than material plenty; it required beauty and something to please the soul. Thus the *Zwázibo* wise men decided to create a new religion, but one without new gods and their power: they wanted to experience the sublime without the gods. Their solution was to create the Cult of the Art Object. They began their quest for the universal truth of beauty, just as they once had done for the truth of thought and numbers. They began to formulate laws for the judgement of beauty, which became the laws of the new religion. Through their formal rules, the wise men became the 'aesthetic police' of the universe, to balance out their role as its 'thought police'.

The Cult of the Art Object was an interesting one. It revolved around a sacred triad comprised of the individual artist, the art object, and the individual contemplator of the object. The *Zwázibo* wise men decreed that all three were to leave what they called the real world. They were to exist instead in a sacred domain separate from the domain of prosaic activities in which people were involved in making artefacts, and in trading and using them. The wise men thereby sacralized the Object of Art, by proclaiming it to be separate from the world of utilitarian objects. They decreed that artefacts used in everyday life could not be beautiful: it was *only when an object had no use* that it could be beautiful, only when created for the contemplation of its beauty alone could it thereby become Art. As one devotee of the cult pronounced: 'the beautiful cannot be the way to what is useful, or to what is good, or to what is holy; it leads only to itself' (Victor Cousin). Or, as another remarked more succinctly, 'art never expresses anything but itself' (Oscar Wilde). The objects of the cult were to function by producing in the individual cult members what the wise men called an 'aesthetic consciousness', and not in any other way.

(It seems now fair to mention the fact that with the development of this Cult of the Self, the *Zwázibo* celebrated by changing their name, and it was universally approved that they henceforth should no longer be called the *Zwázibo*, but the *Borzwázi*.)

The Cult of the Art Object was highly elitist, and for the most part its membership consisted of the *Borzwázi*. In the codification of the laws of the cult, the wise men had dwelt particularly upon the rules for judging, experiencing and enjoying beauty. Such rules were difficult to learn, and knowing and following them became a strong marker of *Borzwázi* status. Thus each *Borzwázi* family trained its children at an early age in these rules for contemplating beauty correctly. When the child was first shown a great Object of Art, he or she was instructed to focus completely upon it, and not to think of everyday, ordinary concerns. In this way, children were taught to appreciate the Art Object in a disinterested way – just as the wise men had decreed – so that they could understand the internal relations of the Object through what the wise men called the detached and 'free play of the imagination' (Immanuel Kant). If done well, they could understand the truth of the object, and 'burn with a hard gemlike flame' (Walter Peter), thereby attaining the sublime. Only a privileged few could experience the universal truth of the object as a piece of pure beauty, and thus gain true freedom from the crassness of everyday life.

In great *Borzwázi* families, one – but not more – male children were sacrificed to the cult to become creators of art objects. To do this a boy had to separate himself from all everyday practical affairs in order to devote himself to a life of artistic creativity. His role, however, was a paradoxical one. *Borzwázi* children were taught not to use their hands in labour, and the value was instilled in them that it was unbecoming to their status to make objects, for such labour was the job of workers. It was only in the area of art, where prosaic utility was not in question, that they could participate in the making of objects, which was then regarded not as work but as an act of creation. The Objects of Art made by the artist that were judged to be beautiful were not understood as mere replicas (as in ordinary making), but each as something exemplary and unprecedented, and therefore as products of a creative impulse. The artist's creation of a 'perfect object' became the great signifier of *Borzwázi* selfhood, indicative of their unique ability to attain the sublime. As one famous *Borzwázi* proclaimed: 'I believe in Michelangelo, Rembrandt; in the might of design, the mystery of colour, the redemption of all things by Beauty everlasting, and the message of Art that has made these hands blessed' (George Bernard Shaw).

Yet the artist was still a sort of labourer, a worker, a maker of objects, and as a consequence his status within *Borzwázi* society was not a high one. The wise men had been shrewd; for in codifying the laws of the cult their emphasis had been upon the aesthetic consciousness of the contemplator of beauty rather than upon that of its creator. Thus they had managed to keep power in their own hands; they decreed that a piece of art became art only when viewed as such by the contemplators. In the end it was the judges who, through their own (and not the artist's) aesthetic consciousness, legitimized, and thus created, an object as sacred (and therefore 'fine') art. Salvation came not so much to the artist, the creator of the object – who could, as often as not, live a life of the damned by the canons of this new religion. Although the cult had many members, salvation could be achieved only by the few: those who discovered its secrets by stringently following the rules formulated by the wise men for the judgement and the experiencing of the beauty of the object.

Now I turn to my Amazonian example. The basic elements of our notion of 'aesthetic consciousness' do not apply to an Amazonian understanding of beautiful production. Among the Piaroa, there do not exist the 'artist', the 'art object' and 'the aesthetically astute subject' – each functioning in sovereign manner. This is not to say that the Piaroa do not have a highly developed tradition of artistic production, for they do. It ranges through what we would call the verbal and poetic, the visual, the musical and the performative arts. But our aesthetics will not help us understand what these 'arts' are for the Piaroa.

I wish to emphasize two related points. First, each of these 'forms of art' is 'technological', and is considered as such by the Piaroa. Because they play an essential role within the productive process, their meaning is socially, politically and cosmologically contextualized. For the Piaroa 'art' is not something that stands alone, outside the context of life. Second, most of these modes of artistic production, the exceptions being ceremonial masks and music, belong to the domain of the everyday, and thus to daily productive activities. Beautification plays a part, first and foremost, in a process of everyday empowerment that enables *both a person and an object* to act productively. When it comes to beautification, people and objects are not so different.

Most of the everyday objects (and not just ceremonial items) that are indigenously made are beautified. Tools are beautiful: they are carefully designed in form, and many carry distinctive patterns. The form and especially the design are understood to be both displays and manifestations of their beauty and their potency – that is, their capacity to deliver effects on the world. Cassava boards carry the design of their potency painted in dark red resin; as do canoe paddles and blow guns. Quivers and basketry carry their distinct and woven designs. And so on. Because everyone has the skills, in accordance with gender capacity, to make the objects, the Piaroa have no category through which to specify a person as an artist or craftsman.[16]

How are the objects conceived? For it is certain that they are not 'objects' as we conceive them to be. Most objects, the Piaroa explain, are products or manifestations of the 'life of thoughts' (*ta'kwarü*) of the person who makes them. Each person receives his or her 'thoughts' from the crystal boxes of the gods, and it is the forces of the 'life of thoughts' that play an essential part in that person's capabilities to have an effect upon the world: to create tools, to have babies, to hunt, and to cure. Indeed, all creation for which a person is responsible is said to be a manifestation of his or her thoughts. Thus, each such creation is said to be a 'thought' (*a'kwa*) of that person. Each created 'object', whether a child, a cassava grater, a garden, or a cure, is also considered to be a product of its creator's fertility. As a thought of a person, the 'object' (as child, cure or tool) contains the potency of its creator. Thus, *object, creator and use are not separated from each other*. What is more, the object has an agency of its own: this is why pots can cook, blowguns kill, cassava graters grate.

We may ask what is the relation of the object to its beauty? The Piaroa answer is that both objects and people are beautiful because of what they *do*. A person's 'life of thoughts' confers beauty on both self and object. Beauty, thoughts and the products of work are conceptually linked, and they also have the same linguistic root – *a'kwa*. The body is beautified by its 'life of thoughts'. The productive, but dangerous, forces of the 'life of thoughts' are safely stored within the body: there, they design the internal self with their beauty. In turn, Piaroa ornamentation (their necklaces, leg and arm bands, their face and body painting) makes manifest on the surface of the body the beauty – and thus the potency – of the productive capacities within. Similarly, the designs and forms of the cassava grater, and of the basket, make manifest their beauty, and hence the potency or the productive capacities of these objects.

In sum, the principles of the Piaroa understanding of artistic production that clearly separate it from *Borzwázi* aesthetics are the following:

(a) The Piaroa notion of beauty cannot be removed from contexts of productive use. Both objects and people are beautiful because of what they can do. Thus, in the Piaroa exegesis of the beautiful and its place in their life, work is not detached from art. This is because (whether speaking of objects or people) beautification empowers, and is enabling of the technological process itself.

(b) The corollary of the above is that in the Piaroa conception, beauty and its creation are not separable from everyday life.

(c) There is no such thing as the 'object' standing alone, over and above the everyday, to be contemplated as such. And there is no spectator. One does not acquire power from the mere viewing of beauty. It is its capacity for use, and not its truth or formal attributes, that makes an object or person beautiful. In Amazonia, it is clear that the technical and the productive, the beautiful and the artistic, the designs giving potency to both tools and the human body, are all considered to be aspects of one and the same process. Without artistic production there could be neither food nor babies.

It is especially the question of everyday utility that is offensive to our aesthetic sensibility; moreover, it opens up an anthropological can of worms. It does so because anthropology itself has not escaped the *Borzwázi* paradigm of aesthetics. The idea of the everyday utility of objects of art is odious to anthropological sensibility because it goes against our conventional wisdom that art is a sphere of activity distinct from the everyday. Art, it is said, belongs to the domain of ritual, and not to everyday life. By contrast, the idea of contextualization is not so problematic. For instance, Alfred Gell, in a recent article where he argues against the universals of aesthetics, contextualizes Trobriand art within what he calls the 'technology of enchantment'. Similarly, Anthony Shelton elegantly places Huichol artistic activity within its cosmological and ethical context, and concludes by demonstrating its productive value.[17] However, both authors assume that artistic endeavours are restricted to ritual occasions, and thereby implicitly separate them from the more mundane and everyday matters of work. In this regard they are following Leach, who argued that art (which he understood to be always on the side of the mysterious, the sacred and the dangerous) is generally reserved for ritual activity.[18] For Gell, art becomes an 'idealized form of production' – it is not the truly true, and therefore is not of the everyday and the real. The idea that art transcends an everyday reality remains central to anthropological sensibility.

One thing becomes clear: the Piaroa view of beauty and its relation to everyday production cannot be understood within our category of aesthetics. Ours is a modernist vision, as the Amazonians' view most definitely is not. The argument is that to overcome our aesthetic consciousness, we must also overcome the modernist vision upon which it rests. This is because the *type of detachment* prescribed by modernist dogma for the accomplishment of successful science is much akin to the detachment prescribed for the successful development of an aesthetic consciousness within our own 'religion of art', or Cult of the Art Object. Thus the wider issue that this debate raises is the question of the degree to which we can successfully accomplish anthropology (that is, attend to indigenous categories of experience and thought) through *any* modernist programme and set of beliefs about the world.

FOR THE MOTION (2)

JEREMY COOTE

If this were an open discussion about aesthetics, unconstrained by the particular wording of the motion, I should devote my time to supporting and illustrating the line taken by Howard Morphy in the opening contribution to the debate. Our views of aesthetics and of the anthropology of aesthetics, while not matching completely, are not very different. But given the wording of the motion before us, I want to take another tack.

There seem to be at least two senses in which a category may be said to be cross-cultural, these two senses perhaps being at the two poles of a continuum. In the first, that taken by Morphy in his contribution, a category is cross-cultural if it is useful in cross-cultural analysis. The more useful it is, perhaps the more cross-cultural it is. While this might be regarded as a weak sense of the phrase 'cross-cultural category', this does not mean it is a weak argument. Far from it. As Morphy has argued, aesthetics is an essential aspect of our being in the world. It should receive far more attention from anthropologists than it has done in the past. If we neglect it, we neglect much of what it is to be human.

Such an understanding of aesthetics seems to be becoming more and more widespread in anthropology. (As usual, one thinks one is saying something new, only to find that one is part of a trend that one did not know existed.) There probably are some anthropological monographs from before the 1970s with the word 'aesthetics' in their titles, but none comes immediately to mind. If there were any, they were few and far between. In the last few years, however, there have been an increasing number. On my own shelves, for example, I find John Forrest's *Lord I'm coming home: everyday aesthetics in Tidewater North Carolina*, published in 1988. In this original work, according to the publisher's synopsis, Forrest 'seeks to document the entire aesthetic experience of a group of people, showing the aesthetic to be an "everyday experience and not some rarefied and pure behavior reserved for an artistic elite".' Among other recent titles are Robert R. Desjarlais' *Body and emotion: the aesthetics of illness and healing in the Nepal Himalayas* (1992); Carol Laderman's *Taming the wind of desire: psychology, medicine, and aesthetics in Malay shamanistic performance* (1991); and, just to show that it is possible to get 'aesthetics' into the title before the colon, Kris L. Hardin's *The aesthetics of action: continuity and change in a West African town* (1993). None of these ethnographies is concerned with art as conventionally understood, nor even with art as unconventionally understood. They are not art books, they are not even anthropology-of-art books. They are all, however, concerned with the aesthetics of other cultures, with aesthetic experience, behaviour and action in all areas of life. For these authors, as for an increasing number of other scholars, 'aesthetics' is clearly a useful cross-cultural category. That is, it is useful in cross-cultural analysis.

Even where authors are not directly concerned with aesthetics, where it does not occur in the titles of their works, they may still find themselves touching on the category and applying it cross-culturally. For example, in her account of religion and healing among the Nilotic-speaking cattle-keeping Mandari of Southern Sudan, Jean Buxton wrote of how 'marking and patterning are very highly estimated in the Mandari visual aesthetic'.[19] In my own work I have tried to amplify this statement for the Mandari and for their Dinka, Nuer and Atuot neighbours. I have tried to show how it is meaningful to talk of Dinka, Nuer, Atuot and Mandari aesthetics and, at another level of abstraction, even of 'Nilotic aesthetics'.[20]

It could be argued, however, that such talk is just that, abstraction. It may be useful, even meaningful, but it is far removed from indigenous discourse where the category of aesthetics does not in fact exist. In another, harder sense of what a cross-cultural category is, the recognition of what *we* take to be aesthetic experience and behaviour in other cultures would count for little. In this harder sense of the phrase, a category must be explicitly recognized in other cultures for it to be cross-cultural.

Categories are not always explicitly recognized in vocabulary, at least not in a simple way. In looking for indigenous categories, however, vocabularies do at least provide a place to start. So far as I know 'aesthetics' does not appear in any Dinka dictionary, though I should argue that this has as much, if not more, to do with the presuppositions of the compilers of Dinka dictionaries as it does with the limitations of Dinka categories. The word 'beautiful' does appear though, with the Dinka term *dheng* (or *dheeng*) proffered as the Dinka equivalent.[21] Fortunately for our purposes this term has been glossed at length by the Dinka scholar and statesman Francis Mading Deng. His ten-page account of the Dinka conception of 'human dignity' focuses on the term *dheeng* and its adjectival form *adheng* and their various meanings and uses.[22] This is a short extract from Deng's account:

> *Dheeng* . . . is a word of multiple meanings – all positive. As a noun, it means nobility, beauty, handsomeness, elegance, charm, grace, gentleness, hospitality, generosity, good manners, discretion, and kindness. . . . Except in prayer or on certain religious occasions, singing and dancing are *dheeng*. Personal decoration, initiation ceremonies, celebration of marriages, the display of 'personality-oxen', indeed, any demonstration of an aesthetic value, is considered *dheeng*. The social background of a man, his physical appearance, the way he walks, talks, eats, or dresses, and the way he behaves towards his fellow men are all factors in determining his *dheeng*.[23]

I need hardly elaborate here on how this Dinka category overlaps in great measure with Western understandings of aesthetics.

Let me turn to another African example, this time from a people with much richer traditions of visual art than those of the Dinka. Over the last twenty years or so a large literature has been created on African aesthetics. For our purposes, the most interesting studies are those that present an explicit indigenous category. And most significant, I think, are those that are written by scholars, like Francis Mading Deng, who can be regarded as members of the cultures about which they write. For this debate, these scholars are my cross-cultural witnesses, for who better to give evidence about the cross-cultural nature of a category than cross-cultural scholars, products of the culture about which they write but also fluent in the culture of Euro-American academe?

More has been written about Yoruba aesthetics than about that of any other African people. Personally I find much of this literature indigestible, littered as it is with hundreds of Yoruba terms with a full panoply of diacritics. Taken as a whole, however, it would seem to establish beyond reasonable doubt the existence of a Yoruba category of aesthetics. This is especially evident when one considers the contribution to this literature of Yoruba authors. For instance, Babatunde Lawal drew not only on fieldwork but on his 'own experience as a Yoruba' in presenting 'some aspects of Yoruba aesthetics' in a contribution to the *British Journal of Aesthetics*.[24] (One is tempted to say that if this journal publishes an essay on Yoruba aesthetics then Yoruba aesthetics must exist.) Another Yoruba scholar, Rowland Abiodun, has made major contributions to the scholarly presentation of Yoruba aesthetics in a number of his own essays and in collaborative projects.[25] As presented by him, Yoruba aesthetics has its foundation in the phrase *iwa l'ewa*, 'character is beauty', and a full understanding of it requires an exploration of the range of meanings of these and related terms. Unsurprisingly perhaps, such an exploration eventually takes in the whole of Yoruba life, culture, morality, religion and politics. Yoruba aesthetics, which can be presented as a set of criteria for the evaluation of art objects, proves to be an aspect of all areas of Yoruba life and culture. Such scholarly writings on Yoruba aesthetics are only the tip of a very large iceberg. They draw on and reflect an extensive discourse on art and life that in turn draws on the Ifa corpus of Yoruba literature. I do not know if there is a term in Yoruba equivalent to 'aesthetics' in English, but there is undoubtedly a discourse that overlaps to a great extent with what is understood as 'aesthetics' in the West. If we are going to call this anything, we are going to have to call it Yoruba aesthetics. Similar accounts have been provided for other West African peoples, for the Igbo of Nigeria for example, and for such Akan-speaking peoples as the Asante of Ghana. Here again there is a substantial literature, much of it by scholars who know the cultures about which they write from the inside.[26] In these cases, at least, there does seem to be explicit indigenous categories of aesthetics, categories that overlap with the Western category sufficiently to warrant the assertion that 'aesthetics is a cross-cultural category'.

There is a paradox here, however, to which I wish to draw attention. The explicit categories that we find in other cultures do, I think, overlap sufficiently with the Western category to warrant the label 'aesthetics'. They are, however, far removed from the sort of definition of aesthetics with which both Morphy and I work, and which we should regard as necessary for cross-cultural analysis. I am not yet able to resolve this apparent paradox to my own satisfaction, but let me finish with a few points that seem to me relevant to its resolution.

First, it would be a great surprise if the categories of the analyst turned out to match the categories of the analysed. The former are conceptual tools refined for particular analytical purposes, the latter are ideological categories that must perform such tasks as legitimation and mystification. If the two categories were perfectly congruent there would be little point in analysis and little point in anthropology. (This is, of course, a difference of degree, rather than an absolute one. Anthropological categories are themselves ideological, and indigenous categories are tools for communicating and for negotiating cultural life. The difference is significant, however.)

Second, the paradox is perhaps not actually a significant one, but only emerges because of the artificiality of the terms of the motion before us. Whichever sense is given to 'cross-cultural category', however, the motion must surely be carried. The two approaches may take rather different paths, but they both come to the same conclusion: aesthetics *is* a cross-cultural category.

Finally, let me conclude with a comparison between two pieces of English poetry, which seems to me to throw light on the problem. In looking for comparisons, say, between English and Dinka aesthetics, one might be led by Deng's presentation of the Dinka concept of *dheeng* to such popular and unsatisfactory statements of aesthetic philosophy as the oft-quoted lines of Keats: 'Beauty is truth, truth beauty, – that is all / Ye know on earth, and all ye need to know.' But as anyone familiar with the Dinka ethnography will readily recognize, a much more powerful comparison is provided by Gerard Manley Hopkins's poem 'Pied Beauty':

> Glory be to God for dappled things—
> For skies of couple-colour as a brinded cow;
> For rose-moles all in stipple upon trout that swim;
> Fresh-firecoal, chestnut-falls; finches' wings;
> Landscape plotted and pieced—fold, fallow, and plough;
> And all trades, their gear and tackle and trim.
>
> All things counter, original, spare, strange;
> Whatever is fickle, freckled (who knows how?)
> With swift, slow; sweet, sour; adazzle, dim;
> He fathers-forth whose beauty is past change:
> Praise him.

The lines from Keats constitute a piece of aesthetic ideology that gives you no idea of what beauty consists in for the writer – that is, it tells you nothing about the visual qualities that make a Grecian urn, for example, beautiful. Hopkins's poem, by contrast, is brimful of references that evoke the rich aesthetic experience presented by pied beauty in everyday life. The Dinka might agree with the sentiments expressed by Keats (actually I'm not sure they would agree with quite that sentiment, but Yoruba might; indeed, the words of Keats are referred to implicitly, if not explicitly, in one account of Yoruba aesthetics[27]), but they wouldn't think much of his poems. Hopkins, however, would provide stiff competition for Dinka songsters.

The anthropologist's job is twofold. The indigenous ideological discourse has to be recorded, analysed, understood and perhaps explained, but so must the aesthetic aspects of the way people live in, experience and create the world they inhabit. The anthropologist must try to see the world as the people he or she studies see it, both ideologically and perceptually. In both pursuits, however, the anthropologist will be applying categories of aesthetics cross-culturally.

AGAINST THE MOTION (2)

PETER GOW

In *Distinction*, Pierre Bourdieu paints, with his characteristic sharp eye and steady hand, a terrifying portrait of aesthetic experience in a Western society.[28] His French informants distinguish. They compare, contrast and judge all things, and especially each other. And they judge each other by how well or badly they compare, contrast and judge. I defy any Western person to read this book without wincing in self-recognition, which even the defensive judgement, 'Oh, but then the French are like that!', cannot quite mask. Bourdieu shows us that our deeply personal feeling for the beautiful, our carefully guarded refuge from all the discriminatory horrors of late capitalist society, is the primary form of discrimination – it *is* the horror of that society.

Bourdieu tells us nothing that we did not already know, for we have all experienced expressions of taste as discrimination, whether against ourselves or against others. This is how we win friends and influence people. But Bourdieu presents us with this knowledge in a new way. He shows us how our aesthetic acts of comparing, contrasting and judging are intrinsically discriminatory in class terms, something we would rather not have known. If capitalism is narcissism with respect to minor differences, it has reached its apotheosis in Western aesthetic discourse. Our aesthetics, our 'possessiveness with regard to the object', as Lévi-Strauss termed it, is the supreme fetishization of our economic system.

'Comparing and contrasting', but not judgement, are one of the central concerns of anthropology. As a method, anthropology seeks the answers to its questions by way of the comparison and contrast between cultures, and since anthropology has been a largely Western project, the comparison and contrast are largely with Western culture. It is this, I assume, that lies behind the desire to treat aesthetics as a cross-cultural category. Aesthetics is a problem, so as anthropologists, we should address it comparatively. 'This is what we do, what do they do?' This is in the time-honoured tradition of anthropology, and I have no quarrel with it. But it won't work with aesthetics. It won't work because Western aesthetics will always outrun us. When we set off to find the answer in comparison and contrast, the Western aesthetic will have got there first, because that is what it is.

The Western aesthetic is primarily discriminatory, with regard to both the object and the subject of aesthetic experience. Because of this, we can never say what it is *other* than discrimination. We can never tie it to any concrete experience for the purposes of comparison, because as soon as we do so, we want to judge that judgement. An example may help here. An anthropologist, Paul Stoller in this case, seeking to elucidate the role of vision in his fieldwork experience, likens himself to Cézanne.[29] He thereby elicits our empathy, our derision or our confusion: we respond variously, 'Oh, yes, I know what you mean!', or 'Hang on, Cézanne was a genius, you're not!', or 'What has a late nineteenth-century French painter got to do with the Songhay?' The Western aesthetic compares, contrasts and judges everything, and you appeal to it at your own risk.

This problem is exacerbated when we attempt to compare aesthetic systems as such. As soon as we hold Western aesthetics still, in order to compare it to some other concrete human aesthetics, we have to exemplify the Western aesthetic. We have to provide an example which we would all agree about. But this is impossible, since the whole movement of the modern Western aesthetic is about disagreement, about personal discrimination. Take Morphy's justly celebrated article, 'From dull to brilliant'.[30] Morphy is here analysing a specific visual effect in Yolngu painting which is thought of as a shimmering quality of light which represents the manifestation of ancestral power. So far, so good. But Morphy then goes on to suggest that this specific visual effect transcends particular contexts, and identifies it also in the work of the British artist Bridget Riley.[31] Here comes the problem. Morphy's analytic claim about the nature of Yolngu painting now becomes a claim about Riley's work. I think that Riley is a charlatan, I think that she can't paint, and I have long wondered about her relative success. That is my aesthetic judgement, my opinion, and it presumably differs from Morphy's. But that is also my point: the Western aesthetic simply discriminates, and any appeal to it invites judgement.

While Riley is right in there in the Western aesthetic project, soliciting our discriminatory opinions, and hence deserves all she gets, the Yolngu ritual painters are not. I am intrigued by Morphy's argument, but I don't want to have to change my opinion of Riley's work in order to follow it. Still less do I want to be invited to make the parallel judgement: do I like Yolngu paintings? The Yolngu are interesting because they are people, not because we think they are good painters. In the Western aesthetic, comparison invites discrimination. Anthropology compares and contrasts but does not judge. It abjures, I hope, discrimination in the sense of aesthetic judgements about the cultures studied, even when these might be favourable.

It is this feature of anthropology, its refusal to judge the cultures it compares and contrasts, which sets it most firmly against the modern Western aesthetic project. Indeed, I would argue that the desire for a comparative aesthetics does not come from within anthropology at all, but is an import from outside. It is non-anthropologists who want answers to issues of comparative aesthetics from anthropologists. Who are these people?

The project of 'comparing and contrasting' Western aesthetics and the aesthetics of other cultures already has a long history in Western culture, one in which anthropology has played virtually no part. This is the project of 'primitive art'. Since the late nineteenth century, the 'primitive' has always been a talisman of authenticity at the heart of the Western aesthetic project. Modernism's radical break with sterile academic tradition, its project of unmediated contact with primordial reality, elevated the primitive to a supreme place. Whenever artists working within the modernist Western aesthetic project have felt a serious gap developing between what they are doing and their intended effect, they have called upon the shamanic powers of 'primitive art' to help them. As Picasso said of the African masks which decorated his studio, 'They are not here as models, but as witnesses to the act of creation.'

Whatever anthropologists might like to imagine, their discipline played virtually no part in this interest in the 'primitive'. Indeed, modernist artists, dealers, collectors and critics were simply irritated by anthropologists' desire to explain these objects, to put them back into their cultural context. Anthropology renders the exotic as the everyday, to borrow Condominas' phrase. Modernist aesthetics did not want that explanation, it wanted these things to be exotic, and the more exotic the better.

Moreover, the specific modernist aesthetic of Primitivism does not want anthropologists' explanations of 'primitive art'; it wants anthropologists to sign up for the project; it wants their agreement. The complaints from the devotees of this project go something like this: 'The Navajo (or whoever) produce these stunningly beautiful works of art, which embody the same elemental energy and primordial quality as do Pollock's drip paintings. Anthropologists explain the Navajo sand paintings by putting them into context, showing how they function in rituals. But they never explain why they are so beautiful, why they have this aesthetic power.'[32]

The question is real, and deserves an answer, but it is not an anthropological problem. An ethnographic account of Navajo sand painting would address Navajo people's experience and actions. It would not have to explain why Navajo sand paintings remind certain non-

Navajo of Pollock's work. Unless proven otherwise by fieldwork, we may presume that Pollock plays no role in the network of action and meaning of Navajo culture, which is what ethnographers would take as their object. I have no objection to devotees of the Primitivist Modern Aesthetic project setting off to discover why Navajo culture is so beautiful, and I would be fascinated by their results. But I suspect few will, for that would require spending far too long away from the metropolitan capitals of modernist culture, and doing tedious things like learning Navajo and getting to know Navajo people on their terms.

I have argued that to treat aesthetics as a cross-cultural category is impossible, and that it is not an anthropological problem. What, then, can anthropologists do with aesthetics?

Of all anthropologists, Lévi-Strauss has most consistently engaged with modern Western aesthetics, whether directly in his art criticism or more indirectly in his anthropological work. There is no question that Lévi-Strauss is an aesthete, with strongly discriminatory opinions. But what is important in his work is that he uses his aesthetic not for comparison with the aesthetics of other cultures, but as a perspective on other cultures.

Consider *The way of the masks*.[33] He starts with an aesthetic problem: the stylistic dissonance of the Salish *swaihwe* masks within American Northwest Coast traditions. He then goes on to place these masks within a system of transformations of masks and of myths in the cultural history of Northwestern America. But nowhere does he suggest that this aesthetic problem is shared by the indigenous people of that area, quite the opposite. He shows that Northwest Coast people thought Salish *swaihwe* and the apparently quite different Kwakiutl *xwexwe* were the same mask. The aesthetic problem is Lévi-Strauss's own problem, and he locates it where it belongs: in his own experience of the Northwest Coast Indian Gallery of the American Museum of Natural History. The solution, which is also his, is located far outside that gallery, in the ceaseless transformational creativity of innumerable anonymous artists who simply tried to follow the paths of tradition.

By making his own aesthetic explicit, Lévi-Strauss is able to escape its constrictions and to use it as a perspective. When he compares indigenous Amazonian myths to the music of Wagner, only the naïve imagine that he is proposing some sort of substantive relationship between the two 'out there in the real world'. The connection is in his own thought, which for Western people is the locus of aesthetic discrimination. But once that linkage is made obvious, it becomes possible to think about these Amazonian myths with the sort of intensity usually reserved by Western people for 'Great Art'. By starting out explicitly as an aesthete, and by making his discriminatory judgements overt, Lévi-Strauss finishes as an anthropologist whose objective is not to engage in the work of non-discriminatory aesthetics, which I have argued is both impossible for anthropology and alien to it, but to gain a perspective on aesthetics itself, which is a quite different thing.

Lévi-Strauss compares, contrasts, and finally judges. But what he judges is the Western aesthetic tradition itself. He judges it and finds it wanting. He turns the Western aesthetic back on itself. That is what anthropology seeks to do, I suggest, and it is what Bourdieu, with impeccable anthropological credentials, is doing in *Distinction*. We will further the anthropological project not by trying to establish aesthetics as a cross-cultural category, but by critical reflection on our own aesthetic projects, upon which anthropology provides us with a perspective.

Part II The debate

ROBERT LAYTON   In her talk, Joanna Overing spoke of art and of the making of beautiful things among the Piaroa. I wonder by what criteria she would identify things as works of beauty or of art.

JOANNA OVERING   I was talking about what the Piaroa themselves said were beautiful – which included almost everything they produced.

ROBERT LAYTON   But the Piaroa were not speaking to you in English...

JOANNA OVERING   They had a term which they used to express both 'beauty' and the potency of 'thoughts'. It would be interesting to try to identify their criteria for beauty. But this quality pertained to such a wide range of things, including the body and its potency. What I did not do was to talk about *their* aesthetics in *our* terms. To do so would mean taking some quality like brilliance and looking to see whether there is any correlation, say, between feather brilliance and pottery designs. In the visual arts of the Piaroa, however, there are no criteria that connect various images such as feather work, paintings, resin figures, or basketry designs. What was most important for them was the fact that the designs themselves were words of the paths of the songs, or words of the paths of the thoughts. It was not the colours but the designs that had potency.

ROBERT LAYTON   In his study of Abelam ceremonial house fronts, Anthony Forge noted that for the Abelam, certain designs were considered more potent because people in the villages using those designs grew larger yams.[34] Yet the designs the Abelam thought most potent were also the ones Forge himself found to be most aesthetically pleasing.

JOANNA OVERING   There is no such concordance in the Piaroa case, nor would I presume to judge what beauty is to the Piaroa within the framework of our own aesthetic standards. Questions that we (Westerners) would consider significant would make little sense to them. For Piaroa standards of judgement are connected to *use*, which automatically carries with it notions of beauty and potency. Thus Western and Piaroa standards of the aesthetically pleasing cannot be compared. Yet you are asking me to do just that: to impose our own aesthetics on their understanding of the beautiful.

ROBERT LAYTON   Of course the problem to which you have drawn our attention, of the historical specificity of the concept of aesthetics, is a perfectly real one. I wonder whether a pre-eighteenth-century concept like 'grace' or 'graciousness' might better capture Piaroa ideals of beauty. A pre-eighteenth-century anthropologist, employing such a concept, might have been able to grasp the essence of the Piaroa view without being encumbered by all the baggage that attaches to the modern notion of aesthetics. Thus the difference between our view and theirs may lie more in the labels we apply, and the significances that accrue to them, than in the nature of the underlying perceptions.

JOANNA OVERING   I would find the concept of grace as difficult to apply to the Piaroa case as the concept of aesthetics. It would be more interesting to consider pre-eighteenth-century ideas about the *relationships* between art, ethics, community and so on. My concern in the debate, however, was with the *category* of aesthetics as it emerged in the eighteenth century.

PETER WADE   There seems to be a lack of agreement between the two sides to this debate, since they start off from different premises. On the one hand, for Morphy, aesthetics is founded in a universal human capacity to attribute qualitative meanings to material stimuli. On the other hand, Overing ties aesthetics to a modernist notion of refined, elite, bourgeois art. Clearly in the first case the concept of aesthetics has cross-cultural applicability, whereas in the second case it does not. Perhaps, however, if Morphy had elaborated on the proposition that all human beings have the capacity for aesthetic response, it would have given the other side something to contest. For would not the operation of such a capacity entail a process of decontextualization – a process which Overing identified as an exclusively modernist phenomenon?

HOWARD MORPHY   There are currently very few detailed anthropological analyses of systems of qualitative evaluation, of the kind that would enable us to develop a strong challenge to the modernist aesthetic. Jeremy Coote and I were clearly not advocating the universality of such an aesthetic. My claim was a relatively weak one: that certain aspects of what might be called an aesthetic process are universal, and that these have to do with the apprehension of particular stimuli, properties, forms or ideas. I do *not* claim that there is anything universal about the way these phenomena are felt and integrated within cultural systems. Our comparative task, then, is to see whether certain properties (for example, the property of 'brilliance') evoke similar feelings and responses in different cultural contexts. From there, one could go on to build a comparative anthropology of aesthetics that would be concerned, not necessarily with universal properties, but with properties that are independent of specific cultural contexts. I think we should direct our efforts towards developing this kind of comparative perspective on human feelings.

JOANNA OVERING   The definition of aesthetics that Morphy gave us may seem innocent enough, but in fact we are very clearly at cross purposes. For the questions that Morphy considers to be central to understanding aesthetic experience are very much bound up with the modernist project. For example, to ask how people evaluate sensations is to invoke a modernist attitude of judgement. To ask how formal qualities are organized into systems – that, too, is a modernist question about people's aesthetic understandings. And to ask how people *feel* about the world – as distinct from what they *think* about it – is to invoke the dichotomy between emotion and reason, just one of the tremendously potent series of dichotomies underlying modernist thought. These dichotomies blind us to indigenous understanding. They need to be unpacked.

MICHAEL O'HANLON   Despite Joanna Overing's last remark, I rather agree with Peter Wade. It did seem to me that Morphy and Overing were talking past each other, and that neither would disagree fundamentally with the other's position. Thus Morphy would surely agree with Overing's view that Western aesthetics is so specifically Western that it cannot be exported. And the examples that Overing presented to us surely lend substance to Morphy's view that humans have a general capacity to assign qualitative values to properties in the world. However, I would like to enter a couple of caveats. First, I disagree with Overing's claim that the term 'aesthetics' has such a specific lineage that it can have no wider purchase. Every word in our anthropological vocabulary has a specific lineage of one kind or another, and anthropological analysis consists, in a sense, in exploring that lineage so that one can go beyond it. Second, the concept of aesthetics does not have its roots in a single lineage. The term, as Overing noted, was coined by Baumgarten. Now Baumgarten's definition was concerned with sensible knowledge, with the perceptual world as confluence, convergence and synthesis. This rather integrative notion of aesthetics was subsequently hijacked by Kant and given a transcendental spin which, I think, we may now be moving away from in a return to a sense of the term that is both closer to Baumgarten's original intention and potentially more appealing to anthropologists.

ALFRED GELL   I would like to add to the point that the two sides must inevitably talk past one another since each appeals to a quite different notion of aesthetics. It is worth noting that aesthetics is one of those words ending in *-ics*, along with economics, politics, and so on, all of which began as denoting a certain kind of academic discourse and ended as purportedly indicating some phenomenon of the real world. For example, politics originally meant the science or philosophy of government and the state. Yet all of us who have taken a degree in anthropology have attended courses on politics which set out from the assumption that politics is something that people everywhere *have*. It may be pretty difficult to see what the politics of (say) the Mbuti Pygmies are, but we do not doubt that they *have* politics. Why? Because it's on the syllabus! What we witness here is the promotion of a word from its original connotation of a philosophical discourse to its use as a label for a class of activities in the real world that apparently existed in advance of the discipline called up to study them, but which was in fact *produced* by the existence of a certain disciplinary focus bearing a particular name and with a certain scope. In the case of aesthetics, I think we should resist this kind of promotion of the term, for the reasons spelled out by Peter Gow. Aesthetics is a branch of philosophy; it consists in a philosophical discourse, indigenous to the West, primarily about art objects and art traditions, though secondarily also about things like landscapes and flowers, which are not obviously art objects but which may be treated as though they were. But we are on a slippery slope. Once it is accepted that aesthetics should be on the curriculum alongside economics and politics, then its subject matter will inevitably be called forth by virtue of this very promotion process. Now is the time, I believe, to call a halt! All the current difficulties in the anthropology of politics arise from the way politics was promoted from being a kind of philosophical discourse to being a set of beliefs about the real world. In the case of aesthetics, we should draw back from the abyss, rather than being seduced by the convenient etymological relationship of the term with words like economics and politics.

JOANNA OVERING   I agree. Let me return to O'Hanlon's remarks about Baumgarten's definition. Baumgarten was looking for universals – of poetic thought, and of beautiful thought. But in looking for universals of aesthetics, politics, economics, or any of these things, we take these categories as being natural to the world. For my part, I do *not* think they are natural to the world, and we should probably be devoting a great deal more effort to throwing them all out – politics and economics included.

HOWARD MORPHY   I would be quite content to see the disappearance of the anthropology of politics and the anthropology of economics. But I would argue very strongly in *favour* of the development of an anthropology of aesthetics. One of the effects of focusing exclusively on the position that the concept of aesthetics has had at a particular stage in the history of Western philosophy is that a whole area of human experience and action is, as it were, subsumed under the Western category, and contaminated through association with it. From there, it is but a short step to the denial that there is anything in the real world to which the category refers. I believe that to limit the scope of aesthetics within the very narrow range afforded by the Western concept is counterproductive, since the association of the concept with particular, set-aside 'art objects' leaves the more general dimensions of human experience that we are concerned with almost untouched. I could not agree more with the idea that anthropology should offer ways of criticizing and moving beyond narrowly defined, Western concepts, but I am glad that anthropology ends with *-ology* and not with *-ics*!

MARCUS BANKS   To demonstrate that aesthetics is a cross-cultural category, Morphy and Coote would only have to show that there are at least two societies in the world that have a concept of aesthetics, and that they can be compared. And that would be hard to deny. Moreover, Overing's observation that the Piaroa have no category of art object or of the professional artist squares very well with Morphy's point that aesthetics is about the sensible qualities of objects and the valuation of these qualities. What I want to stress, however, is that all four participants in this debate are known for their work in non-state societies. No one has put forward the view of a non-European, high art culture. Overing's *Borzwázi* are natives of western Europe, not of the great civilizations of Asia. Yet one cannot deny the existence of categories of the aesthetic in these civilizations, or of native scholars who have devoted themselves to the explication of aesthetic practices and feelings. The fact that the arts of India, for example, are fully aestheticized within their regional context, quite independently of European contact, surely exemplifies the separate development of a category of aesthetics. Thus we already have two categories, one here (Europe), one there (India). There are parallel examples in China, Japan and elsewhere. So to my mind, the outcome of the debate is a foregone conclusion.

SONIA GREGER   The case for the opposition seems to hinge on a modern concept of aesthetics which we are already beginning to question to some extent. But we should recognize that aesthetic discourse, whether or not called by that name, goes back at least to Plato and Aristotle, and that the dialogues and arguments initiated by these classical thinkers still inform contemporary art. Even for modern aesthetics, the concept of art as a form of discrimination is an extremely narrow one. For example, when Kant stressed the autonomy of the aesthetic object, his point was to show that we do not judge it in the way in which judgement is normally exercised. That is why he spoke of the art object's having purposivity without particular purpose. His aim was to discover in what sense each aesthetic object is unique and *not* an object of judgement in the normal sense.

    If I could go back to the ethnographic examples presented by Joanna Overing, I believe that all the contrasts she drew between *Borzwázi* and Piaroa attitudes may equally be found within the history of the Western aesthetic itself. On the one hand, there is the attitude of 'aestheticism'; on the other hand, we find an aesthetic much closer to feeling, and to the rootedness of everyday life. What were Wordsworth and Coleridge doing in their lyrical ballads? What was happening in the art and craft movement (which was virtually the opposite of aestheticism)? Or consider the tension, in modern aesthetics, between Keats and Gerard Manley Hopkins. What was Keats doing? He was going back over the history of Europe, back to linguistic usages from Italy and Greece, back – by way of Milton – to classicism. That was *his* kind of aesthetic. And what was Gerard Manley Hopkins doing? He was going back to Anglo-Saxon linguistic roots, searching for a kind of earthiness.

PETER GOW   I could reply to that by way of another ethnographic example: Bourdieu's study of modern French society. When you talk about Western aesthetics, it is very easy to be selective, choosing the parts you happen to like. But in an ethnographic analysis of Western aesthetic judgement, you are not at liberty to choose the parts you like and to leave aside the parts you dislike. You have to address the fact that people use these things to make radical social discriminations. Following Bourdieu's study, I argued that this is what modern French people are doing, and I am fairly certain that the same is true of modern English people and indeed of people throughout the Western world.

GEORGINA BORN   But what is Bourdieu's work, if not a contribution to an anthropology of aesthetics? If, following Gell's polemic, we do not develop this branch of anthropology, then how are we to address areas of human activity of the kind with which Bourdieu deals? Peter Gow argued that we should be interested in the Yolngu as people, and not just for their artistic practices, paintings, and so on. But if Morphy engages in his work with these practices, it is surely because they occupy such an important place in the lives of the Yolngu themselves. He resists formalism by constantly emphasizing how artistic practices are embedded in the rituals of everyday (and non-everyday) life.

Take the case of the anthropology of politics. This has served a useful purpose in providing us with the analytic tools by which to compare, say, the Asante and the Mbuti. We are able to conclude that for the Asante politics is a significant focus of social life, whereas for the Mbuti it is not. Likewise, we need terms to distinguish between societies where objectified sources of pleasure and stimulus are recognized, and those where they are not, or where they play only a minor role. Without appropriate terms, how can we grasp this variability? The terms we use may have been reified in the history of anthropology, but we still have need of them. Only then can we achieve what Joanna Overing did in her parody: develop a reflexive anthropology of Western aesthetic discourse that would allow us to become better attuned to its ethnocentricity. It would require us, too, to be much more sensitive to the historical *variability* of this discourse.

But the main problem, it seems to me, lies in something that Jeremy Coote mentioned early on in his presentation. He listed a series of monographs that had the words 'aesthetic' and 'poetic' in their titles. The ever increasing use of these terms carries the risk of their debasement through over-generalization. Anthropologists and others are now using 'aesthetics' as a cover for discussions of social life, religious practices, and a host of other things which are only loosely aggregated under the one encompassing rubric. Thus we are faced with the urgent question of how we might draw boundaries around aesthetics, whether as a concept of analysis or as a category of empirical experience. Unless or until we address this question, we shall not know where to draw the line between an anthropology of aesthetics and an anthropology of the emotions, or of the body.

PETER GOW   I should like to make two points in response to Georgina Born's comment. First, when I said that Yolngu are interesting because they are people, obviously I meant that they are interesting as people because of the things they do. They are *not* interesting just because I happen to judge that they can paint well. That is the difference between our ethnographic interest in the Yolngu and our aesthetic interest in Bridget Riley. When you discuss Bridget Riley's work (unless you are an art historian) you do actually have to make a decision beforehand concerning her merits as a painter, since that is what she is.

Second, Georgina Born suggested that Bourdieu's *Distinction* constitutes proof that aesthetics is a cross-cultural category. If so, I should like to ask why his work on the Kabyle of Algeria does not address aesthetics as a core issue. You could not, I suspect, carry out the exercise which Bourdieu described in *Distinction* for the Kabyle. That is because the discriminatory activities in which French people manifestly engage are much less important to people like the Kabyle. Indeed, I would suggest that the evidence from Bourdieu's work points to the conclusion that aesthetics is *not* a useful cross-cultural category.

FELICIA HUGHES-FREELAND   There are two areas of uncertainty surrounding the interpretation of the motion before us. First, it is not clear whether the discussion is to be about categories or about aesthetics. Second, the notion of 'cross-culture', with its connotations of jumping over very high fences into mutually exclusive social domains, has already become highly problematic. I should like, however, to raise a further issue that arises from my own work on dance.

I have long reflected on Nelson Goodman's question: not *what* is art but *when* is art? These reflections lead me to sympathize to some extent with the opposition to the motion. While we might find that evaluative ascriptions such as dullness and brilliance (or in relation to dance, coarseness and refinement) are very widely used, little has been said about how people actually classify these ascriptions. Working in Java, I found my own research on dance being drawn into a wider cultural, political and ideological debate about what kinds of ascriptions could or could not be counted as aesthetic ascriptions. In other words, whether or not an evaluation qualified as aesthetic was a politically sensitive and hotly contested issue.

This leads me to my question. We have heard how the concept of aesthetics was coined in the eighteenth century, but no one has spoken of what is happening now and why we might be thinking about aesthetics in an era of commoditization, tourism and so forth. What is the connection between our current use of the term and the wider historical situation in which we find ourselves?

HOWARD MORPHY   One of the reasons why I feel so strongly about the need for an anthropology of aesthetics is that it should serve to direct our attention towards the products and activities of people in non-European cultures which – given the restricted purview of the concept of aesthetics endorsed by many Western commentators – would otherwise be excluded. I agree, however, that the field of aesthetics, even as it has developed in Europe, is much more complex and varied than this restricted concept would suggest.

TIM INGOLD   I should like to raise three related problems. First, if – as Morphy says – aesthetics is concerned with the qualitative effects of stimuli upon the senses, and if – as presumably they are – non-human animals are affected by stimuli, can there be an aesthetics of non-human animals? In other words, is aesthetics a cross-species category? You might immediately answer: 'No, not at all, because what distinguishes human beings from animals of other species is that we attach values of one sort or another to what we feel.' But that leads to my second problem. In his presentation, Morphy argued that aesthetics really deals with the interrelation between the sensual and the semantic – that is, between what we feel and the values we attach to these feelings. I wonder, however, in what way these are to be separated. I fear that the separation can only be made in terms of a mind–body dualism of some kind. The argument would run as follows: as organisms with certain innate bodily capacities, human beings sense things in certain general ways. Then, depending on the cultural context in which they are brought up, they proceed to attach particular, culturally specific values to these sensations. I am very suspicious, however, of the idea that there are universal human capacities, to which cultural particulars have subsequently been attached, and this is my third problem. I do not believe that there are *any* human capacities that do not themselves emerge in and through the process of development of human beings in particular environmental contexts. When we separate out a general human 'capacity for aesthetic response' from people's specific tendency to respond in this way rather than that (just as when we separate the 'capacity for language' from people's practised ability to speak some languages rather than others), we are reifying what is, at best, a convenient abstraction. We are separating out what seem to be the general aspects of human perception from what seem to be the particular ones and putting the former into the pot labelled 'human universals' and the latter into the pot labelled 'cultural differences'. The same procedure, it seems to me, underlies the separation of the sensual and the semantic. Now, if that is how aesthetics is constituted – as the relation between the sensual and the semantic – then to dissolve that dichotomy is also to dissolve the category of the aesthetic. What we are left with is an anthropology of perception.

CHRISTINA TOREN From what Alfred Gell and Tim Ingold have said, it is clear that we are in a position where we should actually be trying to get rid of terms like aesthetics. The time is surely long past when we would have demarcated these neat domains and then gone out to check whether people do or do not have them. Ingold has brought us back to basics in drawing attention to the fact that each side to the debate has an implicit theory of cognition. Morphy and Coote adhere to the time-honoured notion that we are first born with certain cognitive universals, and then culture comes along and puts differences on top. My own view, to the contrary, is that cognition is, from the very beginning, a historical process. What interests me as an anthropologist is the question of how people become *who* they are. I would want to look at their concerns about the nature of their lives, and to focus on what they feel to be most interesting. To do this does not require that life should be parcelled up into neat domains. Of course we need words, so that we can communicate with one another. We need terms of analysis. But aesthetics is not an analytical category, nor will it ever become one. It is entirely unnecessary. We do not need it in order to study Abelam masks, or Yolngu paintings, or anything else.

HOWARD MORPHY   I disagree fundamentally with almost every word Christina Toren has said. I disagree in part because she seems to set up a theoretical framework of her own which gives exclusive and idiosyncratic meanings to terms such as history, so that it becomes virtually impossible to integrate them into the theoretical frameworks with which, as anthropologists, we are accustomed to deal – frameworks that accord a central place to such concepts as culture and cultural structure. Now of course, I do not hold that aesthetic systems are independent of historical processes. Indeed, one of the reasons why I object to the arguments of the opponents to the motion is that they stick rigidly to a particular, historically based concept of aesthetics – a concept that has played its part in establishing the hegemony of Western academic discourse over the ways in which other cultures are conceived and understood.

In relation to Tim Ingold's first problem, I would not necessarily limit the applicability of the concept of aesthetics to human beings. In fact, from my point of view, the exploration of the aesthetic aspects of perception in non-human populations would form a fundamental part of the general science of aesthetics. It is perhaps harder to carry out cognitive studies that cross the boundaries of species rather than culture, but I would not rule out the possibility. Moreover, I believe it is analytically useful, despite Ingold's objections, to distinguish the semantic from the sensual. The relationship between the two is often very strong, as shown for example in Nancy Munn's *The fame of Gawa*.[35] I do think, however, that the distinction is more than an analytic convenience, and that the sensual and the semantic refer to quite different dimensions of human experience and action. Both are relevant to the understanding of what I would be quite happy to call cultural processes.

PENELOPE HARVEY   I should like to undertake the dangerous task of challenging the status of Jeremy Coote's evidence. He referred us to the work of scholars from non-Western backgrounds such as Yoruba, who have written about the aesthetics of the cultures to which they belong. Such scholars are perfect informants, since they speak the languages both of their cultures of origin and of Western academia. They are of course very complexly positioned in relation to Western academic discourses. In the light of Alfred Gell's remarks, I wonder whether these people also write about politics and economics. And if they do, what are the implications for what they write about aesthetics? I was interested to note that while Morphy wants to broaden the concept of aesthetics so as not to exclude non-Western cultures, he is quite content to see politics and economics disappear as domains of anthropological inquiry. Does that not entail precisely the kind of exclusionary strategy to which Morphy otherwise declares himself opposed?

HOWARD MORPHY   When I referred to the exclusion of politics and economics, I meant that I was not especially concerned with them at that moment in the debate!

MARCUS BANKS   I would share Penelope Harvey's scepticism about Yoruba scholars. We should not be deceived by the counterfeit authenticity that comes when a native person articulates the point of view *we* want to hear – as though it conferred a seal of approval. But it is still the case that there are indigenous aesthetic traditions that have nothing whatsoever to do with European culture and history. People from these traditions resemble Overing's *Borzwázi* in every critical respect. They reify art objects, they mystify art, they talk about non-verbal qualities that only the true aesthete can appreciate – in everything from paintings and poetry to natural landscapes. The Moghuls were great instigators of this kind of discourse in India. My concern is simply that there are other examples of self-contained aesthetic systems, besides the Western one, which need to be unpacked, following the normal procedures of anthropological analysis. To assume that aesthetics was suddenly invented in Western Europe in the eighteenth century is blatantly ethnocentric. If Ingold can make his plea about animals, I make my plea about high cultures. Anthropologists consistently fail to recognize that there are other cultures in the world that *cannot* be called savage, primitive, simple, or whatever the current, politically correct term may be. Yet these cultures have their own traditions. In continuing to take stateless, acephalous societies as our prototype for the non-Western 'other', we fail to account for indigenous philosophies of highly reified, articulate and literate forms, such as are found in the great civilizations of Asia. But as for the Yoruba, I would not be surprised if the scholars whom Coote mentioned had been following art classes!

JOANNA OVERING   It so happens that my ethnographic work has been in Amazonia, so that is the example I gave. I am no expert on India. I do not deny that other peoples have extraordinarily interesting philosophies and understandings of the world. So too, by the way, do the people of the Amazon. What I am concerned with is the emergence of aesthetics as a *metalanguage*. I dare say that Indian discourse on art would be much more recognizable to us because it is situated in a society which, like ours, is stratified, hierarchical and elitist. But this discourse is not, in itself, equivalent to an aesthetics. I do not think that the ancient Greeks, for example, had an aesthetic – certainly not in the sense that we do. They were concerned with beauty as it fitted in with the whole – that is to say, it was contextualized. It had to do with *use*; thus art was placed in the same category alongside skilled crafting. In India, likewise, I am sure that discussions about beauty and artistic activity are situated within social contexts of practical application. To me, what was significant about the birth of the concept of aesthetics was that it signalled the *decontextualization* of art from social life, its separation and detachment from ordinary domains of human experience.

PNINA WERBNER   I would like to respond to Alfred Gell's statement that we have no need for a separate anthropology of aesthetics. If I thought that people's passionate reactions to attacks on what we would take to be their culture were based on utilitarian grounds, as a neo-Marxist interpretation might have it, then I would agree. In other words, if you could understand people's attempts to defend and protect their culture, in the face of external threat, simply in terms of their economic and political interests, then we could indeed do without aesthetics. But if one believes, as I do, that people respond passionately to these kinds of threats in ways that go beyond economics and politics, and equally beyond moral dogma and religious fanaticism, then I think we have to recognize something which we can only call their aesthetics.

PETER GOW   There is nothing wrong with an observer or analyst describing that reaction as an aesthetic reaction. The problem arises when you try to set up aesthetics as a cross-cultural category. For many people aesthetic experience has nothing to do with passion – indeed, the passionate response may be explicitly *excluded* from aesthetic experience. My point was that we have no common language with which to describe our aesthetic judgements because they are intrinsically discriminatory. I have no objection to your adopting an aesthetic perspective, drawn from your own experience, in order to characterize a particular reaction as *more* than simply material and moral. I can read what you say and decide for myself what to think about it. But I do not want this perspective imposed from the outset.

JAMES WEINER   I should like to make one observation, which has to do with the ways in which the aesthetic figures in the writings of Kant. On the one hand, we have the pure aesthetics of the *Critique of judgement*, which seems to have been at issue here. On the other hand, we have the transcendental aesthetic of the *Critique of pure reason*, in which Kant identifies how our perceptual mechanism enables us to recognize form as such – what it is in the way our perceptual framework is structured that allows us to draw forth the forms though which we recognize the world. These are the categories of intuition. Now this latter understanding of the aesthetic is a much more general one. There is no doubt that people everywhere have to deal with the problem of drawing forth an appearance of the world that they can accept as real and can make their way through. This premiss is at the heart of Marilyn Strathern's work,[36] where she undertakes to look at the Melanesian way of life in aesthetic terms – that is, as the manner in which people draw forth the proper forms of their sociality. The difference between these two senses of the aesthetic is apparent from the remarks by Jeremy Coote and Howard Morphy. They seem to envision a mentalistic process which ultimately involves acts of contemplation and attribution. And I think this is what is being rejected in part by the opposers, especially Peter Gow. It is not that aesthetic considerations are not important everywhere. Rather, the ways in which people draw forth their forms might be very different, might have nothing to do with mentation, might have everything to do with the body and intersubjectivity – such that they might be unrecognizable to *us* as aesthetic procedures.

HOWARD MORPHY   I feel that the opposers of the motion were unable to escape from a limited concept of aesthetics that *is* judgemental, that *is* specific to a particular political structure and a particular segment of their own society. On no occasion did Jeremy Coote or I adopt a contemplative perspective on the aesthetics of form. Indeed, we studiously *avoided* the temptation to locate aesthetics in the contemplation of objects reified as art. It was because of their adherence to a peculiar Western definition that the opposers found it necessary to hang their critique on a particular moment in the history of Western philosophy and to call upon the authority of an Oxford professor of English literature. Their approach serves to exemplify the ways in which the discourse of anthropology is allowing itself to be appropriated by narrow Western concerns. Indeed, the very lessons that Peter Gow showed we could learn from Lévi-Strauss's reflections on Western aesthetics are almost denied by the perspective they adopt. I felt that the opposers were trying to force our position into line with a concept of aesthetics that neither Coote nor I hold – for example, in their attempt to associate the concept with a 'set aside' category of art objects. It was significant that in her references to the recent volume edited by Coote and Shelton,[37] Overing cited the articles by Shelton and Gell, both of which deal with cases – among the Trobriand Islanders and the Huichol respectively – where aesthetics is rooted in the areas of religion and ritual and not integrated within everyday life. But in other contributions to the volume (my own and Coote's included), the very opposite perspective is adopted.

JOANNA OVERING   Our opponents did indeed give us a more general definition of aesthetics, but in doing so they did not escape the modernist paradigm. Their concern is to develop a metalanguage of aesthetics for the purposes of cross-cultural translation. It is dangerous, however, to assume that one can separate out analytic terms through which to assess the values of other peoples. The imposition of our categories and our understandings will work against the contextualization of their notions of beauty and the place of it in their lives. No matter how you define aesthetics to begin with, more and more of the modernist value system tends to seep in as the discussion unfolds. We really need to pay attention to this seepage. I have nothing against the use of the term aesthetics, but I do object to its use as a means of translation, or as a means of developing analytic categories that purport to explain, on some separate, deeper level, what is going on in indigenous minds, feelings and culture.

JEREMY COOTE   I shall make just one brief comment. Our opponents seem to want to choose the most ethnocentric definition of aesthetics they can find, so that they can then claim that it cannot apply cross-culturally. This seems to me perverse. What we should be doing is to use our studies of the aesthetics and aesthetic categories of other cultures to reflect on our own categories. Rather than giving up aesthetics because it has been appropriated by the bourgeoisie, or by philosophers, we should be drawing on our own ethnographic experience to criticize the categories of bourgeois philosophy. And in this way we can perhaps try to overcome our modernist assumptions.

PETER GOW   But we *cannot* do that. We cannot idly step outside of the

Western aesthetic as though it were a set of clothes we could discard. It is too intrinsically personal.

Howard Morphy spoke of the establishment of a metalanguage of discourse for translation by which we could compare aesthetic systems, ours being one of them. This approach strikes me as problematic since that very metalanguage remains that of the Western aesthetic. Comparing, contrasting and judging are of the essence of this aesthetic, and you cannot simply step outside of it. We stand accused, by Morphy, of adhering to a very rigid notion of aesthetics. Yet Morphy's entire framework – according to which received sensory stimuli are attributed with qualitative semantic values – is none other than the modernist aesthetic itself. It is the aesthetic of the educated eye. There are of course other critiques of this framework within the Western tradition, such as the Marxist critique to which Overing referred. Let me conclude, however, with a small observation. It is surely far from fortuitous that Coote's best example of an elaborated, non-Western aesthetic comes from the Yoruba. As he was speaking, I wondered to myself, why does the *British Journal of Aesthetics* carry an article by a Yoruba author, about Yoruba aesthetics? The answer, surely, is that Yoruba art is the very prototype for 'primitive art' on the international market. There is an intrinsic desire, on the part of the modern aesthetic, that the Yoruba should *have* aesthetics. So a Yoruba scholar is invited to write this article, to invent a Yoruba aesthetic. And that's my point.

NOTES

1 A. Gell, 'The technology of enchantment and the enchantment of technology', in *Anthropology, art and aesthetics*, eds J. Coote and A. Shelton, Oxford, Clarendon, 1992.

2 J. Baudrillard, *Seduction*, trans. B. Singer, Basingstoke, Macmillan, 1990, p. 151.

3 R. Firth, *Elements of social organization*, London, Tavistock, 1951, p. 156; J. A. W. Forge, 'The Abelam artist', in *Social organisation: essays presented to Raymond Firth*, London, Frank Cass, 1967.

4 M. Fortes, 'Descent, filiation and affinity', *Man* 59, 1959, pp. 193–7.

5 M. Strathern, *The gender of the gift: problems with women and problems with society in Melanesia*, Berkeley, University of California Press, 1988, p. 8.

6 H. Morphy, '"Now you understand": an analysis of the way in which Yolngu have used sacred knowledge to maintain their autonomy', in *Aborigines, land and land rights*, eds N. Peterson and M. Langton, Canberra, Australian Institute of Aboriginal Studies, 1983.

7   K. Thomas, *Religion and the decline of magic*, London, Weidenfeld and Nicolson, 1971.
8   H. Morphy, 'Aesthetics in a cross-cultural perspective: some reflections on Native American basketry', *Journal of the Anthropological Society of Oxford* 23, 1992, pp. 1–16; 'From dull to brilliant: the aesthetics of spiritual power among the Yolngu', in *Anthropology, art, and aesthetics*, eds J. Coote and A. Shelton, Oxford, Clarendon, 1992; 'The anthropology of art', in *Companion Encyclopedia of Anthropology*, ed. T. Ingold, London, Routledge, 1994.
9   See Munn's concept of a qualisign, in N. M. Munn, *The fame of Gawa: a symbolic study of value transformation in a Massim (Papua New Guinea) society*, Cambridge, Cambridge University Press, 1986.
10 R. White, 'Beyond art: towards an understanding of the origins of material representation in Europe', *Annual Review of Anthropology* 21, 1992, pp. 537–64; 'Technological and social dimensions of "Aurignacian-age" body adornments across Europe', in *Before Lascaux: the complex record of the Upper Paleolithic*, Boca-Raton, FL, CRC Press, 1993.
11 N. M. Munn, *The fame of Gawa: a symbolic study of value transformation in a Massim (Papua New Guinea) society*, Cambridge, Cambridge University Press, 1986, pp. 80ff.
12 D. Miller, *Material culture and mass consumption*, Oxford, Blackwell, 1987.
13 H. Morphy, 'From dull to brilliant: the aesthetics of spiritual power among the Yolngu', in *Anthropology, art, and aesthetics*, eds J. Coote and A. Shelton, Oxford, Clarendon, 1992.
14 A. G. Baumgarten, *Reflections on poetry: Alexander Gottlieb Baumgarten's 'Meditationes philosophicae de nonnullis ad poema pertinentibus'*, trans. K. Aschenbrenner and W. B. Holther, Berkeley: University of California Press, 1954.
15 T. Eagleton, *The ideology of the aesthetic*, Oxford, Blackwell, 1990, p. 4.
16 In very recent years some Piaroa have become attuned to the tourist trade and cater to it by selling even ceremonial masks on the market. These masks, which to the Western eye are 'art', have become highly lucrative items of trade, and can even be found in shops in the Venezuelan international airports. Whether certain Piaroa specialize in the making of such objects for the market would be a good topic of study. Even more interesting would be the Piaroa view of such people.
17 A. Gell, 'The technology of enchantment and the enchantment of technology', and A. Shelton, 'Predicates of aesthetic judgement: ontology and value in Huichol material representations', in *Anthropology, art, and aesthetics*, eds J. Coote and A. Shelton, Oxford, Clarendon, 1992.
18 E. R. Leach, 'Levels of communication and problems of taboo in the appreciation of primitive art', in *Primitive art and society*, ed. J. A. W. Forge, London, Oxford University Press, 1973.
19 J. Buxton, *Religion and healing in Mandari*, Oxford, Clarendon, 1973, p. 7.
20 J. Coote, '"Marvels of everyday vision": the anthropology of aesthetics and the cattle-keeping Nilotes', in *Anthropology, art, and aesthetics*, eds J. Coote and A. Shelton, Oxford, Clarendon, 1992.
21 A. Nebel, *Dinka-English, English-Dinka Dictionary: Thong Muonyjang Jam Jang Kek Jieng, Dinka Language Jang and Jieng Dialects* (Museum Combonianum 36), Bologna, Editrice Missionaria Italiana, 1979 [1954], p. 109.

22 F. M. Deng, *The Dinka of the Sudan*, New York, Holt, Rinehart and Winston, 1972, pp. 14–24.

23 *Ibid.*, p. 14.

24 B. Lawal, 'Some aspects of Yoruba aesthetics', *British Journal of Aesthetics* 14, 1974, pp. 239–49.

25 R. Abiodun, 'Identity and the artistic process in the Yoruba aesthetic concept of Iwa', *Journal of Cultures and Ideas* 1, 1983, pp. 13–30; R. Abiodun, H. J. Drewal and J. Pemberton III, *Yoruba art and aesthetics*, Zurich, Museum Rietberg [exhibition catalogue], 1991.

26 H. M. Cole and C. C. Aniakor, *Igbo arts: community and cosmos*, Museum of Cultural History, University of California at Los Angeles [exhibition catalogue], 1984; D. M. Warren and J. K. Andrews, *An ethnoscientific approach to Akan arts and aesthetics* (Working Papers in the Traditional Arts No. 3), Philadelphia, Institute for the Study of Human Issues, 1977.

27 H. J. Drewal, J. Pemberton III and R. Abiodun, 'The Yoruba world', in *Yoruba: nine centuries of African art and thought*, by H. J. Drewal and J. Pemberton III, with R. Abiodun (ed. Allen Wardwell), New York, The Center for African Art, in association with Harry N. Abrams [exhibition catalogue], 1989.

28 P. Bourdieu, *Distinction: a social critique of the judgement of taste*, London, Routledge & Kegan Paul, 1984.

29 P. Stoller, *The taste of ethnographic things: the senses in anthropology*, Philadelphia, University of Pennsylvania Press, 1989, pp. 37–40.

30 H. Morphy, 'From dull to brilliant: the aesthetics of spiritual power among the Yolngu', in *Anthropology, art, and aesthetics*, eds J. Coote and A. Shelton, Oxford, Clarendon, 1992.

31 *Ibid.*, p. 202.

32 The comparison between Navajo sandpaintings and the art of Jackson Pollock is suggested by G. Witherspoon in his *Language and art in the Navajo universe*, Ann Arbor, University of Michigan Press, 1977, pp. 174–7.

33 C. Lévi-Strauss, *The way of the masks*, trans. S. Modelski, London, Cape, 1983.

34 J. A. W. Forge, 'Style and meaning in Sepik art', in *Primitive art and society*, ed. J. A. W. Forge, London, Oxford University Press, p. 175.

35 N. M. Munn, *The fame of Gawa: a symbolic study of value transformation in a Massim (Papua New Guinea) society*, Cambridge, Cambridge University Press, 1986.

36 M. Strathern, *The gender of the gift: problems with women and problems with society in Melanesia*, Berkeley, University of California Press, 1988.

37 J. Coote and A. Shelton, eds, *Anthropology, art, and aesthetics*, Oxford, Clarendon, 1992.

Index

Page numbers in bold denote major chapter/section devoted to subject

Abelam 276
Abiodun, Rowland 268
Abrahams, Ray 41, 49, 53
Abramson, Alan 86
aesthetics: as a cross-cultural category 8, 9, **251–91**; support for motion (Coote) 251, 252, **266–71**, 282–3, 286, 290; (Morphy) 252, **255–60**, 266, 272, 277–8, 280, 284, 286, 287, 288–90, 291; opposition to motion (Gow) 252–3, **271–5**, 279, 282, 283, 288, 290–1; (Overing) 252, 253, **260–6**, 276, 277, 278, 280, 282, 287–8, 290; debate 276–91
Africa(n): aesthetics 267–9, 270; music 126; relations between state and society 84; unhelpfulness of 'construction' in context of 139, 141–2; Yoruba 126, 252, 268–9, 270, 286, 291
Agar, Michael 39
Allen, Woody: on immortality 231–2
Alpers, Svetlana 165
Amazonian cultures 90, 287; Bajo Urubamba 221, 233; Piaroa 253, 263–5, 276, 277, 280
Americans: first encounters between Europeans and 222
animals 106; and aesthetics 284, 286; 'culture' 109–10; dichotomy between humans and 112–13,

117–18, 140; and environment 113, 118; and memory 203
apprenticeship 203
archaeology 180
Arendt, Hannah 81
art(s): and aesthetics 253, 260, 261–5; and language 156, 157, 169–70
'artificial' 209
Asad, Talal 108
Asante 282
Asia 252, 281, 287
Attali, Jacques 127
Australia 27; Hageners' first contact with White Australians 221–2, 237; Yolngu 190, 196, 256–7, 272, 282, 283
Avatip 109

Bach, Johann Sebastian 133–4, 135, 136, 138, 210
Bajo Urubamba 221, 233
ballot results (debate) 14
Balzac, Honoré de 36–7
Banks, Marcus 252, 280–1, 287
Basso, Keith 174
Baudrillard, J. 253
Baumgarten, Alexander Gottlieb 260, 279, 280
Baxandall, Michael 209
Baxter, Paul 92, 192
Beneviste, Emile 187

Berger, Peter 131; and Luckmann, Thomas *The social construction of reality* 103, 124, 139
Bernstein, Leonard 80–1
Bickerton, David 186
biologists 130, 140
biology 31, 62, 114
Bloch, Maurice 164
'body plus' 101, 102, 112, 130
Born, Georgina 282–3
Bourdieu, Pierre 171, 253; *Distinction* 271, 275, 283; and habitus 108, 127, 190, 214; study of French society 282
Borzwázi (was *Zwázibo*) 261–3, 265, 281
Boyarin, Jonathan 218
brain *see* neurophysiology
Britain: and change 207–8
Brydon, Lynn 42, 48
Buxton, Jean 267

Carrithers, Michael 35
Carruthers, Mary J. 239; *The book of memory* 230
Castoriadis, Cornelius 81
categories 267, 269
cave paintings 157
Central Statistical Office (CSO) 71
Chapman, Michael 43–4, 49–50
Chateaubriand, F.R. de 208
chemistry 31, 33–4; differences between anthropology and 30–1
Chernoff, John M. 126
Chewong 109
child development 133, 134, 188, 196; focus on sociality 58, 72–4, 75; and language 153, 162–3, 182, 190; teaching of deaf-blind 107–8
childhood 211
chimpanzees 107, 176, 186–7
China 72
Clifford, James 219
Cohen, Anthony: on social anthropology as a generalizing science 17–18, **26–30**, 43, 45, 46–7, 52–3
collective organization 110–11
Collins, Steven 111
communication 154, 156, 178, 184

comparative anthropology 41, 62, 92, 93
computers 230
concepts 164, 176, 185–6, 187–8
consciousness 109, 180; and memory 226, 227, 233
construction 103–4, 118–19; contrast between engagement and 115, 129; dispute over meaning 131, 134, 139, 141; 'dwelling perspective' 103, 115–16, 117, 124, 125; notion of bricks 120; and state 142
Coote, Jeremy: on aesthetics as a cross-cultural category 251, 252, **266–71**, 282–3, 286, 290
cross-cultural categories 255–6, 266, 267, 269
Crusoe, Robinson 108
CSO (Central Statistical Office) 71
Cult of the Art Object 261–3, 265
cultural construction: of human worlds 6–7, 10; support for motion **101–44**: (James) 101, 102, **105–12**, 130, 133–4, 135, 137, 141–4; (Littlewood) 102, 103, 104, **118–23**, 130, 137–8, 143; opposition to motion (Ingold) 101–2, 103, 104, **112–18**, 129–30, 130–1, 133, 136–7, 139–41, 142, 143; (Richards) 102, 103, **123–8**, 129, 131–2, 134, 139, 210, 229; debate 129–44
culture: and biology 10, 105–7, 113–14; and construction 6–7, 101–44; and language 7, 149–96; notion of 28, 101–2, 106; opposition to society 83, 92, 106, 139

dance 150, 186, 284
Daniel, Valentine 80
Darwin: *The Origin of Species* 37, 50
'data': dichotomy between theory and 2, 59; and fieldwork 2, 3, 4
Davidson, Donald 172
Davis, Natalie Zemon 209
deaf-blind children 107–8
deafness 192
death 231–2, 233

debates 4; ballot results 14; converting to written text 11–12; reading of 12–13; setting up 9–11
Deng, Francis Mading 267–8, 270
design: dichotomy between use and 2
determinism 129, 141
Dharmarajapota 79
dheeng 268, 270
dichotomies 43, 90, 103, 104; advantages of 78, 86–7; Leach on 60; problems with **5–9**, 85, 104, 278
difference 236–7
Dinka: aesthetics of 252, 267–8, 270
discourse, notion of 108, 109
discrimination: and Western aesthetics 271–2, 281
disease 121–2
Distinction (Bourdieu) 271, 275, 283
DNA 102, 111, 114
Dragadze, Tamara 129
Dreyfus, Hurbert 174
Drucker-Brown, Susan 48–9, 83
Dumont, Louis 81–2
Dunmore, Ian 178
Durkheim, Emile 50, 59, 67, 86, 94, 140, 174
Dutch language 165, 192
'dwelling perspective': and construction 103, 115–16, 117, 124, 125

Eagleton, T. 260
Eastern Europe 83, 84
Eccles, Sir John C. 180
economy: opposition with society 60–1
Eilberg-Schwartz, Howard 218
Eisenstein, Sergei 37
Ellen, Roy 139
emotion 106–7
empiricism 51
English (language) 165
Enlightenment 22, 24, 173, 260
environment 116, 121, 125, 132; and animals 113, 118; contrasted with nature 117, 138; distinction between individual and 138, 140; distinction between natural and artificial 136–7; relationship with organisms 123, 130–1, 142

'essences' 154, 159, 171, 172
ethno-classification 156
Europeans: first encounters between Americans and 222
Evans-Pritchard, Sir Edward Evan 39, 45, 158
evolution: and language 159, 160–2, 180
Expo '92, 219–20, 223

Fardon, Richard 85; on human worlds being culturally constructed 132–3; on past as a foreign country 230–1
Feeley-Harnik, Gillian: on past as a foreign country 202, 204, **212–18**, 229, 230, 232, 235–6, 236–7, 238, 239, 241, 242, 243
Ferguson, Adam: *Essay on the History of Civil Society* 69, 70
fiction: meaning of 36–7
Fiddes, Nicholas 42
'fieldwork' 38, 39, 41, 201; and 'data' 2, 3, 4
Fink, Anne 44, 48
'first contact' 221; between Europeans and Americans 222; between Hageners and White Australians 221–2, 237
food gathering 110
foreign countries 219–20, 222, 223
Forge, Anthony 276
forgetting 241, 242–3
Forrest, John 266
Fortes, Meyer 91
France 50
Frankenberg, Ronald 87
Freud, Sigmund 236
Friedman, Jonathan 29
Fuller, Chris 90
'funnel method' 39
future 229–30

Gadamer, Hans-Georg 216, 241
Geertz, Clifford 29, 113, 129, 130, 131
Gell, Alfred: on aesthetics 279–80; on language as the essence of culture 150, 151, 153, **159–65**, 176, 177, 178, 179–80, 181–2, 182–3, 186, 188, 194–5; on past as a foreign

country 234, 239–40; on Trobriand art 253, 265

Gellner, Ernest 84

general: dichotomy between the particular and 5–6, 8, 43

generalization 26–30, 41, 42, 47; types of 17–18

genes 102, 111, 114

gestures 152, 177, 180–1, 182, 186, 187

Giddens, Anthony: *The constitution of society* 67–8

Go-Between, The (Hartley) 201, 206, 207, 212–13, 219, 242

Godelier, Maurice 39

Goethe, Johann Wolfgang von 208

Good, Anthony: on social anthropology as a generalizing science 18, 27, **30–6**, 42, 48, 53

Goodman, Nelson 173, 283–4

Gow, Peter: on aesthetics as a cross-cultural category 252–3, **271–5**, 279, 282, 283, 288, 290–1; on concept of society 90; work on Bajo Urubamba 221, 233

Gramsci, Antonio 80

Greeks 80: and beauty 288; and language 162; 'Method of Loci' 230; and 'society' 68

Greger, Sonia 253, 281

'group': and society 62, 63

Gurney, Ivor: 'The Hedger' 127–8, 132

Guyer, Jane 126, 127, 131, 132

habitus 108, 109, 127, 175, 214

Handel, George Frideric: *Coronation Anthem* 240

Hann, Chris 83–4

Harris, Olivia 223

Harrison, Simon 109

Hart, Keith: on social anthropology as a generalizing science 19, **21–6**, 42–3, 44, 45, 46, 50–1, 52

Hartley, L.P.: *The Go-Between* 201, 206, 207, 212–13, 219, 242

Harvey, David 219

Harvey, Penelope: on aesthetics 286–7; on past as a foreign country 202, 204, **218–24**, 229–30, 232–3, 234–5, 236, 240–1; on societies 93

Hawking, Stephen 235

'Hedger, The' (Gurney) 127–8, 132

Hendry, Joy 47–8

Henley, Paul 90–1

Herodotus 237, 238

historians 47; and past 207, 209, 211, 234, 238

history 208, 222–3; anthropology compared with 47; and past 208; relations between memory and 202–3, 213–14; writing of 236

Hobbes, Thomas 243; *Leviathan* 68

Holding, Andrew 136, 186, 240

Holland 165

Holocaust 217–18

Holy, Ladislav: *Comparative anthropology* 29; on dichotomies 86–7; and Stuchlik, Milan 33

hominization: language and process of 159, 160–2, 163, 187

Homo erectus 160, 161, 176, 186

Homo habilis 160, 161, 176

Homo sapiens 106–7, 160, 161

Hopkins, Gerard Manley 281, 282; 'Pied Beauty' 270

Howell, Signe 109

Hubbard, Ruth 214

Hughes-Freeland, Felicia 283

human beings: dichotomy between animals and 112–13, 117–18, 140; split-level existence of 114–15; suspension in webs of significance 129, 130

humanities: dichotomy between science and 5, 6, 23, 25, 50

Hungary 84

hunter-gatherers 34, 110, 111, 137, 143–4

hypotheses 18, 33, 38–9

Ilongot 109

image-making 226

individual 65; distinction between environment and 138, 140; and society dichotomy 58, 59, 62, 66, 69, 71, 72, 76, 77–8, 86, 87, 90, 92, 94

298   *Index*

Ingold, Tim 41, 91; on aesthetics
284–5; on biology 111, 121; on
comparison 93; on dichotomies 87;
on environment 214; *Evolution and
social life* 68; on human worlds
being culturally constructed 101–2,
103, 104, **112–18**, 129–30, 130–1,
133, 136–7, 139–41, 142, 143; on
language and culture 178–9, 181,
187, 192–3; on past as a foreign
country 231, 239, 242; on science
49, 50
initiation rituals 89, 90–1, 92

James, Wendy: on human worlds
being culturally constructed 101,
102, **105–12**, 130, 133, 133–4, 135,
137, 141–4; *The listening ebony* 29;
on social anthropology as a
generalizing science 45, 46
Japanese 191
juju music 126
Johnson-Laird, Philip 186

Kabyle 283
Kaluli 215–16
Kant, Immanuel 252, 253, 260, 262,
279, 281, 289
Keats, John 270, 281
Keen, Ian 181–2, 186, 190–1, 192
Keesing, Roger 30
Kelly, Elinor 49
Kendon, Adam 179, 185
kinship 27, 30, 221
Knight, Chris 150, 152, 176–7, 179,
180–1, 185–7
Kolakowski, Leszek 44
Kpelle music performance 132
Küchler, Susanne: on past as a
foreign country 202, 220, **224–8**,
230, 232, 233–4, 236, 237, 238
Kuipers, Joel 232
Kula ring 26

Langer, Lawrence L. 218
language 216, 232; concept of as
theoretically obsolete 87–8; [as
essence of culture 7–8, 10, **149–96**;
support for motion (Moeran)
149–50, **166–70**, 184, 191–2, 195;

(Parkin) 10, 149–50, 151, 152,
154–8, 166, 172, 178, 179, 182,
183–4, 185, 190, 191, 193–4;
opposition to motion (Gell) 150,
151, 153, **159–65**, 176, 177, 178,
179–80, 181–2, 186, 188, 194–5;
(Weiner) 150, 152, **171–5**, 178,
180–1, 186, 187–8, 189, 194, 195–6;
debate 176–96]; and society 88, 97
Lawal, Babatunde 268
'laws': anthropological and scientific
34
Layton, Robert 276–7
Leach, Edmund: on art 265; on
society 57, 60–1, 64, 66, 68, 96
Lévi-Strauss, Claude: approach to
music 127, 132; on aesthetics 271,
274–5, 290; and culture of
communication 154; *The way of the
masks* 274
literature: and anthropology 36–7
Littlejohn, James 76
Littlewood, Roland: on human
worlds being culturally constructed
102, 103, 104, **118–23**, 130, 137–8,
143
logocentrism 191, 195–6
Lopasic, Alexander 237–8
Lowenthal, David: on past as a
foreign country 202, 204, **206–12**,
213, 219, 229, 231–2, 238–9, 240,
241–2, 242–3

MacDonald, Maryon 191
Magne, Frank 184
Malagasy 216
Malangan sculptures 220–1, 227, 233
Malinowski, Bronislaw 21, 39, 204,
232
Mann, Michael: *Sources of social
power* 70
Marett, R.R. 204
Martin Guerre 209
Marx, Karl 50, 77, 78, 85; *1844
Manuscripts* 94; on political
economy 69–70
masks 274
mathematics: and language 177, 182
Mauss, Marcel 77, 175; body
techniques 109

Mbuti 282
media, global 251, 252
Melanesia 69, 89, 90–1, 92, 109, 243, 289
memory 203, 204–5, 221, 239; and animals 203; Carruthers' study of techniques 230; and commemoration 203; and consciousness 226, 227, 233; 'ecological' research into 213–14; and food 232; and forgetting 241, 242–3; Langer on 'common' and 'deep' 218; neurophysiology of 214–15; and past 207, 225, 226–7, 228, 233; relations with history 202–3, 213–14
Merleau-Ponty, Maurice 152
metalanguage 256–7, 288, 290, 291
metaphors 207
Mill, John Stuart 78
Millier, Daniel 92–3
Moeran, Brian: on language as essence of culture 49–50, **166–70**, 184, 191–2, 195
monograph 37–8, 41
Morphy, Howard: on aesthetics as a cross-cultural category 252, **255–60**, 266, 272, 277–8, 280, 284, 286, 287, 289–90, 291
Moser, Sir Claus 71
Munn, Nancy 259, 286
Museum of Mankind 92
museums 210
music: approach to anthropology 126–7, 132; African 126; and culture 133–6, 138, 139; and language 151, 152, 177–8, 178–9, 180, 181, 182, 183, 189; and past 210, 240

nation-states 222–3
nationalism 69, 84, 251–2
nature 115; concept of 113; distinction between environment and 117, 138
Navajo sand paintings 273–4
neurophysiology: and language 151, 179, 180, 181, 189, 191, 194; and memory 214–15
New Guinea *see* Papua New Guinea

Newby, Alison 135–6
Nietzsche, Friedrich Wilhelm 126
Nipnip 45
non-human primates 107; and language 176, 178, 185, 186–7
non-verbal communication 7–8, 150, 151, 152, 155, 157, 182, 184
Nuer 45

odours *see* smells
O'Hanlon, Michael 278–9
Okely, Judith: on social anthropology as a generalizing science 18–19, **36–40**, 47, 48, 53–4
ontogeny 153, 159, 162, 179, 188, 189, 190
organisms 101–2, 105, 106, 111, 132, 140, 142–3, 214; and environment 123, 130–1, 142
Orientalism 192
Overing, Joanna: on aesthetics as a cross-cultural category 252, 253, **260–6**, 276, 277, 278, 280, 282, 287–8, 290

Paine, Tom 69
palaeontology 159, 160–2, 176, 177, 178, 179, 182, 186, 191
pantomime 157, 179, 186
Paolozzi, Eduardo 92
Papua New Guinea: Massim region 259, 286; Melanesia 69, 89, 90–1, 92, 109, 243, 289
paradigms 59, 63, 89, 91, 93–4, 95, 96, 97
Parkin, David: on language being essence of culture 10, 149–50, 152, **154–8**, 166, 172, 178, 179, 182, 183–4, 185, 190, 191, 193–4; view of culture 29
Passerini, Luisa 207
past: as a foreign country 8, **201–43**; support for motion (Harvey) 202, 204, **218–24**, 229–30, 232–3, 234–5, 236, 240–1; (Lowenthal) 202, 204, **206–12**, 213, 219, 229, 231–2, 238–9, 240, 241–2, 242–3; opposition to motion (Feeley-Harnik) 202, 204, **212–18**, 229, 230, 232, 235–6, 236–7, 238, 239,

241, 242, 243; (Küchler) 202, 220, **224–8**, 230, 232, 233–4, 236, 237, 238; debate 229–43
pastiche 91–2
'pathology' 121, 122
Peacock, James L.: *The anthropological lens* 26
Peel, John: on concept of society being theoretically obsolete 58, **67–72**, 78, 84–5, 88, 91–2, 96; on the past 213, 237
perception 115, 118, 133, 189, 236, 284, 285
personhood 58, 111, 130, 143
phenomenology 159, 164–5
phylogeny 153, 159, 161, 177
physics 31
Piaroa: and aesthetics 253, 263–5, 276, 277, 280
Picasso, Pablo 273
'Pied Beauty' (Hopkins) 270
Piero della Francesca 209
Pirie, David 182, 192
plant breeding 103, 124–5
politics 279, 280; anthropology of 282; aestheticization of 251–2
Pollock, Jackson 273, 274
pongids 160, 161, 162
Popper, Karl: concept of theory 38; and Eccles, John 180; and science 18, 19, 33, 34, 51
positivism 18, 19, 36, 38–9, 42, 43, 44, 48, 50
practice, notion of 108–9
present 225; ethnographic 201; relations with past 221, 224, 225, 227, 231, 232–3, 240, 241 *see also* presentism
'presentism' 204, 212, 213, 216, 230, 231, 236
Prigogine, Ilya 235
'primitive art' 273–4, 291
Proust, Marcel 227
'pseudo-scientists' 48
Punch 211
pundits: distinction between journeymen and 91

Rapport, Nigel 129
realism 37

reflexivity 29, 39, 185
remembering *see* memory
resonance, concept of 128
Return of Martin Guerre, The 209
Richards, Paul: on human worlds being culturally constructed 102, 103, **123–8**, 129, 131–2, 134, 139, 210, 229
Richardson, Kay 183
Rickets Campaign 49
rights 111, 143
Riley, Bridget 272, 283
rituals 110, 157, 177, 186; initiation 89, 90–1, 92
Rosaldo, Michelle 109
Rosenfield, Israel 226, 227
Rowlands, Michael 41, 43, 51
rugby 166–8

Sacks, Oliver 224–5, 227
Sacred Bundle of the Pawnee Indians 242
Sahlins, Marshall 34
Saussure, Ferdinand de 52, 87, 88, 167, 187
Schieffelin, Edward 129, 131, 136
science(s) 19–20, 22, 24; defined 32–3; dichotomy between humanity and 5, 6, 23, 25, 50; interrelationships of basic 31–2; need for broader conception of as knowledge 6–7; negation of 23, 25; objectives 22; Popper on 18, 19, 33, 34, 51; and positivism 19; social anthropology as generalizing *see* social anthropology
scientism 18–19
scientists 6, 46, 48, 49–50, 53
sculptures, *Malangan* 220–1, 227, 233
Searle-Chatterjee, Mary 51
semantic(s) 9, 155–6; dichotomy between sensual and 285, 286
semiology 155, 156
Shakespeare, William 169, 170
Shelton, Anthony 265
Siegel, James 215
Simmonds, Norman 125
smells 168, 215, 227
social anthropology: as a generalizing science **17–54**: support for motion

(Good) 18, 27, **30–6**, 42, 48, 53; (Hart) 19, **21–6**, 42–3, 44, 45, 46, 50–1, 52; opposition to motion (Cohen) 17–18, **26–30**, 43, 45, 46–7, 52–3; (Okely) 18–19, **36–40**, 47, 48, 53–4; debate 41–54
social theory 68, 69, 71, 77, 81, 251
sociality, concept of 58, 64, 74, 78, 83, 86, 94
socialization, notion of 73, 74, 89, 258; and aesthetics 258–9
society 22, 106, 140; concept of as theoretically obsolete **57–97**; support for motion (Strathern) 57–8, **60–6**, 69, 74, 77, 83, 85, 86, 88–9, 90, 94–6; (Toren) 57–8, **72–6**, 85, 86, 87–8, 96–7; opposition to motion (Peel) 58, **67–72**, 78, 84–5, 88, 91–2, 96; (Spencer) 58, 67, **76–82**, 85, 86, 89–90, 97; debate 83–97
sociobiology 102, 140–1
sociology: distinction between social anthropology and 42–3
speaking 174, 181
speech 150, 155, 173, 175, 183, 187; and song 151, 152
Spencer, Jonathan: on concept of society as theoretically obsolete 58, 67, **76–82**, 85, 86, 89–90, 97; *The Man vs. the State* 71
Spiegelman, Art 217
Sri Lanka 27, 78, 79–80, 81, 85
state: and cultural construction 142; and society 58, 68–9, 71, 72, 79–80, 83–5, 88
Stoller, Paul 272
Stone, Ruth 132
story-telling 8, 203
Strathern, Marilyn 132; on construction 131; on 'first contact' 221; Melanesian studies 69, 89, 90–1, 92, 109, 289; on past as a foreign country 240; on science 10, 43, 44–5; on society as theoretically obsolete 57–8, **60–6**, 69, 74, 77, 83, 85, 86, 88–9, 90, 94–6
structuralism: and theory of language 173
Sudanese Nuer 45

Taylor, Charles 85
testing, critical 33
Thatcher, Margaret (Thatcherism) 65–6, 71, 85, 90, 94
theory **1–5**; dichotomy between design and use 2; division between data and 2, 59; importance of 4–5; musical approach to 126; as ongoing process of argumentation 3–4; Popperian concept of 38; relations between paradigms and 59
thermodynamics 34
Thompson, Valreter 192
time 223, 232; arrow of 235–6; types of temporal series 234–5
Tiv society 68
Tocqueville, Alexis de 69, 71, 84
Tonkin, Elizabeth 41–2, 88, 138
Toren, Christina: on aesthetics 285–6; on concept of society as theoretically obsolete 57–8, **72–6**, 85, 86, 87–8, 96–7; on language 187, 188–90
tourism 211–12
transcendence 253
Trautman, Thomas 217
Trobriand art 253, 265

Uduk 109

van Binsbergen, Wim 44, 47, 53
vervet monkeys 185, 186
Voloshinov, Valentin Nikolaevich 87

Wade, Peter 93–4, 277
Wagner, Roy 174
Wanamaker, Sam 210
Waterman, Christopher A. 126
Weber, Max 31, 50, 67, 85, 129, 171
Weiner, James: on aesthetics 288–9; on language as essence of culture 150, 152, **171–5**, 178, 180–1, 186, 187–8, 189, 194, 195–6; on past as a foreign country 203, 236, 238
Werbner, Pnina 42, 53, 138, 288
Werbner, Richard 178
Wernicke, Carl 180
Western aesthetics 271–2, 273, 274, 275, 278, 280, 281, 282, 287, 291

Western Apache 215
'Western discourse' 1, 4, 137
Whitehead, Alfred North 117
Wilmers, George 177–8, 188, 189
witchcraft 257
Wittgenstein, Ludwig 170, 171, 175
Wolf, Eric 222–3
Wollheim, Richard 156
Woodburn, James 51, 53

words: and concepts 187–8

Yolngu 190, 196, 256–7, 272, 282, 283
Yoruba 126, 252, 268–9, 286, 291;
    aesthetics 268–9, 270

Zen Buddhism 168–9, 191
Zwázibo (later named *Borzwázi*): and
    Cult of the Art Object 261–3, 265